A N

ARCHAEOLOGY OF

ELMINA

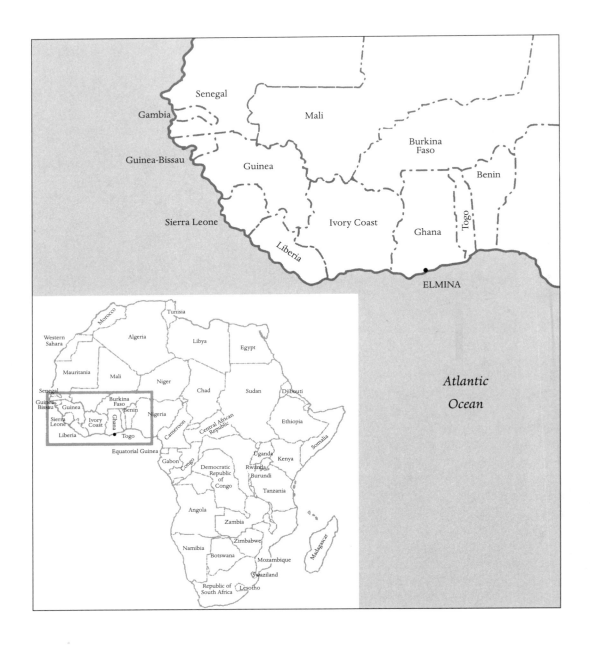

AN ARCHAEOLOGY OF

ELMINA

AFRICANS AND EUROPEANS ON THE GOLD COAST, 1400–1900

Christopher R. DeCorse

❖

SMITHSONIAN INSTITUTION PRESS

Washington and London

COPY EDITOR: Robin Whitaker
PRODUCTION EDITOR: Ruth G. Thomson
DESIGNER: Janice Wheeler

Library of Congress Cataloging-in-Publication Data
DeCorse, Christopher R.
    An archaeology of Elmina : Africans and Europeans on the Gold Coast,
    1400–1900 / Christopher R. DeCorse.
        p.   cm.
    Includes bibliographical references and index.
    ISBN 1-56098-971-8 (alk. paper)
        1. Elmina (Ghana)—History. 2. Europeans—Ghana—Elmina—History.
    3. Slave trade—Ghana—Elmina—History.   4. Excavations (Archaeology)—
    Ghana—Elmina.   5. Elmina (Ghana)—Antiquities.   I. Title.
    DT512.9.E46 D43   2001
    966.7—dc21   00-047005

British Library Cataloguing-in-Publication Data available

♾ The paper used in this publication meets the minimum requirements of the American National Standard for Information Sciences—Permanence of Paper for Printed Library Materials ANSI Z39.48-1984.

For Philip L. Ravenhill, mentor, colleague, and friend

❖

CONTENTS

ACKNOWLEDGMENTS

I owe a great debt to Merrick Posnansky, who initially suggested Elmina as a site for the study of African-European relations. His knowledge and advice have served as a constant inspiration. Financial support was provided by a variety of sources including: a Fulbright-Hays Dissertation Research Grant, the UCLA Friends of Archaeology, University of California Research Grants, the Foundation for Field Research, the Bead Society, a Smithsonian Institution Postdoctoral Fellowship, the Maxwell School Citizenship and Public Affairs, an Appleby-Mosher Research Award, the Center for Field Research, and Syracuse University. Support and facilities were also provided by the University of Ghana and the Ghana Museums and Monuments Board. I greatly appreciate the assistance of Isaac Nyade Debrah, Emmanuel Attuah Asanti, Francis Boakye Duah, Joseph Nkrumah, Maxwell Dzogbenuku, Samuel Francis Dadzie, Vincent Amelor, Joe Gazari, and the rest of the staff of the Ghana National Museum, who were consistently helpful and ensured that my excavation permits were up to date. The Ghana Museums and Monuments Board's permission to use museum facilities at Elmina greatly facilitated the work. In the field, Emmanuel Kofi Agorsah provided a great deal of logistical and personal support. I also owe a vote of thanks to Theresa Singleton, who joined me in Ghana during the 1993 field season. I thank the United States Information Service personnel Roberta Jones, Nick Robertson, and Gene Schaeffer for their help and numerous free meals. Without the support of these people and institutions, the research undertaken would not have been possible. I am grateful for their confidence.

Excavations and laboratory work in the Central Region were facilitated by many individuals. Laboratory and field directors include Bossman Murey, John Ako Okoro, Joseph (Oga) Quansah, Edward Carr, Sam Spiers, Jackie Becker, Keith Bratton, Sarah Terlouw, Elizabeth Gryzmala, Patty Evans, and Seth Danquah. Ghana Museums and Monuments Board staff Raymond Agbo, Kwesi Miles, Ben Kankpeyeng, Alex Mensah, Wallace Kwaw, Alhasan Isaka, George Sackey, Charles Mensah, and Paul Gyim were of great help. The support of Ernest Quayson, Peter King Badu Prah and Sallars Awortwi in Elmina is much appreciated. I also thank Diederik Six for loaning me surveying equipment for work during 1987. I am also especially appreciative of all the chiefs and elders that have given their consent and support to archaeological work.

Navigating the mass of documentary records relevant to the study was made much easier by having several superb guides. I am particularly indebted to Paul E. H. Hair, Gérard Chouin, Adam Jones, Albert van Dantzig, Harvey Feinberg, and Michel Doortmont. In addition to their published work they shared many unpublished references and insights with me. Janet Stanley and Chris Geary of the Smithsonian Institution, National Museum of African Art, were of tremendous help in locating illustrations and sources. I also owe a great debt to librarians, archivists, and curators at many other institutions who provided invaluable help.

Anyone has worked with trade materials of the fifteenth through nineteenth centuries can appreciate the diversity represented and the critical importance of comments from researchers who have seen similar material. Several individuals were of great help with the identification of the European artifacts. The assistance of Jan Baart, Jim Boone, Seymour de Lotbiniere, Paul Huey, Olive Jones, Karlis Karklins, Olga Klimko, Jane Klose, Teresita Majewski, George Miller, Emlen Meyers, Ivor and Audrey Noël Hume, Carmel Schrire, and Peter A. R. Vermeulen was invaluable. K. R. Miller and S. K. Hopkins of the National Army Museum, London, were of particular help in identifying some of the British-period artifacts. Philip Ravenhill, Doran Ross, Cofie Odarty, Tara Tetrault, and Kofi Agorsah provided useful observations on some of the African material culture. Peggy Appiah was kind enough to comment on the possible proverbs that could be attached to the gold weights.

Drawings and photographs of many of the artifacts were completed by Bossman Murey, Ishmael Sowah, Raphael Tonyigoh, Timothy Seymour, Sandra Kaplan, Douglas Pippin, Mark Hauser, Michael Lascomb, Kristy Fritts, Kate Kriezel, and Zesha Skop. Their contributions are gratefully recognized.

I offer special thanks to Gérard Chouin, Greg Cook, Paul Hair, Adam Jones, Sam Spiers, and David S. Whitley, who provided many useful comments on drafts of the manuscript. At the Smithsonian Institution Press, I thank Daniel Goodwin, Scott Mahler, Ruth Thomson, and copy editor Robin Whitaker for their numerous useful suggestions.

Thiis is an archaeological study, but documentary records, oral sources, and ethnographic data have been used to interpret the material record. Elmina is one of the best-illustrated and -described African settlements in sub-Saharan Africa. It is fortunate that many primary sources on Elmina and the Gold Coast have been republished and annotated in English.[1] Several scholars have synthesized Elmina's history and examined Elmina within the broader context of the Gold Coast.[2] Many archives also possess rich holdings of maps and plans. In particular, I was able to examine manuscripts relevant to Elmina at the British Public Record Office, Kew; the Rijksarchief, Amsterdam; the National Maritime Museum, London; the Furley Collection at the University of Ghana; and the National Museum of African Art, Smithsonian Institution, Washington, D.C. I also obtained selected material from a number of other archives including: Bibliotheek der Rijksuniversiteit, Leiden; Stichting Cultuurgeschiedenis van de Nederlanders Overzee (now part of the Rijksmuseum), Amsterdam; the *Illustrated London News* Picture Library; and the Algemeen Rijksarchief, The Hague. A variety of documentary sources have been quoted at length in the text. These provide substantive information as well as colorful descriptions by European visitors to the coast. Irregularities in spelling and grammar have been retained as they appear in the original works or translations. Unless these confuse the meaning of the passage, they have not been identified in the text.

Despite the wealth of documentary sources, the records are by no means complete. Information on the lower Guinea coast, the area that extends from Liberia to Cameroon, during the Portuguese period is particularly limited. The records that do exist almost exclusively concern trade and navigational peculiarities.[3] Much fuller accounts are available for later periods, but their value in historical reconstruction is variable. In some instances, as with the sixteenth-century writings of Duarte Pacheco Pereira and Willem Bosman's later work, *A New and Accurate Description of the Coast of Guinea*, the accounts are by Europeans who participated in the events described and played key roles in African-European relations.[4] Other narratives are by minor functionaries who plagiarized other writers and offer little new information (see, e.g., Feinberg 1979; Jones 1980, 1986). The Asante War and the British military expedition of 1873–74 resulted in the publication of a mass of popular books and accounts in English; for the most part they are of limited direct relevance to Elmina, but some provide useful information (e.g., Allen 1874; Beaton 1873; Boyle 1874; *Daily News* Special Correspondent 1874; Hay 1874; Stanley 1874).[5] Above all, many of the documents reflect European economic interests, the vast majority consisting of observations and reports of trade relations, often made rather dense by bureaucratic excess.

From an archaeological standpoint the documentary records are disappointing. There is a dearth of information on settlement organization and housing within the town. Descriptions are vague at best, and no detailed maps exist. No architectural plans of Elmina Castle itself are known until after the Dutch capture in 1637, or at least no earlier plans survive. The illustrations that do exist suggest a steady increase in the size of the settlement and, to some extent, the incorporation of European elements into house construction. Yet they are also indicative of the limitations of European source material in general: They are lacking in scale and perspective, concentrate on the European presence, and often present widely differing viewpoints.[6] There are, for the most part, no detailed property records, deeds, or wills prior to the late nineteenth century. Notable exceptions are sources such as the second West India Company's *dagregisters* (daily journals), *lijsten van overlijden* (annual lists of the dead), and correspondence. These, as well as occasional references in other sources, briefly describe the homes of specific individuals. In the absence of more detailed maps, however, this information cannot be related to specific archaeological provenances. In any case, the few documents that record estate inventories or properties refer to only a minute portion of the population. The identities of the individuals who lived, worked, and were buried in the houses uncovered during archaeological work are unknown.[7]

ORAL TRADITIONS AND HISTORIES

To provide more holistic analyses of African societies, many researchers have supplemented documentary records with oral histories and traditions as well as ethnographic data.[8] Other researchers have surveyed and recorded these data with regard to Elmina, but this information, for the most part, was not directly relevant to the current research.[9] Interviews, oral histories and traditions, and ethnographic data were collected during each field season. Much of the data recorded related to specific activities such as salt production, butchering practices, potting traditions, and fishing, and they also included the memories of recent activities that may have impacted the archaeological site.[10]

Oral traditions—narratives of the past passed down over generations—relevant to the early history of Elmina survive. These sources were, however, of minimal use in interpreting the town's past. There is a general consensus within the town that oral traditions no longer exist: "[A]ll the old people who knew about this are now dead" (Feinberg 1969:x–xv; 1989:xiii). In his study of eighteenth-century Elmina-Dutch relations, Harvey Feinberg obtained very little historical information from his informants. In fact, there likely never were formalized mechanisms or positions for preserving oral traditions, such as there are in many African societies, and there may never have been substantial traditions to pass on. Feinberg also noted the chaotic political situation after the town's destruction in 1873 as a possible reason for the paucity of the kind of information these sources can sometimes provide.

The interpretation of oral traditions within Elmina, and within coastal Ghana in general, is further complicated by a process David Henige (1973, 1974) has referred to as "feedback." Many of the people of coastal Ghana are literate, have been so for centuries, and have had access to published materials on Ghanaian history. Elements of these sources, correct or incorrect, have been incorporated into indigenous renditions of Elmina's past. Henige illustrates the problem by citing the influence of early, published European historiography on traditional lists of the paramount stool lineages, including those recounted in a local history published in the 1950s by J. Sylvanus Wartemberg (1951).[11] These traditions include references to Caramansa, the African ruler named in early European sources as the one who met with the Portuguese at the founding of Castelo de São Jorge da Mina. In examining Elmina traditions, Henige found that Caramansa does not appear in recorded lists of Elmina rulers until the late nineteenth century, a period when printed accounts of African-European interactions and references to Caramansa became more widely accessible in Elmina.

Wartemberg, in turn, has become a principal source in contemporary oral traditions (Feinberg 1989:xiii). This point was clearly illustrated during my own research. While interviewing an elder, I was surprised at some of the facts that he was able to recount regarding the history of the town and the settlement's origins. As I rapidly scribbled things down in my notebook, he kindly mentioned that there was no need for me to do so, for he would loan me the book— a copy of Wartemberg. Other traditions that were recorded during fieldwork referred to Caramansa and clearly drew information from Wartemberg. Further traditions of doubtful historical merit were also mentioned, including the proposition that a French outpost had been located at Elmina prior to the arrival of the Portuguese.[12]

More helpful than oral traditions were the memories, personal reminiscences, and eyewitness accounts provided by oral histories. This information was principally confined to information relevant to the last 50 years. For example, awareness of grading the parade ground for Queen Elizabeth's visit in the early 1960s and use of the site by the Ghana police helped explain some of the surface features and artifact patterns noted during archaeological survey and excavation. Even this information was often quite limited, however. There was no memory, for example, of a structure located southeast of the castle, which archaeological evidence indicates was associated with the occupation by the Ghana police during the 1950s. Nor could any insight be obtained into the restoration work and clearing of portions of the site undertaken during the 1950s under A. W. Lawrence's direction.[13] Memories of the discovery of skeletal remains and artifacts were useful in identifying the location of archaeological deposits and the extent of archaeological features, many of which had been obliterated by more recent activity. Ethnohistorical information on some cultural practices—pottery manufacture, fishing, and butchering practices—provided useful analogs for the uses of material discovered archaeologically.

ARCHAEOLOGICAL RESEARCH

Much of sub-Saharan Africa remains poorly known archaeologically compared with some world areas.[14] Site inventories, artifact chronologies, and culture histories are still important concerns, which is true in terms of the present study. Although Ghana has been the focus of more archaeological research than many areas, only limited work has specifically dealt with sites associated with African-European interactions.[15] Research on European sites has generally been limited in scope, concentrating on the identification and description of structures and on architectural history, with little attention given to the associated archaeological materials. This characterization applies to work in Ghana as well as Africa in general (DeCorse 1996:42–43). The history and construction of the forts and castles of coastal Ghana have received substantial attention. The most comprehensive study remains Lawrence 1963, but Dahmen and Elteren 1992, Groll 1968, O'Neil 1951, and van Dantzig 1980a provide useful overviews. The majority of the other works are relatively short and primarily aimed at more general audiences.[16] Detailed plans of the castle were recently prepared by students from Delft University and as part of current renovation work (Hyland 1995; Joustra and Six 1988). The limited amount of archaeological research undertaken in conjunction with this work has dealt with overarching reconstruction concerns and not the recovery of archaeological data that would help in the interpretation of African or European lifeways (Anquandah 1992, 1993, 1997; Joustra and Six 1988).

Elmina's archaeological potential has been long recognized, but no systematic work had been undertaken on the site when the current work began in 1985.[17] Lawrence (1963:169) noted the presence of stone foundations but provided no additional information. Other researchers reported isolated archaeological features and surface finds.[18] Bernard Golden evaluated the site as part of the 1969 coastal survey, but his assessment of the site's archaeological potential was negative, concluding that "[t]here has been considerable modification of the terrain here and the deposits in the thin layer of soil covering bedrock are no doubt disturbed" (1969:124).

More intensive excavations were undertaken by David Calvocoressi (1968, 1977) during the 1960s at Veersche Schans (known in the British period as Fort de Veer), a small redoubt built in 1811 on the landward side of the Elmina peninsula, west of the old town. The impetus for the archaeological research was oral traditions that suggested that the location had been the site of a

French outpost that predated the arrival of the Portuguese. The traditions are problematic in a number of ways, and Calvocoressi's work uncovered no evidence of pre-Portuguese European occupation. The excavation, however, did produce material predating construction of Veersche Schans, including burials probably dating to the eighteenth century and earlier midden deposits that were likely pre-sixteenth-century in age. These finds provided material useful for comparison with pre-nineteenth-century artifacts from the Elmina excavations.

Prior to the present work, research on African sites on adjacent parts of the coast had also been limited, and there has still not been a comprehensive survey of the Central Region as a whole, though information is now accumulating. Preliminary surveys had been undertaken.[19] Excavations of the historical Fante capitals of Efutu by Agorsah (1975, 1993) and Asebu by Nunoo (1957) illustrate the potential of these sites, but the research undertaken was limited in scope. Farther into the hinterland, important comparative information about change in coastal Ghana during the post-European-contact period comes from the work of Bellis (1972, 1982, 1987) and Kiyaga-Mulindwa (1978, 1982). To the east, Ozanne's (1963) survey of sites in Accra and Shai complements some of the observations made here concerning the transition to more nucleated settlements between the late fifteenth and seventeenth centuries. To the west of Elmina, the sites of Komenda and Sekondi also provide some comparative information.[20]

My initial research on the Elmina settlement was conducted between 1985 and 1987 (DeCorse 1987a, b, 1989a, 1992a, b). This work and the 1990 field season focused entirely on the Elmina site. Archaeological work in 1993, 1997, 1998, and 2000 included additional excavation and survey at Elmina, but work was extended to neighboring areas to help place the Elmina site in broader cultural and historical context (DeCorse 1998a). The specific objective of this research was to locate and retrieve diagnostic artifacts to establish some chronological control for a further understanding of late prehistoric and historic occupations in the areas around Elmina. This collaborative effort has been integrated into the Central Region Project. Archaeological remains at Elmina itself cover an area of almost 81 ha (200 acres), but the earliest and densest areas of past occupation are concentrated on the 8 ha (20 acres) closest to the castle. Portions of the site related to the pre-European-contact village and the Portuguese-period town occupy even more restricted areas. Deposits today lie buried under destruction debris or fill ranging from a few centimeters (less than an inch) to over 2.5 m (8.2 feet). Although portions of the site have been heavily affected by recent development, many areas remain well preserved. Over 40 stone-walled structures were excavated, some with walls still standing to a height of 2 m (6.5 feet). The nineteenth century, the time of the settlement's destruction, is best represented, but the remains span the fifteenth through the nineteenth centuries. A complete survey of the coast 10 km (6.2 miles) east and west of Elmina has now been completed, and most historically and archaeologically identified African settlements and European trade posts throughout the Central Region have been visited. All standing European structures have been mapped. Material from excavations and from unstratified surface collections has provided a much more detailed understanding of the occupation of the Central Region coast over the past 1,000 years.

A particularly significant aspect of the Elmina excavations was the large proportion of European trade materials recovered. Interpretations of African art and material culture are often limited by their dependency on objects that have been removed from their cultural and historical contexts (see Cole 1979; Posnansky 1970, 1979). The close chronological control provided by European trade materials is very helpful in dating associated objects of African manufacture, such as metal vessels, gold weights, beads, and ceramics.

The preceding sources allow for interpretation of the lifeways of the Elmina people and a means of examining developments within the Elmina settlement over the past 500 years. The history of Elmina, as reconstructed from documentary and traditional sources, is presented in Chapters 1 and 2. The first chapter concentrates on sociopolitical developments and the demography of the settlement; Chapter 2 focuses on records and traditions relating to the town site, spatial organization within the settlement, and town life. These discussions are followed by a survey of the archaeological research undertaken (Chapter 3). The subsequent chapters examine different aspects of the Elmina past, drawing together documentary, ethnographic, and archaeological data. Transformations in subsistence, craft production, and trade are considered first (Chapter 4). Archaeological research provides a closely dated selection of local ceramics, indigenous metalworking, ivory carving, bead production, and other local industries. These data suggest important insights into indigenous technology and necessitate reevaluation of current interpretations. European trade materials dominate the assemblage, and this aspect of the artifact inventory is considered in Chapter 5. Ceramics, glass, tobacco pipes, firearms, and beads outnumber items of local manufacture. The trade in these materials, as well as aspects of European trade poorly perceived archaeologically, is considered. The concluding chapter considers artifacts within the cultural system, the variable meanings assigned to European trade materials, and archaeological perceptions of culture contact.

I

HISTORICAL

BACKGROUND

The African settlement of Elmina in coastal Ghana encapsulates the years of European contact, trade, and colonization better than any other site in Africa. The town was the major trade entrepôt in the portion of West Africa the Europeans called Mina or the Mine and, later, the Gold Coast because of the gold that could be obtained there.[1] The Portuguese stronghold of Castelo de São Jorge da Mina, founded in 1482 adjacent to an existing African settlement, was the first fortified European trade post in sub-Saharan Africa (Figures 1.1 and 1.2).[2] Elmina Castle, as the fortress eventually came to be known, played a crucial role in Portuguese attempts to monopolize the trade in coastal Ghana, and it became a focal point of European rivalry in the region (Figures 1.3 and 1.4). The Dutch captured the castle in 1637, and Elmina remained the headquarters of Dutch mercantile interests in West Africa until its transfer to the British in 1872. The destruction of the African town by the British in 1873 and the subsequent abandonment of the site illustrate dramatic

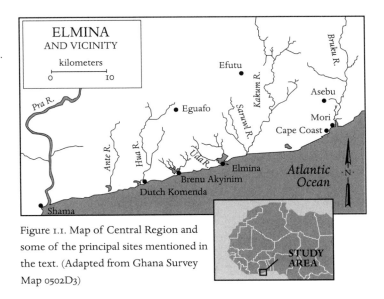

Figure 1.1. Map of Central Region and some of the principal sites mentioned in the text. (Adapted from Ghana Survey Map 0502D3)

Figure 1.2. Map of
Elmina today.
(Illustration courtesy of
Christopher R.
DeCorse)

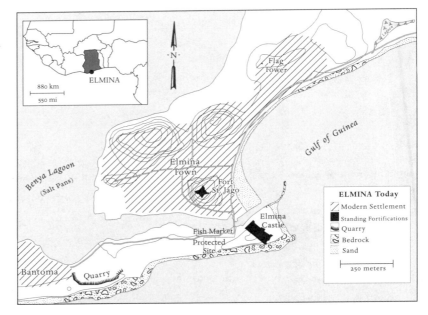

Figure 1.3. An idealized
view of Castelo de São
Jorge da Mina in the
sixteenth century. More
accurate depictions of
Elmina Castle do not
appear until the
seventeenth century.
(From Georg Braun
and Franz Hogenberg,
*Beschreibung und
Contrafactur der
vornembster Stat der Welt*
[1575]; reproduced
courtesy of Christraud
M. Geary)

changes in African-European interactions. The late nineteenth century witnessed much more overt European involvement in African affairs and the beginning of the colonial partition of Africa.

The interactions and transformations that ensued at Elmina during the 400
years spanning the first contact with Europeans and the destruction of the town

Figure 1.4. View of Elmina Castle and the old town site as seen from Fort St. Jago in 1986. Some of the excavations can be seen on the peninsula. (Photograph by Christopher R. DeCorse)

are varied, complex, and illustrative of the challenges present in evaluating the intersection of Europe with the non-Western world. Despite tensions with the Europeans the African settlement flourished. The population climbed from a few hundred during the fifteenth century to perhaps 18,000–20,000 inhabitants by the mid-nineteenth century. The growth of Elmina and other coastal trading centers marked a reorientation away from long-established trans-Saharan routes toward a new frontier of opportunity provided by European coastal trade. Although fifteenth-century Elmina was likely subservient to the neighboring Fante states of Eguafo and Fetu, the population had, by the mid-sixteenth century, come to regard itself as politically distinct from the surrounding African population. These developments are only partly revealed by documentary sources. European narratives provide limited, Eurocentric understanding of the events that transpired, conveying little about the African population, their beliefs, or indigenous perceptions of the Europeans.[3]

This book considers Elmina's past in light of 15 years of archaeological research in coastal Ghana. The data presented represent one of the largest settlement studies of its kind undertaken in West Africa.[4] Excavation cannot provide the detailed chronicle of people and events that documentary records or oral histories at times afford. Archaeology does, however, offer independent information not accessible through other sources. These data both expand our knowledge and furnish a means of evaluating other sources of information for a more holistic understanding of the past.

CONCEPTUALIZING THE PAST

Archaeological research at Elmina had two overarching concerns. The foremost of these was the story of the African settlement of Elmina. This narrative is more about the everyday life of the Elmina people than the great historical events of which they were part. Elmina was an African settlement, but the majority of the population left no written records, and the documentary sources that outline the town's history and tell the story of the individuals who lived there were written by Europeans. House foundations, pottery sherds, bottles, bone, and metal fragments furnish a more complete interpretation of the settlement and of the diet, craft specialization, trade contacts, activities, and the beliefs of its inhabitants—the past lifeways of the Elmina people.[5]

The other primary objective of the archaeological study was to place Elmina in broader context and examine developments within the settlement in light of models of European expansion and the processes of sociocultural change in general, particularly how these phenomena can be perceived and investigated archaeologically. The European buildings and the myriad of trade goods offer clear testament to the European presence, but inferring what these material remains convey about change in the belief system, values, ideals—the *worldview*—of the African population is more challenging. Physical traces do, however, provide insights into both change and continuity in how the Elmina people ordered their lives and conceptualized the world.

Much of the data discussed in this volume deal with the impacts and consequences of the expansion of a European-centered economic system into the non-Western world between the fifteenth and the nineteenth centuries. The European trade, territorial claims, and eventual colonization had far-reaching effects on West African exchange systems, economies, and sociopolitical organization. From the onset, Africa was an integral part of European expansion. It was in Africa that European maritime exploration and colonial expansion began and where the models of colonization unfolded.[6] The islands off the northwest coast of Africa were settled in the early fifteenth century. Castelo de São Jorge da Mina was founded 10 years prior to Columbus's first voyage to the Americas, and Columbus, in fact, sailed with a Portuguese trading mission to West Africa between 1482 and 1484 (Hair 1990:115). There he may have witnessed the final stages of the construction of São Jorge. The technical and practical expertise in navigation and expedition planning and the knowledge of trade that Columbus gained on this voyage were crucial in his succeeding voyages of discovery. Whatever the rationale for the Spanish court's acceptance of his proposed ventures, Columbus brought current, detailed knowledge of Atlantic exploration.

Connections among Africa, Asia, Europe, and the Americas were essential to the developments that influenced much of the character of the world we see today (see Thornton 1995).[7] West African gold provided incentive for European trade during the fifteenth and sixteenth centuries, and it remained an important motive even after the realization of Asian and American riches.[8] Beginning in the sixteenth century the emerging plantation economies of the Americas demanded more labor—demands that were filled through increasing exports of enslaved Africans. This trade dominated European interests in the region between 1650 and 1850, with a peak during the late eighteenth century. The Atlantic slave trade engulfed vast portions of the western and central African coasts and hinterlands and brought 12 million to 15.4 million individuals across the Atlantic.[9] This trade initiated a variety of changes in indigenous societies as Africa was drawn into a worldwide economic system. The immediate result was the strengthening of sociopolitical structures that facilitated and controlled exchange. By the mid-nineteenth century new conditions had emerged. The Atlantic slave trade was abolished, and raw materials such as palm oil and rubber increasingly became the staples of the West African trade. European mass-produced commodities arrived in increasing variety and quantity. The nineteenth century also brought intensified Christian missionary activity. All of these developments foreshadowed, led to, and culminated with European partition of Africa into spheres of influence by the beginning of the twentieth century (Boahen 1991; Pakenham 1991).

It was trade that brought the Europeans, and it was within this arena that their activities took place. It is not surprising, therefore, that examinations of European interactions with Africans have often been conceptualized in terms of changing trade relations and economic impacts.[10] Many models have been posited to chart these interactions. Among the best articulated is world-system theory, developed by Immanuel Wallerstein (1976a, b, 1980, 1986).[11] For social scientists, this theory provides insight into the economic and political connections that have shaped the world during the past 500 years. Its potential for contextualizing the appearance of European trade materials in the archaeological record makes it particularly seductive to archaeologists examining the record of European expansion.[12] Wallerstein identified several historical phases during which Africa was incorporated into the global economy. He considers African economies prior to the eighteenth century to have largely functioned independently. European trade consisted mainly of nonessential commodities, and demand was primarily dependent on European productive capacities and supply lines. By 1750 the coastal regions of Africa had been brought into the economic periphery. This period was, first and foremost, characterized by the growth of slave labor as an integral part of the European economy. The growth of the trade, Wallerstein argues, in turn precipitated changes in sociopolitical organizations within the slave-exporting regions. During the next 150 years, the rest of West Africa was incorporated into the economic periphery.

The world-system model is particularly relevant here because the majority of this volume deals with the effects that occurred in African societies as a result of European trade and the economic, political, and social changes it engendered. The data from Elmina are illustrative of dramatic transformation, ranging from innovation in subsistence and diet to urbanization and state formation. Despite these changes, an overarching perspective in this book has been the examination of the material record in terms of *cultural continuity* rather than change in African belief systems. This is not to imply a stasis or lack of change in African societies: Africa and Elmina did not remain "primitive, static, and asleep or in a Hobbesian state of nature" during the period under study (Boahen 1991:23).[13] Rather, examination of continuities is a recognition of the way in which history at once is shaped by and shapes the cultural context in which it unfolds and the diversity of local responses.[14] World-system theory and similar models provide a macroscopic view of the contact setting, offering a holistic means of conceptualizing the economic and historical processes and the political constraints that shaped European expansion. They afford a less satisfactory explanation of developments internal to African societies. Addressing variation in the contact setting, Wallerstein notes: "It is not that there are no particularities of each acting group. Quite the contrary. It is that the alternatives available for each unit are constrained by the framework of the whole, even while each actor opting for a given alternative in fact alters the framework of the whole" (1986:101). Yet it is reasonable to question, as many have, to what extent the same Eurocentric "framework" constrained individual parts of the global economy (e.g., Mintz 1977; Thornton 1995; Wolf 1982). Although European interactions in West Africa can be painted in broad strokes, active agency on the part of African societies in shaping the nature of the contact setting and the diversity of the interactions that occurred needs to be underscored. Even in our recognition of the potential explanatory value of larger systems, understanding of how change occurs is best examined through case studies of individual societies (e.g., Marcus 1995). Elmina is such a study. What this research dramatically illustrates is the ways in which local rules uniquely articulate with and mitigate global patterns.

Although changes in economic relations may have necessitated particular structural changes and emphasis on the trade in certain commodities, the nature of African-European interactions varied at different times and in different locales, as did the specific European policies initiated, the materials exchanged, and the volume of trade. Portuguese settlements in North Africa, such as Qsar es-Seghir, can be viewed as ill-fated colonial experiments: cultural transplants and economic failures that remained economically and culturally isolated from the hinterland and the interior trade (Redman 1986). In contrast the lucrative traffic along the West African coast was at first conducted entirely from ships, which remained the predominant pattern in some parts of the coast. It is not coincidental that two of the regions of West Africa that saw the most intensive European activity were areas that afforded comparatively easy access to the gold-producing areas of the interior. Gold was found relatively close to the coast of modern-day Ghana, and the Europeans established fortified outposts to secure trade and allow for the accumulation and storage of goods. In the Senegambia, European trade posts were located along the Gambia and Sénégal river valleys. These enclaves were military garrisons, predominantly staffed by men and comparatively small (Posnansky and DeCorse 1986; van Dantzig 1980a; Wood 1967).

Nor did the various African societies that came in contact with Europeans encounter a monolithic "European" or national cultural tradition. In coastal Ghana, the Portuguese, Dutch, French, British, Swedes, Danes, and Brandenburgers vied for trade. Typically, however, the different nations relied on recruits from all over Europe, and staffs of individual garrisons were ethnically heterogeneous. In 1672, for example, the entire complement of Danish Fort Christiansborg consisted of a Danish commander, a Greek assistant, and 40 slaves (Lawrence 1963:201). Shifting European alliances often resulted in rapid changes in relations among different European powers and, hence, in the policies and the specifics of the contact settings that unfolded. Yet conditions in Europe cannot be equated with those in West Africa, where actions were mitigated by local issues and concerns. There are many instances of commandants of different nationalities continuing to eat and drink together while their countrymen fought in Europe (Nørregård 1966:26–27). On the other hand, the Dutch aided the Danes during their 1658 war with Sweden, but this did not stop them from attempting to capture the Danish outposts in West Africa. France occupied the Dutch Republic in 1795, yet the Dutch flag continued to fly over the Gold Coast outposts (Brukum 1985:19). It is doubtful that specific national characters emerged under these conditions. This does not, however, suggest that Africans perceived no differences among the Europeans they encountered.[15]

African responses to contact were similarly diverse. There is ample evidence that West African societies witnessed extensive change in sociopolitical and economic relations during the past 500 years. Africa has presented a diversity of cultures that have evinced a variety of sociopolitical organizations ranging from comparatively decentralized societies to groups that have been categorized as chiefdoms and states.[16] Indigenes responded to and interacted with Europeans in different ways and shaped the consequences of these interactions to varying degrees. Political and technological sophistication allowed many West African societies to manipulate European relations, to effectively play one group off against another, or to actively restrict European ventures. Some African polities forged close alliances with the Europeans, whereas others vigorously opposed or regulated their activities. On the Gold Coast many of the coastal states allied themselves with European powers and proved key in European competition for trade and possession of trade forts. The trans-Saharan trade and trading towns of the forest-savanna ecotone declined while coastal states thrived along the new frontier of opportunity provided by the European trade. States rose and fell, new trade entrepôts flourished, and millions of Africans were enslaved and transported to the Americas. A multitude of non-Western cultures became linked through European trade to an increasingly global economy, but a particular stage of economic development—of "core-periphery" relations—did not correspond to a particular stage of acculturation. Ethnographic studies vividly demonstrate the variable nature of the causal factors involved in change and the specific processes through which change occurs (e.g., Bascom and Herskovits 1963; Curtin 1972; Herskovits 1962; Serageldin and Taboroff 1994; Steward 1972; Tessler, O'Barr, and Spain 1973; Wallerstein 1966). Explication of these distinctive, culturally mitigated conditions is germane to many of the questions and concerns central to anthropology.

In examining the African-European interactions at Elmina, I address the preceding concerns through the archaeological record, European documentary sources, and oral histories and traditions. Each of these sources affords insight into the ways in which the past unfolded. Such interdisciplinary resources are the strength of historical archaeology. Methodologically, however, researchers are confronted with differences in the kinds and scale of information each source provides. In addition to necessitating different research strategies, different source materials structure the kind or type of information that can be investigated. Details on certain topics are more complete or more readily available than others. For example, if archaeological data and the documentary record both confirm the growth of European trade at Elmina, they provide quite different perspectives. Archaeologically, imported ceramics are among the most common trade items found. Over 6,000 sherds of imported ceramics were recovered at Elmina, roughly a quarter of the number of local pottery fragments. The imported wares include more than 100 type varieties from Europe, Britain, Asia, and America. Ceramics clearly constitute an important part of the European commodities trade from an archaeological standpoint. Nevertheless, documentary records and trade lists of the fifteenth through the nineteenth centuries make only minor reference to ceramics and certainly give no indication of the large amount found relative to the rest of the archaeological assemblage.

Far more common in the documentary records are references to cloth. Dozens of terms for Indian and European linens, cotton prints, batiks, and silks pervade trade lists and occur with regularity in European accounts of the West African trade. A diversity of cloth was also woven locally using native cotton and imported threads. Unfortunately, cloth's composition and its functional versatility make it an unlikely material to be recovered archaeologically. A worn-out bedspread might continue in use as a wrap, rag, and eventually a lamp wick. Organic fibers do not survive well in humid climates, and discarded fragments are likely to disappear long before they are uncovered by the archaeologist's trowel. What must have been a vast cloth trade at Elmina is represented archaeologically by a single lead bale seal with the coat of arms of the city of Leiden (Figure 1.5) and a few shreds or impressions of fabric preserved with copper alloy objects.

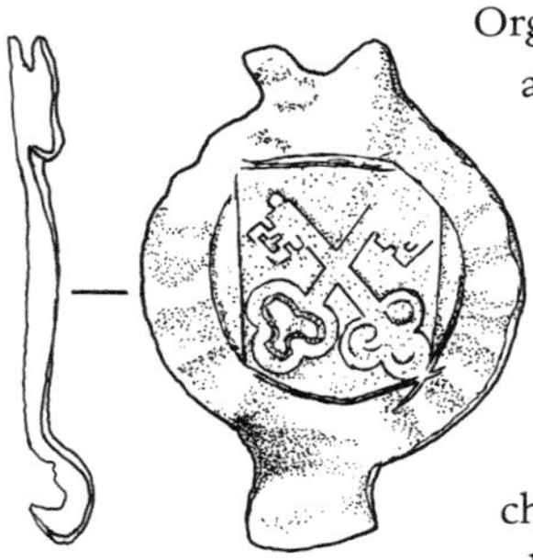

Similar disparities of scope, scale, and coign of vantage are seen in the interpretation of the Elmina settlement as a whole. Locating the site archaeologically was not a challenge. Elmina is one of the most written about and illustrated precolonial African settlements in sub-Saharan Africa. It is mentioned in copious documentary records and pictured in numerous European illustrations from the sixteenth through the nineteenth century. European records describe the military action of 1873 in detail and list the British officers and soldiers who participated in the conflict. Oral traditions also recount versions of the town's founding and interactions with the Europeans. Although many inhabitants of modern Elmina were surprised by the archaeological discoveries at the old town site, the location of the settlement was certainly known, and elders could narrate elements of Elmina's past and the destruction of the settlement.

Given this wealth of information, some Elmina people felt that digging up the old site was an entertaining though somewhat strange pursuit, and some historians might agree.[17] In fact, what is often striking when considering written and oral accounts of Elmina's past is the paucity of information and the lack of detail available on certain topics. The relative contribution of archaeological data speaks directly to the potential of archaeological research, as well as to the differences between historical and archaeological inquiry, the data sets each employs, and their distinct epistemologies. Archaeological data have alternatively been seen as an independent means of historical discovery and as

Figure 1.5.
A lead bale seal with the coat of arms of the city of Leiden (shown from front and side; seal measures 3.3 by 2.4 by 0.1 cm [1.3 by 0.95 by 0.05 inches]).
(Illustration by Christopher R. DeCorse)

the pursuit of data anecdotal to historical studies, on one hand providing the framework for historical narrative, on the other detailing the specifics lacking in written records (e.g., Oliver 1966:371; Vansina 1985:185, 187–188).[18] Archaeology can meet these objectives—and more. The material record is, in fact, particularly good at demonstrating the timing and kind of change that occurred in subsistence, technology, and indigenous artistic traditions. It can also assess some of the specific types of goods—ceramics, glass, tobacco pipes, and firearms—that were traded and their temporal ranges. But archaeology can also contribute to broader historical and anthropological debate through examination of changes in settlement patterns, artifact inventory, and archaeological features that can be used to interpret historical processes. With regard to the post-European-contact period in West Africa, perhaps the greatest potential contribution of archaeology lies in the delineation of the impact and consequences of the Atlantic slave trade on African populations, not solely those on the coastal margins occasionally mentioned in documentary records, but also those in the vast hinterland from which many enslaved Africans originated (DeCorse 1991, 2000b).[19]

The real strength lies in the interdisciplinary study of both historical and cultural phenomena. Use of different sources allows for a fuller interpretation of specific sites, features, and artifacts in a manner impossible in prehistoric studies. Documentary data provide not just the particularities of site occupation but also insight into the economic, social, political, and cultural contexts represented in the material record. This includes understanding of specific events, such as the destruction of Elmina by the British in 1873, as well as the patterns observed archaeologically that are representative of the culturally shaped historical processes that produced them. The historical background of African-European interactions on the Gold Coast briefly presented here—itself partly based on archaeological data—affords only a brief outline of the complex events and interactions that took place between the fifteenth century and the present. It nevertheless provides a context for archaeological examination of the economic, social, and cultural transformations of the past 500 years.

Problems faced in interpreting the past have been compounded by the fact that historians and archaeologists alike have, at times, viewed the archaeological record as a direct expression of an ethnographic past. The material record or even individual artifact classes have been seen as essentializing cultural or ethnic identities, as "actors on the historical stage, playing the role for prehistory that known individuals and groups have in documentary history" (Shennan 1989:6; see also DeCorse 1998b, c; Lightfoot 1995). As a result, researchers examining the archaeological record of European expansion have had a tendency to view the advent of trade materials representative of European trade and merchant capitalism as concomitant with equally dramatic changes in nonmaterial aspects of non-Western cultures, marking the erosion of values, the circumvention of traditional beliefs, and the devastation of cultural norms in the face of mass-produced products, technological superiority, and hegemonic policies of Europe. Because of the peculiarities of their data set, archaeologists have tended to underconceptualize the past.[20]

There is, in fact, no simple correspondence between material culture and nonmaterial sociocultural constructs. Many cultures maintained non-Western values and beliefs and, in doing so, turned European trade items to new purposes and ends. This is equally true with regard to sociocultural precepts as technological innovation. Trade materials are of interest not solely because of their usefulness in establishing site chronology or because of the insight they provide into technological innovation and trade but also because of what they convey about the impact of European trade on indigenous cultural systems. Technological superiority has been an integral part of cross-cultural change throughout history and a crucial factor in European interactions with indigenes (Headrick 1981). European maritime technology, communications, medical science, and firearms were the tools of empire that secured Europe's dominions in Africa and Asia in the nineteenth century. There is little question that the conflict that destroyed Elmina in 1873 would have had a different outcome if the Asante had possessed Snider repeating rifles and the British aging flintlocks. Technology was integral to the European expansion. But in viewing this technological maelstrom, we often forget that imported objects were not accepted en masse by non-Western peoples. Nor do they immediately imply an acceptance of nonmaterial European beliefs and practices. Trade materials were adopted, transformed, or rejected within the indigenous cultural traditions in a myriad of different ways. Such *entanglements* have often been ignored by archaeologists who have assessed cultural or ethnic identities—and change—in terms of artifacts whose cultural meanings are left poorly defined.[21] Reaching beyond trade lists and artifact inventories to understand how indigenes used and transformed artifacts is basic to an anthropological perception of cultural contact, continuity, and change.

Ethnoarchaeological research in West Africa serves to underscore both the prospects and problems in the archaeological delineation of ethnographically discernible cultural boundaries and changes in worldview. The archaeological record and cultural reality can be seen as complementary, each at once shaped by and an expression of the other. The archaeological record may provide material expression of ethnographically perceived boundaries. Ceramics, for example, may serve as an important expression of cosmology, religion, and symbolic structures, justifying their use as material indicators of ethnicity (e.g., David et al. 1988:365; Vansina 1995:382–383). Artifact patterning, the use of space, and settlement organization have also been shown to be useful for exploring past cognitive systems (e.g., Agorsah 1983a, b; David 1971). However, recognition of the potential of such inferences must also include awareness that such correspondences are not constant in all cultural settings. Equally varied as patterns of cultural change and the nature of African-European interaction are the ways in which these phenomena are represented archaeologically. Although artifacts are concrete, survive in the ground, and provide testament to past behavior, they were recontextualized and reinterpreted in a diversity of cultural settings in ways that may have been quite different from those that their manufacturer intended.

ELMINA IN PERSPECTIVE

The contact setting at Elmina was very different from those that unfolded in other parts of West Africa, even in adjacent portions of the Gold Coast, and Elmina presents a dramatic contrast to the many regions of Africa that remained isolated from direct European contact throughout the nineteenth century.[22] Even in areas relatively close to the coast, a combination of geographical, technological, and cultural factors limited European activities and constrained European expansion.[23] African-European interactions prior to the late nineteenth century had a distinctive character as a result of these constraints. Some areas stand out as nexuses of activity: the Sénégal and Gambia river valleys, coastal Ghana, and the small concentrations of European outposts in coastal Benin and Nigeria. But during much of the nineteenth century, the hinterland was known to only a handful of European explorers, many of whom died in their attempts to reach the interior (see McLynn 1992).[24] Disease was a major impediment to European expansion throughout West Africa until the late nineteenth century. Malaria, sleeping sickness, dysentery, yellow fever, and a host of other plagues unfamiliar to Europeans were endemic to tropical Africa. The death rate among Europeans serving on the West African coast was staggering.[25] The consequence of these impediments was that some three and a half centuries after the founding of Castelo de São Jorge da Mina the vast majority of the West African hinterland lay largely unknown to Europeans. By the 1850s it was still convenient to show most of the fruits of European exploration in West Africa on a single map.[26]

African-European interactions and European involvement in Elmina affairs were far more direct, the most important consequence being the political independence of Elmina from neighboring polities. By the mid-sixteenth century, the settlement was an independent state, which expanded with the assistance of the Portuguese and the Dutch during the following centuries.[27] Written accounts also suggest the formation of new sociopolitical institutions and practices. European officials at Elmina settled disputes, levied fish tolls, and were called upon to recognize newly elected African rulers (e.g., Baesjou 1979b; Feinberg 1989:99–104, 115–126).[28] The power the Europeans exercised was not, however, absolute. If European policies became too difficult, the people could simply abandon the town, a situation the Europeans considered alarming because it was injurious to trade. A 1523 letter from King John III to the Portuguese governor of Castelo de São Jorge da Mina expressed concern that the "knights" of Elmina were being treated harshly and that as a result the village was becoming depopulated. The king noted that this was detrimental to the maintenance of good trade relations and that the people should rather be defended, protected, and instructed (e.g., Blake 1942:46–47, 133–134).[29] Similar concerns were cited during the Dutch period (e.g., Feinberg 1969:125; van Dantzig 1978:81).[30] The Portuguese undoubtedly tried to claim rights to adjacent portions of the coast, but this was not recognized by the Dutch or, more important, by the surrounding African polities.

We have no detailed descriptions of Elmina at the time of contact, and the precise changes that took place in coastal African culture over the past 500 years will probably never be known. We can, however, point to ethnographic, documentary, and archaeological data that underscore continuity rather than change in African beliefs. This apparent continuity is particularly interesting because it occurs within the midst of a great deal of technological and sociopolitical change. Documentary sources and oral traditions attest to Elmina's central role as a trade entrepôt, and, not surprisingly, a striking aspect of the Elmina excavations was the vast amount of European trade goods recovered. This assemblage can be dramatically contrasted with data from other sites. Indeed, throughout much of sub-Saharan Africa the arrival of the Europeans on the Atlantic coast and hinterland is not a dramatic event archaeologically. Even colonial-era sites a short distance into the interior present only small numbers of European artifacts.[31] Yet the predominance of imported objects in the Elmina artifact inventory cannot be equated with ipso facto evidence of change in nonmaterial beliefs. Food preparation and eating practices, the use of space, and ritual practices illustrate continuity in Elmina culture with the surrounding, largely Akan, cultural tradition. Interpretations of both change and continuity are facilitated by a wealth of source material.

Prologue

On the eve of European contact, settlements were scattered along all of coastal Ghana and throughout the adjacent hinterland. Most were likely small fishing villages or farming communities. This pattern would dramatically change in the following centuries. Population growth along the coastal margin and concomitant changes in sociopolitical structures characterize the post-European-contact period. During the fifteenth century, however, the larger population centers were still located in the West African interior, and coastal settlements were small and dispersed. Describing coastal Ghana in 1479, Eustache de la Fosse noted Shama and Elmina as the only significant harbors. Even here it took four or five days for news of a ship's arrival to spread and for the merchants to gather (Hair 1994b:129).[32] Another fifteenth-century account of the trade comments that ". . . when any of the [European] ships reached that land, the people of the land immediately summoned each other with trumpets because they lived in the countryside, and would all assemble at the ports to trade their gold" (Hair 1994b:115).[33]

Archaeological data from coastal Ghana suggest that this pattern of dispersed settlement extends back at least 1,000 years, probably much earlier.[34] Pre-European-contact coastal sites are represented by low-density scatters of ceramics with occasional stone beads, iron artifacts, and smelting debris. Some of these sites are quite sizable. At Brenu Akyinim, for example, pottery sherds can be found for almost a kilometer (about two-thirds of a mile) along the shore.[35] This distribution, however, is likely the result of a series of small, shifting settlements over a long period of time rather than a single large occupation. Substantial midden deposits, large settlement mounds, or embankments, features that characterize later sites, are absent. Similar observations have been made for other parts of coastal Ghana.[36]

The inhabitants of these settlements spoke Akan languages. This inference is based on linguistic evidence and, to a lesser extent, on ethnohistorical data.

Surveying European sources, Paul Hair deduced that vocabularies and word references to the local language from the late fifteenth century onward are Akan.[37] This attribution provides no indications of dialectical differences or more subtle ethnolinguistic divisions. Akan languages are closely related, forming one of the major subdivisions within the Volta-Comoé Group (Dolphyne and Kropp Dakubu 1988).[38] They are currently spoken in a continuous geographical spread from southeastern Ivory Coast to the Volta River in eastern Ghana. Today the principal Akan group of central, coastal Ghana—including Elmina—is Fante, which is bordered on the west by Ahanta speakers and in the east by the Ga and Guan. To a large extent the various Akan languages are mutually intelligible. Although Akan is purely a linguistic classification, a high degree of cultural homogeneity also characterizes groups within the language family.[39] The people are historically agriculturists, relying on shifting hoe cultivation and fallowing, with fishing providing an important subsistence stratagem among the coastal Fante. Akan sociocultural organization is characterized by highly extended exogamous matriclans, or *mmusua* (sing., *abusua*), which have been historically important as a unifying factor of Akan identity and a means of assimilating non-Akan cultural elements into Akan society. The matrilineage is the locus of an individual's identity, determining inheritance of property, sociopolitical status, eligibility for state office, and links with the spiritual world. A high degree of ideological and ritual conformity within Akan groups is enforced by the clan elders. Patrilateral ties of varying kinds, including the spiritual links of the *ntɔrɔ,* crosscut and complement the overarching matrilineal framework.[40] These kinship ties are associated with a wide variety of rituals, taboos, and totems. Other Akan commonalties include certain aspects of origin traditions, a 42-day calendrical system, naming procedures, elements of sociopolitical organization, and shared aspects of worldview.

Akan studies have been overshadowed by the Asante, who are the best described ethnographically and thus are frequently used to characterize the Akan as a whole (e.g., Kiyaga-Mulindwa 1980; Wilks 1993).[41] The Asante state expanded throughout much of central Ghana in the eighteenth century, incorporating groups that had formerly been autonomous polities. Asante culture traits, particularly language, sociopolitical organization, and state craft, were imprinted on non-Asante groups. Asante cultural influences can also be seen in the archaeological record. This is particularly the case in ceramics, which in parts of southern Ghana become increasingly dominated by black burnished, carinated Asante forms in the eighteenth and nineteenth centuries (e.g., Bellis 1987; Crossland 1973, 1989).[42] On the other hand, features of other groups, including those of the non-Akan Ewe-, Ga-, Guan-, and Dangme-speaking peoples were welded into a distinct and fairly homogeneous Akan culture. It is reasonable to assume that during the fifteenth century the Akan inhabitants of coastal Ghana shared ideological, ritual, and sociocultural features, the distinctive expression of which may be traced in the documentary, ethnographic, and archaeological records.[43]

The political organization of the fifteenth-century Akan coast is more difficult to assess. Political relations probably consisted of small chiefdoms or in-

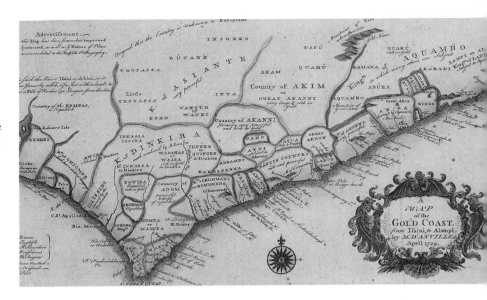

Figure 1.6. A map of the Gold Coast by M. d'Anville, 1729. The relative positions of the coastal settlements and polities are shown relatively accurately, but European knowledge of the interior was much more limited. (Reproduced courtesy of Christraud M. Geary)

cipient state-level polities centered on major settlements, with the larger political aggregates located in the interior closer to the forest-savanna ecotone. Actual empirical evidence for this is, however, limited. Surveys of place names and African states mentioned in early European accounts suggest a correspondence with the general location, if not the specific organization and extent, of polities identified in later periods (see Figure 1.6). Maps of the coast by Luis Teixeira in 1602 and also in a Dutch manuscript of 1629 show Eguafo (Guaffo, Great Comendo, or Comane) to the west of Elmina and the country of Fetu (Futu, Afutu) to the east (see comments in Blake 1987; Chouin 1998a:191–193; Cortesão and Teixeira de Mota 1960, 3:67–70; Daaku 1970:182–184; Daaku and van Dantzig 1966; de Marees 1987:xxii–xxv; Kea 1982:23–28; and by Müller in Jones 1983).[44] These names, and possibly the lineal descendants of the polities represented, still exist. Fetu, with its capital at Efutu, is known to have controlled much of the territory east of Elmina, with the principal coastal settlement being Cape Coast (Cabo Cors). The Eguafo polity, with its seat at the town of Eguafo, controlled lands to the northwest and west of Elmina. Fetu and Eguafo may both have laid claim to Elmina during the fifteenth century.

Archaeological survey and excavation that might help assess the development of sociopolitical complexity have not been undertaken, though information is accumulating.[45] The sites of Eguafo and Efutu, as well as other historically known Fante settlements, have extensive archaeological deposits. European trade materials dating to the sixteenth through the nineteenth centuries have been recovered from test excavations, surface collections, and poorly documented finds made by gold prospectors. Thermoluminescence dates on ceramics from recent excavations at Eguafo suggest that the settlement had been occupied by early in the second millennium A.D., but the majority of the deposits likely reflect later occupation.

The Europeans on the Gold Coast

Portuguese mariners began explorations of the African coast in the early fifteenth century. Isolated travelers' accounts from antiquity provided scant information on the lands south of the Sahara, but the West African coast and hinterland were completely unknown (Boxer 1972:9–10).[46] Waters south of Cape Bojador on the Moroccan coast were believed to be a dead zone with no wind and temperatures too hot to endure—the lands peopled with legendary creatures. This situation dramatically changed by the end of the century. Political, social, and economic conditions, combined with more refined sailing technology, allowed Portugal to enter a century of maritime expansion.[47] Ships were trading at the mouth of the Pra River by 1471, but isolated visits may have occurred earlier.[48] The Portuguese first traded from ships, but the advantages of a strong base were soon realized. A fortress would serve as a deterrent to other European traders and also would allow for the accumulation and storage of goods prior to a ship's arrival. The latter may have been especially critical given the time it took for merchants to assemble.[49] The result of these concerns was the founding of Castelo de São Jorge da Mina.

Several things made Elmina a logical choice for a fortress.[50] The foremost of these was the presence of a sizable African settlement, which afforded trade opportunities and labor. The physical setting was also advantageous. The African town and the future site of the castle were on a narrow rocky peninsula formed by the Benya Lagoon and the ocean. The peninsula provided an easily defensible position, and the lagoon offered a safe anchorage and a place to careen vessels. Finally, an abundance of quarriable stone to be used in the castle's construction made the site a logical choice. Commander Diogo de Azambuja arrived in Elmina in January 1482.[51] He sailed with an expedition of 10 caravels, 500 soldiers and servants, and 100 masons, carpenters, and craftsmen. The ships carried precut stone for the castle's foundations, arches, and windows. The precut stone from Portugal and quarried Elminian sandstone were used to erect a rectangular enclosure at the eastern end of the Elmina peninsula. Although modified by later Dutch and British additions, the basic plan still conforms to the later Portuguese fortification. Some Portuguese elements are still readily discernible, including the Portuguese church in the central courtyard, remodeled by the Dutch and used as a warehouse and soldiers' mess.

The Portuguese established smaller trade posts on the Gold Coast at Axim, Shama, and Accra. With these and the garrison at Elmina, Portugal attempted to maintain, through force and legal sanctions, a monopoly on European trade on the Gold Coast. Information about the trade was a closely guarded secret, and royal decrees forbade the passing of knowledge to foreigners. Portugal claimed exclusive trading rights in Guinea on the basis of several papal bulls that granted rights to profits obtained from the lands discovered between Cape Bojador (Morocco) and the East Indies (Blake 1977:20–23).[52] This authority provided the Portuguese with political leverage and prevented the overt intervention of other European powers.

Interloping could not, however, always be regulated through political channels. As early as 1480, instructions were given to Portuguese captains sailing to Guinea to seize the ships and cargoes of any other nation and cast their crews into the sea—a policy that continued until the middle of the next century (e.g., Blake 1977:54, 118; Teixeira da Mota and Hair 1988:11).[53] Heavily armed galleons were dispatched from Lisbon to protect the caravels returning from Elmina, and coastal patrols were used to suppress illicit trade. Elmina and its environs were patrolled by armed galleys. Villages whose inhabitants traded with other European nations were burned (e.g., Feinberg 1969:22, 30; Vogt 1979:96, 103, 109, 129; Jones 1983:78; Teixeira da Mota and Hair 1988:10–11.).

Rivalries

Despite Portuguese efforts, other European nations vied for a share of the trade. Voyages to Guinea by Flemish, Spanish, and, possibly, Genoese merchants occurred before 1500 (Blake 1977:37–39; Vogt 1979:12–18). Perhaps even more serious than unsanctioned trade were attacks on Portuguese ships. As early as 1492 French privateers seized a Portuguese caravel returning from Elmina (Blake 1977:107). *The Letters of John III* (Ford 1931) indicates that French pirates captured more than 300 Portuguese ships between 1500 and 1531. At least a portion of these were involved in the Guinea trade. With the Treaties of Alcovas in 1478 and Tordesillas in 1494 and Castile's increased preoccupation with the Americas, the Spanish threat lessened, but incursions by other nations proved more serious. Initially, the chief Portuguese rival was France, but Dutch and English voyages became equally common by the end of the century (Blake 1977:106). By 1530, 50 years of "quiet consolidation" had come to an abrupt end (Blake 1977:96).[54] At the close of the sixteenth century, voyages to Guinea were so common that there was no "winter or summer" of navigation, as many as 25 ships anchoring at a time (Thilmans 1968:17–18).[55] "Illegitimate" trade by other Europeans soon surpassed the trade of the Portuguese.

Elmina remained the Portuguese stronghold, albeit ill supplied and plagued by inefficient bureaucracy.[56] The model of governance that the Portuguese employed continued to rely on royal authority from Lisbon, which in practical terms provided limited direction in the empire's far-flung outposts. The Portuguese crown's central concern was the potential revenue from the trade. Attention was focused on luxury items, such as spices, ivory, and gold, the last being the primary trade item at Elmina. Royal monopolies and leases over trade in particular regions and key commodities were granted to merchants in exchange for rent. The merchant community further supported expansive energies by sharing the costs with the government and by the use of private vessels. In fact, the trading rights and support granted by Lisbon were unenforceable and of limited use in West Africa. Portugal also lacked an administrative bureaucracy to support and resupply outposts efficiently and regularly, and garrisons were often left to fend for themselves. By the mid-sixteenth century, profits from Elmina were often insufficient to cover the cost of maintaining the garrison (Teixeira da Mota and Hair 1988:26–33; see also Ballong-Wen-Mewuda 1984, 1993; Fage 1973; Vogt 1979:144, 218–219). The loss in revenue at Elmina and problems with Portugal's trade in Brazil and Asia can be traced to foreign competition and the growing illicit trade carried on by Portuguese officials (Birmingham 1970; Blake 1942:49–51; Boxer 1972:18–19; Elbl 1997; Rodney 1965; Tomlinson 1970; Vogt 1974). Despite regulation, government posts were regarded as a means of amassing personal fortunes. While the trade of other nations expanded, Portuguese commerce remained hampered by economic problems and a cumbersome bureaucracy.

Figure 1.7. Dutch Fort Nassau at Mori. Founded in 1612, the fort was the first non-Portuguese, fortified trade post established on the Gold Coast. The ruins include many of the distinctive yellow Dutch bricks used in construction. (Photograph by Christopher R. DeCorse)

Between 1580 and 1640, Portugal was united with the Spanish monarchy.[57] Although this may have provided a brief reinvestment in Mina trade, São Jorge remained more a liability than an asset (Vogt 1979:114, 127–169; de Marees 1987:212–217, 221). Fewer and fewer supply ships came to Elmina during the closing years of the sixteenth century. The Elmina garrison prevented other European ships from anchoring there, but competitors' ships in neighboring areas drew trade away. The Portuguese position became increasingly tenuous, and other European powers competed to fill the vacancy. The Dutch and the French had established trade posts in the Senegambia by the seventeenth century.[58] On the Gold Coast the Dutch established a fort at Mori (Mouri, Moure) just 16 km (10 miles) east of Elmina in 1612 (Figure 1.7) (Vogt 1979:164–165; de Marees 1987:81–84; Feinberg 1989:30).[59] The Dutch had been actively trading at this location since the late fifteenth century. Dutch merchants had, in fact, started to fortify the site several years earlier. The fortress was established with the support of the chief of the Asebu state, who sent two ambassadors to Holland on a Dutch ship with the request that a fort be built in defiance of the Portuguese (van Dantzig 1980b:32). Mori subsequently became the center of Dutch mercantile activity.

These incursions were an immediate threat to the Portuguese. The Dutch unsuccessfully attempted to capture São Jorge da Mina in 1596, 1603, 1606, 1615, and 1625. In all of these cases they were driven off with the help of Africans from Elmina (Chouin 1998a:39–45; de Marees 1987:108, 219; Feinberg 1969:30–31; Ulsheimer in Jones 1983:21–22; Vogt 1979:148, 155–157, 166–167, 179–184).[60] The success of the Dutch attack in August 1637 was largely due to the support of the African states of Eguafo and Asebu and to the incapacitation of the Portuguese garrison (Figures 1.8 and 1.9). A force of 800 Dutch soldiers, with another 1,000–1,400 men from Asebu and Eguafo, reportedly gathered at the coastal town of Komenda and marched toward Elmina (Vogt 1979:166, 187–192).[61] The

Figure 1.8. A 1637 view of Elmina Castle and town from the southeast. Note the wall or stockade between the southern side of the castle and the shore. (From *Rerum per Octennium in Brasilia et Alibi Nuper Gestarum . . . Historia* by Caspar Balaraeus. Reproduced courtesy of the Bibliotheek der Rijksuniversiteit, Leiden [20069 A2])

Figure 1.9. Plan of Elmina Castle and town circa 1637. Although the location of the town is indicated, the houses are represented in schematic form and do not correspond to the actual layout of the settlement. (Reproduced courtesy of the Algemeen Rijksarchief, Afdeling Kaarten en Tekeningen [VELH 619-77])

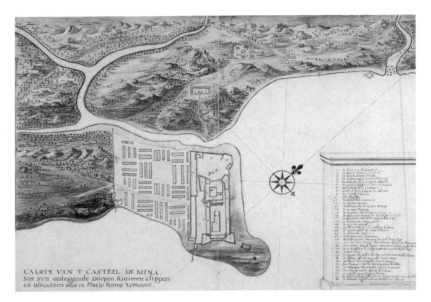

Portuguese garrison at Elmina at this time consisted of 35 officials and soldiers. The Dutch succeeded in overwhelming the Portuguese and Elmina forces protecting the small redoubt on the top of St. Jago Hill, a small rise north of the Benya Lagoon. Here they positioned artillery pieces to bombard the Portuguese garrison into submission. The castle subsequently replaced Fort Nassau at Mori as the Dutch headquarters in Guinea, and it remained Dutch for the next 235 years.

Mercantilism

The capture of Elmina was indicative of changes in political, social, and especially economic conditions in Europe. By 1600 European centers of commerce, finance, and industry were in northwest Europe: Holland and Zeeland; England (especially London and East Anglia); and later in northern and western France (Wallerstein 1980:37–71).[62] Unquestionably the nexus was the provinces of the emerging state of the Netherlands, which, at the end of the sixteenth century, were just beginning to extract themselves from Spanish rule. Particularly important was the Dutch textile industry, centered at Leiden, which dominated

European production through much of the seventeenth century. There were also rapid developments in agriculture, mechanical technology, distilling, paper production, brick making, ceramics, tobacco pipe manufacture, and a host of other industries. The Dutch also brought craftsmen from Venice, the center of glass bead production, to Amsterdam. This productive output was combined with efficient commercial organization and the Dutch shipbuilding industry (for general reviews, see Boxer 1990; Wallerstein 1980).

Many of the commodities produced in northwestern Europe were of major importance in the Africa trade. Portugal lacked the productive capabilities and, thus, was placed at a disadvantage. Dutch and other European traders on the Gold Coast brought goods of a quality similar to or better than those offered by the Portuguese and offered them at better prices. The Portuguese attempted to bolster their position through the use of Asian metalware and cloth, but these too could not be supplied on a regular basis (Vogt 1979:146–147, 153). Writing in 1602, Pieter de Marees painted the picture: "[T]hey [the Portuguese] are faring quite badly and are much in decline, so that nowadays the Castle d'Mina gives the King of Spain more loss than profit; and this is because the trade of the Portuguese is totally ruined . . . as a result of competition from the Dutch Ships, which offer trade-goods here for about the same price as the Portuguese have to pay in Portugal" (1987:214, see also 55).[63] The predominance of Dutch pipes, wine and gin bottles, and yellow brick on archaeological sites, along with

the occasional finds of tobacco boxes and delftware sherds, is testament to the commercial success of the Dutch during the seventeenth and eighteenth centuries (Figure 1.10). Unlike the earlier Portuguese trade that had been an archaic *feitoria* system governed by royal *regimentos* and personal representatives of the crown, the Dutch trade of the seventeenth and eighteenth centuries was guided by chartered mercantile companies (see Brukum 1985; Feinberg 1969, 1989). The first of these was the first West India Company, which was organized in 1621. The company failed in 1674 and was replaced by the second West India Company. The organization of the second company was much the same as the first, but it was less ambitious and narrower in scope than its predecessor. By 1725 there were 15 Dutch forts on the Gold Coast (Feinberg 1989:35).

Figure 1.10. An eighteenth-century brass tobacco box discovered by gold miners at Eguafo. A similar find was also recovered from an eighteenth-century context at Elmina (shown from front and side; box measures 10.8 by 6.6 by 3.2 cm [4.25 by 2.55 by 1.25 inches]). (Photograph by Douglas Pippin)

The seventeenth and eighteenth centuries were the age of the Dutch seaborne empire. By 1700 this small European nation had extended trade and established outposts in western and southern Africa, Asia, and the Americas. Dutch commercial interests were not, however, unchallenged. Other European nations launched their own trading ventures in West Africa. By 1800 over 30 forts, castles, lodges, and plantations belonging to various European nations were scattered along the 500-km (310-mile) shore of the Gold Coast (Figure 1.11) (Lawrence 1963; van Dantzig 1980a).[64] Ship trade also remained important. Although French efforts to establish trade posts were short lived, they nevertheless maintained an active trade (e.g., see Chouin 1998a:91–127, 149–181; van Dantzig 1980a:41–42; Vogt 1979:96–98).[65] The Portuguese, who were unable to maintain an outpost on the Gold Coast after their loss of São Antonio de Axem (Axim) in 1642 and Fort St. Francis Xavier (Osu) in 1683, also remained active,

Figure 1.11. European trade posts in West Africa during the eighteenth century. The enlargement of the Gold Coast was probably added before 1773. (British Crown copyright photograph supplied courtesy of the Public Record Office [Document MPK45])

particularly trading in Brazilian tobacco and slaves (e.g., Brukum 1985:41; van Dantzig 1978:152; Vogt 1979:194–204). Dutch free traders, who operated outside the West India Company's jurisdiction, were also active (e.g., see van Dantzig 1978:9, 237).

Of critical significance in the seventeenth and eighteenth centuries was the continued growth of the Atlantic slave trade. During the seventeenth century slaves replaced gold as the primary export from the Gold Coast. The timing, reasons, and implications of this shift have been the subject of extensive scholarship.[66] At the core of a variety of economic, social, and political transformations were the labor requirements of the emerging plantation system in the Americas. These developments had important consequences in West Africa. Prior to the seventeenth century, European coastal trade was essentially the same as that of the trans-Saharan and Indian Ocean systems, which had begun centuries earlier. The items involved consisted of many commodities and luxury items for which there was already demand. African gold was exchanged for metal goods, cowrie shells, clothing, and beads (see Chapter 5). The volume of trade was dependent on European production and supply capabilities, as well as on African trade and distribution networks. Initially, African economies remained self-sustaining and largely functioned independently. The slave trade, however, increasingly enmeshed the African economies that supplied the slaves, in many instances through raiding.[67]

The historical and archaeological data that are available are insufficient to assess fully the consequences of the slave trade on African populations. The majority of the documentary sources and, hence, much of the history on the topic focus on the coastal ports through which enslaved Africans passed, not on their actual ethnic origins. Understanding of the African impacts, as well as the cultural heritage of Africans in the diaspora, is dependent on much fuller knowledge of developments in the vast hinterland of Africa, from which the slaves were drawn (DeCorse 1991, 1999, 2000b).[68] What is clear is that the impact of trade varied in individual social, cultural, and historical settings. Some societies were directly involved in slave procurement and trading, whereas others were extensively raided for slaves. The negative effect was much greater in the latter situation, the ultimate consequence being interference in the societies' ability to reproduce biologically. Archaeologically, the disruption of social systems may be inferred by alterations in settlement patterns, appearance of fortifications, evidence of depopulation, rapid change in pottery styles, and changes in the artifact inventory.

At Elmina the historical context was quite distinct from other areas of West Africa and even from adjacent portions of the coast and hinterland. The settlement and immediate vicinity were generally not a substantial source of slaves. There are examples of Elmina citizens being *panyarred,* or sold into slavery because of debt, and others were enslaved as war captives in conflicts with neighboring Fante states, but these were limited occurrences rather than the norm.[69] The Portuguese, in fact, imported slaves to Elmina throughout the late fifteenth and early sixteenth centuries. The Portuguese, and later the Dutch, prohibited the taking of slaves on the Gold Coast, the presumption being that it was detrimental to the trade in gold (de Marees 1987:48 n. 2; Rodney 1969; Vogt 1979:168).[70] This proved to be the case in the eighteenth century when the increased demand for slaves for the Atlantic trade led to kidnapping, slaving, and the disruption of trading caravans (Rodney 1969:19).[71] A royal decree of 1615 permitted the capture and enslavement of Africans on the Gold Coast only beyond a distance of 10 leagues (approximately 50 km or 30 miles) from Elmina, and the Dutch refer to the limited number of slaves available on the central Gold Coast through the seventeenth century.

The complexities of the Atlantic slave trade and the paucity of detailed records on ethnic origins make it difficult to determine how many captive Africans actually from Elmina were taken to the Americas. Given the population size of the town and its immediate environs relative to the overall volume of the trade, the number had to have been comparatively small. Europeans generally failed to recognize differences in African ethnicities and language dialects. Hence, in many instances the identity of captives became associated with the region or port of export through which they passed, resulting in the amalgamation of numerous distinct cultural and ethnic identities into a few, broad categories (Geggus 1989; Kea 1996; Lovejoy 1989). Elmina, variously listed as Mina, Amina, Aminra, and Aminer, became a trope for Akan-speaking people from the Gold Coast. Many other enslaved Africans who passed through ports such as Elmina were from other regions and representative of ethnic groups quite distinct from the indigenous population. These complexities are well illustrated in the difficulties faced in tracing the connections between Elmina and Curaçao in the Netherlands Antilles, which served as a major Dutch distribution point for captive Africans in the Americas (Haviser and DeCorse 1991). Documentary accounts indicate that many of the slaves that reached Curaçao via Elmina were actually brought by ship from other parts of the coast, particularly the Bight of Benin. Many were subsequently dispersed to other parts of the Americas. Such intricacies make it difficult to identify African continuities in American settings.

Limited historical sources suggest that slave traders considered the "Elmina"— the term here including individuals from other areas as well as the actual Elmina settlement—as mutinous, savage, and vicious, the worst of slaves, and thus regarded them as a poor resource. Slaves from Elmina were said to have been the instigators of the 1733 slave revolt in the Danish West Indies, which left them in control of the island of St. John for six months.[72] It is possible that a few of the Elmina held responsible were free people, merchants or individuals of some prominence from the Elmina settlement (Pope 1969:134–135). However, the majority of "Elmina" slaves in the St. John revolt were likely Akwamu and Adangme men and women, from the eastern Gold Coast, who were sold to agents of the Danish West India and Guinea Company between 1730 and 1733, following the collapse of the Akwamu state in 1730 (Kea 1996; Wilks 1957).

If the town of Elmina and its immediate environs were not a primary source of slaves, they nevertheless provide dramatic illustration of the consequences of an expanding Eurocentric economic system and the emergence of the Atlantic trade. This is reflected in change in African sociopolitical institutions, as well as in the urbanization, growth of material wealth, and the alteration of behavior patterns detailed by the archaeological record. As discussed below, it is during this time period that some of the town's distinctive political structures likely emerged.

Consolidation and Colonialism

Competition between European nations was fierce. This rivalry was played out against a backdrop of shifting alliances, wars, and political intrigue. Accounts of trade present an array of conflicting perceptions and images. Ships' captains of different nationalities might enjoy a pleasant dinner together and yet view each other as bitter enemies a few weeks later. Vast fortunes were amassed, but competition brought lower prices and increasingly shrewd buyers. European nations unable to compete simply gave up. By the late eighteenth century the last of the major coastal forts on the Gold Coast had been built. The succeeding century was a period of reevaluation, consolidation, and retrenchment. Three nations controlled the outposts: Britain, the Netherlands, and Denmark. The Danes dominated the eastern Gold Coast, including all of the forts between Christiansborg Castle, Osu, and Fort Prindsensteen on the Keta Lagoon. British and Dutch holdings were interspersed at irregular intervals to the west. The British headquarters was at Cape Coast Castle, only about 13 km (8 miles) from the Dutch headquarters at Elmina. Of these three nations, only Britain would remain in 1872.

The precipitator of changes on the Gold Coast was the abolition of the slave trade. The moral and economic rational for the trade in slavery was debated throughout Europe in the eighteenth century. After 1772, slaves reaching England were increasingly deemed to have free status, and Denmark outlawed the importation of slaves in 1803. Other European countries and finally the United States (in 1865) and Brazil (in 1888) followed suit. New areas of commerce had to be explored, and it was Britain that was in the best position to do this. By the nineteenth century Britain had developed as the economic nexus of Europe. Birmingham brass, Manchester cotton, and Staffordshire pottery were starting to dominate trade. Britain alone was able to take advantage of the changing economic conditions and seize the potential of new markets.[73] During the nineteenth century the gross tonnage of British shipping involved in West Africa burgeoned, climbing from about 52,000 t (57,000 tons) in 1854 to about 458,000 t (504,000 tons) in 1874 (Reynolds 1974:119). Even as a crude measure, such figures illustrate the increasing volume of trade and growing commercial concern.

This was an era of détente in intra-European relations on the Gold Coast. In contrast with the military rivalry of the preceding centuries, relations among European nations were harmonious to the extent that conflicts were primarily resolved through political accord. Forts were no longer needed to secure trade from other European nations. They became, instead, administrative centers and bases for the antislavery squadrons that patrolled the coast. The economic rational for outposts was, however, never more carefully scrutinized, and competition never more intense. Ultimately, commercial enterprise would be important in rationalizing the colonial expansion later in the century, but in the preceding decades the economic worth of the West African outposts was far from obvious. Treaties sought to consolidate holdings and secure revenue. There was an increasing perception of territorial rights to the lands beyond the confines of the small coastal enclaves, a foundation or rationale for the territorial claims that would typify the end of the century.

As the nineteenth century progressed, Denmark was the first nation to decide its Gold Coast holdings were not worth maintaining. The Danish crown had purchased the troubled Danish West India and Guinea Company in 1754 (Nørregård 1966).[74] Despite a resurgence during the American Revolution, Danish West African enterprises were largely unsuccessful. The nineteenth century began with the destruction of the Danish fleet at Copenhagen by the British, a move perhaps motivated by commercial rather than military interests. Tranquebar on the Indian coast was ceded to Britain in 1845, and the Danish possessions on the Gold Coast followed five years later in exchange for a payment of £10,000.

Britain and Holland also considered abandoning their outposts.[75] The London Committee of Merchants discussed the declining revenues and the fate of the Gold Coast outposts for several years. These issues were resolved in 1821 when the British government took over management of the forts. In 1828 the British government decided to give up the forts, but the merchants of Cape Coast protested and the plan was dropped. Nevertheless, the economic benefits remained elusive, and losses continued through the following decades. Dutch interests also waxed and waned. During the late eighteenth century, the West India Company outposts were troubled by periodic shortages of trade goods and supplies. Despite reorganization and budgetary cutbacks, there was a steady decrease in revenue. The second West India Company failed in 1790. The Dutch government assumed responsibility for the company's possessions, and in 1795 these were placed under the Ministry of Colonies. Sale to Britain was considered in the 1850s.[76] When rumors that the Dutch might abandon Elmina reached the coast, the chiefs of the settlement sent a long letter to the Dutch king. The document emphasized Elmina's many years of service to the Dutch and, actually, began the town's history with the Dutch capture of the castle in 1637. This move is not surprising considering Elmina's past. Elmina had frequently fought with the Dutch against the British and their African allies, including the Fante. Now these antagonists were to control the castle.

The sale did not proceed for reasons that probably have less to do with the Elmina petition than with the continued hope of economic return. Both Britain and the Netherlands were by this time claiming jurisdiction over adjacent settlements and territories. The limits of British and Dutch territories were, how-

Figure 1.12.
Bombardment of
Elmina by launches
from British warships,
June 13, 1873. This view
is looking east from the
inside of the Benya
Lagoon. Elmina Castle
and the town appear on
the right and Fort St.
Jago on the hilltop to
the left. (Reproduced
courtesy of the
Illustrated London
News Picture Library
[vol. 63, no. 1768, July
19, 1873])

ever, ill defined, and there were constant disagreements about the extent of jurisdiction. In an attempt to resolve these differences and consolidate territory,
an exchange was agreed on in 1867 (see Coombs 1963). English forts west of the
mouth of the Sweet or Kakum River (between Elmina and Cape Coast) were
ceded to the Dutch, and Dutch forts to the east became British. The forts' military role increased, not as protection from European interlopers, but because
of the threat of African polities who challenged European territorial claims. A
series of defensive works were built by the Dutch around the Elmina settlement during the nineteenth century. These included Fort Beekestein, Veersche
Schans, Fort Schomerus, Fort Java, Fort Nagtglas, and the watchtower in Government Gardens (see discussions in Chapters 2 and 3). Although these were
termed forts, they were really small defensive redoubts with a few cannons,
were staffed by no more than a few men, and were designed to act as deterrents
to an approaching army. The British lookout towers of Fort William and Fort
Victoria on the hills above Cape Coast also date to this period.

The Dutch decided to give up their Gold Coast possessions in February 1871,
with the actual exchange taking place the following year (*British Parliamentary
Papers* 1970a:9–236; Coombs 1963; Crooks 1923:393–429). When the transfer to
the British was effected in 1872, much of the Elmina population refused to recognize the British authority. The situation reached a crisis in June 1873, when
the Asante moved to the coast, defeating the Fante. Dutch, and hence Elmina's,
trade alliances had long been with the Asante. Britain, on the other hand, had
actively encouraged Fante independence from Asante.

The British responded to the Elmina insurrection by proclaiming martial law
and ordering the surrender of all arms at the castle. The West Indian Regiment
was supported by marines and sailors from the *H.M.S. Decoy, Barracouta, Druid,
Seagull,* and *Argus.* On June 13, 1873, the "disaffected" portion of the town, lying
immediately in front of the castle, was surrounded. At about 12:00 noon, after

several ultimatums went unanswered, the British "opened fire with artillery all round the disaffected quarter for the purpose of destroying the town" (*British Parliamentary Papers* 1970a:452).[77] The town was shortly in flames, and the attack was discontinued after about a quarter of an hour. No one was killed in the bombardment of the town, a number of armed Elmina soldiers having escaped westward along the peninsula and many women and children having taken shelter in the castle (*British Parliamentary Papers* 1970a:445, 447, 474) (Figure 1.12). Over 200 Asante, however, later died in fighting near the town.

TRANSFORMATIONS

The first and most striking change in African societies in the Ghanaian coast and hinterland during the post-European-contact period was increasing urbanization, the concentration of population into larger aggregates. This began as a gradual process during the fifteenth and sixteenth centuries but culminated during the following centuries. Detailed demographic information is regrettably limited. Census figures are not available for any part of the Gold Coast until the late nineteenth century.[78] More information is available on Elmina than on many other areas, and this can be used to typify developments, as well as illustrate problems in demographic studies of African populations between the fifteenth and the nineteenth centuries. The sources involved clearly represent a variety of phenomena and measurements: Many observations may have been little more than wild guesses.[79] Given these limitations it is difficult to assess demographic change. How, for example, should an estimate of 300–400 canoes in 1640 be contrasted with 1,000 militiamen in 1702? Whatever information can be extracted provides no information on age or sex ratios or on the mortality rate. Some indication of the relative increase in coastal populations may be indirectly gleaned through the examination of natural resources available, such as the prevalence of the wild animals along the coastal margin and the relative decline in these populations in the centuries following European contact. But actual estimates of human populations remain elusive.[80]

With these ambiguities in mind, we clearly see from the data that Elmina's population increased substantially between the fifteenth and the nineteenth centuries. Although estimates before the mid-seventeenth century suggest a population in the hundreds, the succeeding figures are more suggestive of numbers in the thousands or tens of thousands. Elmina was considered a "large" settlement when the Portuguese arrived. There is little indication of what this meant, but the population probably numbered only a few hundred. During the following four centuries, the town became one of the largest, if not *the* largest, settlement on the coast. This may already have been true by the late sixteenth century, when Elmina, followed by Shama, was said to be larger than settlements of the coastal hinterland, such as Efutu (Hair 1994b:77 n. 126). Harvey Feinberg (1989:85) estimates Elmina's population at between 12,000 and 16,000 during much of the eighteenth century, and Larry Yarak (1990:48) suggests similar figures for the 1820s. During the late nineteenth century the number of inhabitants may have been somewhat higher. A Dutch report of 1859 estimated a total population between 18,000 and 20,000 (Feinberg 1989:95 n. 42; see also Baesjou 1979a: 214–224; Kea 1982:32–39).[81]

These estimates are striking when the sizes of the major seventeenth- and eighteenth-century trade entrepôts of the Americas are considered. In 1692, Port Royal, Jamaica, the largest English harbor in the Americas at the time, had a population of between 6,500 and 10,000 (Pawson and Buisseret 1975). Williamsburg, Virginia, the Anglo-colonial capital, had a population of approximately 2,000 on the eve of the Revolutionary War, and the population of Spanish St. Augustine numbered just over 3,000 (Deagan 1983; Olmert 1990). The crucial difference between these settlements and Elmina is in their population composition: The Elmina population was primarily composed of indigenous African—mostly Akan—people, whereas the populations of the Americas were heterogeneous mixtures of European settlers, enslaved Africans, Amerindians, and people of mixed ancestry.

The small population of coastal African settlements during the early period of European contact reflects the interior orientation of West African trade prior to the late fifteenth century. Earlier trade routes had linked Elmina to a wider network prior to the European arrival, but the larger urban centers were located in the interior along the forest-savanna ecotone and the inland Niger Delta (e.g., Boachie-Ansah 1986; McIntosh 1999; Posnansky 1971; Shinnie and Kense 1989). These were the frontiers of different resource spheres. European coastal trade moved sites like Elmina from the periphery of a trade network to key markets in the distribution of European goods along a new frontier of opportunity. Not only merchants were settled in coastal sites but also boatmen for landing people and cargoes, clerks, soldiers, carpenters, masons, and a myriad of other workers employed by the Europeans. Craftsmen concentrated in the settlements and contributed to a florescence of art. Urban settlements were also foci of power and authority. More important, larger towns afforded protection. Warfare, political instability, and raids characterize the seventeenth- and eighteenth-century Gold Coast.[82] During the seventeenth century, coastal Akan society became dominated by the Fante, who expanded westward from the area around Mankesim. There were also lengthy conflicts with Eguafo and Efutu. These conflicts contributed to population dislocations and demographic shifts. Multifunctionality and socioeconomic heterogeneity characterized urban settlements (see Kea 1982:13).

Population growth within urban centers was partly supported by a variety of American and Asian domesticates. Introduced species commonly cultivated today include: tomato, pineapple, peanut, guava, papaw, avocado, breadfruit, cashew, coffee, cocoa, sugar cane, coconut, cassava (manioc), orange, plantain, sweet potato, mango, corn, and several species of bean (Mauny 1954; Miracle 1965, 1972; Juhe-Beaulaton 1990; Alpern 1992; Chastanet 1998). Some of these plants were known in other parts of Africa prior to the fifteenth century, but European sea trade facilitated their introduction along the West African coast. Introduced animals, including species of sheep, pig, cow, and goose also supplemented earlier food resources. Archaeological and documentary data suggest change in the technology used in the exploitation of marine resources and perhaps also in the kind of resources gathered (see Chapter 4). As will be seen, the primary consequences of these innovations were likely in the increased variety and potential caloric value of the resources available, not in the manner in which food was prepared and eaten. There is, however, no question that en masse these introductions affected diet. Foods made from introduced domesticates, such as *kenkey* from corn, became staples in many areas. *Fufu,* still predominately prepared with boiled and pounded indigenous species of yam, may also be made with cassava and plantain.

Substantial immigration, as well as natural increase, accounts for Elmina's increasing population during the post-European-contact period.[83] Initially the settlement's growth was likely the result of the amalgamation of smaller Akan villages in the vicinity—a transition from a dispersed settlement pattern to larger centers. This pattern is also reflected in the expansion of other towns in the coastal hinterland, such as Eguafo and Efutu. Archaeological data indicate that small coastal settlements that had been occupied during the early historic period were abandoned in favor of these growing urban concentrations. During the eighteenth and nineteenth centuries, increasing numbers of immigrants from farther afield settled in these growing urban centers. Elmina's population became more heterogeneous, incorporating other Akan and non-Akan peoples. It is impossible to determine what percentage of the settlement these groups may have accounted for, yet there are clues. Most notable are the traders from the interior, many of whom were identified as Akani, a vague term often applied to Akan traders from the interior (i.e., both Akan-speaking peoples and traders from what became the Asante state) but possibly also referring to people from farther north (Daaku 1970:146, 202; Kiyaga-Mulindwa 1980).[84] The interior Akan figured prominently in Portuguese trade, and merchants and representatives from the Akan hinterland were present at Elmina from the early sixteenth century. References to Asante traders continue throughout the Dutch period, and by the early nineteenth century there may have been as many as 1,000 Asante traders and officials at Elmina.

People from other portions of the coast requested permission to settle at Elmina throughout the Dutch period (de Marrée 1818:51; Feinberg 1989:81–85). In the seventeenth and eighteenth centuries, people from Fetu, Eguafo, Simbo, Akim, and Denkyira, refugees from conflicts with the Asante and Wasa, settled at Elmina. Other immigrants may have included Ewe and Ga fishermen from eastern Ghana. The modern village of Bantoma, on the inland side of the Elmina peninsula, has a large Ewe population, and it is possible that the Ewe have long formed a part of Elmina society. A small number of Dyula and Mande traders from the northern savanna and the Sahel may also have contributed to the settlement's heterogeneity. Culturally and linguistically they are distinct from the Akan, and they have figured in interpretations of Elmina's early history.[85] Notably, Dutch permission was sought for outsiders to settle in Elmina, and an oath of allegiance was sometimes sworn, including a clause promising service to the Europeans. These "strangers" may have made up distinct groups within the town, and it is possible that the third "quarter," which appeared by the seventeenth century, may have been a quarter for strangers.[86]

Slaves   Captive Africans brought to Elmina by the Portuguese and Dutch also contributed to Elmina's heterogeneity. African slavery, its characteristics, origins,
and development are poorly documented.[87] There is no historical evidence that
slaves existed at Elmina prior to the advent of the European trade. They were,
however, being brought to Elmina by the 1470s, prior to the founding of São
Jorge da Mina, and there are many references to them on the Gold Coast in
sixteenth- and seventeenth-century sources (Elbl 1997; see also Ballong-Wen-
Mewuda 1984, 1993; Bean 1974; Hair 1994b; Rodney 1969; and Vogt 1973a, 1974,
1979).[88] They were used to meet the labor needs of the Portuguese garrison, as
well as to help African merchants transport goods to the interior. Between 1500
and 1535 the Portuguese may have imported 10,000–12,000 slaves to Elmina, primarily from the Niger Delta and the Bight of Biafra (Vogt 1973a:464–465; see
also Elbl 1997).[89] It has been estimated that 10 percent of the gold bought by the
Portuguese crown at Elmina before 1540 was paid for in slaves (Vogt 1979:76).
The importation of slaves to Elmina continued into the Dutch period, when,
as will be seen below, slaves made up an important component of the town's
population. Some captives brought to Elmina were obtained in Ghana, but
most came from other parts of the West African coast and were both linguistically and culturally distinct from the indigenous Akan population.

  The earliest reference to slaves being brought to Elmina is by Eustache de
la Fosse in 1479, who describes the arrival of caravels from the "River of Slaves."
These ships carried "a good 200 [slaves] each," most of whom were sold at the
"Mine of Gold" (quoted in Hair 1994b:128–131).[90] The "River of Slaves" likely
refers to the Niger Delta area of modern Nigeria, some 500 miles farther east.
The Portuguese also sometimes obtained slaves from lands to the west in modern Liberia and from Arguim on the Mauritanian coast. Beginning early in the
sixteenth century, São Tomé and Príncipe were used as distribution points for
slaves obtained on the Slave Coast, and as many as 673 slaves per year were
transported to Elmina. Although the slaves may have originated at Ouidah or
São Tomé, these areas were collection points, and the captive Africans likely included many different ethnolinguistic groups. Some of these people were taken
to the interior, but others stayed at Elmina. As many as 20 or 30 slaves were kept
at São Jorge to assist with the maintenance of the garrison (Vogt 1973a:454).[91]
Others may have been retained by merchants in the town, but aside from their
service as porters, their numbers and occupations within the Elmina settlement
are uncertain. The importation of slaves dropped after 1535, perhaps a result
of both the disruption of trade routes to the interior and the expansion of the
trade in slaves to Portugal and the Americas (Vogt 1973a:466–467).

  The number of slaves in Elmina increased during the Dutch period. Letters
from the Dutch director general on the Gold Coast frequently referred to the
need to bring more slaves from Ouidah on the coast of Benin. Harvey Feinberg
(1969:36) estimates that the West India Company maintained approximately 600
slaves on the Gold Coast during the eighteenth century, about half of whom
were at Elmina.[92] In 1812, Henry Meredith (1967:86) placed the number of
Dutch West India Company slaves in the town at about 900, perhaps 4–8 percent of the total population.[93]

These figures relate only to company slaves, and, as in the case of the Portuguese period, the number and activities of slaves owned by the townspeople are difficult to infer. Documentary records do provide some indication of their presence.[94] Slaves remained important for the transport of trade goods to the interior, as illustrated by an early seventeenth-century account that describes merchants employing 200 or 300 slaves in a caravan (Hemmersam in Jones 1983:115). In addition, as in Asante, they were likely integral to the production of crops, and they may also have assisted in gold mining and with the harvesting of kola, two principal export commodities of the Gold Coast besides the slaves themselves (Hair 1994a:51 n. 51; Yarak 1990:13).[95] At least some slaves and servants lived in the houses in which they worked (de Marrée 1818). Domestic slaves also were used as sacrificial victims at funerals.[96]

The role of slaves at Elmina and the institution of slavery in Akan society provide an important contrast to plantation systems in the Americas.[97] Unlike the latter, slaves in coastal Ghana exercised a relative degree of freedom. They were important to the functioning of the European outposts, and they made up an important component of the Elmina settlement. In Akan society, slaves captured in warfare or purchased became part of the matrilineage (*abusua*) of their owners, and thus became part of a family, linked by marriage ties and kin relations (Christensen 1954:38–41).[98] In many regions, oral traditions refer to slave villages or slave families. During the Dutch period the *trainslaven,* or "company slaves," also seem to have had some degree of freedom. They lived within the town and formed a distinct segment of the Elmina population (Feinberg 1969:36–37; Meredith 1967:86). Many slaves became masons, carpenters, and craftsmen. For example, Meredith (1967:86), writing in 1812, noted some of the slaves of the Dutch West India Company as being "excellent artificers." Significantly, one of the later *asafo* companies, the Brofonkowa, was made up of West India Company slaves. These were military companies that helped defend the town. At least occasionally they were embroiled in European-African conflicts. During hostilities between the Dutch and Elmina in 1739, the *trainslaven* caught in the town were either put to death or sold (Feinberg 1970a:361). Because these people were integrated into local communities, they have poor visibility archaeologically, and documentary sources and oral traditions provide only a very limited indication of their role in the town of Elmina.

Europeans

The European population at Elmina is better documented than the African population. Their numbers were always small and by no means stable. Disease and the undesirability of the post caused constant staffing problems. Portuguese records frequently refer to the ill health of the garrison and the need for replacements. When Azambuja established Castelo de São Jorge da Mina, only 63 Europeans remained with him. Throughout the Portuguese period the number was never larger than this and was often much smaller (Hair 1994b:36; Vogt 1974). In 1615 the Portuguese garrison was reduced to 25 men, and at the time of the Dutch takeover there were only 35. The actual composition of the Portuguese population is difficult to assess. The most important personages, such as the commander, would have been people of some prominence, yet the varied qualifications of the Mina commanders in terms of their age, experience, and careers are striking. The majority were drawn from the lower nobility (*fidalgos* and *escudeiros*) (Ballong-Wen-Mewuda 1984:210–265; Vogt 1979: 42–44). However, others in the early Portuguese company were likely convicts, or *degredados,* sentenced to exile in Mina (Hair 1994a:91 n. 196).[99]

The size of the European company increased during the Dutch period, reflecting both the greater importance of Elmina as a trading center and the increasing competition on the coast (Feinberg 1974, 1989:29–42). Figures for the seventeenth century suggest a European garrison at Elmina of over 100.[100] During the eighteenth century the Gold Coast staff ranged from as many as 377 in 1728 to a low of 138 in 1757, generally averaging over 175 men. Elmina was the headquarters, so the majority of these people were probably stationed there.

Prior to the eighteenth century most of these soldiers, administrators, and sailors were European, but they presented a culturally varied group. Soldiers, the group that made up the largest portion, were drawn from all over Europe. Hence the "Dutch" garrison at Elmina might have included individuals from portions of the Continent that are today part of France, Germany, and Belgium. Many were also lower-class, culled from the orphanages, prisons, and workhouses of Rotterdam, the "dregs of the Dutch nation" enlisted by labor recruiters (Boxer 1990:89–93; Feinberg 1989:86). This was particularly true of the military personnel; West India Company employment was not seen as desirable by most middle- and upper-class Dutch men, and even senior officials and directors general were of ambiguous background.[101]

In the second half of the eighteenth century more Africans and individuals of African-European descent were employed by the West India Company, possibly as means of cutting costs and replacing losses from illness (Feinberg 1969:39–40). By the end of the eighteenth century the entire garrison consisted of Africans or men of African-European ancestry. Under the Dutch government, the number of Dutchmen in Elmina was drastically reduced, and during the nineteenth century they probably never numbered more than about 20 (Yarak 1986a:34).

African-European
Descendants

A significant feature of the European population was the small number of European women (Hair 1994b:36). Only three remained with the original Portuguese garrison, and there was never a significant number. A *regimento,* or set of regulations, set down for the outpost in 1529 listed four women, who were required to cook, nurse, and, for a set fee, provide sexual services to the men (Hair 1994b:36, 91; see also Ballong-Wen-Mewuda 1984:303–304; Birmingham 1970:2). These women may have been *degredadas.* Consequently, beginning early on in European-African interactions, European men relied on African women for domestic and marital relations. Though it is difficult to determine their numbers, mulattos were already recognized as a distinct segment of the population during the sixteenth century (Feinberg 1989:36, 88–92; Vogt 1979:182).[102] They were distinguished by their dress, which was influenced by European clothing. Writing on the Portuguese treatment of mulatto women in 1602, Pieter de Marees noted: "They maintain these Wives in grand style and keep them in splendid clothes, and they always dress more ostentatiously and stand out more than any other Indigenous women. They can be easily recognized, for they shave the hair on their heads very short, just as do the Men, which is not the habit of the other Women; and they also have far more ornaments on their cloths and all over their bodies, a habit which the other women do not have either" (1987:217). The Portuguese mulatto population was of sufficient importance that special permission was obtained for them to accompany the Portuguese garrison to São Tomé following the 1637 surrender, although at least 200 appear to have remained in Elmina under the Dutch (Feinberg 1969:24–25).

There were formal marriages between Dutch men and Elmina women, but these were sufficiently uncommon in the early eighteenth century that the permission of the Dutch director general was sought (Kerkdijk 1978:153–155; van Dantzig 1978:176).[103] Dutch officers and merchants, however, frequently maintained common-law wives, and there were children from these unions. In 1700 the director general and members of the council decreed that Dutch men having children out of wedlock would be required either to take their offspring back to Holland or to provide "a proper sum for honest maintenance and Christian education" (van Dantzig 1978:60; also see Feinberg 1969:123).[104] It was further agreed that a communal house would be built in Elmina for all such children to be brought at the age of five or six years, where they would be separated from both the Africans and the Europeans. Here they were to be educated in the art of letters, the foundation of economics, and some crafts, as well as in the making of plantations.

Using documentary sources, Harvey Feinberg has identified over 250 mulattos living on the entire Gold Coast during the eighteenth century, approximately two-thirds of which he estimates were born in Elmina (Feinberg 1989:89). The Dutch called them *tapoeijers,* possibly because their skin color was similar to the Tapuya Indians in Brazil (de Marees 1987:26 n. 3; Feinberg 1989:97 n. 71). Many mulattos worked for the European trading companies on the coast. Some became successful independent traders (Feinberg 1989:85–92; Priestley 1969; Yarak 1989).[105] One of the most important Elmina citizens was Jan Niezer (Brukum 1985:165–179; Lever 1970).[106] He visited Europe several times and was probably the first African merchant at Elmina to order his goods directly from American and European companies. Because he was highly regarded by both the African and the European communities, he was consulted on several occasions to settle disputes.

Some descendants of Elmina women and Dutch men were granted special status. This group was known as the *vrijburgers,* which can be translated from Dutch as "free citizens" or "free people," and they were given the rights and privileges afforded by Dutch law (Feinberg 1969:124; Yarak 1986a:34).[107] During the late eighteenth century the *vrijburgers* were recognized as a distinct group within the town that organized *asafo* company number seven, "Akrampa." They had their own *burgemeester,* or mayor, who signed agreements with the Europeans. The *vrijburgers* were exempt from some duties and were also allowed to have a crown on their company flag and to carry swords because of their special status.

SOCIOPOLITICAL CHANGE

Despite the heterogeneous nature of the Elmina population and occasional conflict between different segments, the town functioned as a political unit. A variety of informal crosscutting links served to unify the settlement (Yarak 1986a:35). These included intermarriage, the general importance of trade, economic competition with surrounding Fante groups, and Akan culture. These factors provided a cohesiveness in the settlement's internal political organization and relationships with neighboring polities.

The advent of colonial rule at Elmina during the late nineteenth and twentieth centuries reflects dramatic change in European objectives and concerns, as well as African-European relations. The colonial administration exercised increasingly overt control over many aspects of African society and imposed, or at least attempted to impose, European government, society, and cultural ideals. But during the preceding centuries African-European interactions were quite different. Europeans played roles that were much more narrowly defined. Although the Portuguese referred to the town's inhabitants as "our subjects," it was, in fact, only the castle that was granted the status of "city" by the Portuguese crown (Blake 1977:99).[108] The town itself might be better described as a self-governing republic or the Commonwealth of Mina (Blake 1942:45). The Dutch likewise sought to avoid municipal disputes. Although the Dutch tried cases, these were almost invariably heard jointly with Elmina leaders (Feinberg 1969:208–217). The Dutch factors made every effort to maintain equable relations with the African population to avoid any interruption in the trade. Africans could file charges against Europeans, and unpopular factors were quickly replaced. Oppressive European policies could result in the cession of trade, riots, or abandonment of the settlement (Blake 1942:46, 54–55; Bosman 1967:43; Feinberg 1989:145–150; van Dantzig 1978:9, 80–81, 212–213, 243–244).

The European presence, nevertheless, wrought important changes, especially in political and social relations within the town and in interpolity interactions. This was influenced by both formal and informal policies. Europeans encouraged Elmina's independence from adjacent polities and fostered connections with other African states. African rulers were given Dutch sanction through payment of an annual gift, or *kostgeld*. The most influential people in the eighteenth century, at least from the vantage of Europeans, were individuals in the most advantageous positions to benefit from the European trade (Baesjou 1979b:37; Feinberg 1969:241; Priestley 1969). This observation might be colored by dependence on European perceptions that provide limited insight into African views. Elmina and neighboring coastal Akan communities evolved political and social institutions that, at least in some respects, were distinct from those of other Akan groups. There is little doubt, however, that the structure, makeup, and expression of these institutions were African in their underlying epistemology and manifestations. Their antecedents were the kin-based Akan organizations; their models, the institutions and government of the neighboring Akan states.

The organization and development of Elmina and adjacent polities during the late nineteenth and twentieth centuries are clear. However, their antecedents and the transformations that occurred between the fifteenth and nineteenth centuries are more difficult to trace (see Hair 1994b:52–56 nn. 31, 35, and 37; see also Ballong-Wen-Mewuda 1984:75–106; Blake 1977:99–100; and Vogt 1979). The political structures that are found in more recent periods did not appear fully formed but rather gradually evolved in the preceding centuries. Although the relationship between Elmina and neighboring polities at the time of European contact cannot be fully evaluated, it is clear that fifteenth-century Elmina was not an independent state: What would become the Edina (Elmina) state emerged over the last five centuries. At the time of initial European contact the Eguafo state, centered at the Eguafo settlement, and Fetu, centered at Efutu, may have both claimed territorial rights to Elmina. Some Elmina oral traditions recount that the founder of Elmina was Kwa Amankwaa, a member of the Eguafo royal family who came to Elmina to hunt (Meyerowitz 1952a, 1974:76–77; Feinberg 1969:8–14; Fynn 1974b:3–4).[109] Support for Fetu claims, on the other hand, primarily comes from documentary sources. The principal source is a Dutch map of 1629 that states, "[I]n the old days one half [of Elmina] used to be under Great Commendo [Eguafo] and the other Futu, who came there to collect their contribution" (translated in Feinberg 1969:12–13).[110] This division is repeated in later sources. A nineteenth-century oral tradition further traces the founding of Elmina to a hunter from Simbo (Simeo, a town now part of Edina but originally belonging to Fetu) and a fisherman from Cape Coast (Feinberg 1969:12).[111] Regardless of the political claims that may have existed, the Elmina settlement became increasingly autonomous after the founding of the Castelo de São Jorge da Mina, and by the second decade of the sixteenth century it had established its independence from both Fetu and Eguafo (Vogt 1979:86–87).

Kingship

Elmina's sociopolitical structure presents a number of distinctive aspects, which can be first illustrated by the evolution of kingship. Today, the head of the Edina state is the *ɔmanhen,* who rules through monarchical succession. He is viewed as the political, military, and religious leader of the Edina state. In contrast with most other Akan groups, inheritance of the position is considered patrilineal. The *ɔmanhen* must also be a member of Enyampa Asafo and a member of either the Anona or Nsona clans. Other important officials are the state linguist (*ɔman ɔkyeame*), the heads of families (*nguabadofo*), the heads of the *asafo* companies (*asafohene*), and the divisional chiefs.

Although the organization of the modern Edina state may appear clear, the origins and structure of these features are complex. A single king and the central role of the *ɔmanhen* did not emerge until the eighteenth century.[112] Caramansa, the African ruler who met with Azambuja at the foundation of Castelo de São Jorge da Mina, is unmentioned after his initial appearance, never to be referred to in European records again. Although some writers have described him as the king of Elmina, his actual position is unclear. On the basis of the limited contemporary documentation available, Caramansa can only be described as a ruler, possibly either from or subservient to a neighboring polity, but whatever his position, it likely did not conform to any contemporary European notions of status and power.[113] Although the lack of reference to a single ruler is negative evidence, it seems unlikely that a principal figure with whom the Portuguese interacted would be left unnoted.

There is, in fact, some evidence to the contrary. A 1572 Portuguese report on Elmina discusses how it is unfitting for any of the African rulers to be referred to as kings: "[I]t may seem that nothing is lost by permitting this, yet it is very important, since when one of these blacks is called 'King,' or wants to be called 'King,' he then thinks that being King of Cumani or King of Afuto, which are villages of not more than one hundred huts or shacks, is the same as being King of Portugal, which is a kingdom worthy of the name" (Teixeira da Mota and Hair 1988:74; also see Birmingham 1970). In 1639 the Dutch director general noted that the Elmina people customarily "communicate all occurrences to the [Dutch] General, because they have no king; and they stand so firmly upon their rights that they would rather place their lives in peril than be robbed of them by any of the neighboring kings" (quoted in Feinberg 1970b:24). Throughout the seventeenth century Dutch references to political relations within the settlement point to more than one ruler. Beginning in 1629 three different "quarters" were noted as each having its own *caboceer,* or captain, the people being organized "as a republic of their own," mostly governed by the Portuguese (Henige 1974:505; Feinberg 1989:99–103).[114] References to kings appear in European records only after 1732. At this date the Dutch appear to have been unfamiliar with the position and viewed it as a new office. Eighteenth-century references usually refer to a first or upper king, a second or under king, and a third king. This may denote the formalization of the office of the "king," or *ɔhen.*[115] The specific powers and authority associated with the office likely evolved even more slowly.

Succession of the position also appears to have varied. The position may have rotated among lesser kings, power eventually being centralized in a paramount king, or *ɔmanhen,* though consideration of king lists indicates that the precise line of descent was variable. Although succession of the position is now regarded as patrilineal—a feature that distinguishes the office from those in most other coastal Akan communities—king lists suggest that the actual line of inheritance has been variable. In fact, the issue of succession remains the source of great debate in modern Elmina.[116] The Elmina royal court was likely initially undistinguished, with the importance of the *ɔmanhen* and the royal court becoming fully solidified during the late nineteenth and early twentieth centuries. Even then the head of the state appears as only one of a series of political balances, the most important of which were the *asafo.*

Asafo

The *asafo* are associations based on lineal descent, often connected with specific areas within a town.[117] They are characteristic of the coastal Akan, particularly within the Fante states. Membership is by patrilineal descent, which contrasts with the matrilineal orientation of other aspects of Akan office succession and kinship (Arhin 1966; Christensen 1954:108; Chukwukere 1970, 1980; Danquah 1928:16–20, 199–121; Datta and Porter 1971:281; de Graft-Johnson 1932; Ffoulkes 1907; Hayford 1903:85–92; Sarbah 1968:26–32).[118] Certain aspects of *asafo* organization, pageantry, and symbolism suggest European influences: the company

organization, the flags, the representation of European warships, guns, planes, and uniforms in shrines (Figure 1.13). Nevertheless, the groups are clearly indigenous in form and conceptualization.[119] They may represent indigenous institutions, such as the young men's associations in Asante (*mmerante*) that evolved to include new elements and nontraditional groups like company slaves, *vrijburgers,* and Europeans.[120] They provided a mechanism through which young men and commoners could express their opinions. Although often characterized as serving primarily military or social functions, the *asafo* are validated through rituals and fealty oaths. Each *asafo* has its own shrine in which offerings are made.

At Elmina the origin of *asafo* likely predates the office of ɔmanhen. Beginning in the late seventeenth or early eighteenth century, the number of leaders noted in Dutch records increased, possibly an indication of the development or expansion of the *asafo* system (Henige 1974:505–506; see also Baesjou 1979a:19; Christensen 1954:107; Feinberg 1989:104–108; Wartemberg 1951:53–55).

Figure 1.13. *Asafo* shrine at Elmina. Although such shrines incorporate European elements, the underlying epistemology is African. (Photograph by Christopher R. DeCorse)

The *asafo* organization may have started to emerge in neighboring coastal states at about the same time.[121] Elmina's seven core *asafo* were recognized by 1724, but three others were added during the late eighteenth and nineteenth centuries. Two of the additions consisted of refugees from Simbo and Eguafo, displaced by the Fante war of 1810. The final *asafo* was the Akrampa, consisting of the Dutch West India Company slaves and their descendants. This brought the total number of *asafo* to 10—more than any other settlement.[122] Their role in Elmina politics contrasted with other coastal Akan polities, for the *asafo* appear to have had a preeminent position in the political hierarchy. The election of the *edenahen* (kings) was determined by the *asafo* (Henige 1973:226; 1974:506–507). The political structure of Elmina is also distinct in its lack of divisional chiefs (prior to 1873), and the nineteenth-century creation of the *besonfo*, a council of wealthy Elmina people that also originated from the *asafo* (Feinberg 1969:72–89; 1970b, 1989; Yarak 1986a:33–34). These institutions to some extent counterbalanced one another, but within the Elmina polity all initially were of secondary importance to the patrilineally linked *asafo*.

The Dutch clearly recognized the primary importance of the *asafo*. The overall leader of the *asafo* (*ekuwessonhin*) and the individual company heads all received a larger allowance than the king (Feinberg 1969:86; 1970b). Such favoritism may have fostered a vested interest in the *asafo* relations with the Dutch. The formation of companies made up of Dutch West India Company slaves and of mulattos also may have served to legitimize a degree of European influence in local politics through a quasi-indigenous mechanism.

Elmina and Its
Neighbors

The growing infrastructure of the Elmina polity was commensurate with increasing political autonomy from the neighboring states of Fetu and Eguafo and the emergence of Elmina as a competitor for territory. Elmina originally was limited to the settlement area and adjacent farmlands. With the emergence of Elmina as an independent polity, additional land was incorporated with the help of the Portuguese and the Dutch. By 1813 it had extended as far to the east as the Sweet or Kakum River, the location of the modern boundary (Feinberg 1989:77). Presently, the Edina state with Elmina as the capital includes the towns of Ampenyi, Ankwanda, Atabadze, Bantoma, Brenu Akyinim, Dutch Komenda, Essaman, Simew, Yesunkwa, and several smaller settlements. It is bounded by the stools of British Komenda in the west, Oguaa (Cape Coast) in the east, and Eguafo to the northwest. Oral traditions suggest that some of the villages currently incorporated within the Edina state were part of Eguafo until the nineteenth century (Fynn 1974b:21).

Relations between Elmina and the neighboring polities are primarily gleaned through European sources. Portuguese accounts record that in requesting permission to found Castelo de São Jorge da Mina the Portuguese promised always to afford the people of Elmina protection. Barros writes that the African ruler Caramansa was told that he "would become powerful in his land, and lord of his neighbors, for no one would trouble him since that same house, and the power of the [Portuguese] King, would be there to defend him" (1967:119; see also Blake 1942:40–46, 74). Barros does not provide a firsthand account, but the sentiment expressed may well have characterized early Portuguese policy. The political expansion of Elmina strained relations with the neighboring Fante states. Fetu and Eguafo did not recognize Portugal's claim to exclusive trading rights in Guinea, and they were quick to welcome trade from French and Dutch interlopers. These factors led to a series of conflicts spanning the sixteenth through the nineteenth century (e.g., Coombs 1963:52; de Marees 1987:8, 91; Feinberg 1970b:23–24; Vogt 1979:86, 124–125). A European policy that encouraged independence reinforced Elmina's isolation from the adjacent polities, and it can be used to explain, at least partly, the town's distinctive, self-perceived identity.

Conflict with the neighboring states also fostered Elmina's long-term ties with the Asante. The Asante state coalesced from a loose confederation of Akan polities during the late seventeenth and early eighteenth centuries. By 1750 it had reached its greatest extent, having incorporated much of modern Ghana, and become a major power in coastal politics (Fynn 1971; McCaskie 1995; Wilks 1993). Nineteenth-century British policy, particularly under Governor Charles MacCarthy, encouraged Fante independence from Asante (Baesjou 1979a:8–17; Fynn 1971:142–147; Sanders 1979). This interrupted the supply of goods from the coast (including guns, powder, and shot) and threatened the Asante position as middlemen with the interior. Elmina was seen as a natural ally, and long-standing links among Elmina, the Dutch, and Asante were strengthened (Baesjou 1979a:17–28; Brukum 1985:34–39; Coombs 1963:1–13; Yarak 1986a:34).[123]

These close relations between Elmina and Asante no doubt helped precipitate the forcible treatment of the town by the British in 1873. The bombardment and leveling of the settlement in June 1873 largely destroyed Elmina's economic importance. Much of the town's population was dispersed, climbing to its pre-1873 levels only during the present century (*British Parliamentary Papers* 1970b:269).[124] The town, nevertheless, continued to receive much of the Asante trade until 1900, and buildings dating to this period can be seen in the present town on the north side of the Benya River.

2

THE ELMINA

SETTLEMENT

I must tell you something about this little territory of Mina. It is of small extent, being only three leagues in circumference; and the only place it has on the coast is the large village of La Mina, which is situated on a tongue of land below the cannon of the castle, St. Georges del Mina, three leagues from Little Commendo. The buildings in this village are closely packed together in the manner of the Portuguese; the streets are irregular, tortuous, and dirty during the rains; most of the houses are of masonry, one or two stories high.

The village is extremely long, containing about 1,200 huts, with so many people in them one can count almost 6,000 men bearing arms, and there are almost six times as many wives and children.

JEAN BARBOT,
Barbot on Guinea

Elmina is today a settlement of more than 17,000 people crowded among the low hills adjacent to the Atlantic coast. Its appearance is the same as many other towns in coastal Ghana, a mixture of one- and two-storied dwellings, shops, churches, restaurants, and bars. There are clues to the settlement's history. Fort Coenraadsburg, built by the Dutch in the seventeenth century and recently refurbished, commands a view of much of the town. Nineteenth-century buildings cluster on the southeastern side of the settlement, particularly along Liverpool Street. Distinctive yellow Dutch bricks appear in the facades of many of the old houses, reminders of the presence of the Dutch from 1637 to 1872 (Figure 2.1). The modern settlement ends at the Benya Lagoon, a narrow inlet that extends from the Atlantic Ocean in the east to salt pans in the west. The Benya separates the modern settlement from the Elmina peninsula, a thin strip of reddish brown Elminian sandstone that lies between the Atlantic Ocean and the Benya Lagoon. The peninsula stretches over 1.5 km (just under a mile) from its tip to the mainland, generally measuring only 100–250 m (100–275 yards) across. This rocky strip of land, barren except for a handful of palms, is the site of the original Elmina settlement. The castle still dominates the eastern end of the peninsula, as it has for the past 500 years.

Modern Elmina offers little insight into the organization, appearance, and life within the old settlement. A unique aspect of Elmina's history was the abandonment of the old town after the 1873 bombardment. Many of the people fled prior to the British attack, leaving the settlement deserted. Some buildings were destroyed by the British guns and the subsequent conflagration. The unprotected buildings and stores were then looted. Even before the bombardment the British regarded the town's proximity to the castle as a security risk, and they were quick to relocate the settlement.

Figure 2.1. An 1888 photograph of Fort St. Jago looking north from the old town site. Twentieth-century renovations have roofed the bastions and reduced the height of the tower. Note the thatch roof on the stone-walled house at the foot of the hill. (Reproduced courtesy of the Koninklijk Instituut voor Taal-, Land- en Volkenkunde, Royal Institute of Linguistics and Anthropology, Leiden [NR9731/42000/2.27.49])

No rebuilding was allowed on the peninsula after 1873, and the settlement was relocated to its present position. The area in front of the castle was filled with rubble and leveled for use as a parade ground,[1] first by the British military and later by the Gold Coast police force and the Ghana police.

The old buildings north of the Benya Lagoon are an important part of Elmina's heritage. These are, however, reminders of the more recent past, testament to the nineteenth-century expansion of the town beyond the peninsula and development subsequent to the settlement's relocation. Elmina's earlier growth, the town's plan, house locations, and roads—information of critical importance in archaeological research—must be gleaned through the documentary records and oral histories. These sources are, however, frustratingly incomplete, and the information that is available cannot be linked to specific archaeological features. Oral histories were of limited help in guiding archaeological research. Although many individuals knew the old town's location, it was difficult to evaluate the information provided. Many people were familiar with published accounts of Elmina's past, especially Wartemberg's (1951) history, and drew on these sources when making comments, as discussed in the Introduction. The most important information provided by informants was contained in personal accounts of discoveries of artifacts, burials, and traces of buildings. Documentary sources that discuss Elmina's social, economic, and cultural history afford only scant insight into the spatial aspects of these phenomena. It is, indeed, illustrative that Barbot's brief 1680s description, seen above as the opening epigraph, provides one of the most detailed accounts of early Elmina. Information on the Portuguese period is especially limited. Documents concentrate on trade relations with occasional comments on African

Figure 2.2. Elmina in an 1869 hand-tinted photograph of a drawing, looking south from St. Jago Hill. Note the buildings north of the Benya Lagoon. (Reproduced courtesy of the Rijksmuseum, Amsterdam [RP-T-1994-99])

sociopolitical relations. Fewer still dwell on the town's physical appearance. The site is depicted in a few Portuguese-period illustrations, but most of these were probably done by cartographers who had never visited West Africa. In many instances drawings were simply copied from the work of previous illustrators. For example, the illustration of the castle reproduced in Figure 1.3 appears in various works of the sixteenth and seventeenth centuries.

More detailed information is available for the Dutch period. Several published descriptions are available, including references by the most well-known writers of the period: Olfert Dapper (1676), Jean Barbot (1732), and Willem Bosman (1704).[2] Drawings are also more prevalent, but they vary tremendously in quality, ranging from quite fanciful renderings to what would appear to be fairly accurate depictions. The best illustrations date to the nineteenth century. These include a striking 1869 hand-colored drawing of the Elmina settlement, looking south from St. Jago Hill (Figure 2.2). It shows several houses north of the Benya Lagoon, Elmina Castle, and the old town stretching along the Elmina peninsula. Plan and maps exist, but they offer limited insight into the arrangement of the town. Although the drawings of the fortifications, at least in some instances, clearly present architectural particulars in some detail, the town's size and complexity made it too difficult for early draftsmen to depict with any accuracy.

The concern in this chapter is to identify those aspects of the written record that may offer insight into the archaeological past, particularly the extent, organization, and physical characteristics of the settlement. Written records and illustrations attest to the growth of the settlement from a small town to a crowded settlement, stretching westward along the entire peninsula. They offer approximate positions of some of the town's features, such as the market, defenses, churches, and burial grounds. Documents also offer some clues to the spatial aspects of the cultural and socioeconomic divisions within the settlement. These observations helped plan archaeological research and provide means of evaluating the archaeological findings. In this respect, this discussion provides logical background to the more specific, particularistic archaeological data considered in Chapter 3.

THE EARLY SETTLEMENT

The appearance of Elmina and the immediate vicinity in the fifteenth century was quite different from that of the densely packed urban sprawl of the modern town. The fifteenth-century population was far sparser; the settlement, smaller and more open. Much of the western end of the peninsula and the land north of the Benya would have been covered with transitional forest and farm bush, punctuated with mixed farms. This would not have been the tropical forest that is still found farther to the west and the north. As is the case today, the fifteenth-century littoral of central and eastern Ghana, Togo, and Benin likely exhibited a dry, more savannalike climatic regime, a result of the way winds and ocean currents strike the land. Mangroves and brush covered the Benya Lagoon and the poorly drained areas of the Elmina peninsula. Writing in the early eighteenth century, Willem Bosman (1967:48) noted that there were not enough people to give the land "its proper tillage" and that the trees stood "thick together" and until relatively recently much of the area remained covered with brush.[3] Nineteenth-century plans of Elmina show only narrow watercourses within the Benya Lagoon, not the large open salt pans that are the striking feature of the site today. The *Illustrated London News* depiction of the 1873 Elmina bombardment shows mangroves and brush covering the western end of the peninsula, and military accounts consistently refer to the thick brush in this area and the need to clear it (*British Parliamentary Papers* 1970a:447, 452; 1970b:57, 331, 360, 361).[4] Many early writers referred to the abundance of wildlife around Elmina. Documentary sources, as well as archaeological research, suggest that the peninsula, at least the areas immediately adjacent to the castle, was rocky and, very likely, covered with little vegetation. This environment was increasingly impacted by the growth of the Elmina settlement during the following centuries.

Pre-nineteenth-century Elmina concentrated on the peninsula.[5] At the time of Portuguese contact it likely extended all the way to the eastern tip (Figure 2.3). This is inferred by a reference in Rui de Pina's description of the founding of Castelo de São Jorge da Mina, which notes the destruction of some of the African settlement during the castle's construction. Pina states: "[T]he surround of the castle was forthwith begun, for which it was necessary to demolish some houses of the negroes, and this they and their women consented easily and without taking offense in return for large reparations and the gifts which were given to them" (translated in Blake 1942:77).[6] Little can be said about the spatial organization of the African community, which perhaps numbered several hundred people, but there are some clues. The most detailed information is actually provided by Eustache de la Fosse, a French sailor captured by the Portuguese and imprisoned at Elmina. He describes a walk through the "Aldea das

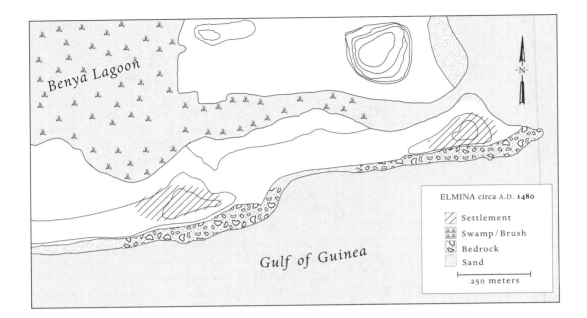

Benya Lagoon

Gulf of Guinea

-N-

ELMINA circa A.D. 1480

Settlement
Swamp/Brush
Bedrock
Sand

250 meters

Figure 2.3. Map of
Elmina and vicinity in
the fifteenth century.
(Illustration courtesy
of Christopher R.
DeCorse)

Duas Partes," or the "Village of Two Parts," so-called because the settlement
consisted of "two villages, a bow shot one from the other" (translated in Hair
1994b:129). Portuguese sources deal with the early settlement within the context of the founding of the castle. The toponym "Village of Two Parts" appears
in these accounts but is not used after that.[7] Although the documents suggest
that one portion of the settlement was located near the castle, there is no indication where the other part was. As will be discussed in Chapter 3, archaeological data suggest that if the village had two parts both were likely located on
the peninsula, not on either side of the Benya Lagoon.

Various theories have attempted to assess the implications of the village's
"two parts." The best explanation lies in an understanding of African settlement patterns and the unique topography of the Elmina peninsula. Many
African villages and towns have discrete clusters of houses or quarters that reflect ethnic or religious differences, areas occupied by craft specialists or clan
and phratry groupings.[8] Any of these divisions might account for early Elmina
having been viewed as a village of two parts. Two such sections or quarters
located even a short distance from each other on the narrow Elmina peninsula could have been clearly discerned from ships in the Gulf of Guinea. Such
a division would not be so striking in other topographical settings.[9] After the
construction of São Jorge da Mina, the castle became the settlement's defining characteristic. This would have been especially true if the most eastern
"quarter" at the end of the peninsula had been destroyed or relocated during
the castle's construction.

The specific sociocultural implications of the village's two sections can only
be guessed at. Because of Elmina's position at the border of the Fetu and
Eguafo states, it has been suggested that the parts may have represented the
two neighboring states.[10] This interpretation is, however, afforded scarce vali-

dation by early documentary sources. Although the polities' claims to Elmina are clearly documented beginning in the early seventeenth century, evidence for a jointly controlled, divided Elmina settlement at the time of European contact is more tenuous. Portuguese narratives of the castle's founding clearly describe negotiations with a single African ruler, something that presumably would not have been the case if the approval of two different states had been required (see Feinberg 1969:14; Hair 1994b:55–56). Caramansa, who alone negotiated with Azambuja, can logically be seen as either a ruler of an independent Elmina or a leader of a neighboring polity. Given the limited evidence for kingship at Elmina prior to the eighteenth century, the latter inference is more likely.

Those who propose another alternative view suggest that the two parts were separate quarters for an Akan settlement and a community of Mande traders.[11] This supposition is, however, also given limited support by the documentary sources. There is no question that southern Ghana was incorporated into northern trade networks, which included Mande people, yet evidence for a fifteenth-century Mande presence in Elmina is very limited. The primary evidence cited is the term *mansa* (as in *caramansa*), which is applied to the ruler of Elmina in several instances. This word means "ruler" in many Mande languages, but usage by the people of Elmina during the fifteenth century remains ambiguous. It is possible that the term was actually introduced by the Portuguese or their African interpreters, who brought it with them from Mande areas in the upper Guinea coast, with which they had long familiarity.[12] A Mande settlement at Elmina is not consistent with other linguistic evidence, which indicates an entirely Akan orthography of local languages from the fifteenth century onward. Apart from the earliest descriptions, *mansa* does not appear in European accounts.

Given the available information, divisions of early Elmina into either Eguafo-Fetu or Mande-Akan quarters remain speculative. Neither is stronger than the possibility that any division implied by the village's presumed two parts was based on clan or ethnic divisions, and these explanations may, in fact, be more likely. It was Elmina's distinctive topographic character, rather than unique sociopolitical or historical factors, that lent its name to the site.

The town's growth after the fifteenth century was constrained by both the confines of the Elmina peninsula and European policies. After the castle's construction the Portuguese restricted access to the eastern end of the peninsula. The adjacent areas north and northeast of the castle were used by the Europeans to unload ships. Goods were then brought into the castle through entrances into the north bastion and the riverside yard (Barbot 1992:380; Lawrence 1963:118–119, 178–179). These activities and the castle's walls precluded any African settlement. The area today is level and sandy with a narrow grassy strip separating the castle from the beach, but there is little indication of what this would have been in the fifteenth century. Archaeological data indicate that the area open to settlement may have been limited to the tongue of bedrock southeast of the castle, and even here filling was necessary to make the area suitable for habitation (see Chapter 3).[13] It is also likely that the Portuguese re-

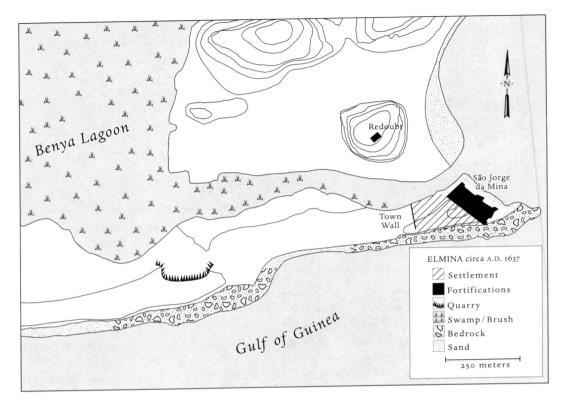

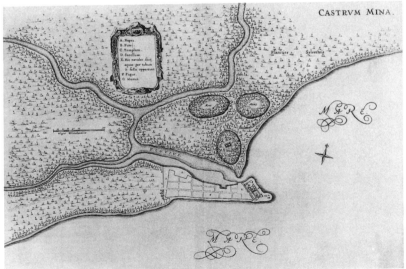

Figure 2.4. Map of Elmina circa 1637. (Illustration courtesy of Christopher R. DeCorse)

Figure 2.5. Caspar Barlaeus's (1647) plan of Elmina. The position of the town is shown, but the regular street pattern is a fictional representation. The defensive wall built by the Portuguese marks the western border of the town. (Reproduced courtesy of the Bibliotheek der Rijksuniversiteit te Leiden [20069 A2])

stricted access to these areas. Dutch plans and illustrations done shortly after 1637 show a wall running between the castle and the ocean (see Figures 1.8 and 1.9).[14] The rocky foreshore is less than 5 m (16.4 feet) across at this point, and a wall, combined with the pounding surf, would have effectively isolated the end of the peninsula.

The African settlement began beneath the castle's walls and gradually expanded westward.[15] Tensions during and immediately following the castle's construction may have led to a temporary abandonment or relocation of the village toward the landward side of the peninsula.[16] But if such a move took place it was temporary. By the first decades of the sixteenth century the settlement was already asserting its independence from the neighboring polities, and the interdependent relations that would characterize African-European interactions for the next 350 years were emerging (Hair 1994b:38–41; Ballong-Wen-Mewuda 1984:passim; Vogt 1979:85–86, 124–125, 155–157, 180–182). The military and economic support of their African allies was of key concern to the Portuguese. As early as 1514 the Elmina people were acting together with the Portuguese in military engagements. Elmina warriors manned the castle's walls and, together with the Portuguese, formed an integrated military unit. For the Africans, the proximity of the town to the castle would have been desirable because of the protection it afforded. The castle's walls were high enough to allow the effective use of artillery to protect the approaches to the settlement without endangering the town. If the town was overrun, the castle provided a place of refuge, as during the Dutch attack of 1606, when all of the women and children of the village, along with their livestock, were brought into the castle (Vogt 1979:156).[17]

To defend the settlement further, the Portuguese built a wall across the inland side of the peninsula, west of the settlement (Figures 2.4 and 2.5). The wall clearly appears on the plans of 1637 and 1647, but it may have been built during the second half of the sixteenth century.[18] In the late seventeenth century Olfert Dapper (1676:74) sketchily described a strong wall that extended from the seashore to the riverside and was defended by iron cannons.[19] Such defenses would have placed the town in a very strong position. The Atlantic Ocean provided an effective barrier to the south and the east, and the northern limits were protected by the Benya Lagoon. Attacking armies, therefore, had to approach the settlement and castle from the western side of the peninsula. The site's one weakness was the high ground of St. Jago Hill, located on the north side of the Benya. It was this hill that provided the Dutch with the means of bombarding the castle into submission.

Archaeological research may have identified the possible location of the Portuguese wall, but its exact position can be no more than a surmise. It was, however, located closer to the castle than later eighteenth- and nineteenth-century redoubts designed to protect a much larger settlement. The maps, of uncertain accuracy, suggest it began on the southern side of the peninsula where the land juts to the south, about 560 m (about a quarter of a mile) west of the castle's entrance. A more probable location is closer to the castle just east of the point where the land slopes down to a slightly lower, depressed portion of the peninsula, an area that still collects water and floods at extreme high tide.[20] This interpretation is consistent with archaeological evidence that suggests that the settlement expanded to the west in the eighteenth and nineteenth centuries. The topography of the peninsula was altered by the leveling and filling of the site after the 1873 bombardment. The depression noted, however, is a consequence of the underlying bedrock and so would have still been relatively low compared with the land to the southern margin of the peninsula and the area to the east. A wall on the high ground at this point would have taken advantage of the natural terrain. These defenses would have enclosed a space of approximately 3 ha (7 acres). This is a substantially smaller area than that covered by the later town, but one that would have been sufficient to enclose a settlement of several hundred people.

Expansion

The settlement expanded during the Dutch period (Figures 2.6 and 2.7). This is indicated by scattered references to the town's population, as well as by illustrations.[21] Plans done in 1637, 1647, 1671, 1799, 1828, and 1829 provide clues to the town's arrangement and extent, but they do not depict individual dwellings. Their schematic nature is illustrated by the strikingly different ways the town is represented. The 1637 plans show the houses in a regular, barrackslike arrangement, whereas the 1799 plan represents the settlement using an angular, geometric pattern. The 1829 plan is, perhaps, the most accurate (Bech and Hyland 1978:30–31). The landforms represented seem to conform best to the actual topography, and the relative positions of the features are approximately correct. The 1829 plan also depicts gardens and individual houses north of the Benya Lagoon. The peninsula settlement, however, is represented by 200 or so rectangular buildings, a picture that accords with neither the larger number of houses mentioned in documentary references nor the archaeological evidence.[22] Hence, this plan also likely represents a schematic representation. Both the 1799 and 1829 plans show the settlement becoming narrower to the west. This may reflect limited occupation of the rocky foreshore along the southern side of the peninsula and the absence of houses in the low-lying land to the north.

As estimates of the town's population increased from hundreds to thousands or tens of thousands, estimates of the number of houses also increased. Barbot (1992:373) guessed there were 1,200 dwellings in Elmina in the late seventeenth century, and an 1859 estimate places the number at 3,358 (Baesjou 1979a:214). By the early eighteenth century the settlement had likely extended beyond the location of the old Portuguese wall, which is no longer mentioned in written accounts, nor does it appear in eighteenth-century illustrations.[23] The wall's disappearance is probably related to the fact that it no longer provided effective protection for the town, which had grown beyond it and extended into and around the sunken part of the peninsula. This lower area is very likely the area described as a square with coconut trees by J. A. de Marrée in 1818 (translated in Feinberg 1969:115). The same area is likely represented by what appears to be ponds on the 1799 plan and as an open area in 1829.

During the Dutch period, houses were also built south and southeast of the castle. Illustrations of the seventeenth through nineteenth centuries regularly show structures of some kind in this location, and no wall is depicted between the southwest bastion and the ocean.[24] The conclusive information is provided by archaeological data, which clearly indicate that there was no settlement prior

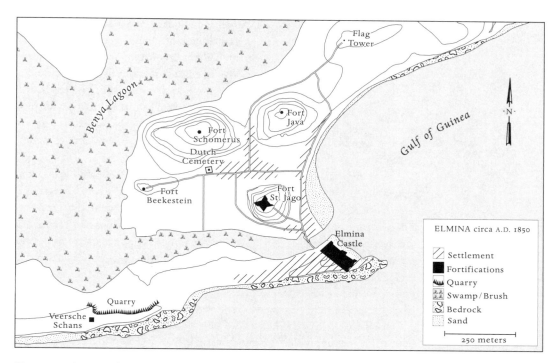

Figure 2.6. Elmina and vicinity circa 1850. (Illustration courtesy of Christopher R. DeCorse)

Figure 2.7. Plan of Elmina in 1799. A bridge extends across the Benya Lagoon, and the settlement has expanded north of the lagoon, around St. Jago Hill. (Reproduced courtesy of the Algemeen Rijksarchief, Afdeling Kaarten en Tekeningen [VEL 781])

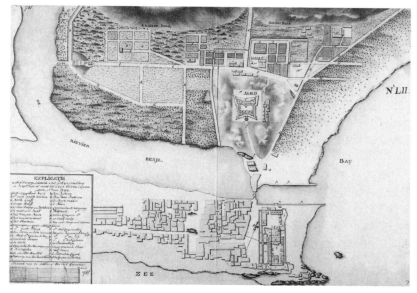

to this period. A clue to the inhabitants may be provided by the 1873 *Illustrated London News* drawing of the bombardment of Elmina, which labels this part of the town the "fisherman's village." References to the *fisherkrom* also occur in the eighteenth century.[25]

The settlement also started to expand north of the Benya Lagoon. During the seventeenth and early eighteenth centuries, potting and salt-making villages were located 2 or 3 km (about 1.25 or 1.85 miles) to the north, but only Fort

Coenraadsburg on St. Jago Hill, gardens, and farms occupied the lands closer to the lagoon. These cultivated areas included the Dutch West India Company gardens as well as those of private individuals. In the late seventeenth century the garden of the Dutch director general, close to the foot of St. Jago, was described as having walks "lined with orange and lemon trees, palms, Palma Christi, and several other kinds of trees unknown in Europe" and as having produced a "large quantity" of European vegetables, herbs, roots, salads, and grains (Barbot 1992:380).[26] During the following century the gardens were relocated to the lands north of St. Jago Hill.[27]

Access to the fort and gardens, as well as to the roads to Fetu and Cape Coast, was facilitated by a bridge built across the lagoon during the seventeenth century. Barbot describes the bridge as having had "a break in the middle (to form a drawbridge), both for the security of the place and to let ships pass further up the river in order to refit. At each end of the bridge is a large guard-house, and there is a lifting-device in the middle" (1992:380).[28] The security aspect of the bridge remained important into the nineteenth century, when J. A. de Marrée noted "a bridge with a gate, serving for a sort of barrier, so that no foreign negroes can come into the village" (1818, translated in Feinberg 1969:117).[29]

During the Dutch period, modifications were also made to the course of the Benya. These were the first of modifications that have continued up until the present, aimed at minimizing flooding and, probably more important, increasing the usable areas along the peninsula's eastern and northern margins. It is reasonable to presume that some modifications were initiated with the building of the bridge, earlier constructions being renovated and replaced in the succeeding centuries.[30] Whenever the modifications were first undertaken, they were undoubtedly in need of constant repair up until the present day (see discussion of archaeological data in Chapter 3). Eighteenth-century illustrations suggest that a retaining wall was built along the shoreline from the bridge to the mouth of the lagoon (Lawrence 1963:164, Plate 13a) (Figure 2.7). Although the accuracy of such illustrations must be considered with circumspection, walls were likely built on the foreshore and would have slightly increased the space available north of the castle. It is unlikely, however, that these substantially altered the inlet's channel. A quay, or landing area, was built on the interior side of lagoon west of the bridge. This, in fact, may have been an area of naturally occurring shallow water.[31] Describing his 1727 visit, William Smith (1967:131) noted a "fine Key," but it is probable that a landing of some kind was present much earlier.[32] This is suggested by the 1647 plan, which shows a recess in the peninsula's shoreline immediately west of the bridge.

The first houses appear immediately north of the Benya in the 1700s, and more follow during the next century. They at first clustered along the coastal road (present Liverpool Street) and then extended up High Street, Cemetery Road, and Lime Street around St. Jago Hill (see Figure 2.6). The owners and unique histories of many of these buildings are known.[33] Several were impressive buildings, built of brick and stone and owned by wealthy Dutch or mulatto merchants. Many others were apparently less impressive, and they receive little comment in contemporary descriptions. Their existence is attested by the

1799 and 1829 plans, which locate numerous smaller houses along Cemetery Road, High Street, and Lime Street. Notably, the 1829 plan shows no houses on the hill immediately north of St. Jago Hill. By the mid-nineteenth century this area had become known as Java Hill, after the African recruits who served with the Royal Dutch East Indian Army and settled in the area.[34] During the early nineteenth century the Societeit, a gentlemen's club, was built on the corner of High and Liverpool streets—over 0.5 km (0.3 mile) from the Benya and well beyond St. Jago Hill (van Dantzig 1980a:75).[35] From this point the town continued still farther to the north and northeast.

Fortifications

The Dutch built a number of new redoubts and defensive works around the town. The first of these was on top of St. Jago Hill, so named for an early Portuguese church. This chapel was dismantled in the late sixteenth century, possibly because the Portuguese became aware of the threat of the high ground north of the Benya.[36] In anticipation of the Dutch attack of 1637, the Portuguese constructed a small defensive redoubt on the site (Figure 2.1). The strategic position of St. Jago Hill was noted by de Marees (1987:219).[37] Conscious of the hill's strategic importance, the Dutch replaced the earlier fortification—probably a low earthwork and defensive ditch—in 1666 with a stone structure, christened Fort Coenraadsburg, which was further expanded in 1671 to include the outer enclosure still seen today.[38] The fort's distinctive ravelin appears to have been added at a still later date.

Although the purpose of Fort St. Jago was to secure the high ground above the castle, the reason for all subsequent fortifications was the protection of the expanding town. These later defenses thus provide a useful indicator of the settlement's limits. One remains standing; traces of the others were identified archaeologically (see Chapter 3). Most of these defenses were insubstantial gun emplacements mounted with a few cannons, with only limited shelter. For this reason they may have been manned only intermittently during times of conflict.[39] The first to be built was Beekestein, which dates to 1792 or 1793. It was a circular redoubt built of stone and clay, located west of St. Jago Hill near the edge of the Benya Lagoon. A watchtower at the outermost end of the new settlement north of the Benya probably also dates to this period. It was located on a low rise and commanded a sweeping view of the northern approaches to the settlement (Lawrence 1963:165) (Figure 2.8).[40] It nevertheless had no defenses and so could not have been of much strategic importance.

Another redoubt was built during the Fante siege of 1811. This fortification, named Waakzaamheid, or "Vigilance," was located to guard the landward approach to the settlement, as the earlier Portuguese wall had been. J. A. de Mar-

Figure 2.8. The flag tower. During the nineteenth century the tower commanded a view from a small rise at what was then the northern margin of the settlement. (Photograph by Christopher R. DeCorse)

rée describes it as having been located "at the end of the village, to cover, as much as possible, against all attacks from that side" (1818, translated in Feinberg 1969:115–116). It was, however, farther west than the wall, for de Marrée, in walking through the town, continued past the site of the old Portuguese chapel, then on "about five hundred footsteps higher up, westwards from the village." Waakzaamheid was soon in disrepair and, so, was replaced between 1817 and 1829 with Veersche Schans, named after Jacobus A. de Veer, the Dutch director general.[41] Fort de Veer, as it was called by the British, was a square redoubt built of stone and was entered by means of a ladder. Its parapet walls had "loopholes and embrasures both for musketry and artillery fire" (British Parliamentary Papers 1970b:361).

Redoubts were also constructed on the two hills north and northwest of St. Jago, known, respectively, as "Cattoenbergh" (Cotton Hill) and "Coebergh" (Cow Hill).[42] Fort Schomerus on Coebergh probably dates to the 1820s, and it appears as a square redoubt on the 1829 plan. It was, however, reconstructed in 1843 and probably expanded. In 1873 it was described as a pentagonal fort, entered by a removable ladder, and had limestone gun platforms and a sunken magazine. Another redoubt, circular in plan, existed on Cattoenbergh by the late 1820s, because it appears on the 1829 plan. It was rebuilt and named Fort Java in 1855, testament to the returned Royal Dutch East Indian soldiers. It remained, however, a small defensive work. By 1873 the parapet had entirely fallen away, leaving only a platform for three "six-pounder" iron guns and a small brass field piece. Finally, in 1869 on the eve of the transfer of Dutch possessions to the British, Fort Nagtglas was built beyond the tower on the coast northeast of Elmina. It was a "square-shaped redoubt with a command of 8 feet . . . surrounded with a wet ditch about 10 feet in depth and 16 feet in width" (British Parliamentary Papers 1970b:360). Its walls were already crumbling, and its guns unserviceable by 1873.

By the mid-nineteenth century these defensive works collectively encompassed an area of almost 81 ha (200 acres), an area substantially larger than the actual settlement, most of which continued to concentrate on 8 ha (20 acres) of the Elmina peninsula. The redoubts, therefore, extended protection to some outlying farms, gardens, and open spaces, as well as to the few houses scattered north of the Benya.

SETTLEMENT ORGANIZATION

Although providing some idea of the town's boundaries, documentary sources make it difficult to determine the social, economic, and cultural variables that influenced the town's organization and divisions. Europeans referred to portions of the town by various physical and historical features that had little reference to the sociocultural context. The Dutch called the area closest to the castle the lower village, and the western area was known as the upper or chapel town (Feinberg 1969:104; 1989:80). "Chapel" was likely a reference to the old Portuguese chapel used by the Dutch as a guardhouse during the eighteenth century. The reference to the upper and lower villages is somewhat confusing because the highest portion of the peninsula was actually the land to the east. The terms were likely in reference to the perspective of the farther, western end of the village when it was viewed from the castle. During the nineteenth century, the new settlement north of the Benya became known as de Tuin, or the Garden Town (see Gramberg 1861). During the hostilities of 1873 the British referred to the area north of the Benya as the loyal quarter, and the old settlement on the peninsula was called the king's quarter. The latter was a reference to the old town's loyalty to King (Ɔmanhen) Nana Kobena Igyan of Elmina, who refused to recognize British authority and was exiled to Sierra Leone in 1873. It is, however, unclear if the term *quarter* in these contexts can be equated with usage in other, earlier contexts. In fact, four of the eight *asafo* companies the British recognized in Elmina in 1873 were "loyal" to the British (*British Parliamentary Papers* 1970a:445–446, 473–474).

References such as these complicate any assessment of the economic, occupational, and sociocultural variables that influenced the town's physical arrangement and, thus, interpretation of the archaeological record. Several factors were important in structuring social patterns within the community. Economic status was clearly significant, but sociocultural ties, which in the eighteenth and nineteenth centuries were clearly linked to the *asafo* system, were also important. Differences in economic status were expressed in the larger, ostentatious stone houses of the wealthier people, which were crowded close to the castle around the market. The less imposing dwellings were located to the west. A clear statement of this division was provided by J. A. de Marrée in the early nineteenth century. Describing the area around the market, he notes several large houses, including his own, and "various good buildings of stone, which are occupied by important negroes, from which the remaining common negro huts exclude themselves" (translated in Feinberg 1969:115). The western side of the town, toward the landward side of the peninsula, was less crowded. It was this area that de Marrée described as the place where most of the Dutch West India Company slaves lived.

Socioeconomic status, at least during the eighteenth and nineteenth centuries, would thus appear to have been an important means of determining who could own or build houses in certain areas. Evaluation of who actually lived in specific structures is, however, more problematic.[43] Though difficult to assess on the basis of documentary sources, household composition was likely quite heterogeneous. Servants and slaves lived and worked in the houses, along with the owners. J. A. de Marrée (1818) suggests that in the larger residences the spaces beneath the roofs were used as kitchens and as living spaces for "slaves, servants and women," and the remaining rooms served 10–20 people. Marriage and kin ties would have further included people of different status and background. As a result of these complexities, archaeological data provide a poor indicator of the more subtle variations in kinship ties, *asafo* membership, and other features of sociocultural organization.

The *asafo* are historically important—in the case of Elmina preeminently so—in the sociopolitical organization of Fante settlements. Most significant from an archaeological standpoint is the fact that the *asafo* also have a strong spatial component, certain *asafo* being closely associated with specific "wards," or *bron,* within a settlement.[44] In their comprehensive review of the *asafo* system, Datta and Porter conclude that "[t]raditionally, members of a [*asafo*] company tended to settle together in the particular part of a town where the company post, including the abode of its principal god, had been established. . . . The correspondence between the ward division and the company division was so complete that, in course of time, many *asafo* companies were given names that seem to have been primarily meant for wards" (1971:280). At Elmina, the earliest unambiguous evidence for a clearly defined *asafo* system comparable to that observed ethnographically in twentieth-century Fante settlements dates to the 1700s. These findings are consistent with data from other coastal settlements (Datta and Porter 1971:284–287; Feinberg 1989:104). However, evidence for wards, or spatial divisions within the settlement, as well as other indications of the social and cultural components that later distinguish the *asafo,* extend back much further in time. By the early seventeenth century several sources note that Elmina had three quarters, each with its own leader. These divisions may have represented an expansion of the "two parts" described in the fifteenth-century settlement, the third quarter representing an immigrant settlement (Feinberg 1989:104–105). Alternatively, they may have reflected divisions that emerged after the castle's foundation. Corresponding with the settlement's expansion in the succeeding centuries was the appearance of more quarters. Perhaps by the late seventeenth century but definitely by the early 1700s, four more wards were added to the existing three. In 1724 the wards, which corresponded to seven *asafo* companies, were identified. These were: Ankobia, Akim, Encodjo, Apendjafoe (Benyafoe, Benya, Wombir), Abesi, Allade (Adjadie, Abadie, Adadie), and Enyampa. These coincide with the seven principal companies today (Amissah 1975; Feinberg 1969:81; 1989:106; Fynn 1974b:72).

Unfortunately, aside from the fact that the entire settlement concentrated near the castle, there is little indication of the location of the wards. Surveying eighteenth-century sources, Harvey Feinberg (1989:106) attempted to identify their size and location. Allade and Enyampa were located at the western end of the settlement in the upper, or chapel, village. Abesi was located, at least in part, adjacent to the lagoon, perhaps having begun just to the west of the bridge. The Ankobia ward was described in the early nineteenth century as consisting of the servants of the Europeans and the men who traded for them, which may suggest that the ward was located close to the castle. The Apendjafoe were canoe paddlers and fishermen. Hence this ward may have been located near the Benya or, alternatively, in the area southeast of the castle—the area identified as *fisherkrom.* Feinberg identified no references to the location of the Akim or Encodjo *asafo.* On the basis of the location of the other wards, he suggests they may have been located in the middle of the settlement near the southern side.

Other wards or groups were distinguished, though these were somewhat different from the other companies. Most notable was the voluntary association of mulattos that was formed in the 1780s. This group was the *vrijburger,* or Akrampa, quarter, which was recognized by the Dutch as a distinct ward. Although this was clearly an influential group within the town, it is unclear if the *vrijburger* quarter had a spatial component. Many of the more important mulattos had houses north of the Benya, and it is possible that this area was the Akrampa quarter. The *makelaar* Abocan's followers also formed a distinct group that was recognized by the Dutch, if not by the Elmina, as a distinct quarter during the late eighteenth century (Feinberg 1989:110–111). The political importance of the Asante community was also viewed as being on par with the Elmina *asafo* or wards (Yarak 1990:48). Divisions such as these may very well have had clearly delineated spatial components, but there is no evidence that they did.

There was also no distinct European quarter, and it is unclear how many Portuguese or Dutch men may have lived in the town. Pieter de Marees (1987:220) suggests that during the early seventeenth century most of the Portuguese garrison lived in the town and went to the castle only to perform their duties. De Marees was, however, Dutch, and he could not have visited the Portuguese stronghold himself. The majority of the Europeans may have lived in the castle prior to the eighteenth century. The Portuguese attempted to restrict the degree of interaction between the garrison and the Elmina people, particularly with regard to trade.[45] Similarly, Dutch West India Company policy forbade members of the garrison to spend the night in the town (van Dantzig 1980a:84).

Such strictures may have restricted some aspects of African-European interactions, but given the garrison's dependence on the local population for food and other provisions, as well as for defense, it is unlikely the garrison was isolated from the town. Europeans living in the town, or at least references to them, are more common in the later Dutch period, and many were wealthier merchants. In his description of the settlement close to the castle, J. A. de Marrée (1818) presents a mixed picture of African, mulatto, and European houses. These individuals would have represented only a small portion of a European population of varied means. Most of the European garrison, drawn from the poorer classes, could not have afforded to build large houses.

THE BUILT ENVIRONMENT

The settlement's position on the narrow Elmina peninsula made it a crowded, convoluted place. It had few streets, many narrow alleys, and numerous cul-de-sacs: Its complex arrangement likely explains why European illustrators failed to provide detailed maps. By the eighteenth century only two main roads or pathways ran through the town. One led along the front of the castle, north to the bridge that spanned the Benya Lagoon. The other road followed a tortuous route, west from the castle through the town, eventually ending at the lagoon. The paths were ill-kempt, and many writers refer to the dirty, unhealthful conditions in the town (Barbot 1992:373; Feinberg 1969:116; Meredith 1967:83; Robertson 1819:119). This was a characteristic of the coastal towns commented on by many European writers, who often contrasted them with the more open settlements in the interior. In 1602 de Marees (1987:77) wrote that when wind blew from the landward side, the towns could be smelled 2.5 km (1.5 miles) out to sea (see also Barbot 1992:511).

Elmina's only open space of note was a square located directly in front of the castle. This appears in most town plans, though it varies substantially in size, shape, and precise location (Figures 2.5 and 2.7). It was paved with square stones in 1675 by the Dutch director general Heerman Abramsz, who was also responsible for the construction of a "sun-compass," a surviving version of which is located to the left of the castle's main entrance.[46] Although it is tempting to liken the square to the central plazas that were the focal point of public activities in many European cities and the Hispanic colonial world, Elmina was not a European city and the analogy is inappropriate. Located at the intersection of major avenues, plazas were bounded by the chief administrative and religious buildings, banks, and the homes of wealthy merchants and political functionaries. At Elmina, many houses of the wealthy commercial elite were located near the square, but it lacked the political, commercial, and religious foci of a plaza. The location of these functions at Elmina was more nebulous and diffuse, without clearly bounded spaces. African and European perceptions of the square's function may have differed, and its use possibly changed through time. The Dutch, at least occasionally, attempted to regulate conduct within the square. In 1739 they forbade anyone to "go on the Square with a cap on one's head, a cloth over one's shoulder and a pipe in one's mouth."[47] The space also served as a meeting place for negotiations between the Dutch and the townspeople. These activities would seem to suggest more formal functions, yet, by the early nineteenth century, the square was serving as a market area, which may have long been its primary function (de Marrée 1818, translated in Feinberg 1969:115).[48]

The market's presence in the square cannot be equated with a business or commercial quarter. Although many of the people who lived around the square may have been involved in trade, there is no indication that stores and shops concentrated in this area. During the Dutch period, European factors conducted trade within the castle's courtyard, or the "House of Trade," whereas much of the commerce of the local population was undertaken in the town. The Elmina market, such as it was, was not large, and people frequently had to go to neighboring villages to buy food stuffs. People undoubtedly also conducted trade in their homes, but the pattern of clearly defined shops with storefronts is likely a characteristic that emerged only in the late nineteenth and twentieth centuries. It is known that at least two British merchants maintained stores in the settlement in the 1870s, because they unsuccessfully petitioned the British crown for recompense after the town's destruction. The stores' locations are not indicated, but they may very well have been located near the lagoon (*British Parliamentary Papers* 1970b:256).

There was another open space within the town. A second square, or at least a clearing, was located at the western end of the settlement. This was described by J. A. de Marrée in 1818: "At the end of this long street [leading west from the castle], one comes to the beach and moreover on a square, where various coconut trees stand . . ." (translated in Feinberg 1969:115). This likely corresponds to the open areas shown in the 1799 and 1829 plans. There is no indication what the function of this space was; as noted earlier, it simply may have been left open because of intermittent flooding. The central, northern side of the peninsula still gradually slopes down to the shore, today serving as the fish market. Archaeological data indicate that this area was filled in during the late nineteenth century.

There were occasional, unsuccessful efforts by the Dutch to reorganize the town and widen the streets. Given the limited room the peninsula afforded, land was at a premium, and it is not surprising that the people resisted attempts to cut new roads. After fires destroyed 90 houses in 1837, the Dutch governor attempted to lay out new streets by marking out a plan with bamboo stakes. However, the townspeople, instigated by the women, uttered "riotous cries" and removed the stakes.[49] The report on the incident goes on to say that the king and some of the elders were subsequently imprisoned and a new plan was marked out. After 10 days the old walls were still not removed, and 32 recruits with battering rams were sent to break down the buildings. The lack of success in these efforts is best indicated by the continued references to the town's convoluted, mazelike aspect in the following decades.

The response to the 1837 efforts to reorganize the town may provide an inkling of the growth of the private ownership of property and the fixed nature of the town's plan by the nineteenth century. Unfortunately, precolonial policies of land tenure are difficult to reconstruct.[50] Landownership among the Akan was traditionally vested in the chiefs (*ahene*), who apportioned it to individuals, the land returning to the custodianship of the chief upon an individual's death. The chief could also give land to immigrants, who paid tribute to him. Change in how ownership was conceptualized may have begun during the late seventeenth and eighteenth centuries as chiefs increasingly attempted to control and profit from the land. Perception of the commercial value of land and private ownership, in the European sense, did not become widespread in Ghana until the advent of twentieth-century cash cropping. At Elmina, the earliest mention of private property (*erfgrond*) dates to the early 1700s. In 1718 a certificate was issued indicating that a certain piece of land belonged to a woman named Accoma, who had allowed "one Negro Jas" to build a house on it but that after his death the land would return to her.[51] In 1736 a Dutch West India Company broker ceded his house "on the sea shore" to the *tapoeijer* William Matthysse and certain Elmina Negroes.[52] Other isolated references occur during the next century. They account for only a minute fraction of the houses within the settlement (e.g., Kerdijk 1978:153, 201).[53] In most instances, at least one of the principals is a European or mulatto, probably an indication that the European concept of titled land—or at least the recording of landownership—was not widespread in the rest of the community. In the early nineteenth century, J. A. de Marrée (1818) noted that he had obtained the land on which he built his house from an African woman of the Abrotoe family, who had full ownership, which was "rare" (translated account in Feinberg 1969:115).[54] A corollary of the fact that the office of ɔmanhen did not emerge at Elmina until the eighteenth century may have been comparatively limited control over the profits afforded by land tenure. Occupation of houses, if not their private ownership, likely ensured ownership within the town. In the surrounding farmlands of the expanding Edina state, allocation by divisional chiefs and lineages may have continued to be the means through which land rights were established.

The crowded nature of the town and the proximity of the houses caused constant health and fire hazards, problems that were further complicated by Elmina's poor water supply. It was impossible to dig wells in the shallow soil and bedrock of the peninsula, and the Benya Lagoon itself was brackish.[55] The nearest available sources were the small drainages north and northwest of the lagoon (designated the Udu and Anwin on the 1:125,000 topographic sheet).[56] Both still have freshwater, though they may dry seasonally. In the 1640s, Michael Hemmersam may have been referring to one of these sources when he described a freshwater river a mile (about 1.5 km) from the castle, which he often bathed in, and further reported that the king of Fetu blocked the path "by which we were otherwise accustomed to fetch our water, which was a mile from our castle" (in Jones 1983:107–198, 125).[57]

Another and often the principal water source was the effluence of the Kakum and Saruwi rivers, which flow into the ocean near the village of Iture, almost 4.8 km (3 miles) distant and roughly halfway between Elmina and Cape Coast. Water, therefore, had to be carried to the settlement from some distance. The effort expended on this can only be imagined. In the eighteenth and early nineteenth centuries Dutch estimates suggest that 700–800 people went to the rivers' mouth each day to get water (Feinberg 1989:81). The limited water supply posed a problem to both the castle and the town, and a threat during times of unrest was to cut off the water supply. The castle had several large cisterns that, at least by the eighteenth century, were efficiently fed by rainwater (Bosman 1967:42; Lawrence 1963:163–164).[58] Remarkably, when the piped water supply to the town failed during 1987, people were able to obtain water from a basin at the southern end of the castle's inner defensive ditch.

Housing

A unique feature of the Elmina settlement was the large number of stone houses mentioned by writers of the seventeenth through nineteenth centuries. This type of construction was not typical of the West African coast. The more usual method was to use timber and clay, or "wattle and daub." A detailed account of this type of construction is provided by Pieter de Marees in his early seventeenth-century account of the Gold Coast:

First, they take four forked Posts or Trees, which they erect on the ground so as to make a square. Then they lay other Trees on top of the Posts and fasten them well. Between the posts they place many thin sticks, thus forming the house; and they bind them together with Laths so tightly that one can hardly squeeze one's hand in between. Then they make Mud out of yellow earth, which they take from the open country, and pound it till it is fine and thin like Potter's earth. They slap handfuls of this mud against the framework of the house, all around, from top to bottom, front and back, wherever they want it to be filled. They press the mud in between this wattle with their hands, so that it will stick to the supports. Once they have filled the walls of their House with this mud, [making them] nearly half a foot thick, they let it dry and become hard as brick. After it has dried, they make a very thin Pap of red earth and plenty of water, and, taking a straw-brush in their hand, they besmear all the inside of their house, using this mixture instead of Paint. They like to Paint their houses in this way, some with red, others with white or black earth, as if it were for a contest. (1987:75)[59]

De Marees's account is probably an apt description of the type of construction used at Elmina prior to the seventeenth century. In 1555, for example, Martin Frobisher reported that " the howses abowt the said forte and castell [of Elmina] . . . be made all of canes and reedes" (quoted in Blake 1942:359–360).[60] By the late seventeenth century, however, Elmina was noted for its masonry building, the first reference to which may be Jean Barbot's allusion to multi-storied stone buildings (Barbot 1992:373).[61] In 1704 Willem Bosman could contrast Elmina with other settlements, noting: "The Houses [of Elmina] are built with Rock-Stone in which it differs from all other Places, as in other places . . . they are only made of clay or loam intertwined with wood" (1967:42–43; cf. van Dantzig 1975:205). This distinctive feature was still noted in the late nineteenth century.[62] Not all the houses were made of stone, however. In the early nineteenth century most were said to be made from "reed and loam or clay," and others were built of rock (de Marrée 1818; see also Gramberg 1861:88–90).

Stone construction is likely a European building technology appropriated by Elmina craftsman for use in the African settlement during the early Dutch period. The Portuguese built in stone, but they relied on European masons—men who were always in short supply. The *regimentos* provided for masons throughout the Portuguese period, but many succumbed to diseases on the coast.[63] A 1557 letter from the acting governor of Mina notes: "Previously, whatever number of quarrymen came here none escaped and all died, and up to now I have kept the stone-quarrying going by using three or four blacks whom I ordered to be taught this . . ." (Teixeira da Mota and Hair 1988:63). The last refers to the quarrying of ballast stones for ships returning to Portugal, but the letter adds that Africans might be taken to Portugal to be trained, for such people "would have been in great service, not only in stone-breaking but in all the other tasks, because they [black artisans] are lacking here, and High Highness would be able to excuse whitemen who put their lives at such risk" (Teixeira da Mota and Hair 1988:63–64).[64]

Despite these concerns, no local artisans were apparently trained during the Portuguese period. When a bastion collapsed during the earthquake of 1615, repairs could not be undertaken because the only stonemason at the post had died the previous year. Repairs were not completed until after the arrival of two masons from Portugal in 1617, a delay that would be unlikely if local masons had been available. European masons were also relied on in the early years of the Dutch occupation, and it is likely significant that the earliest Dutch descriptions of the coast do not mention stone buildings within the town of Elmina.[65] Company slaves were, however, being used to quarry stone by 1739.[66]

The documentary records afford little indication of the arrangement, construction, and architectural details of these structures, and these details are better examined archaeologically (see Chapter 3). The single feature that recurs in documentary descriptions is the crowded, irregular plan: "so entangled that no

European can find his way in the maze of corners, holes, passages, and sloughs" (Gramberg 1861:88).[67] Illustrations of houses that do appear show a densely packed settlement, the building appearing suspiciously regular and European in style. Many houses are depicted as having been rectangular in plan with gabled roofs, doorways centered on the gabled ends, and windows at regular intervals. This regularity accords with neither the written descriptions nor the archaeological data. Apart from the obvious similarity in construction material, the African stone buildings present a number of technical and functional contrasts with European structures.

The majority of the roofs were likely to have been ridged with a gable at either end. Roofs of this form, framed with poles and covered with a thatching of palm, grass, or other material, are traditional along the entire coast. Examples can still be seen in many villages and towns and can occasionally be found on two-storied, masonry buildings. In the nineteenth century the more opulent houses had tile or slate roofs, but others were still covered with thatch (de Marrée 1818).[68]

Figure 2.9. Houses at the village of Ekon (Akrong), east of Cape Coast, with flat, timber and clay roofs. Note the thatching on the top of the wall. (Photograph by Christopher R. DeCorse)

Drawings of both the peninsula and the new town show thatch roofs on several structures. Although the limitations of these illustrations are apparent, late nineteenth-century photographs looking north from the castle clearly show thatch roofs on some buildings (Figures 1.12, 2.1, and 2.2). This is consistent with archaeological and documentary sources (see Chapter 3; also de Marrée 1818:10; Hawthorne 1845:137). The many references to fire within the town also likely attest to the prevalence of thatch roofs.

Other buildings are notable for their flat roofs—an innovation that, along with stone construction, is distinctive of the Fante coast. The origins and development of this building tradition are unclear. Flat roofs are not characteristic of the West African coast but, rather, are more typical of northern Ghana and the West African Sahel. They may have become popular at Elmina following the Dutch arrival in 1637. Among the first architectural changes effected in the castle was the replacement of ridged roofs with flat surfaces (Lawrence 1963:151–152, 214). The earliest reference to flat roofs in African coastal settlements is by Barbot (1992:513) in the late seventeenth century, although illustrations date somewhat later. Flat roofs were relatively common in coastal towns such as Cape Coast until 15 or 20 years ago, and many can still be seen there and in the small settlements of Ekon and Biriwa to the east (Figure 2.9). This may have been the preferred method of roofing on the more elaborate houses of the Europeans and wealthy Africans in the late nineteenth century.[69]

Flat-roof building techniques may have been introduced to the coast by

Figure 2.10. A 1792
drawing by C.
Bergeman of the house
of merchant Johan
Neizer, Elmina. The
building is depicted as
multistoried, with
exterior lamps and a
flat roof. (Reproduced
courtesy of the Leiden
University Library,
Collectie Bodel
Nijenhuis [P.314-IN.97])

northerners and adapted for use on the coast by both Africans and Europeans.
This is suggested by the timber and clay construction employed: Europeans
typically constructed flat roofs with planks supported by joists, which were then
covered with brick and *tarras,* a waterproof cement made from ground bricks
and shell (Lawrence 1963:193; van Dantzig 1980a:83).[70] In contrast, flat roofs in
both coastal Ghana and the north are made with poles, which extend hori-
zontally into the clay walls, the weight in most instances being born by vertical wooden posts. The latticework of poles is then covered with a layer of clay
up to 30 cm (1 foot) thick. The wall is extended upward to encase the ends of
the poles and to form a low parapet around the roof. Spouts are inserted
through the walls to carry rainwater off the roof. Flat, open roofs would have
been advantageous in crowded coastal towns like Elmina, providing additional
space and reducing the risk of thatch fire. Typically the roof also serves as a
work area, a place for drying crops, or even a place to sleep in good weather,
access being provided by a ladder on the side of the building. Although efficient, they are not well suited for the heavier rainfall that sometimes occurs on
the coast, and they frequently leak and require replacement. Examples at the
village of Ekon, east of Cape Coast, have thatch along the tops of the wall to
provide some additional protection from rain.

Some of the eighteenth-century stone structures at Elmina were quite impressive, as illustrated by the 1792 drawing of the Johan Niezer house by C.
Bergeman (Figure 2.10). The structure is shown three stories high with a stairway leading up to a flat roof. The windows have shutters, and those on the
ground floor appear to be paned with glass. Two lighting fixtures are mounted
on the exterior walls. This structure may be one of the larger, multistoried
structures shown in the center of the 1873 illustration of the bombardment of
Elmina, but not enough detail is present to be certain. Further clues to the
larger buildings may also be gleaned from photographs of the New Town taken
in the late nineteenth century. These also include views of Bridge House, which
was located just north of the lagoon until its collapse in 1981.[71]

Few accounts offer any suggestion of what the interior of these houses
looked like. Seventeenth-century descriptions of the Gold Coast suggest only
limited furnishings: "[A] few wooden seats, a small chest, a few pots for cooking or drinking, and some weapons hung on the walls" (Barbot 1992:512). J. S.
G. Gramberg (1861:88–90) made similar, though somewhat more extensive,

comments specifically on Elmina in 1861. He noted that most dwellings were poorly lit and that they had no chimneys and only small windows and doors. The furnishings were "utterly sparse" and often consisted of only a couple of benches or low stools, a little table, and a wooden chest to keep cloth in. There might also be a small mirror and some prints or paintings. A couch made with boards was a luxury. In contrast, the houses of the more well-to-do African and mulatto merchants were "roomy, well furnished and even neat dwellings."

Ritual Space

Gramberg also affords a glimpse into ritual and sacred space within the town. With reference to the typical African house, he says: "In another cubicle one may find what makes the house complete . . . a pot containing some offering for the House-fetish" (1861:88–89). Such shrines, dedicated to *asaman* (the spirits of the ancestors) are characteristic of the Akan. They may be located in a special area within a compound or in an individual's room. Other shrines were dedicated to *ɔbosom*, spirits that inhabit things such as groves, rivers, and rocks. Their role in Akan worldview and their archaeological manifestations will be discussed in Chapter 6. Accounts of such sacred spaces occur in documentary records, but they are only occasional and probably account for only a small fraction of such special locations found within the settlement.

Only slightly better described than African shrines are Christian churches, several of which were built within the castle for the service of the Europeans.[72] There were, however, several chapels built outside the castle. The first of these may have been on top of St. Jago Hill. John Vogt suggests that it was built in 1503 to commemorate the conversion of the king of Efutu.[73] It was this structure that was torn down in 1596 and replaced, eventually, with Fort Coenraadsburg. The plan of 1647 and accompanying illustration show another chapel, or "Sacellum," at the western end of the settlement just beyond the town wall. This remained standing during the Dutch period, when it functioned as a guard post.[74] Its ruins could still be discerned as late as 1802 (de Marrée 1818, translated in Feinberg 1969:115). Finally, during the Dutch period a Roman Catholic chapel was built north of the Benya Lagoon to accommodate the Brazilian traders who visited Elmina. Although shown as a substantial building on the 1799 plan, it was probably a simple building of clay and stone (Feinberg 1969:116; 1989:80).

References to both African and European cemeteries and burial grounds are also of note. These data are of particular interest because of the data on burial practices that were recovered during archaeological work. The limited documentary information at hand makes it impossible to determine the temporal, social, or cultural variables represented. However, these references, as well as the archaeological data, serve to underscore variation in indigenous burial practices. Whereas Christian Europeans primarily conceive of sacred spaces in terms of discrete burial grounds, African burial practices exhibit much more variation, even within cultural groups.[75] The archaeological data from Elmina indicate both burial within households and the use of separate burial grounds. It is also likely there was substantial variation in the placement of the bodies, associated grave goods, and the presence or absence of above-ground markers.

Figure 2.11. The Dutch cemetery with its central mausoleum, established north of St. Jago Hill in the early nineteenth century. (Photograph by Christopher R. DeCorse)

The earliest allusion to a burial ground within the town is found in two tantalizing references in Barbot's seventeenth-century account (Barbot 1992:380). Barbot's account is of interest because it affords the only documentary reference to the use of the land north of the Benya Lagoon as a burial ground. Confirmation of the use of this area, now east of Liverpool Street, as a burial ground came from the personal reminiscences of a number of Elmina people who recalled finding human bones and grave goods exposed by heavy rains and construction.[76] The area is recalled as *asamanpomu,* or the "ghost bush."[77] Limited information indicates African burials in at least two other locations during the early history of the settlement. A burial ground is currently located on the landward side of the peninsula, at the eastern margin of the village of Bantoma. This is marked on the 1965 (1:2,500) Ghana survey maps, but there are no other documentary references. The antiquity of burial within this area was determined by archaeological research. The other area is around Coebergh, which was reputedly the place where soldiers and artisans were buried (Feinberg 1989:80).[78]

There were also several European burial grounds. The oldest may have been located outside the castle at the site "where the first mass was said" (Barros, translated in Hair 1994b:36). This site might possibly be associated with the peninsula chapel described above. Better known is the location of a burial ground inside the castle in the northwest corner of the riverside yard, adjacent to the small chapel. The earliest evidence for the use of this cemetery dates to the Dutch period, but it was likely used earlier. It may have been full by the time of the epidemic between 1645 and 1646, when members of the garrison were buried in other parts of the riverside yard, as well as in the main courtyard (Lawrence 1963:127).[79] The first of the European cemeteries outside the castle was located immediately south of its entrance. This "old" Dutch cemetery remained in use until new ones were established on the northern side of St. Jago Hill in the late eighteenth or early nineteenth century.[80] The first of these may have been located on the northern side of chapel square, at the junction of Liverpool Street and Cemetery Road.[81] By 1806 a burial ground was established farther west. This "new" Dutch cemetery is well maintained and can be seen on the north side of Cemetery Road (Figure 2.11). It continued in use by Elmina people through the twentieth century, though interments have been infrequent.

THE TOWN SITE SINCE 1873

Elmina Castle, Fort Coenraadsburg, the old town site, and the nineteenth-century buildings of the modern town make Elmina a unique, collective historic monument. Survey of the site's history subsequent to its destruction is important as a means of assessing archaeological formation processes and identifying areas of disturbance. This information, in turn, helped determine excavation strategies and the interpretation of archaeological remains. Information on the site's history also has important implications for the development of management plans and preservation efforts. The old town site remained protected during the late nineteenth and early twentieth centuries. This was due to limited population growth and the lack of development rather than any protective legislation. The harbor was closed to trade in 1921, and the coast road bypassed the town, reducing the town's commercial importance. Young people were attracted to jobs in growing national centers such as Accra or Takoradi. With a population under 4,000, Elmina remained a sleepy backwater throughout the earlier twentieth century.

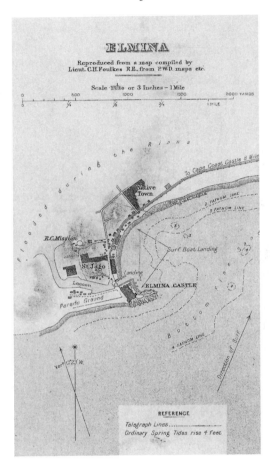

Figure 2.12. Plan of Elmina, 1898. By this time the old town site had been leveled to make a parade ground. (British Crown copyright photograph supplied courtesy of the Public Record Office [WO78/5393])

Following the town's initial destruction, the use of the peninsula was limited. Although the digging of fill for the parade ground likely damaged some sections of the old town site, the rubble protected the 400 m (437 yards) lying closest to the castle on its western side. Building activity remained severely restricted through the colonial period. Wartemberg comments: "No justifiable reason exists why the natives may not return to their ancestral lands if they so desire. The presumption that the Government confiscated the lands at the bombardment is without substance" (1951:66 fn. 2). Although this may have been true in the late 1940s, it was certainly not true in the late nineteenth century, when the castle's military role was still a consideration. British reports of the 1870s specifically note the town as encroaching too close to the castle and the security risk it presented. A British Public Works Department plan of 1898 shows only eight buildings northwest of the parade ground in the area of the present fish market (Figure 2.12). Some of these may actually have been buildings that survived the bombardment and continued in use. Alternatively, these may be late nineteenth-century constructions.

The later Dutch defensive works remained standing at the time of the conflict of 1873, but they were left unmanned by the British. The castle remained in active use for a variety of functions, including its use as a national training center for police recruits and more recently as a school and district administration offices. The colonial government added garages and housing for the police north and east of the castle. These were demolished during renovation work in the 1990s. Minor improvements and renovations were also periodically made to the harbor. The margins of the Benya Lagoon were straightened, and a new bridge was constructed across the lagoon. The breakwater was also strengthened and extended. In 1873 the western end of the peninsula was still covered with low bush and mangroves. The irregular ground allowed for the escape of Elmina soldiers during the 1873 bombardment, and it was an effective impediment to British troops. After that event, some of this vegetation was removed. It was, however, only in the twentieth century that the lagoon was cleared for salt pans.[82]

Ghana was one of the first African countries to develop an antiquities program.[83] Indeed, much of the early preservation legislation, conservation work, and archaeological research was directed at the forts and castles. The historical and architectural significance of the forts and castles was recognized after the Second World War. The pioneering work of B. H. St. J. O'Neil was followed by extensive survey and restoration efforts by A. W. Lawrence in the 1950s (O'Neil 1951; Lawrence 1963). Custodianship of the castle was turned over to the Ghana Museums and Monuments Board in 1972. In the early 1970s a comprehensive conservation study of Elmina was put forward by Neils Bech and Anthony Hyland (Bech and Hyland 1978). This called for a holistic perspective of the entire settlement and its historic quarters. Their recommendations included the designation of conservation areas, the restoration and rehabilitation of some structures, and the complete reconstruction of two ruined buildings. The proposal was aimed at international funding agencies, but with the idea that the management of sites would eventually become self-sustaining. Unfortunately, the proposal came at a time of increasing economic and political uncertainty in Ghana, and no action could be taken. Lacking funds, resources, and a trained staff, and facing the maintenance of sites and structures with many complex conservation problems, the Ghana Museums and Monuments Board could undertake only limited work.

In Elmina, the town's archaeological resources and historical landscape have been increasingly affected during the past decade. This situation started to change with the expansion of the town's population during the present century, which had grown to 8,534 by 1960 and increased another 50 percent by 10 years later. Pictures of the peninsula taken in the 1960s and 1970s show several small structures along the southern shoreline both to the east and to the west of the castle.[84] The area immediately in front of the castle remained free of construction, but it was damaged as a result of further leveling of the parade ground, possibly in connection with Queen Elizabeth's visit in 1960. This activity impacted the pre-1806 Dutch burials outside the castle, which were partly graded. A reconstructed eighteenth-century gravestone exposed at this time can presently be seen just outside the castle's main entrance.[85]

The central portion of the peninsula, which had been used only as a soccer field, became the town lorry park during the late 1980s. At this time, kiosks, a chop bar, fish drying, canoe building, and increased settlement of the landward side of the peninsula also expanded dramatically. Although these small structures and the increased activity had no immediate subsurface impact, they caused further erosion. The area farther west was graded for use as a playing field. Also during this period the ocean shore on the south side of the peninsula was used to dump trash. Although unsightly, this may have actually helped protect the site, for the greatest threat in this area is from the ocean, which breaks uninterrupted onto the shore. Within the last five years, an increasing squatter settlement has extended up the peninsula between the site of Veersche Schans and the castle.

The greatest impact was on the land north of the Benya. Unrestricted growth and lack of maintenance resulted in the erosion of the hill, the loss of many of the old structures and defensive works, and the destruction of archaeological deposits. Many of the nineteenth-century buildings have fallen into disrepair or have collapsed. These developments are dramatically illustrated by photographs of the site taken in 1888, 1950, and 1985.

Not until 1992 was a comprehensive five-year preservation program initiated (Hyland 1995).[86] Elmina Castle and Fort Coenraadsburg, along with Cape Coast Castle, have been the target of a multimillion-dollar renovation program funded by USAID. The work undertaken illustrates all the intricacies of balancing historic-site management with modern needs. Elmina is seen, at least by some, as key to Ghana's rapidly expanding tourist industry. Protection of a portion of the Elmina old town site has been provided by a wall bordering the modern road on the northern side of the peninsula. However, much of the development threatening the old town site and historic structures within the old town has gone unchecked. Without better cultural resource management planning, the site still remains threatened. The major portion of the old Elmina site on the eastern end of the peninsula, directly in front of the castle is protected by the Ghana Museums and Monuments Board. In 1990, walls were constructed from the castle along the southern side of the road and at the western end of the site to protect the area further. This encloses the majority of the old settlement, and, presumably, any development in this area will include provision for archaeological assessment, though trash dumping on the site has continued unchecked. No protection exists in other areas. Some archaeological sites such as Veersche Schans at Bantoma, the redoubts, and the early merchant houses north of the Benya Lagoon receive no protection. Current conservation efforts by the Save Elmina Association have focused on some of the historic buildings in the new town, but these efforts have concentrated on preservation and reconstruction, not on the management and protection of archaeological resources. Although government archaeologists should, ideally, monitor all construction, any such efforts are plagued by a lack of funding.

3

THE ARCHAEOLOGY

OF AN

AFRICAN TOWN

Sankofa: Return and pick it up. That
is, learn from or build on the past.
Pick up the gems of the past.
AKAN PROVERB, QUOTED IN A.
K. QUARCOO,
The Language of Andinkra Patterns

ankofa is "a constant reminder that the past is not all shame-
ful and that the future may profitably be built on aspects of the
past. Indeed, there must be movement with the times but as the forward march proceeds, the gems must be picked from behind and
carried forward on the march" (Quarcoo 1994:17).[1] Elmina's archaeological past stands in dramatic contrast to many sites. Unlike the majority of settlements associated with the beginnings of African-
European interaction, the ancient town has not been obliterated by
modern settlement.[2] The early African towns associated with the
British headquarters at Cape Coast and the Danish Christiansborg
Castle, Accra, have been continuously occupied by thriving communities, and urban development has obliterated or rendered inac-
cessible many of the early archaeological deposits. In contrast, much
of the Elmina settlement lies buried on the peninsula, comparatively
well preserved and accessible, providing a unique opportunity to examine archaeological aspects of culture contact at a major African
trade center. Foundations, burnt daub, and occasional artifacts lie
exposed on the surface, testament to the richness of the deposits.
Archaeological research was directed at obtaining as comprehensive
an understanding of the past settlement as possible. Libation to the
ancestors was offered by the then–acting chief of Elmina, Nana
Kojo Nquandoh III, on March 11, 1986, and excavations began.[3]
Work at Elmina was undertaken with the help of University of
Ghana and Syracuse University archaeology students, the Ghana
Museums and Monuments Board staff, and Earthwatch and Foun-
dation for Field Research volunteers. The vast majority of fieldwork,
however, was completed by paid workers from Elmina.

Although documentary sources could be used to delineate the
approximate margins of the settlement, especially between the seventeenth and the nineteenth centuries, archaeological data were

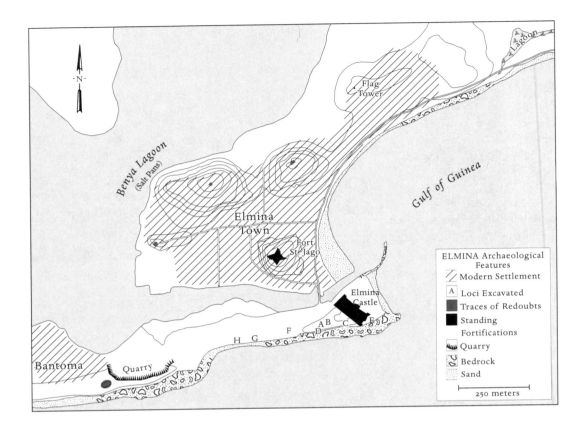

Figure 3.1. Map of modern Elmina showing archaeological features. (Illustration courtesy of Christopher R. DeCorse)

used to assess this information and clarify the extent of the pre-seventeenth-century occupations. Prior to 1985 there had been no systematic work on the site, and the most detailed survey that had been undertaken suggested that the archaeological deposits were disturbed, consisting of a "thin layer of soil covering bedrock" (Golden 1969:124).[4] Fortunately, this initial assessment proved incorrect. Archaeological surveys and excavations during the 1985–87, 1990, 1993, 1997, 1998, and 2000 field seasons examined the entire peninsula and much of the present town for archaeological remains (Figure 3.1) (DeCorse 1987a, b, 1988, 1989a, 1992a, b, 1998a). The data obtained allowed for archaeological assessment of the fifteenth- through nineteenth-century Elmina settlement.

The most intensive archaeological work focused on areas closest to the castle, particularly the portions of the site to the west and the southeast, which include the earliest and most densely settled sections of the town. The area immediately west of the castle, covering an area of almost 100,000 m² (about 25 acres), is the portion of the old town that was leveled and used as a parade ground by the British during the late nineteenth and twentieth centuries. It includes areas arbitrarily designated Loci A, B, C, and D (see Figure 3.1). These areas, thus, had the potential of yielding the longest sequence of occupation. Accounts of the founding of Castelo São Jorge da Mina note that some of the town was destroyed during its construction, hence traces of the pre-European occupation might be found adjacent to or near the castle. Following the construction of the castle, the African town clearly concentrated beneath the castle's walls to the west. During the eighteenth and the nineteenth centuries, this portion of the settlement included the market, an area that had been surrounded by the stone houses of wealthy merchants, from which the dwellings of the "common Negroes" were excluded, and it likely included several *bron,* or wards.[5] Excavation in this area also afforded the most information on trade materials, an important concern in developing artifact chronologies for Elmina and adjacent areas of the coast.

The buildings excavated from the areas closest to the castle clearly represent the town's economic elite—a population known to have built impressive stone houses, possessed a myriad of trade materials, and enjoyed a privileged position in trade with the Europeans. In assessing the consequences of culture contact, we might expect these areas of the settlement to have presented the greatest contrasts with traditional African lifeways: Did these individuals adopt behavioral practices and a worldview distinct from the adjacent population? The portions of the site located southeast of the castle (Locus E) and areas located farther west, including Loci F, G, and H, were more recently settled and the less affluent sections of the town, possibly including sections of the settlement occupied by slaves. The area to the southeast of the castle was, by the late nineteenth century, identified as *fisherkrom,* or the "fisherman's village."

FIELD METHODS

Four interrelated levels of archaeological recovery were used to evaluate the settlement. These included surface surveys, test excavations, trenches, and larger area excavations. The depth of the archaeological deposits proved to be an important concern in planning archaeological research. Despite the suggestion that the deposits covering the site were thin, much of the old settlement lies buried under layers of fill and stone rubble, at times over 2 m (6.5 feet) thick. Shovel testing or auguring has proven useful in delineating settlement areas in some contexts (e.g., Deagan 1983:51–53), and it was thought that this sampling method could be used at Elmina. However, the depth and compact stony nature of the deposits made this impossible in the majority of the Elmina site. Archaeological research was guided by these constraints. Throughout the project the same recording methods, excavation techniques, and analysis procedures were used.[6] This allowed for continuity in analysis, facilitated comparison, and enabled features to be readily relocated. Survey concentrated on evaluating the extent of the site through the identification of foundations, stone scatters, burnt daub, traces of structural remains, and artifacts across the 80 ha (200 acres) covering the potential area of archaeological resources relevant to the maximum extent of the nineteenth-century settlement.[7] All features on the peninsula were mapped at 1:100 metric scale, and more detailed 1:10 drawings were used to prepare plans of structures and features. Finds north of the Benya were plotted on the 1:2,500 series topographic map.[8] The term *locus* has been used as a convenient means to refer to areas of the site that were the focus of archaeological excavation. These are intended to provide only general locations and do not refer to areas of specific size or grid designation.

Surface data provided important information on settlement size, site occupation, and activity areas. For example, at Veersche Schans, on the western end of the peninsula, the surface material closely paralleled observations based on excavations. In many areas, however, the evaluation of surface data was problematic because of extensive use of fill, modern development, and intensive use. The portions of the site closer to the castle were the areas of the site best monitored by the Ghana Museums and Monuments Board when research was initiated. No modern structures covered the excavation sites, vehicular traffic was prohibited, and other activities were also limited. The most substantial pastimes undertaken at the site consisted of mending nets, landing fish, and bathing. In contrast, during the late 1980s and 1990s other areas were the focus of increasing development. Fragments of material of sixteenth- through twentieth-century age were noted across the peninsula and in areas of the modern settlement north of the Benya, but most artifacts relate to twentieth-century activity. In some cases, surface finds have become much more common in the last five years as a result of the erosion caused by the more intensive use of the site. On the other hand, the 1997 excavations at Locus G, the possible location of the nineteenth-century Dutch redoubt, Waakzaamheid, were abandoned because of settlement by squatters of this portion of the peninsula. An even greater logistical problem was the disposal of trash on the peninsula, particularly along the southern shore. Twentieth-century rubbish covers portions of Locus D and the adjacent areas to the west to a depth of 3 m (9.8 feet) in places.[9] Because of the extensive deposits of trash dumped on the site in the previous three years, excavations of the Locus D structures planned for 1993 were limited to a few test units.

North of the Benya Lagoon, the areas most relevant to archaeological investigation of the early settlement had long been covered by modern settlement. Survey, supplemented by test excavations, provided the principal source of information.[10] This is the location of the present town, and many of the areas of potential archaeological significance were covered by late nineteenth- and twentieth-century construction and roads and were used intensively. Houses, adjacent living areas, and trash-covered ground surfaces obscure archaeological visibility. Examination of much of this portion of the town, out of necessity, concentrated on accessible areas. The land immediately north of the Benya, south and east of Fort St. Jago, was examined most thoroughly. Several things made this area of particular interest. Some scholars had suggested that one part of the early African settlement may have been located in this area. In addition, seventeenth-century accounts and recent oral histories suggested the presence of a burial ground in this vicinity. Construction exposed buried deposits in several instances. Although detrimental to the archaeological site, such exposures were usefully exploited during survey, and they provided an important way of assessing the presence or lack of archaeological deposits. Artifacts or artifact scatters were noted but, with few exceptions, not collected.[11]

Archaeological excavation concentrated on the peninsula (Figure 3.2). Small

Figure 3.2. Elmina old town site, as viewed today from Elmina Castle. The Atlantic Ocean is on the left, and the Benya Lagoon is to the right, outside the frame of the picture. (Photograph by Christopher R. DeCorse)

test units of 1–6 m² (10.8–64.6 square feet) at Loci D, F, G, and H were aimed at delineating the extent of the site. Trenches, however, proved more useful for sampling because they provided long profiles that were helpful in defining the stratigraphic relationship of numerous interrelated structures and features. Trench I extended 14 m (45.8 feet) through Locus A, Trench II cut 40 m (131.2 feet) through Locus B, and Trench III extended 52 m (170.6 feet) across Loci A and D. The trenches were all extended to bedrock, which varied in depth between 1 and 2.5 m (3.3 and 8.2 feet). Larger area excavations concentrated on the exposure of structures at Loci A, B, and E. Surface soil was also cleared from an additional 300 m² (about 360 square yards) to expose foundations and trace walls.

All excavation was undertaken in 1 by 1 m (3.3 by 3.3 feet) units, excavated by natural strata whenever possible. If natural strata could not be defined, artificial levels ranging from 1 to 40 cm (0.39 to 15.6 inches) thick were used in order to maintain close horizontal and vertical control. The thickness of a level was dictated by individual archaeological contexts. Larger divisions were used when large sections of contemporaneous fill needed to be removed, whereas smaller increments were used to delineate floor contexts. Exposed artifacts, stones, and features were plotted on unit-level records, and soil colors and artifactual remains were noted. Effort was made to locate all artifacts in situ, but to ensure maximum recovery all excavated soil was passed through 3-mm (⅛-inch) mesh screen.[12]

Washing, labeling, and the initial cataloging of all material were completed in the field.[13] Sorting and tabulating all of the artifactual material were completed in Ghana, and the data were keyed for computer entry in the United States.[14] The objects were then deposited at the Department of Archaeology, University of Ghana, Legon, or at the West African Historical Museum, Cape Coast.[15] Reanalysis of locally produced and imported ceramics, beads, and tobacco pipes depended on small study collections.

THE DOCUMENTARY RECORD AND
THE ARCHAEOLOGICAL PAST

Because much of the peninsula settlement was the focus of intensive activity for hundreds of years, the archaeological deposits were exceedingly complex. A typical 1 by 1 m unit, 1.5 m (4.9 feet) deep, might include a meter of fill and destruction rubble, several clay and sand floors, a stone floor, four burials, a wall, and pockets of undisturbed midden deposits. Because of the large amount of European trade materials recovered, the dating of Elmina's archaeological finds was much more precise than for most West African archaeological sites that are generally dependent on radiometric dating or oral traditions for chronology. Imported ceramics, pipes, metal goods, glass, beads, gunflints, and other finds can often be dated to within a few decades or even years. This is important in tracing the occurrence of artifact types, features, and building construction.

The primary means of ordering the archaeological deposits was the *terminus post quem*, provided by the stratigraphic context and the initial date of manufacture of the most recent artifact recovered. *Terminus ante quem* for a building's construction was provided by artifacts in the floors and fill layers that sealed earlier deposits. Mean ceramic dates (MCDs) were also calculated for some stratigraphic layers, but these proved misleading. This technique is based on the production ranges of varieties of European trade ceramics and their relative frequency in archaeological deposits.[16] In some settings these calculations have been shown to correspond closely to the median occupation date of a site. At Elmina, however, the extensive use of fill at times led to the mixing of artifacts of quite different ages, thus frequently presenting MCDs earlier than the probable age of the deposits. For example, a layer of floor fill bracketed by nineteenth-century levels might produce an eighteenth-century MCD because of sixteenth- to eighteenth-century ceramics included in the fill.

For comparative purposes the thousands of archaeological levels were placed into one of several temporal contexts on the basis of stratigraphic position, dated archaeological materials, and, in the case of 1873 floor contexts, the archaeological evidence for a particular historical event. The divisions are useful in making some observations about the presence, absence, or frequency of certain artifact types or archaeological features and summarizing the development of the site. The temporal phases used are: pre-European-contact period (circa A.D. 1000–1471); Portuguese period (circa 1471–1637); seventeenth century (circa 1637–1700); eighteenth century (circa 1700–1800); nineteenth century (circa 1800–73); 1873 floor context; British period (circa 1873–80); colonial period (circa 1880–1900); and twentieth century. These divisions are somewhat arbitrary, and they relate to known historical events, such as the arrival and departure of the Portuguese, in only in a general way. The earlier divisions are broader and more generally defined. Later time periods could be more clearly delineated because of both the archaeological features represented and the greater amounts of closely dated trade materials. The "pre-European-contact period," for example, spans almost 1,500 years, whereas the nineteenth century has four divisions. In practice, the ordering and interpretation of data began with the detailed evaluation of individual contexts.[17]

Despite the comparatively precise dating afforded by trade materials, the archaeological past cannot, for the most part, be correlated with specific historically known events. For instance, portions of the town are known to have been destroyed by flooding, fires, and bombardment during the eighteenth century, yet these events have no archaeological visibility.[18] Following these occurrences the town was reoccupied, and the houses cleaned or rebuilt. Individual structures often presented many phases of renovation or construction—new floors, added walls—but no lenses of water-laid deposits, charcoal, or destruction debris distinguished individual layers that could be traced across wide areas of the site. The single striking exception was the clearly delineated floor levels associated with the 1873 destruction of the site and the massive layers of rubble that covered them.

The formation processes that produced the stratigraphic layers—the archaeological contexts—represented a variety of cultural and environmental factors. Different types of formation processes are more characteristic of some periods than others. Recognition of these different processes is important when comparing assemblages from different periods. The majority of the pre-eighteenth-century material consisted of shallow midden deposits resting on bedrock, which had often been disturbed by later burials and wall construction. The timber and clay building methods that predominated during this period left little archaeological footprint. Pre-eighteenth-century burials were represented, but none of them was articulated. In contrast, eighteenth- and nineteenth-century contexts produced the majority of the structures identified. All of these buildings were still occupied at the time of the 1873 bombardment. The stone and packed clay floors of the houses were probably kept well swept, but small numbers of beads and fragments of ceramic and glass were recovered from the surfaces of the clay floors and between floor stones. These artifacts, including some dating to the eighteenth century, provide limited indication of activity areas. In contrast, although portions of the site had been affected by its more recent use, 1873 contexts proved to be quite well preserved in most of the areas tested. In some cases building walls still stood at a height of almost 2 m (6.6 feet). Because the town was destroyed and the buildings abandoned, 1873 floor levels produced more in situ material at locations where it was used than is often represented in archaeological sites (Figure 3.3). These contexts were readily distinguished by masses of charcoal and broken artifacts, usually covered with remnants of stone walls, burnt daub, and rubble from building destruction. Floors dating to 1873 also produced a larger proportion of intact and reconstructible vessels than other contexts.[19] Such deposits provide a more direct indication of human behavior and artifact use. A number of floors also produced cannonballs and shell fragments from the 1873 bombardment.

The presence of fill, often containing material of mixed age, was a common problem in interpreting deposits of all ages. Because much of the early town

Figure 3.3. Many of the structures excavated produced in situ artifacts from 1873 floor contexts. In this photograph, a variety of local pottery bowls and pots, imported ceramics, glass, and bone beads are shown resting on an 1873 floor exposed at Locus B during the 1986 excavations. Scale shows 5-cm increments. (Photograph by Christopher R. DeCorse)

Figure 3.4. Collage of British-period artifacts, clockwise from the upper left: general service button with the royal coat of arms, circa 1871–1902; Gold Coast police buckle; Robinson Crusoe belt buckle, probably late nineteenth century; lion's-mask belt clip of the type worn by British cavalry and staff prior to 1855; "Piver" tin closure; a shell casing made into a whistle; military buttons; late nineteenth-century British pipe. (Illustration courtesy of Christopher R. DeCorse)

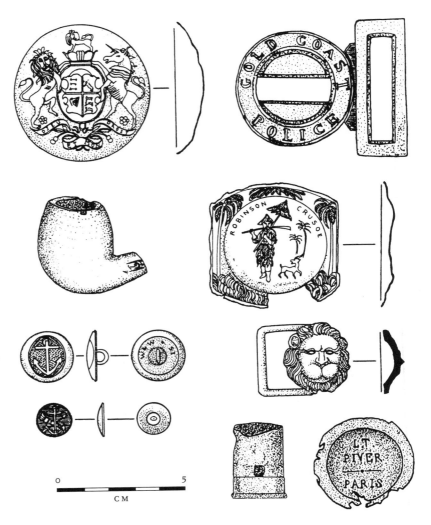

site was covered by exposed bedrock, fill derived from earlier midden deposits was frequently used to create building areas and level floors. In addition, the British apparently dug soil from other parts of the town site to level the parade ground. As a result, in several places artifacts of sixteenth- through eighteenth-century age were found overlying 1873 surfaces. Burials cutting into these deposits from various levels also mixed material from different temporal contexts. Fortunately, the stratigraphy of the site was generally very well defined, and individual deposits could be closely dated by the plethora of trade materials, and the age of individual provenances could be assessed on the basis of surrounding deposits.

The discard of human waste and trash was likely an important concern in the densely occupied settlement. Much material was probably discarded along the shore, yet only occasional water-worn artifacts were found in this area. In many instances buildings were constructed beyond the shoreline, and trash could have been dumped directly into the sea.[20] It is also possible that latrines were located on platforms that extended over the sea, but there is no evidence for this.[21] Refuse and human waste were also disposed of in narrow corridors and alleyways adjacent to buildings (see discussion of Locus B below). Deposition of trash, particularly by the British military, continued after the destruction of the town. Refuse dumped around the margins of the parade ground includes military buckles, shell casings, and insignia (Figure 3.4). A large portion of material from the late nineteenth-century context (circa 1873–1900) may have come from the British garrison, but trash from the town's inhabitants may also be represented. During the late nineteenth century a limited number of African burials were also located on the old town site, notably at Loci A, B, and E.[22] During the twentieth-century occupation of the castle by the Gold Coast and Ghana police force, trash dumping and filling of the site were limited. A thin layer of sterile gravel covered the parade ground, which was likely kept cleanly swept.[23]

The complexity of the disposal patterns makes it difficult to readily associate midden deposits with particular households.[24] The diverse formation processes represented also had important implications for the analysis of archaeological data. Comparison of faunal remains from different levels, change in the proportion of pottery styles represented, and the frequency of artifact types are of limited value without recognition of whether midden deposits, floor contexts, or tertiary fill deposits are represented.

THE SETTLEMENT

The extent of the nineteenth-century settlement could be readily defined by comparing the historical plans and descriptions with the archaeological features, especially traces of the defensive works. North of Benya Lagoon only Fort St. Jago and the flag tower remain standing. Some artifactual evidence of pre-nineteenth-century occupation was found on St. Jago Hill, where surface surveys revealed a very thin distribution of artifacts of seventeenth- through twentieth-century age.[25] Examination of construction and erosional surfaces, including channels cut for drains and large excavations for cesspits, revealed no evidence of midden deposits immediately north or west of the fort. Areas to the south and southeast were heavily impacted by the construction of fish-smoking ovens in the late 1980s. The compact, clayey soil used to make the ovens was dug out of the hillside, and in other places erosion exposed bedrock. Survey of these areas and the soil used in the construction of the ovens revealed no artifacts of pre-nineteenth-century age. The majority of surface finds were noted east of the fort. A more recent survey undertaken in conjunction with architectural renovation work reported that foundations and artifacts of an age of circa 1650–1850 had been exposed in this area (Anquandah 1992:44; 1993:7, 19–20).[26] Test excavations, also undertaken in conjunction with 1992 restoration work, exposed buried deposits in several locations, particularly adjacent to the fort's southeast bastion (Anquandah 1992, 1993). These deposits include material of mixed age, and they may have been affected by more recent construction or restoration work.[27] Both the surface artifacts and the excavated mate-

Figure 3.5 (*above*). Photograph of the site of Fort Beekestein. The original redoubt has long been obliterated by modern construction, but a cannon, visible to the right of the steps, and some nineteenth-century artifacts still mark the location. (Photograph by Christopher R. DeCorse)

Figure 3.6 (*opposite*). Java Hill (Cattoenbergh): the site as it appears today and a copper alloy bell recovered during survey work. The redoubt has been heavily impacted by modern construction, and cannons and a few artifacts are the only traces that remain. (Photograph and illustration by Christopher R. DeCorse)

rial are likely associated with the activities of the European military garrison in Fort St. Jago rather than the African population.[28]

Traces of three of the four other outlying redoubts constructed north of the Benya could be identified. The bastions themselves have long since crumbled, but cannons, a few artifacts, and some traces of foundations mark their location. Only Fort Nagtglas remains totally obscured, probably located beneath the Methodist primary school on the northeastern side of the town. It may, in fact, have been dismantled and much of the armament removed by the British during the nineteenth century.[29] Cannons from Fort Schomerus lie in the Catholic mission school compound, and those of Fort Beekestein mark the grounds of the old local council school at the end of Cemetery Road (Figure 3.5).[30] The site of Fort Java has been largely obliterated by modern housing. A small semicircle of stone that was identified may consist of remnants of the redoubt's fortifications, but the site is principally marked by four iron cannons and a small artifact scatter.

The artifacts collected from Fort Java may represent midden deposits displaced by modern construction (Figure 3.6).[31] The size of the collection makes it of limited value, yet it affords an interesting contrast with material from the town site. Diagnostic ceramics were almost entirely dated to the mid-nineteenth century, which is consistent with the construction and renovation of the redoubt and its occupation of circa 1820–73. The finds also included a nineteenth-century brass bell that was likely associated with the redoubt. Diagnostic ceramics consistent with the mid-nineteenth-century occupation include undecorated whiteware fragments and decorated sherds with hand-painted floral motifs; bands of pink and blue; dendritic and hand-painted finger swirls; black, brown, and flow blue transfer-printed ceramics; and cut-sponge-stamped vessels. The proportion of decorated vessels is higher and the number and variety of vessel forms more diverse than assemblages of comparable age from the peninsula settlement. Some post-1873 material was clearly present, for example, a single fragment of a polychrome transfer-printed plate commemorating King George VI's 1937 coronation. The only three manufacturer marks on tobacco pipe stems and bowl fragments also are British and, hence, are also indicative of British-period occupation. This material clearly postdates the use of the redoubt and, thus, may relate to the African settlement of the hill after 1873.

In addition to the military construction, some of the old Dutch merchant houses can be seen, particularly along Liverpool Street. These include the Quayson (or Plange) and Viala houses and the ruins of the Simons and Bridge houses (Bech and Hyland 1978; van den Nieuwenhof 1991). The Catholic mission buildings, the Methodist church, and houses along Cemetery Road and Buitenrust Lane date to the late nineteenth and early twentieth centuries. The pillars, which marked the entrance to the nineteenth-century Dutch government gardens, were also located. These were reconstructed, and one was slightly moved by A. W. Lawrence (1963:165) during reconstruction work in the 1950s.[32] A plan

of the roads laid out during the nineteenth century nicely corresponds to the town's present principal avenues. The large stone-lined channel that extends from north of Cemetery Road down to the Benya Lagoon may be part of the nineteenth-century irrigation system for the plantations that were located in this area.[33]

Surface material provided a less satisfactory indication of nineteenth-century occupation. Survey of the ruins and collapsed portions of the Bridge and Quayson houses noted some fragments of late nineteenth-century glass. However, compounds in the densely occupied areas of the modern town are kept clear of vegetation and regularly swept. This results in the redistribution or removal of artifacts and quite probably the relocation of some pre-twentieth-century midden deposits to the foreshore and municipal trash dumps. Sweeping and heavy pedestrian traffic contributed to a striking amount of erosion, in some instances the ground surface lying several feet below the original house foundations. Erosion was particularly a problem on the hillsides. Despite the report of the discovery of exposed burials in past decades in the area immediately north of the bridge, the vast majority of artifactual material noted during survey consisted of twentieth-century artifacts with a limited amount of material of late nineteenth-century age. Archaeological excavations behind Bridge House indicate that it and the other structures along the Benya Lagoon to the east were built on the beach and that floors within the foundations were leveled with fill. The absence of earlier African artifacts is consistent with the supposition that the area north of the Benya was not the site of early African settlement.[34]

The Peninsula

On the peninsula, surface artifacts are consistent with the concentration of the settlement west and southeast of the castle. The area east of the castle produced no evidence of pre-1873 occupation, and the shore likely extended to just below the castle walls until the early twentieth century. The area was tested with a series of excavations in 1997, and the construction of a drainage channel provided a useful cross section from the castle through the shallow beach.[35] The exposed soil consisted of sand fill and artifacts of late nineteenth- or twentieth-century age. This is consistent with early illustrations that depict the shoreline parallel to the castle's eastern wall (see Figures 2.5 and 2.12). The current beach was likely created only in the twentieth century following the construction of the break wall. North of the castle, the present retaining wall along the Benya is likely of similar age.[36] Prior to the twentieth century the shoreline

Figure 3.7. Photograph of house foundations along the southern shore of the Elmina peninsula. Many foundations extended over the shoreline and included some imported European bricks. Scale shows quarter-meter increments. (Photograph by Christopher R. DeCorse)

was likely closer to the riverside yard, and, thus, there would have been even less useable space north of the castle than at present. This area may, however, have been the location of limited African settlement during the eighteenth century.[37] Both the areas north and east of the castle were intensively used by the Gold Coast and Ghana police during the twentieth century.[38]

Excavations at the site of Locus E (*fisherkrom*), located on the narrow sliver of land south and southeast of the castle, confirm the absence of settlement in this area until the Dutch period (1637–1872). Several foundations were exposed along the shoreline and on the surface. Excavations exposed the shallow foundation of a small twentieth-century structure covering the foundations of a large late eighteenth- to nineteenth-century building, constructed on uneven bedrock outcrops and pockets of Portuguese-period midden material. Without the building foundations and covering fill, this portion of the peninsula would have been periodically washed by high tides. During the Portuguese period, African access may have been restricted. The Portuguese-period midden deposits likely represent trash thrown off the castle's southeast bastion.

West of the castle, the most visible surface indications of past settlement on the peninsula are the foundations that can be seen almost continuously along the southern shore, beginning southwest of the castle and extending for 280 m (about 300 yards) westward (Figure 3.7). Archaeological testing proved that some of the foundations on the surface were, in fact, twentieth-century, but these proved to be very shallow, and they had a minor impact on earlier deposits. At Locus C, for example, modern surface foundations were separated from the layers of circa 1873 by over 2 m (6.5 feet). In all, excavations and surface survey identified over 40 stone-walled buildings on the peninsula contemporaneous with the old town site. Stone foundations along the shoreline probably provide a good measure of the extent of the most densely settled part of the site. Excavations at Loci A, B, C, D, F, and G sampled 18 or 20 structures.

Not surprisingly, excavations on the parade ground produced the earliest and

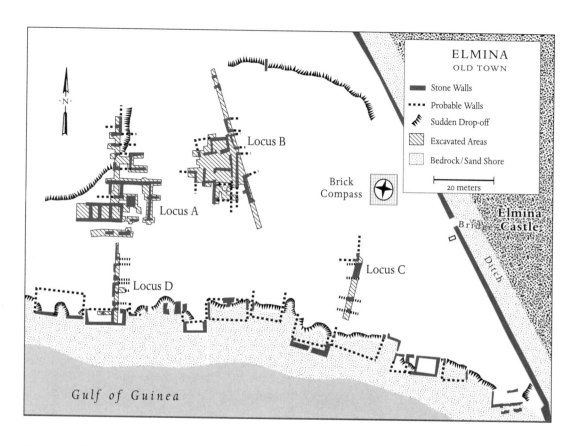

Figure 3.8. Map showing archaeological features and locations excavated immediately west of Elmina Castle. (Illustration by Christopher R. DeCorse)

most extensive evidence of occupation. Loci A, B, C, and D all produced traces of Late Iron Age or Portuguese-period occupation, though these traces were limited to shallow pockets of midden soil resting on bedrock and pre-seventeenth-century material mixed with later deposits (Figure 3.8). Only limited evidence of structural remains was noted (see discussion below). Much more substantial remnants of eighteenth- to nineteenth-century stone-walled structures were found in all of the units excavated.

The areas beyond Loci A and D, west along the peninsula, provided additional evidence of nineteenth-century occupation. This portion of the peninsula is slightly lower in elevation, and the archaeological deposits are unprotected by the fill that covers the parade ground. Pedestrian traffic, fish drying, and the site's use as a lorry park exposed mortared foundations, burnt daub, and artifacts in an almost continuous band along the southern half of the peninsula (Locus F) (Figure 3.9). The remains identified included stone foundations of several structures, destroyed during or immediately subsequent to the 1873 bombardment. The foundations and some of the floors of these structures rested directly on bedrock, and the 1873 floors were only thinly covered with soil. Caches of nineteenth-century bottles and an iron pot were recovered in situ from floor levels. Further confirmation of nineteenth-century settlement in this area was provided by test excavations and the building trench for a wall constructed by the Ghana Museums and Monuments Board.[39]

Figure 3.9. Plan of
Locus F. Erosion and
use of the site as a lorry
park in the early 1990s
exposed the foundations
and floors of many
structures in this area.
(Illustration courtesy of
Christopher R.
DeCorse)

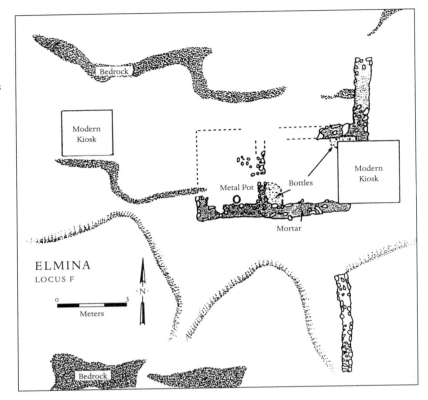

The Locus F finds are significant because they provide clear indication of the nineteenth-century expansion of the settlement westward along the peninsula. This settlement, however, appears to have been limited to the southern side, an observation consistent with nineteenth-century plans and the 1869 photograph of the town. Archaeological testing to the north revealed extensive nineteenth-century deposits. These materials were waterlogged, and the units flooded at a depth of 1 m (3.3 feet). The lower levels produced some deposits of sixteenth- to eighteenth-century age. These data indicate that this portion of the peninsula was a swampy marshy area until the late nineteenth or the twentieth century. It likely corresponds to the area of ponds noted in documentary accounts and illustrations of the settlement. Without the fill, roadway, and modern fish market, even the higher southern margin of the peninsula would have been more susceptible to flooding during flood tides and storms. This is consistent with historical descriptions that make reference to flooding in the town. Foundations of some early stone buildings were incorporated into the twentieth-century State Fishing Corporation building on the north side of the peninsula, on the western side of the fish market.[40] These building foundations likely date to the nineteenth century, but it is unclear if any or all of them relate to the pre-1873 occupation. Buildings appear in this location in the 1869 image and on the 1898 British plan of Elmina, and it is possible the foundations predate the town's destruction. No surface artifacts were located in this area.

Beyond Locus F, evidence for occupation was increasingly limited. The cen-

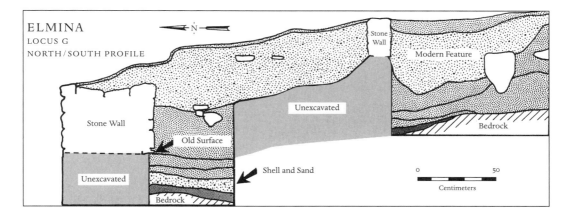

ELMINA
LOCUS G
NORTH/SOUTH PROFILE

Stone Wall

Modern Feature

Unexcavated

Bedrock

Stone Wall

Old Surface

Unexcavated

Shell and Sand

Bedrock

0   50
Centimeters

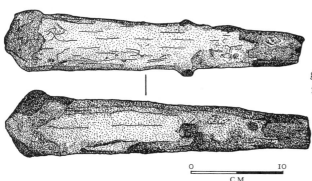

0   10
C M

Figure 3.10. Profile of Locus G excavations and a swivel cannon from the site. This may have been the location of Fort Waakzaamheid, built in 1811. (Illustrations by Christopher R. DeCorse)

ter and northern portions of the peninsula are level and rest less than a meter (only a few feet) above sea level. In 1990 this lower-lying portion of the peninsula was graded and temporarily used as a soccer field. The exposed deposits were fine grained and probably water laid. Stone foundations extended west from Locus F along the southern side of the peninsula. Surface artifacts dated to the nineteenth century. The grading also exposed a small iron swivel cannon and stone foundations, designated Locus G (Figure 3.10). The cannon likely had a bore of less than 5 cm (2 inches), but it is so badly corroded that it is difficult to give more than a general identification. Its construction and size suggest it may have been a Dutch naval gun, dismounted for use on land fortifications.[41] Test excavations (three units, 1 by 1 m) revealed that the stones were from a thick stone foundation. The foundations, almost 70 cm (27 inches) across, are substantially wider than those found in the African settlement, though they are consistent with the walls of the nineteenth-century Dutch redoubt Veersche Schans. The structure's position is notable, located on the southern margin of the peninsula at what then must have been the western edge of the settlement. The stone construction, the location, and the presence of the swivel cannon may suggest the presence of a redoubt, perhaps Fort Waakzaamheid, built in 1811 and described as being in a ruinous state by J. A. de Marrée in 1818 (translated in Feinberg 1969:115). The foundations were laid directly on the ground without building trenches, possibly having been quickly constructed.[42] The soft sand would have provided poor support, and it would not be surprising if the redoubt sank into a ruinous state only a few years after it was built.

The Locus G structure dates to the nineteenth century, but the layers beneath the structure provide indications of earlier use. The structure disturbed earlier burials that probably date to the eighteenth century. These, in turn, covered a shallow shell midden with pre-European-contact (circa A.D. 1000–1471) or

Portuguese-period (circa 1471–1637) African ceramics. Beneath this lies some evidence of earlier occupation, represented by shallow depressions cut into bedrock. This tripartite occupation, consisting of a nineteenth-century redoubt, an eighteenth-century African burial ground, and an occupation of circa A.D. 1000–1471, is analogous to that found at Veersche Schans and may provide important clues to the nature of the Village of Two Parts described in early documentary accounts. Other foundations exposed in this area were far less substantial and represent the nineteenth-century expansion of the town.

West of Locus G evidence for settlement is very limited. No surface finds were noted, nor were any buried features exposed by the grading. Excavations at Locus H, 75 m (246 feet) west of Locus G, exposed uniform sandy soil to a depth of 2 m (6.5 feet). The excavated material included a limited concentration of local pottery that, at the lower levels, was consistent with an age of circa A.D. 1000–1480. European material found with the later ceramics was all nineteenth-century. There was no evidence of foundations, floors, or structures. From Locus H the land rises slightly to an area of exposed bedrock and deep irregular depressions that mark an area long quarried for stone. References to the quarry occur in the nineteenth century, but it may have been a source of stone during the preceding centuries.[43] This area would have provided a ready exposure of bedrock beyond the African settlement and a source of building stone for both the castle and the settlement. Stone is still quarried there today, and fish-smoking ovens and piggeries also dot the area. Regrettably, this continued use of the site has obliterated any vestiges of the early use.

Veersche Schans and the Village of Two Parts

The site of Veersche Schans (or Fort de Veer) lies beyond the old quarries, approximately 0.5 km (0.3 mile) west of Locus H (Figures 3.1 and 3.11). The fort itself is marked by a low mound, six heavily corroded iron cannons, and several pieces of iron gun carriages. Although this nineteenth-century feature dominates the site, surface finds and excavations indicate an earlier and more complex past. The material reflects differences in both the time periods and the activities represented, including a pre-European-contact or contact-period African settlement, an eighteenth-century African burial ground, and the remains of the nineteenth-century redoubt.

Isolated artifacts were noted east and north of the fort as far as the quarry pits, but the majority of the material was located west of the redoubt. The earliest occupation was represented by pottery and occasional stone beads characteristic of the Late Iron Age or early historic periods.[44] Similar finds are thinly scattered along the beach and exposures for 2 km (1.2 miles) to the west.[45] The thin artifact scatter and the pottery are analogous to finds from Elmina and Brenu Akyinim that have produced thermoluminescence dates of circa A.D. 1000.[46] A groundstone celt and occasional quartz flakes provide some indication of earlier settlement.[47] Datable European trade materials were limited to occasional fragments of eighteenth- and nineteenth-century glass bottles, ceramics, beads, and tobacco pipes. This material has a much more limited distribution than the Iron Age finds. Although isolated finds of trade material were noted 0.5 km (0.3 mile) farther west, the majority occurred within 50 m

Figure 3.11. Plan of
Veersche Schans,
Bantoma. Traces of the
nineteenth-century
fortifications overlie
eighteenth-century
burials and earlier
settlement middens.
Much of this site has
been obliterated by
development within the
past five years.
(Illustration courtesy of
Christopher R.
DeCorse)

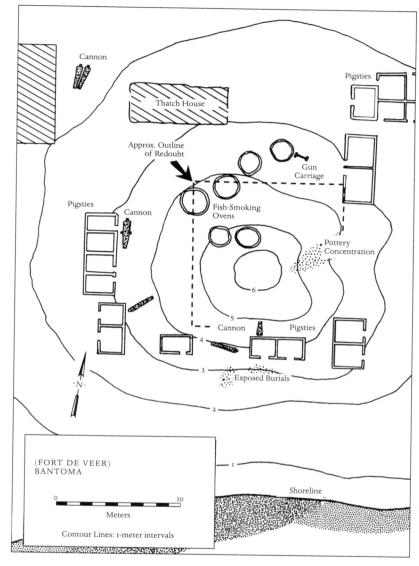

(164 feet) of the redoubt.[48] This material seems to represent two sources: a thin
scatter of refuse associated with the nineteenth-century redoubt, and earlier
artifacts associated with African burials. Several of the latter were exposed on
the surface between the southern side of the redoubt and the shoreline.[49] These
were separated spatially and temporally from the modern graveyard that begins slightly to the west-northwest. The modern cemetery, which includes
many above-ground monuments, is still used by the inhabitants of Bantoma.

Insight into the relationship of these finds was provided by excavations undertaken by David Calvocoressi in the 1960s. This work concerned the evaluation of oral traditions stating that the redoubt was the site of a late fourteenth-
or early fifteenth-century French outpost predating Castelo de São Jorge da Mina

(Calvocoressi 1968, 1977).[50] At the time of excavation the mound was flat topped and measured 4.5 m (14.8 feet) high and 22 m (72.2 feet) across. A number of large masonry fragments, not located during more recent archaeological work, were scattered around the mound. Excavation identified three discrete phases of occupation. These were numbered 1 through 3, beginning with the earliest.

Phase 1 consisted of shallow midden deposits primarily made up of sandy deposits and *Arca senilis* shell. Pottery was the only type of artifact recovered. Vessel forms and decorations correspond to the ceramics noted on pre-European-contact or contact-period sites and the earliest African ceramics from the Elmina excavations. Phase 2 occupation was clearly delineated statigraphically and by the cultural material represented. It consisted of shallow sandy deposits and 15 fragmentary or complete burials.[51] No evidence of structural remains was identified. The assemblage of locally produced ceramics contrasts dramatically with those of Phase 1, including smudged surfaces, micaceous wares, carinated vessel forms, and distinct decorations. Stylistically, some of these are similar to seventeenth- and eighteenth-century ceramics from Akan funerary sites like Twifo Heman and Ahinsan (Calvocoressi 1977:125–128; see also Bellis 1972). Reanalysis of beads associated with two of Calvocoressi's Phase 2 burials indicates that these are consistent with an eighteenth-century age. Phase 3 is represented by the walls of Veersche Schans, built between 1817 and 1829 and manned by the British in 1873. Construction of the redoubt's wall disturbed some of the Phase 2 burials. The stone foundations for the redoubt measured approximately 12.5 m² (129 square feet). The walls were constructed of roughly shaped stone blocks, cemented together with shell mortar and coated on the exterior with white lime plaster. A terrace extended along the eastern side of the structure. The imported material recovered was principally derived from fill in the redoubt and a small amount of secondary refuse associated with the redoubt's occupation.

The finds at Bantoma have nothing to do with early French traders but a great deal to do with the early African settlement of the Elmina peninsula. The Phase 1 finds at Veersche Schans, as well as the discovery of Late Iron Age ceramics to the east and the west, are indicative of the thin, dispersed settlement pattern found on the coast until the post-European-contact period. Notably, the castle's parade ground and Veersche Schans represent the two highest points on the Elmina peninsula. These may have been the locations of the "two villages a bowshot apart," described by Eustache de la Fosse in 1479 (Hair 1994b:129).[52] The lower area in between, occasionally flooded and offering a rise of only a few meters above sea level, would have afforded a less desirable location for a settlement. This area may have been the "Vale of St. Sebastian," where the meeting between Caramansa and the first Portuguese emissaries took place.[53]

Notably, aside from the enigmatic reference to the Village of Two Parts, no documentary references mention either an African settlement or the presence of an African burial ground immediately west of the settlement. If such a settlement had existed, it would seem surprising for it to go completely unmentioned in documentary sources. Hence, it is likely that this did not remain settled for very long after the Portuguese arrival. The abandonment of the western settlement and the concentration of the village adjacent to the castle are consistent with the lack of references to the settlement's "two parts" after the founding of São Jorge da Mina. Less surprising is the lack of reference to burials beyond the peninsula. Although references to burial practices occur in documentary sources, these are not detailed (see Chapter 6). The graves likely lacked any surface marking and were indicated only by shallow depressions in the ground that lasted a few years after interment.

The archaeological data thus indicate settlement on the Elmina peninsula for the last 1,000 years, perhaps longer. The earliest occupation, represented by scatters of ceramics and *Arca senilis* shell, extend from the area immediately west of the castle to the landward side of the peninsula, with a possible gap in occupation where the bedrock narrows and the lower northern side of the peninsula was swampy. This occupation may also have some evidence of timber and clay or thatch construction. This pattern of occupation continued at Elmina, as well as on adjacent portions of the coast until after European contact. Following the construction of São Jorge da Mina in 1482, the African settlement focused immediately west of the castle. During the sixteenth and seventeenth centuries the town remained concentrated in the area immediately west of the castle. In the following centuries the settlement expanded farther down the peninsula and north of the Benya Lagoon, the margins bordered by defensive redoubts.

STRUCTURES

Archaeological excavation afforded a great deal of insight into house forms and construction within the African settlement. The majority of this evidence relates to stone buildings of eighteenth- or nineteenth-century age: The timber and clay architecture used in the two centuries following European contact is difficult to identify archaeologically.[54] Clues to some of the early, pre-eighteenth-century construction may be found in the bedrock itself. These are the cup-shaped depressions that appear to have been systematically cut into the soft stone of the peninsula exposed at Loci A, B, C, D, and G. These depressions may have been made to hold wooden supports for traditional timber and clay construction. Unfortunately, the areas uncovered were too small and the patterns too irregular to discern any building plans, though some were in lines possibly representing wall alignments. The depressions generally did not correspond to other features such as later stone foundations or burials. In one instance, similar depressions were noted adjacent to a stone foundation on the peninsula's southern shore, where the depressions formed a rectangle extending over 1 m (3.3 feet) outward along the entire width of the structure on the ocean shore. They may have held wooden braces or some type of support for a patio or small addition.[55]

Stone foundations appear by the late seventeenth and early eighteenth centuries. Archaeological data support the view of a crowded, convoluted town provided by documentary sources. The property pattern seems to have become increasingly fixed, possibly a consequence of the population growth during the early Dutch period. Buildings were modified: Rooms were divided, additional space was enclosed, and new floors were laid down. These modifications, however, generally indicate renovation or a more intensive use of space rather than the realignment of walls or the construction of new houses. Once constructed, the stone dwellings seem to have remained basically the same in location and plan until their abandonment in the 1870s.

The buildings were at times unsymmetrical, irregular in plan, and the dimensions of rooms and the angles of the walls varied. Construction was confined by the limited room available for expansion on the peninsula, and buildings were squeezed in where space was available. Small structures and rooms were interconnected and fitted in where possible. Buildings along the southern side of the peninsula extended out over the high-water mark on mortared stone foundations, the interior of the rooms leveled with fill. The character of the town is that of a densely occupied urban environment with no delineated "yard" areas or open spaces between structures.

The houses exposed archaeologically can be contrasted with nineteenth-century buildings still standing north of the Benya Lagoon. Some of these, which are more consistent with formalized European building traditions, were built and occupied by wealthy African merchants and Europeans (Bech and Hyland 1978; Hyland 1970; van den Nieuwenhof 1991).[56] They were multistoried and included brick window and door arches and verandahs. European architecture journals were brought to Elmina, and missionary housing from other parts of the coast influenced construction.[57] Some of the foundations located on the peninsula similarly appear to conform to European plans. For example, the partly excavated Locus A structure discussed below seems to have incorporated many of these later innovations. Built in the first half of the nineteenth century, the building was more regular in plan and somewhat better constructed. The strong, mortared foundations likely supported a second story. Yet dwellings such as these were probably not representative of the majority of structures built on the peninsula or the majority of nineteenth-century houses north of the Benya Lagoon. Many were far less formal in appearance than the European-style manor houses. To some extent they embodied less reflective perceptions and more informal folk or vernacular styles.[58] However, they also provided important expression of nonmaterial perceptions of the use of space and the social and cultural beliefs that structured them. Although stone construction is indicative of new building techniques, the conceptualization of the built environment and the use of space within these structures represent continuity with African ideals and worldview.

Some buildings examined archaeologically, especially the Locus B structure, are comparable in arrangement to houses throughout the Akan and Guan areas, having linear arrangements of small unspecialized rooms around a central courtyard.[59] The courtyard was characteristically a semiprivate area used for cooking, eating, food processing, and a variety of other activities. It may even have been used as a sleeping area on hot nights. In function it seems to have changed little between the early seventeenth century and the present. Describing African housing in 1602, Pieter de Marees wrote: "They link together three or four such Huts, standing next to each other so as to form a square, so that the women have a place in the middle where they cook" (1987:76; see also Agorsah 1986:33; Jones 1983:86, 202). Ethnoarchaeological observations of modern Fante and Guan settlements indicate that the only rooms having a purely specialized function are shrines.[60] Other rooms observed ethnographically were frequently shared by individuals and used as repositories for personal property. Hearths, used for both warmth and cooking, and large stacks of pots were characteristic of adult female rooms. This pattern of multipurpose use seems to be reflected in some structures identified archaeologically.

The construction of all the buildings tested was very similar. All had stone walls that, in many cases, rested directly on bedrock. A large number of bricks were recovered during excavation, but their use in house walls was rare. Bricks, including various types and sizes of red brick and yellow brick associated with the Dutch, were occasionally incorporated into house walls, foundations, and steps. In these instances they appear to have been used no differently from stone. There are instances of bricks being used in a similar manner in standing houses north of the Benya. The walls also were generally left unplastered. There were instances of shell mortar or clay plastering on walls, which may have been a feature of houses of some of the more prominent Elmina residents (see discussion of Locus B below).[61] This was, however, atypical of most of the structures excavated, which showed no traces of plastering. Another distinctive aspect of building construction was the frequent absence of builders' trenches. During the fifteenth and sixteenth centuries the Elmina peninsula was only thinly covered with soil.[62] Foundations, therefore, were built directly on exposed bedrock, and the enclosed space was filled with soil. The few builders' trenches that were identified were shallow and dug into thin middens of fifteenth- through eighteenth-century age.

The stone walls throughout the site generally measure between 40 and 55 cm (15.6 and 21.5 inches) wide, averaging around 45 cm (17.5 inches). They consisted almost exclusively of unshaped blocks of Elminian sandstone, the material that forms the bedrock of the peninsula. When wet and newly exposed, this distinctive purplish brown stone may be quite soft and can be cut with a trowel. After drying, however, it becomes sufficiently hard for building.[63] It was also used for building on adjacent parts of the coast, for example, Fort Amsterdam (Abanze), the little fort at Anomabu, and houses at Ekon. Though there is no documentary evidence for this, it is possible that the quarried stone for these buildings was obtained at Elmina.

The walls in the town of Elmina were, for the most part, left unmortared except where additional strength was needed at corners, steps, and doorways, and in foundations along the shoreline. Mortar appears relatively uncommon compared with European structures of eighteenth- and nineteenth-century age.[64] The mortar was made of lime obtained from the baking of shell, particularly *Arca senilis*. This matches mortar that can be found in many portions of Elmina Castle, Fort St. Jago, and other European outposts. This lime mortar was a building material introduced by the Europeans, probably early in the

Dutch period. However, exactly when *Arca senilis* and other local shell became commonly used for mortar on the coast is somewhat uncertain. In the mid-sixteenth century the Portuguese were still relying on imported lime or the raw material to make it. A 1557 document translated by Teixeira da Mota and Hair (1988:63) notes that the garrison's masons and artisans had not undertaken any major work on the fortress because there was no lime, "there having been no stone to make it"—the necessary materials having just arrived by ship. Teixeira da Mota and Hair (1988:71 n. 25) suggest the limestone may have been brought from the Cape Verde Islands. An early seventeenth-century Dutch reference also refers to the importation of lime, as well as stones from Holland, for building, but such imports may not have been typical in later decades.[65]

Local shell specifically for the purpose of producing lime could be purchased on the coast by the third decade of the seventeenth century. A 1629 map discussing the people of Little Incassa describes how they "burn great heaps of lime and bring that for sale at Atchyn . . . from whom they have learnt how to burn lime, but at Atchyn itself most lime is burnt for the maintenance of both her (Portugal's) castles at Atchyn and El Myna [Elmina]" (translated in Daaku 1970:182). The practice of using burnt shell appears to have come into general use on the coast during the seventeenth century, and it was likely the principal source of lime until the late nineteenth century.[66] The shell could have been readily collected from the lagoons and possibly also mined from midden deposits along the coast. Some of the villages on the interior of the Benya Lagoon are, in fact, still known as places where shell was collected. Wall plastering and mortaring of the Locus B structure, discussed below, indicate that mortar made from local shell was being used in the African settlement by the late seventeenth or early eighteenth century, and it is reasonable to assume that shell mortar was used in the earliest mortared stone buildings in the town.

Most of the buildings excavated have some stone flooring, also of Elminian sandstone, though in many cases it is poorly dressed or completely unworked. In the case of the nineteenth-century structure at Locus A, the flooring stones were very neatly cut and set with sand. The stones are shale or slate with beveled edges on the bottom, and it is possible these were imported. Imported marble and cut flagstone flooring can be seen in some of the extant nineteenth-century merchant houses in Elmina, Anomabu, and Cape Coast. At Elmina thin layers of sand, used as a bed for floor stone, were noted in some structures. This technique has been a characteristic of Dutch and other European construction for centuries.[67] Many house floors at Elmina rested just above bedrock, with only a few centimeters space between. Following initial construction, new floors were made by adding layers of fill, sand, clay, or stone.[68]

The excavated structures lacked any evidence of specially prepared lintels, thresholds, or decorative architectural features. There was no evidence of chimneys and only one window, observations that correspond to documentary sources. In the majority of archaeological examples, walls did not extend higher than 1–1.5 m (3.3–4.9 feet) above the floor, and it is possible that windows were present. The one window identified was from the southwestern room of the

Locus A structure. It measured 90 cm (35 inches) across at the bottom and was located approximately 50 cm (19.5 feet) above floor level.

Several hundred fragments of window glass were recovered, and a variety of pane sizes and thicknesses are represented. On the basis of documentary data, we know that some of the more elaborate structures clearly did have windows and possibly glass panes, but these were likely comparatively rare. An 1874 description of Cape Coast suggests the windows in the African settlement had neither glass panes nor shutters: "This effect [of a ruinous appearance] is increased by the absence of glass from the windows, which consist usually of mere holes in the walls" (*Daily News* Special Correspondent 1874:40). Most of the window glass recovered archaeologically was from 1873 destruction debris or later deposits that cannot be clearly related to a particular structure or to the pre-1873 town and, hence, may relate to the British occupation. Several iron pintles were also found. They may have been used to secure doors or wooden window shutters, but none was located in situ. The pintles vary substantially in size and form. All were fabricated by hand out of iron, but it is uncertain if these items were produced by African or European craftsmen.[69]

Most of the buildings probably had thatch roofs, a material not represented archaeologically. Clear indication of flat, timber and clay roofing was found at the Locus B and Locus F structures, discussed below.[70] It is possible that some of the more elaborate structures on the peninsula had tile roofs or incorporated tiles into some part of their construction, but these would have been costly, and tile roofs were likely rare in the town, if present at all. Seven hundred forty-three roofing tiles of unglazed red earthenware were recovered, but these were found in disparate archaeological contexts and not associated with particular structures. It is likely that the tiles represent material removed from the castle.[71]

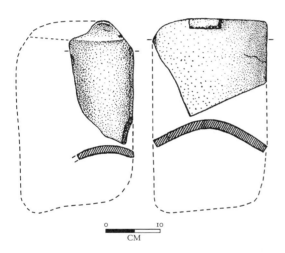

Figure 3.12. Dutch roof tiles from Fort Ruychaver, on the Ankobra River in western Ghana. Comparable tiles were excavated at Elmina. (Reproduced courtesy of Merrick Posnansky)

The tiles are European imports: Their paste is more fine-grained than locally produced ceramics, and they are also more highly fired. They are, for the most part, fragmentary and could represent either Portuguese or Dutch manufacture. Some are simple semicircular tiles, probably 20–40 cm (7.8–15.6 inches) long when intact, that would have tapered at one end to allow overlap with the tile above. These may represent Portuguese imports.[72] Other, more intact tiles are of a form characteristically associated with Dutch sites. They are slightly convex, with curved edges to overlap adjacent tiles and a catch at one end to secure them to the roof (Figure 3.12). When intact they probably measured approximately 36 by 22 cm (14 by 8.6 inches). Petrological analysis of similar tiles from the site of Fort Ruychaver, in the Western Region, suggests that the tiles were shipped from Holland.[73]

Three structures illustrate characteristics and some of the variation in the buildings. They represent the oldest to the most recent structures excavated. The first is in Locus B, which lies between 66 and 78 m (72 and 85 yards) west of the castle in the central part of the parade ground. The second is in Locus E, southeast of the castle, a late eighteenth- or early nineteenth-century build-ing located in *fisherkrom*. Finally, the Locus A structure was built, or perhaps re-constructed, during the nineteenth century.

Locus B

The Locus B structure (see Figures 3.13 and 3.14) was probably located near or adjacent to the market. Excavations to the southeast of this structure uncov-ered only layers of rubble fill over an irregular bedrock surface. Evidence for structures was absent or limited, suggesting the area may have been relatively open. A total of 132 m² (158 square yards) of the structure were excavated. Twenty-nine units (22 percent of the Locus B excavation units) were subjec-tively selected to sample the material below the structure. Midden deposits and a single burial beneath the building contained only Iberian ceramics dating to the seventeenth century or earlier, suggesting that the original construction of portions of the Locus B structure may have been early in the Dutch period. The building was multiroomed with stone walls and roughly dressed stone flooring. Four or five small rooms surrounded an unroofed courtyard. No evi-dence of a wall was exposed along the western side, and it may have been partly open or bounded by a barrier of perishable material.[74] The room on the south-ern side of the courtyard may have been added by subdividing a larger room, because the common wall covered earlier plastering. Traces of shell mortar plastering, up to 1 cm (0.39 inches) thick, were present on the inte-rior walls of the courtyard and adjacent rooms. However, most of the walls had only occasional traces of mortar adhering to them, and few traces of wall plaster were found in floor contexts during excavation. The plaster was, therefore, likely in a poor state of preservation by the 1870s.

A narrow corridor was added to the east-ern exterior side of the structure during the late eighteenth or early nineteenth century. It joins with similar spaces that extended along the exterior of the buildings to the north and northeast. There are entrances to the corri-dor through the courtyard and the room to the southeast (rooms A and C). No exterior openings were found in the corridor, but traces of a blocked doorway were found on the eastern side. The corridor had a roughly laid surface of natural cobbles at approxi-mately the same floor level as the adjacent

Figure 3.13. View of Locus B excavation in 1986. Elmina Castle is visible in the background. (Photograph by Christopher R. DeCorse)

Figure 3.14. Plan of the Locus B excavation. Portions of this building date to the late seventeenth or early eighteenth century. The structure was occupied at the time of the 1873 bombardment. Several smaller rooms surrounded an open courtyard, and a narrow corridor ran along the eastern side of the building. (Illustration by Christopher R. DeCorse)

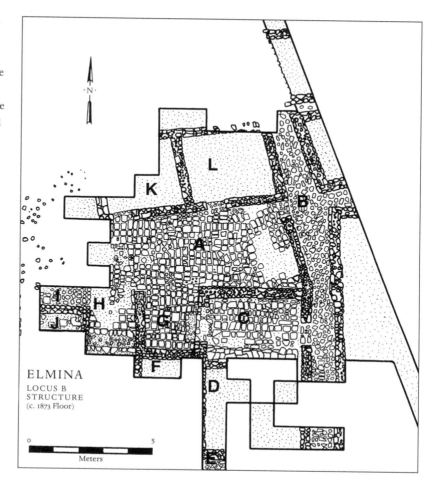

ELMINA
LOCUS B
STRUCTURE
(c. 1873 Floor)

rooms. This floor rested on over a meter of sandy lenses of midden soil with a high content of charcoal, organic material, and artifacts dating to the nineteenth century. The lenses of sand continued above the cobbled floor in the corridor for another 20–30 cm (7.8–11.7 inches). The 1,148 sherds of imported ceramics recovered from these upper levels produced a mean ceramic date of 1846. The ashy, sandy midden deposits within the corridor clearly represent distinct depositional contexts that are not unique to the Locus B structure. Corridors of this type are a feature found in many of the buildings excavated. Similar features in other structures tested may have been original components of the house design, but in some cases they were clearly added. The sandy, artifact-rich fill may have been the product of compound sweepings, or the sand may have been intentionally laid down as floor covering. This practice is still used today to provide dry surfaces during the rainy season. The corridors may have been used as wash yards or, possibly, for the deposition of night soil. Similar features serving in this manner were observed in isolated spaces behind houses in modern coastal settlements.

The roof of the Locus B structure was of timber and clay. Fragments of burnt daub with impressions of wooden poles were recovered from most areas at Locus B but were absent in the central part of the courtyard, the rooms along the northern side of the building, and the narrow corridor. This type of construction, sometimes called wattle and daub, was made by covering wood lashes with clay (discussed in Chapter 2). Impressions of poles in daub fragments indicate poles 3–4 cm (1.2–1.6 inches) in diameter, with a roof 15–20 cm (5.9–7.8 inches) thick. The daub is unfired, and the construction is comparable to that still found in neighboring communities such as Biriwa and Ekon, east of Cape Coast. It is also similar to traditional house construction in much of northern Ghana and neighboring parts of the Sahel.

Traces of fire-and-destruction debris were found in all parts of the Locus B structure. Portions of the building were apparently salvaged shortly after the 1873 bombardment. In places there was evidence that the rubble had been dug through to the 1873 floor level, possibly in attempts to salvage items lost in the building's destruction. Stone flooring from the northeast room and small sections of flooring in other rooms were removed, perhaps for use in the new town or to strengthen British fortifications. After their removal, some flooring

Figure 3.15. Plan of Locus E. Located southeast of Elmina Castle, this structure was not built until the early nineteenth century. It was constructed on top of Portuguese-period midden deposits. (Illustration courtesy of Christopher R. DeCorse)

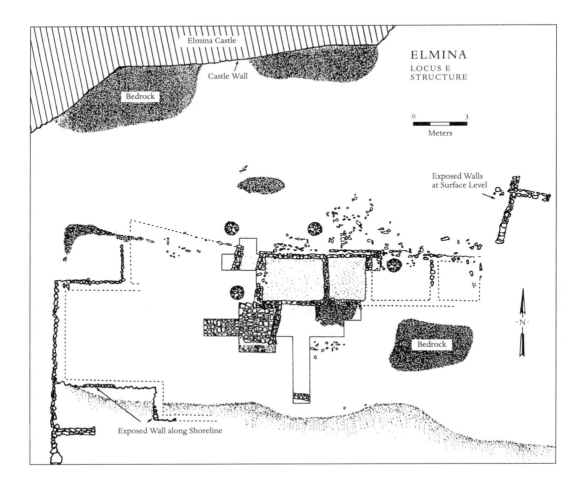

ELMINA
LOCUS E
STRUCTURE

stones were not taken away but left stacked against the southern side of the room southeast of the courtyard. Artifacts found in situ on the floor include fragments of imported and local pottery, glass, metal artifacts, and beads.

There was less evidence of disturbance in the room adjoining the south side of the Locus B structure (room D). No effort was made to salvage this room's contents after it burned and collapsed, preserving a wealth of artifactual material and details about the building's construction. Although no doorway was exposed connecting this room with the rest of the Locus B structure, it was probably part of the same building, for the narrow corridor continues along the east side of the room. Artifacts recovered from floor contexts include a variety associated with food preparation, including local pottery bowls, a coal pot, and the remains of a large barrel with a brass spigot. In places these were overlaid by the charred remains of wooden boxes (the contents of which had burned away), glass toiletry bottles, pieces of an eighteenth-century brass-barreled pistol, and shell beads. Charred pieces of wooden plank suggest that some of these later items were resting on a table or possibly a wooden loft above the floor. The floor was sand and clay, and the stone walls were plastered with sandy daub 1 cm (0.39 inch) thick.

In terms of the uses and activities represented, similar artifact concentrations were found in each of the rooms. The greatest anomalies were rooms G and H. Room H was probably a vestibule and produced no artifacts from the floor. The low artifact density in Room G can probably also be explained by its position as a passage to room C. Significantly, direct evidence for cooking activities (fire-scorched hearth areas and coal pots) was found in rooms A, C, D, G, and L. The data from room D are distinct in involving a relatively lower percentage of artifacts relating to cooking and food processing. Instead, there is a large amount of unidentified metal, much of it probably deriving from metal trunks or material that was stored in the trunks.

Locus E

Locus E, located southeast of the castle, has many similarities with Locus B, but it also has a number of distinctive features (Figure 3.15). Over 30 m² (323 square feet) were excavated to bedrock, which ranged in depth from just below ground surface to over 2 m (6.6 feet). As is the case with Locus B, the building's plan is somewhat irregular, and the rooms vary in shape and size. At least 10 rooms are represented. The earliest cultural deposits, however, do not relate to the structure. They consist of sandy midden deposits of local and Portuguese ceramics in deep pockets of undulating bedrock. During this period the entire area was probably flooded with water at high tide. In the late eighteenth century the area was leveled with fill, and stone walls were laid on bedrock outcrops. The walls extended out several meters beyond the original shoreline. They were largely left unmortared, except on the foundation walls along the shore. Given the size of the foundations and their construction, it seems unlikely that they supported a second story. A significant portion of the structure along the shore has been washed away by wave action, and only traces of mortared walls remain on bedrock outcrops.

The building is large, having originally covered an area of almost 200 m² (about 2,150 square feet).[75] A row of small rooms was located along the north side, and a larger room(s) was located to the southwest. The area south of the smaller rooms was likely unroofed, and it probably served as an open courtyard. Thus the rooms form an L-shaped plan, open on the sea side, a pattern also represented in traditional Akan construction. Initially, the courtyard surface was at least partly exposed bedrock. However, this earlier surface was later covered with a meter of fill, which buried several large cooking or storage pots in situ. Sandy clay floors, containing hundreds of mid-nineteenth-century tobacco pipe stems, covered this surface.

The primary entrance to the building was probably through a corridor in the center of the northern side. The southeastern room measured roughly 5 by 10 m (16 by 33 feet). It was the most elaborate room, being the only one covered with flagstone flooring. This consisted of roughly dressed cobbles of Elminian sandstone set in sand. The smaller rooms along the north side measured between 4.5 and 8 m² (48.4 and 86 square feet). The smaller rooms opened onto the courtyard, except for the westernmost one, which opened to the west into the small corridor.

Archaeological data provide little indication of the specialized activities suggested by the area's name. There was little activity-related material found in situ in floor contexts. This area was not bombarded in the 1873 conflict. Although occupants were forced to abandon their homes, they likely were allowed to pack their belongings. A single broken coal pot was found at the entrance on the northern side.

Locus A

The Locus A structure is the most complex building excavated (Figures 3.16 and 3.17). Although the majority of the foundations represented are nineteenth-century, some of the features may relate to the earliest European presence at the site. More than one structure and different phases of construction are represented. The walls that are present reflect extensive renovation or rebuilding during the nineteenth century. However, portions of the foundations and some features may represent the footprint of the Portuguese chapel and the Dutch guardhouse located adjacent to the old town wall, which were later modified and incorporated into a larger nineteenth-century structure. The building's plan in 1873 presents several European-style features. The principal rooms are bordered on the south and east by a verandah or terrace, which was likely covered by a roof supported with well-mortared columns. A stairway, probably at the main entrance, was located on the eastern side. This led to a central corridor separating the northern and southern rooms. It is possible that the walls and columns supported a second story or loft, but there was no clear evidence of this. The southeastern room has a stone floor of well-dressed slate, squared into regular rectangular shapes with the edges beveled on the bottom. These are set into a thick layer of sand. The area to the northwest may have been open. The structure was occupied at the time of the 1873 bombardment. Although few artifacts were found in situ in the eastern rooms, the two rooms to the southwest produced extensive material from 1873 floor contexts.

The terrace, the stone flooring, the stairs, and the southwestern and north-

Figure 3.16. Plan of Locus A. The foundations illustrated are from a nineteenth-century structure built over earlier features. (Illustration by Christopher R. DeCorse)

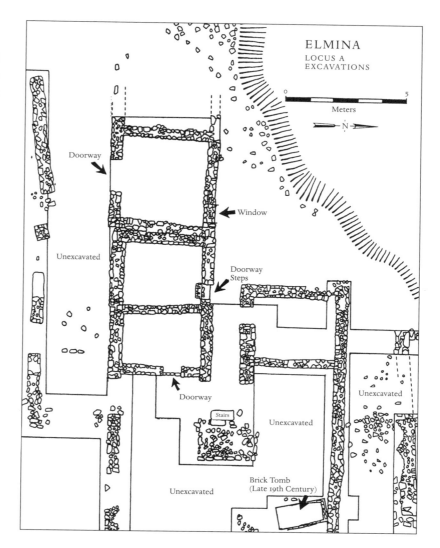

ELMINA
LOCUS A
EXCAVATIONS

0   5
Meters

N

Doorway

Window

Unexcavated

Doorway
Steps

Doorway

Stairs

Unexcavated

Unexcavated

Brick Tomb
(Late 19th Century)

Unexcavated

Figure 3.17. Photograph of Locus A excavations in 1997, facing south with the Atlantic Ocean in the background. (Photograph by Gérard Chouin)

eastern rooms clearly date to the nineteenth century. The two rooms in the southeast, however, represent the reuse or remodeling of earlier stone walling, perhaps dating to the Portuguese period. They appear to have formed a single room that was divided when the nineteenth-century flooring was added. The partitioning wall is thin and rests on top of an earlier floor. The exterior walls, which are 50–55 cm (19.5–21.5 inches) thick, rest directly on bedrock and have traces of shell mortar. The lower levels beneath both of these rooms produced artifacts of the fifteenth and sixteenth centuries, including fragments of brown Rhenish stoneware and tin- and lead-glazed Iberian earthenware. The room to the west also produced a feature consisting of Dutch brick, laid flat, which may represent an even earlier floor. The north and west walls of the room also had small openings that may have served as drains. These early features were heavily impacted by a number of burials below the nineteenth-century floors (see discussion in Chapter 6). The eastern wall of the room farthest to the southeast was reconstructed in the nineteenth century. Deposits around the wall and beneath the adjacent terrace also date to the nineteenth century.

The two southeastern rooms of Locus A clearly represent earlier construction incorporated into a larger nineteenth-century structure. Although the original construction is too fragmentary to evaluate its plan, the early walls and associated features may have been part of the Portuguese chapel or the defensive wall located at the western margin of the settlement during the sixteenth and seventeenth centuries (see Chapter 2), the chapel later serving as a Dutch guardhouse. The remnants of these features were then incorporated into a private house, probably belonging to a wealthy African or European merchant. The former may be indicated by the presence of a nineteenth-century shrine and articulated burials beneath the nineteenth-century floors. The latter included a variety of beads, *forowa,* local pottery, and other grave goods and are consistent with other African burials from the site.

FEATURES

Aside from the construction discussed, burials represented the principal archaeological features identified. There were, for example, no subfloor storage areas or cellars uncovered.[76] The excavation of burials was not a primary part of the research design. It was, however, expected that some human remains would be discovered because of traditional Akan burial practices. Cemeteries are common outside modern settlements, and documentary sources indicate that separate burial grounds were in use in some areas by the seventeenth century, but burial within the house also appears to have been common (see Chapter 6). Chiefs may still be buried in this manner. During the later Dutch period the Europeans attempted to prevent burial within houses because of health concerns. Archaeological work focused on structural remains and the delineation of the site, and burials were initially excavated within this context. Nevertheless, burials constituted the principal cultural features located during excavations.[77] The rituals they represent provide important insight into African worldview (see Chapter 6). Human remains were recovered from over 50 percent of the exca-

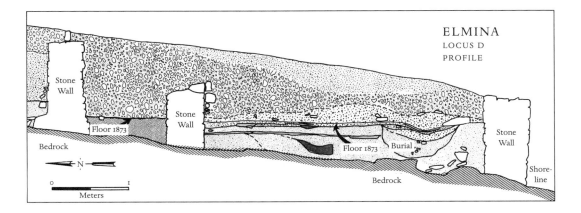

ELMINA
LOCUS D
PROFILE

Stone Wall

Floor 1873

Stone Wall

Bedrock

N

0   1

Meters

Floor 1873   Burial

Stone Wall

Bedrock

Shore-line

Figure 3.18. Excavation profile of Locus D. The foundation was constructed on bedrock beyond the high-water mark and the floor leveled with fill. Note the burial resting just below the 1873 floor surface. (Illustration by Christopher R. DeCorse)

vation units, with approximately 150–200 individuals represented. The majority of burials from all loci were found beneath house floors, but burials located at Locus G and at Veersche Schans and the burials north of the Benya Lagoon referred to in documentary sources represent separate burial areas that would have been outside the settlement at the time of interment. The majority of burials found within the town site were not articulated, having been disturbed by later burials and construction. The disturbed nature of many of the burials poses special difficulties in their interpretation. The collection is, however, the largest excavated in West Africa, and it clearly represents an important data set. It can potentially contribute a great deal to the understanding of the Elmina population and the impact of European diseases on indigenous African populations. The burials span the post-European-contact occupation of the site, but most date to the eighteenth and nineteenth centuries.

The graves were dug into the irregular pockets of soil resting on bedrock. The soil of the Elmina peninsula is thin, and graves frequently extended only 30 cm (less than 1 foot) below living floors (Figure 3.18). No evidence of the use of coffins was recovered in deposits predating 1873. Materials intentionally placed with individuals included a wide variety of glass, stone, shell, ivory and metal beads, European ceramics, metal goods, tobacco pipes, and glass. These imported artifacts were very useful, because they often allowed the burials to be fairly closely dated, despite the disturbed nature of some of the interments.

The caskets and masonry tombs that are present postdate the 1873 destruction of the town. They are found in late nineteenth-century contexts and illustrate the town's limited use as a burial ground following its destruction.[78] The two brick tombs were both located at Locus A. Though both were made of brick, they differed markedly in their construction. One was a cement shaft, coffin shaped in plan, extending almost 2 m (6.5 feet) deep from the modern ground surface. It had no covering, and the tomb had likely been opened and the contents removed during the late nineteenth or early twentieth century. The other was built at the bottom a shaft with no visible indication at the ground surface and, hence, likely predates the complete filling and leveling of the parade ground. The tomb was brick and 40 cm (15.6 inches) deep, with parallel sides and an arched roof. This tomb contained two burials, both disturbed, but one clearly postdating the other. Single post-1873 burials were found at Loci B and E. The scattered, erratic distribution of these interments, as opposed to location in a discrete burial ground, raises the possibility that they may represent an attempt to have located them within particular houses or sections of the settlement, a vivid memory of which would have survived in the late nineteenth century. However, informants could provide no information of their placement.

Evidence for coffin burial was also confined to post-1873 contexts. None was uncovered in undisturbed contexts, but coffin hardware was found.[79] The one coffin-shaped tomb of Locus A is also suggestive, but no evidence of coffins was found in either tomb. The coffins appear to have been made of wood with decorative bosses cut from copper sheets appointed with brads. Handles were made of iron or brass rods, secured by plates of the same materials. This type of decoration occurred in European coffins of the eighteenth and nineteenth centuries. Coffin hardware was mass produced in England, particularly Birmingham, in the latter half of the eighteenth century.[80] Such items were, however, likely produced on the European continent as well. The archaeological examples from Elmina are consistent with the techniques used on European coffin hardware, and they were likely imported.

PICK UP THE GEMS OF THE PAST

The preceding discussion introduces the archaeology of the Elmina settlement and some of the details of the town that can be provided only through archaeological research. Like scanning a bibliography to assess the documentary sources relevant to a particular place or event, discussion of the archaeological research allows us to evaluate the amount and kind of information provided by the material record. People often think of archaeology in terms of the objects recovered, and, indeed, much of the archaeological work examined thus far deals with the discovery of artifacts of certain ages and their location. What was the extent of the settlement? What were the houses of Elmina like? How was trash disposed of? Collectively these rather mundane, particularistic details contribute to a fuller understanding of the settlement's physical layout, chronology, and details of everyday life that were largely omitted in documentary sources.

The information provided by archaeology can, however, assess questions of broader scope. The material record of Elmina and neighboring sites in coastal Ghana furnishes a record of some of the changes and transformations that occurred during the period of European contact and trade. Examination of the broader patterns of which artifacts and sites are part, combined with the documentary record and oral traditions, allows us to examine some of the changes in subsistence, technology, trade, and African culture that occurred in coastal Ghana over the past 1,000 years. These transformations are the focus of the following chapters.

4

SUBSISTENCE, CRAFT SPECIALIZATION, AND TRADE

When young people reach the stage where they have their own household, they must themselves decide how to seek their sustenance. They have several methods and ways of doing this, but the main ones are: 1. Agriculture. 2. Fishing. 3. Livestock husbandry. 4. Hunting. 5. Trading. 6. All kinds of crafts.

WILHELM JOHANN MÜLLER, 1673, TRANSLATED BY ADAM JONES, "German Sources for West African History 1599–1669"

❖

They were traders, farmers and fishermen.

AN ELMINA ELDER, QUOTED BY JOHN FYNN, "EDINA (ELMINA)," *Oral Traditions of the Fante States*

Subsistence, craft production, and trade in coastal Ghana during the past 500 years can be reconstructed through documentary and archaeological sources.[1] These data are incomplete, particularly for the period of early African and Portuguese interactions, but they provide important clues to changes in African society. A complete description of the archaeological assemblage is not intended here.[2] This discussion and those in the following chapters concentrate on those data that highlight change and development in local subsistence strategies and industries, the nature of the Elmina settlement, its trade, and aspects of the Elmina worldview.

As will be seen, European trade impacted some aspects of indigenous subsistence, the crops raised, and African fishing technology. Transformation and continuity in these strategies are particularly interesting because they provide a means of examining the consequences of the biological expansion of Europe (Crosby 1986). Between the fifteenth and the seventeenth centuries there was also increasing settlement of the coast. With urbanization came traders as well as a variety of craft specialists. Five local industries will be briefly discussed: ceramics, metalworking, salt making, bead production, and ivory carving. Although these industries have long histories in West Africa, substantially predating European contact, production was limited on the coast, and much of it was likely located in the interior. Urbanization, expanding trade, and access to European imports facilitated and contributed to the elaboration of these industries. At Elmina, there is little direct evidence of on-site manufacture, but a significant number of the artifacts examined were likely produced in Elmina and its environs. There is also some indication of materials brought from more northern areas and, possibly, adjacent coastal regions.

SUBSISTENCE

At the time of European contact, agriculturists relying on mixed farming with hoe cultivation had likely been on the coast for thousands of years. The earliest evidence for domestication in Ghana comes from Kintampo complex sites in the northern forest and savanna, which suggest the intensification of settled life and possible food production after 2000 B.C.[3] On the central coast, archaeological data on domestication and agricultural origins are especially lacking. European accounts of the fifteenth through the seventeenth centuries refer to the fish, wild game, and indigenous domesticates that were present. These descriptions are not particularly complete or necessarily accurate, but, as yet, archaeological information on subsistence relies on limited data from a small number of sites.[4] The sum total of paleobotanical remains consists of a handful of palm kernels (*Elaeis guineensis*) postdating European contact.[5]

The data that are available on coastal Ghana indicate some transformation in the foods exploited but also consistency in the manner in which food was procured, prepared, and eaten. Rather than an examination of food solely in terms of production, a more holistic consideration within its cultural context is useful. The interrelated system of food conceptualization, procurement, distribution, preservation, preparation, and consumption shared by members of a cultural group can be referred to as the foodways system (Deetz 1996:50). Certain aspects of this system such as food remains, food-processing equipment, serving vessels, cutlery, and tableware survive in the archeological record and may be used to monitor changes in eating practices and customs. Mixed reliance on domesticated and wild resources likely represents a distinctive West African pattern of subsistence, components of which extend back well into the Iron Age.

Although it is possible to discuss generalized "West African" dietary practices, there has been substantial variation in terms of the subsistence strategies employed and the specific foods exploited. Today, mixed soups and stews served on starchy carbohydrates are widely preferred. In much of modern West Africa carbohydrates constitute as much as 80 percent of the diet, almost twice the 45–50 percent they make up in industrialized countries (Latham 1979:58). There are, however, differences in the crops utilized. In the upper Guinea coast, rice is the preferred food, whereas in the savanna and forest to the east yams are much more popular.[6] Pounded yam, cassava (manioc), or plantain, called *fufu,* is currently a staple in much of Ghana. Among the coastal Fante, *kenkey,* a dish made from soaked and partly fermented corn, is very common. Soups or stews served with these dishes are made from an array of different plants and often include a variety of wild and domesticated animals, as well as fish, land snails, crustaceans, and shellfish. Food is commonly pulverized using a grinding stone or pottery mortar prior to cooking. Meals are eaten with the hand or a spoon, which was also the case in the past (e.g., de Marees 1987:43).

Coastal and Marine Resources

Coastal adaptations during the pre- and post-European-contact periods made extensive use of lagoon and marine resources (Figure 4.1). Ethnographic and archaeological information indicates that a wide variety of gastropods, mol-

lusks, and crustacean species were traditionally used as a food resource, and, indeed, shellfish may have constituted an important portion of the diet prior to the seventeenth century.[7] Small middens, principally made up of *Arca senilis* shell, are characteristic of Late Iron Age–early historic period occupations.[8] This bivalve ranges from 20 to 150 mm (0.8 to 6 inches) across and is common in lagoons and estuaries (Edmunds 1978:63–64).[9] At Elmina and elsewhere, the presence of ceramics, distinct from later wares in paste, form, and decoration, and the absence of European trade materials characterize these assemblages. Given the limited size of the shell middens present in coastal Ghana, it is unlikely that mollusks were the primary basis of subsistence but rather a complement to other lagoonal, marine, and agricultural resources. This pattern may reflect a practice of temporary use or seasonal occupation. Yet, it is perhaps significant that some of the major sites producing late prehistoric to early historic period (circa A.D. 1000–1637) ceramics are actually located not on the ocean shore but on the interior sides of lagoons. Such sites would clearly not have facilitated access to marine resources

Figure 4.1. A view of fishing canoes in the Benya Lagoon. Although there has been long-term exploitation of marine resources on the coast, the nature of fishing today has changed to include introduced technologies such as large seine nets and gasoline engines. (Photograph by Christopher R. DeCorse)

but were well positioned to exploit mollusks and fish in the lagoons. The small size of the shell middens may also serve as another indicator of lower population densities prior to the seventeenth century.

At Elmina, shellfish continued to be a significant part of subsistence during the post-European-contact period. European descriptions mention mussels, oysters, lobsters, and crabs, but the references are unclear to what extent these resources were being utilized by the African population.[10] Marine mollusks (classes Gastropoda, Bivalvia, and Scaphopoda) were, however, common in all parts of the Elmina excavations (Table 4.1). Some 10-cm (3.9-inch) levels in 1 by 1 m excavation units produced over 24 kg (53 pounds) of shell.[11] Several discrete middens of seventeenth- and eighteenth-century age were discovered. They consisted almost entirely of *Arca senilis* shell, with small quantities of *Thais haemastoma, Ostrea* spp., *Tagelus angulatus, Donax rugosa, Semifusus morio,* and *Mytilus perna.* Isolated shells, primarily *Arca senilis,* can be found over much of the peninsula.[12] A small amount was also recovered from excavations in and around Fort St. Jago.[13] There is little doubt that the majority of this shell represents food-related waste.[14] Informants at Elmina indicated that virtually all of the mollusk species found archaeologically are, at least occasionally, exploited for food. Those not identified as food resources are primarily unrecognized offshore species or uncommon varieties. Although shellfish is commonly eaten, ethnographic observation indicates that today it is an insignificant com-

Table 4.1

Mollusks Recovered Archaeologically at Elmina

(Classes Gastropoda, Bivalvia, Scaphopoda, and Cephalopoda)

	Habitat	Comment[†]
Arca senilis	Lagoons and estuaries	Collected for food
Archachatina degneri	Terrestrial	Collected for food
Cardium costatum	Offshore, washed up	Edible
Cardium ringens	Offshore, washed up	Edible
Cerithium atratum	Rocky shores	Unrecognized
Clanculus guineensis	Rocky shores	Edible
Clanculus kraussi	Rocky shores	Edible
Cymbium sp.	Mud and sandy shore below low tide	Edible
Cypraea stercoraria	Low on rocky shores, pools	Unrecognized
Dentalium sp.	Offshore	Unrecognized
Donax rugosus	Low on beach	Collected for food
Mactra nitida	Offshore, washed up	Edible
Murex sp.	Shallow water	Unrecognized
Mytilus perna	Mid- to lower shore, attached by byssus	Collected for food
Natica collaria	Offshore, rarely low on sandy shores and washed up	Unrecognized
Natica marochiensis	Common: estuaries, offshore, sandy beaches, etc.	Edible
Nerita senegalensis	Rocky shores, low tide–upper shore	Edible
Olivancillaria hiatula	Low tide, estuaries, offshore	Collected for food
Ostrea sp.	Mid- to upper shore	Collected for food
Patella safiana	Low to midshore, sometimes higher	Collected for food
Pecten sp.	Offshore, washed up	Edible
Pitaria tumens	Offshore, washed up	Collected for food
Semifusus morio	Shore below tide level in estuaries and mangroves	Edible
Tagelus angulatus	Estuaries	Collected for food
Terebra sp.?	Offshore, washed up	Edible
Thais callifera	Lagoons, estuaries	Collected for food
Thais haemastoma	Lower to upper rocky shores	Collected for food
Thais nodosa	Low on rocky shores	Collected for food
Sepia officinalis	Offshore, washed up	Edible
Strombus latus	Offshore	Edible

[†]*Sources of comments:* Elmina interviews 1987; Edmunds 1978; Hodasi 1995.

Note: List does not include species used as currency (i.e., *Cypaea moneta* and *C. annulus*).

ponent of diet compared with fish, chicken, and goat. The small size of many mollusk species makes them of limited importance, except as an occasional resource gathered by children.

Today, marine fishing using beach seine nets, the ali net, and the more recent purse seine nets used by trawlers is a key aspect of coastal life, with the months between June and September being particularly productive for fisherman, but these techniques are recent innovations, and the pattern represented now was not necessarily the same in the past. Because of the importance of marine fishing in post-European-contact times, mostly known from documentary sources dating to the seventeenth century or later, some have assumed that it was also

Table 4.2

Marine Organisms on the Gold Coast

(as represented in documentary accounts)[†]

PHYLUM CHORDATA
*Class Chondrichthyes**
Blue shark or sharp-nosed shark	*Sphyraena guachancho*
Eagle ray	*Myliobatis aguila*
Hammerhead shark	*Sphyrna zygaena*
Sting ray	*Trygon margarita*

Class Mammalia
African manatee	*Trichechus senegalensis*
Sperm whale	*Physeter catodon*

*Class Osteichthyes**
African carp	*Cyprinus carpio*
Barracuda	*Sphyraena guachancho*
Bonito	*Sarda sarda* or *Parathunnus regius*
Burrito	*Brachydeuterus auritus*
Dorado (Fante) or dolphinfish	*Coryphaena hippurus*
False albacore	*Euthynnus alleteratus*
Flying fish or flying gurnard	*Cypsilurus lutkeni* or *Cephalacanthus* sp.
Guitarfish	*Rhinobatus rasus* or *R. albomaculatus*
Herring or sardines	*Sardinella aurita; S. cameronensis*
Kingfish or Spanish mackerel	*Scomberomoros tritor*
Little tunny	*Parathunnus obesus*
Moonfish	*Lampris* sp.?
Opher	*Lampris regius*
Pilot fish	*Naucrates ductor*
Red mullet or goatfish	*Upeneus prayensis* or *Pagellus erythrinus*
Remora	*Echeneis naucrates*
Sea bream	*Trachinotus goreensis*
Sea pike	*Esox* sp.?
Sole	*Symphurus* sp.?
Spanish mackerel	*Scomber colias*
Threadfin or snub-nose fish	*Galeoides decadactylus*
Weever	*Trachinus radiatus*

PHYLUM ANTHROPODA
Class Crustacea
Lobster	*Scyllarides latus*
Crab	*Callinectes latimanus* or *C. gladiator*
Prawn	*Palaemon paucidens* or *Penaeus velutinus*

[†]*Sources of documentary accounts:* Barbot 1992; Bourque 1997; de Marees 1987; Jones 1983; Pennak 1964.

*Found archaeologically.

the principal aspect of subsistence during the pre-European-contact period and a feature of pre-European-contact trade with the interior (Table 4.2).[15] There is no question that marine fishing using canoes played a significant role in coastal subsistence; however, given the evidence currently available, large-scale marine fishing, continuity with ethnographically documented technologies, and an early interior trade in smoked fish cannot be taken for granted. No sites from the Ghanaian hinterland have produced bones of ocean fish, and, more notably, only small amounts of marine or terrestrial vertebrates are represented in the early coastal middens that have been examined.[16]

Ocean fishing using canoes, possibly including sails, long predated European contact with West African populations.[17] The *regimento* of 1529 states: "I [the king] am informed that the blacks of the village [Elmina] have many canoes in which they go fishing and spend much time at sea" (Hair 1994b:78 n. 130, see also 71 n. 97; and Pereira 1967:121). Fish bone makes up a principal component of the archaeological bone at Elmina. Significantly, seventeenth-century archaeological contexts at Elmina include shark centra (Bourque 1997:34).[18] Their presence is notable because shark sink when they die and typically do not wash up on shore. Hence, their presence in seventeenth- and post-seventeenth-century contexts is a good indication of marine, as opposed to lagoon, fishing. Some shark centra also have clear butchering marks (Bourque 1997:Figure 15). Documentary references provide more detail. Jean Barbot, writing in the late seventeenth century, commented: "After that of merchant, the trade of fisherman is the most esteemed and commonest. Fathers bring their children up to it from the age of nine or ten. Every morning (except Tuesday, which is their Sunday), a very large number of fishermen come out from the land for up to two leagues. There are many of them at Axim, Anta, Comendo, Mina, Corso, Mourée, and Cormentin, but more at Comendo and Mina than elsewhere" (1992:519).[19]

Yet, the same sources indicate that fishing methods relied on smaller nets, iron hooks, and spears rather than the large nets that characterize modern practices. In the seventeenth century, marine fishing was said to have been done with hooks, both on drop lines and in barbed lines that were dragged through the water (Figure 4.2). Although large nets (up to 18 m [60 feet] long) were used, the technique seems quite distinct from the predominant modern methods.[20] The sizes of the canoes also seem to have been somewhat smaller than the canoes used for fishing today.[21] Modern canoes are often upward of 10 m (nearly 33 feet) long and are principally powered by outboard motors, though paddles may occasionally be used. Throughout the Late Iron Age until after European contact, the exploitation of fish and shellfish from lagoons and the coastal littoral may have remained an important aspect of subsistence.[22] Fish may have been caught in lagoons using wicker traps or cast nets, methods that are still commonly used today.[23] The harvesting of fish by torchlight in rocky pools was described in the seventeenth century, and, indeed, fish, lobsters, and crabs are still caught this way (de Marees 1987:121; Müller in Jones 1983:232–233, 238). These techniques are likely more characteristic of pre-nineteenth-century subsistence strategies than the seine net fishing used in the later nineteenth and twentieth centuries.[24]

Increasing urbanization along the coastal margin may have stimulated growth in marine fishing by expanding the local market, and access to Euro-

Figure 4.2. How they fished on the Gold Coast, as illustrated in de Marees (1602:Plate 96). Some of the techniques discussed in De Marees's accompanying text, including the use of cast nets, are still used today. (Reproduced courtesy of the Rare Books Division, the New York Public Library, Astor, Lenox and Tilden Foundations)

pean trade materials facilitated local production and innovation. The earliest reference to fishhooks on the central Gold Coast may be in an English account of the 1550s: "[Y]ron worke they can make very fine, of all such things as they doe occupy, as darts, fishookes, hooking yrons, yron heades, and great daggers" (Hakluyt 1589, cited in Hair 1994b:52 n. 29). This technology likely predates European contact, but increasing accessibility of imported metals would have aided such production. Large European sewing needles were fashioned into fishhooks (Müller in Jones 1983:232). Mass-produced European manufactures also became available. In December 1645 Dutch traders at Elmina had on hand over 360,000 fishhooks of various sizes (Alpern 1995:15; see also Bennett and Brooks 1965:41–42; Jones 1983:232). The nine fishhooks recovered archaeologically are all copper alloy (probably brass) and imported.[25] The largest Elmina example is 2.5 cm (nearly 1 inch), somewhat small for marine fishing. European trade also increased availability of rope, twine, and string that could have been used in the manufacture of larger nets for marine fishing. Traditionally, nets and lines were made of cords of twisted bark (de Marees 1987:122–123; Towerson in Blake 1942:379). A variety of lead net weights were found at Elmina, almost exclusively in nineteenth-century contexts. Several imported varieties are represented. Most, however, are irregular fragments of lead sheeting that were folded or clipped over the edge of the net. These were locally made from imported lead.[26] Virtually indistinguishable weights continue in use today. Such weights are typically attached to the bottom of seine nets. Somewhat surprisingly, the weights and the fishhooks recovered archaeologically were found at Loci A, B, and D, whereas none came from Locus E, the site of the erstwhile "fisherman's village."

Hunters and Farmers

A wide variety of cultigens were present in West Africa before the fifteenth century (Clark and Brandt 1984; Lewicki 1974; Mauny 1954, 1961; Shaw et al. 1993). African rice (*Oryza glaberrima*), oil palm (*Elaeis guineensis*), millet (*Pennisetum* sp.), shea nut (*Butyrospermun parkii*), malaguetta pepper, cowpeas (*Vina unguiculata*),

Table 4.3

Terrestrial Animals on the Gold Coast

(as represented in documentary accounts)†

CLASS MAMMALIA
Order Artiodactyla
    Black duiker*   *Cephalophus niger*
    Buffalo   *Syncerus* sp.?
    Deer   Cervidae spp.?
    Duiker or Maxwell's duiker*   *Cephalophus maxwelli*
    Royal antelope   *Neotragus pygmaeus*
    Warthog*   *Potomochoerus porcus*
    Wild pig*   *Potomochoerus proms*

Order Carnivora
    Black-back jackal*   *Canis mesomelas*
    Civet cat   *Viverra civetta*
    Forest genet*   *Genetta maculata*
    Golden cat   *Felis aurata*
    Leopard   *Panthera pardus*
    Palm civet cat*   *Nandinia binotata*
    Serval   *Felis serval*
    Side-striped jackal*   *Canis adustus*

Order Lagomorpha
    Hare   *Lepus whytei*

Order Primates
    Baboon   *Papio anubis*
    Chimpanzee   *Pan troglodytes*
    Diana monkey   *Cercopithecus diana*
    Greater white-nosed monkey   *Cercopithecus nictitans*
    Lesser white-nosed monkey   *Cercopithecus petaurista*
    Olive colobus monkey*   *Procolobus verus*
    White-collared mangabey   *Cercocebus torquatus*

Order Proboscidea
    African elephant   *Loxodonta africana*

Order Rodentia
    Brush-tail porcupine*   *Atherurus africanus*
    Cane rat*   *Cricetomys gambianus*
    Crested porcupine   *Hystrix cristata*
    Giant rat*   *Cricetomys gambianus*
    Grasscutter*   *Thryonomys swinderianus*

CLASS REPTILIA
    African python   *Python sebae*
    Chameleon   *Chamaeleo* sp.?
    Giant ground pangolin   *Manis gigantea*
    Monitor lizard   *Varanus giganteus*
    Nile monitor   *Varanus niloticus*
    Sharp-nose crocodile or Nile crocodile*   *Crocodylus niloticus*
    Tortoise*   *Kinixys* spp.?

Table 4.3 (continued)

CLASS GASTROPODA
  Giant land snail*   *Archachatina degneri*

DOMESTICATED SPECIES
  Chicken*   *Gallus gallus*
  Cow*   *Bos taurus*
  Dog*   *Canis familiaris*
  Dwarf shorthorn   *Bos* sp.?
  Goat*   *Capra* sp.
  Guinea fowl*   *Numida meleagris*
  Pig*   *Sus* sp.
  Sheep*   *Ovis aries*

†*Sources of documentary accounts:* Barbot 1992; Booth 1960; de Marees 1987; Happold 1973; Hodasi 1995; Jones 1983; Pennak 1964.

*Species identified archaeologically in southern Ghana (*Sources:* Bourque 1997; Kiyaga-Mulindwa 1978; Nunoo 1957; Shaw 1961).

fonio (*Digitaria exilis*), hackberry (*Celtis* sp.), sorghum (*Sorghum vulgare*), and numerous species of yam (*Dioscorea* spp.) were grown. The principal tools used in clearing land and cultivating were likely the cutlass (machete), billhook, and hoe, utensils that remain in use today (see, e.g., Barbot 1992:529; de Marees 1987:28, 52, III; Jones 1983:220–221). Hoes that were found archaeologically, dated to the nineteenth century, are comparable to those produced today. These consist of an iron blade with a tang that is inserted into a wooden handle.

Domesticated animals known before European contact include cattle, sheep, goats, chickens, and the guinea fowl. Evidence for the origins of these domesticates largely comes from archaeological sites in the interior. On the coast and in the coastal hinterland of the Central Region, evidence for the use of domesticated animals, as well as marine and terrestrial vertebrates, before the seventeenth century is very limited (Table 4.3). Terrestrial species found at Iron Age period sites possibly include domesticated cattle (*Bos*) and goat or sheep, but antelope and other undomesticated Bovidae may also be represented (Calvocoressi 1977:130).[27] At Elmina, domesticated sheep, goat, and cattle may have become more widely available during the nineteenth century.[28]

European introductions had a major impact on consumption patterns and the variety of foods that were available in West Africa (Figure 4.3). After the fifteenth century, a variety of crops and domesticated animals were introduced, particularly from the Americas and Asia.[29] This may also have led to innovations in the technology needed to process some foods.[30] For example, grinding stones occur in West African sites from the Late Stone Age on, but the need to grind corn may have made them more prevalent. The baking of bread and preparation of *kenkey* may have resulted in subtle changes in the number and kind of vessel forms represented in the ceramic inventory. More significant, however, was the greater diversity and potential caloric value that introduced species provided to increasing coastal populations. There is no question that en masse these had great influence on West African diet. Introduced species com-

Figure 4.3. De Marees's 1602 description of the Gold Coast includes references to "plants brought here by the Portuguese," as well as indigenous domesticates such as the yam. (Reproduced courtesy of the Rare Books Division, the New York Public Library, Astor, Lenox and Tilden Foundations)

monly cultivated today include: cherry tomato, pineapple, peanut, guava, papaw, avocado, breadfruit, cashew, coffee, cocoa, sugar cane, coconut, cassava, orange, sweet potato, mango, corn, and several species of bean. Some of these plants were known or were domesticated in other parts of Africa prior to the fifteenth century, but European sea trade facilitated their spread throughout West Africa. Many were probably brought to coastal Ghana during the Portuguese period.[31] By the early seventeenth century, sweet potatoes, pineapples, sugar cane, and oranges were grown in the Elmina area. Coconut, peanuts, and plantain were added by the end of the century. Wheat does not grow in tropical climates. However, bread and *kenkey* made from corn were common along the coast by the seventeenth century.[32]

Perhaps equally important in the transformation of coastal subsistence patterns was the migration of Akan farming populations to the coast, where they were then able to exploit the introduced species and fallow land. Innovations in agricultural technology and, more especially, the desirability of agricultural lands and the transformations in the organization of land tenure have been seen as key aspects in the emergence of the Akan state (Wilks 1993:95–100). The availability of undeveloped land, as much as the opportunities provided by European trade, may have provided incentive for the immigration of settlers. Large-scale land clearance specifically for maize production may have begun on parts of the coast in the late sixteenth century.[33] This may have been one of the factors that enabled population growth to be sustained in the following centuries, but direct evidence is very limited. Also the amount of cleared land needs to be considered in relative terms. Although the number of farms likely steadily increased throughout the coastal hinterland over the past five centuries, as examined in Chapter 2, much of Elmina's immediate environs remained covered with forest or secondary bush until the late nineteenth century.

Despite West Africans' familiarity with both introduced and indigenous species, their exploitation of a diversity of wild flora and fauna continued.

Ethnographic observations reveal that Ghanaian farmers utilize as many as 200 different wild plants (Posnansky 1984a). Some of these are used on a regular basis, whereas others are "hungry food" gathered only in periods of famine.[34] Such wild resources are dealt with only peripherally in early documentary sources, the principal references focusing on domesticated plants and herbs used in medicines. Both archaeological data and ethnographic evidence from some areas of the Akan hinterland suggest a consistent and heavy reliance on wild fauna, both before European contact and during the succeeding centuries.[35] In the Birim Valley, 100 km (62 miles) north of Elmina, the inventory of faunal remains included no domesticates in either the pre- or the post-European-contact assemblages (Kiyaga-Mulindwa 1978:123–127; see also Posnansky 1984a:149–151).[36] Local hunting strategies typically rely on hiding in perches or blinds near game trails or lighting fires to drive game out of hiding. Bows and iron-tipped arrows and spears would have been traditionally used, increasingly supplemented by firearms during the later seventeenth century.[37] Even during later periods, however, guns likely played a minimal role in procuring game. A diversity of traps are referred to, and these remain the principal means of obtaining game animals on the coast, as well as in other parts of Ghana.

Wild fauna on the Mina coast included various species of deer, buffalo, antelope, monkey, chimpanzee, wild fowl, leopard, civet cat, warthog, wild pig, jackal, hare, rabbit, porcupine, elephant, pangolin, snake, lizard, crocodile, tortoise, and giant land snail (see Table 4.3). Small game, especially grasscutter (*Thryonomys swinderianus*), is still common in the coastal thicket and grasslands east of Elmina. Similar to the ground hog in size and habitat, the grasscutter is regarded as a delicacy, and the prices of bush meat commonly sold along the Accra-Elmina road may be comparable to beef and pork. Larger game is less common.[38] One of the consequences of increasing urbanization along the coast between the seventeenth and the nineteenth centuries may have been the overhunting of some of the indigenous fauna. This would be a consequence of increasing human settlement and the associated habitat destruction. Lists of animal species utilized on the Mina coast can be culled from documentary sources, but their role in subsistence and the changing importance of different species are difficult to evaluate (e.g., Barbot 1992: 468–478; de Marees 1987:40–43, 89, 126–153; Jones 1983:124–127, 240–243).

Animal bone from the Elmina excavations included a subset of those species referred to in documentary accounts (Bourque 1997). Given the diversity of archaeological contexts represented, inferences about the relative importance of these resources, even within a particular period, are tenuous at best. The majority of the bone is probably food-related refuse from within the African settlement, but most consisted of fragments in fill deposits that could only be poorly associated with specific occupation areas. A minor amount was recovered from ritual contexts.[39] Only about two-thirds was discovered in well-dated deposits. Fish bone made up the largest portion of the archaeological assemblage by count, which is consistent with documentary and ethnographic information, emphasizing the importance of fishing. Yet the prevalence of wild and domesticated terrestrial fauna is of note. Undomesticated terrestrial fauna is a consistent portion of the assemblage: Although there may have been a decrease in game in the coastal zone, wild game has continued to be widely eaten. The giant land snail (*Archachatina degneri*) also makes up a small but consistent part of archaeological assemblages.[40]

Foodways at Elmina   Documentary accounts provide some indication of changing dietary practices. By the early nineteenth century some of Elmina's residents had clearly adopted European customs. In 1823 George Howland, an American ship captain, wrote: "I, having to do all the business of trade ashore, was often invited to dine with them [the African merchants]. They live in good style, having rich chased silver plates and dishes and silver and gold handled knives and forks and spoons. Their dinners consist of several courses, soup, meats, chickens, fish &c, all well cooked, and fruits, nuts, and sweet-meats for desserts, and choice wines licquors, and porter, for drink" (quoted in Bennett and Brooks 1965:118). Despite such accounts, these dietary practices are likely not typical of the majority of the population in coastal Ghana during the nineteenth century. Food preparation and consumption are represented by several artifact categories, which can be used to monitor changes in food-preparation practices. In western Europe, the change from mixed dishes to separate servings of various kinds of food is indicated by the replacement of bowls with plates as the primary serving dish during the late eighteenth century. Forks and knives became more common, and the spoon was increasingly used as a serving utensil. Sawn cuts of meat, served in individual portions, replaced the more fragmentary cuts used in soups in stews. This transformation did not occur in West Africa. Although some individuals at Elmina may have adopted European mannerisms, for the most part food preparation and consumption seem to have remained relatively unchanged over the past 500 years.

The extremely fragmentary and shattered condition of the archaeological bone is consistent with ethnographically observed practices.[41] Butchering marks, left by cutting, chopping, and hacking, are found on many remains. Some long bones display longitudinal splitting and marks on their interior, possibly indicating the splitting for marrow extraction (Bourque 1997:26–27). Species with clear traces of butchering include caprids (sheep/goats), fish, sharks, *Bos* sp., *Canis* sp., rodents, bovids (wild species), and unidentified small mammals.[42] Significantly, only three nineteenth-century fragments possibly show evidence of saw marks. In Europe, the saw began to be commonly used in butchering at the end of the eighteenth century (Deetz 1996:171). The presumption here is that the saw marks on the Elmina bone are the result of butchering done locally. It is possible, however, that these represent imports. Pickled and salted meats and fish were commonly sold at Elmina by American traders during the nineteenth century (e.g., Bennett and Brooks 1965:38–39).[43] Sawn cuts of meat are still uncommon in Ghana. Meat is generally chopped with a cleaver and sold by weight at a uniform price regardless of cut. The meat is then commonly cooked in soups or stews, and the bone is cracked during consumption to extract the marrow. The ingestion of small mammals and fish bone might have further modified the quantity and variety of species represented archaeologically.

At Elmina, the most common lithic tools recovered were grinding stones and pestles, which would have been primarily used in food preparation. Grinders can be placed on the ground or mounted on a clay platform to be used while standing. These have a long ancestry and have remained essentially unchanged in form from prehistoric times to the present century.[44] Documentary records indicate they were commonly used for the grinding of millet and corn and probably also served to pulverize ingredients for stew (e.g., de Marees 1987:40; Jones 1983:85, 207–208).[45] The majority of the archaeological examples from Elmina date to the nineteenth century, including four pestles and one slab from 1873 living floors.[46] Two pestles and two grinding stones were found in eighteenth-century levels, and a single pestle of seventeenth-century age was discovered.

Imported and local ceramics include a wide range of vessel forms, but bowls predominate as the principal type of food-serving vessel. This is comparable to the pattern that seems to be present at pre-European-contact sites such as Brenu Akyinim and Coconut Grove. Twenty-six knives, two spoons, and no forks were found in the Elmina excavations. The number of knives probably indicates their importance in food preparation rather than in consumption. Despite the introduction of a variety of new crops, the primary European influence was the cultivation of plant species with greater caloric value, not the manner in which food was prepared and eaten. Undomesticated terrestrial fauna and marine resources continued to be exploited.

In contrast with the changes in African foodways, the European diet at Elmina was probably modified to a much greater degree as a result of their dependence on local foods and cooks. The archaeological data on European subsistence on the coast are more limited than the data on the African population.[47] Documentary records, however, speak volumes on the dependence of the Europeans on local foods. The Portuguese garrison was reliant on imported food, and sixteenth-century instructions laid out procedures for bringing flour, wine, oil, honey, vegetables, livestock, and other foodstuffs to Elmina from Portugal and São Tomé. The irregularity of supply was, however, always problematic (see Hair 1994b:72 fn. 98).[48] During the Dutch period, most of the European staff at Elmina were dependent on the food that could be purchased in Elmina's market, and their diet was, as a result, much the same as the local African population: "fish, maize, cassava, or yam, miscellaneous vegetables, and dry lean Hen" (Feinberg 1989:86). Somewhat better fare was provided for the director and some of the "Principal Men," but other members of the garrison made do with much less (Bosman 1967:106–107; cf. van Dantzig 1976:108). A similar pattern has been noted in colonial America (e.g., Lightfoot, Martinez, and Schiff 1998; Super 1988:2).

SPECIALIZATION

There is a dearth of information on the technology and the organization of production in coastal Ghana prior to the fifteenth century.[49] The majority of the coastal population may have been fishermen and subsistence farmers. Craft production was probably limited and dependent on part-time specialists, with more elaborate items traded from the interior. We can point to the documentary records of the succeeding centuries for reference to increasing specialization and evidence of production within the coastal communities. Similarly, surveying the archaeological record, we can perceive an increasingly diverse material inventory, the elaboration of art forms, and transformations in earlier areas of production. Sites such as Elmina, which emerged as urban centers during the post-European-contact period, produce increasing evidence of specialized industries, including pottery manufacture, metalworking, bead production and modification, ivory carving, and salt making, a pattern which dramatically contrasts with the absence of such evidence on the coast during the preceding centuries.[50]

Ceramics

Ceramic production long predates European contact, and pottery forms a major component of all archaeological assemblages predating the twentieth century. There is a dramatic dichotomy between the ceramics of the Late Iron Age through the Portuguese period (circa A.D. 1000–1637) and those from later periods. No sites have been excavated thoroughly enough to provide a comprehensive assessment of Late Iron Age ceramic traditions. However, excavated material from Elmina, Eguafo, Brenu Akyinim, and Coconut Grove and surface collections from other Central Region sites allow for a preliminary assessment. These ceramics are typically a uniform yellowish red to yellowish brown in color, without cores.[51] Sherds invariably have gritty worn surfaces and are frequently eroded and friable, probably an indication of short, open firings at relatively low temperatures. Their fragmentary condition makes it difficult to examine manufacture. No evidence of coiling is represented, and some pots were clearly fabricated by pinching and molding. Temper is generally very fine to medium grains of rounded quartz, which probably occurred naturally as inclusions in the clay. Pebble inclusions, up to 1 cm (0.39 inch) across, and micaceous temper are present in minute portions of the assemblage.[52] The vessels are thin walled compared with later ceramics: 2.7–10.0 mm (0.1–0.4 inch) thick, with a mean around 5 mm (0.2 inch). Vessel forms include jars, bowls, and globular pots. Rim and lip forms are distinct from later assemblages, including flanged everted rims. Decoration primarily consists of simple incising or stamping on the rims and necks, particularly the former. Bands of impressed wavy lines, which closely correspond to the impressions of the corrugated edges of *Arca senilis* shell, also occur. Less than 3 percent of the sherds from Brenu Akyinim were decorated, a smaller percentage than is found in later assemblages.[53]

Local ceramics associated with European trade materials probably dating to the seventeenth century or later can be distinguished from earlier ceramics on the basis of their condition, vessel forms, surface finish, and decoration. Distinctive smudged, carinated vessels with shallow groove incising, ethnographically associated with the Asante, appear in eighteenth- and nineteenth-century contexts. Ceramics with these characteristics appear substantially earlier in Asante, and their presence on the coast may provide indication of increasing

Figure 4.4. An Elmina potter examining local pottery recovered archaeologically. Several vessels are comparable to forms still produced. Note the clay hearth in the upper left corner. (Photograph by Christopher R. DeCorse)

connections and exchange with the Akan populations of the interior.[54] Pottery production at Elmina resembles techniques ethnographically described throughout the Akan area, and observations of modern Elmina and Fante potters provide insight into the cultural context and manufacture of archaeologically recovered ceramics (Figure 4.4).[55] There is minor variation in the methods of digging the clay, preparation, manufacture, and firing. This may, however, simply reflect slight differences in customary practices or adaptations to local variation in clay sources. Generally, there is a great deal of similarity in the methods employed throughout the Akan area. These methods contrast with those of potters in eastern Ghana, where coil manufacture is commonly used (Quarcoo and Johnson 1968).

The timing of the transition from the Late Iron Age ceramics to the ethnographically documented industry is difficult to determine. Few sites provide a clear stratigraphic transition between the Late Iron Age assemblages and later occupations of the Akan coast.[56] To what extent the change represents alteration of the method of manufacture or the organization of ceramic production, as opposed to stylistic change, is also uncertain. However, the changes represented seem to have come about very rapidly. Indication of the timing of the transition is provided by the presence or lack of associated trade materials and thermoluminescence dates on ceramics from Brenu Akyinim, Eguafo, and Elmina.[57] These data place the Late Iron Age ceramics—and the associated pattern of dispersed settlement in which they are found—between the ninth and the seventeenth centuries A.D. Similar changes have been noted in ceramic assemblages from other parts of Ghana. In Accra and Shai, Paul Ozanne (1962, 1963, 1964a) noted a dramatic difference between the pottery of the late sixteenth century and that of the mid-seventeenth century. As is the case in the Central Region, the earlier pottery is more poorly fired and distinct in both the forms and decorations represented. Research by Kiyaga-Mulindwa (1978, 1982) on the earthworks of the Birim Valley reveals a similar transformation. Here two ware types were distinguished on the basis of form, decoration, and associated settlement patterns: an older ware associated with the construction of earthworks, and later "Atweafo" pottery possibly related to the arrival of the present occupants of the valley sometime between the sixteenth and eighteenth centuries.[58] Stylistically the forms, rim, profiles, and some of the decoration of these ceramics are indistinguishable from corresponding early and late assemblages on the coast.[59]

The reason for the change in ceramics has been evaluated from a variety of perspectives, including sociocultural transformations and population replacement. Surveying information from the Birim Valley, Kiyaga-Mulindwa (1982:73) linked the change in pottery to the abandonment of the area as a result of slave raiding and a reoccupation by the ancestors of the present Akan inhabitants. However, as Bellis (1987) has observed, the discontinuity appears to be present in pottery sequences throughout southern Ghana.[60] Because it is unlikely that this entire area was depopulated, the observed changes in the ceramics are more likely indicative, in the first instance, of technological innovation and, in the second, of other changes in the sociocultural systems of the indigenous population. This interpretation is more consistent with ethnolinguistic and ethnohistorical data that indicate a continuity in Akan populations on the coast over the past 500 years.

Production may have become increasingly specialized over the past five centuries. Prior to the fifteenth century, pottery production in coastal Ghana was possibly limited and primarily for local consumption. During the past few centuries, there has been a tendency toward specialization and standardization in some areas. This pattern is typical of the Akan. Under the Asante Empire, villages were established outside Kumasi to provide pottery for the *asantehene*'s court, the capital, and much of the remainder of the population (Johnson 1982:212). Between the eighteenth and nineteenth centuries the use and manufacture of distinctive Asante-style pottery extended outward into other areas. Such specialization seems to be represented in the documentary accounts of the coast. In the seventeenth century Müller reported that certain families and villages were known for their potters (in Jones 1983:91, 253). In his nineteenth-century account, J. A. de Marrée (1818) described a small potters' village north of the Benya River below St. Jago Hill. This village, he wrote, "consists of about fifty huts, occupied by negroes, whose women keep busy with the preparation of all sorts of pots" (translated in Feinberg 1969:117). Notably perhaps, some of the last remaining Elmina potters lived in the vicinity of the potting village described by de Marrée, now part of modern Elmina.

The majority of the local pottery excavated at Elmina is associated with production between the seventeenth and nineteenth centuries.[61] With some variation, the collection bears a great deal of similarity to material of seventeenth- through nineteenth-century age from adjacent parts of the Akan coast and hinterland. Pottery has been recovered from a number of excavations close to Elmina, including Bantoma, Efutu, Asebu, and, most recently, from test excavations at Eguafo (Agorsah 1975, 1993; Calvocoressi 1975b, 1977; Davies 1961a; DeCorse 1998a; Golden 1969; Nunoo 1957).[62] As a whole the pottery lacks the eroded, friable character typical of the earlier ceramics, and it may have been better fired: open fired using coconut husks, wood shavings, and grass for fuel, as in ethnographically observed examples. Manufacture, when it could be inferred, was clearly the pinch pot–slab method used throughout the Akan area.

At Elmina, as in most ethnographic examples from Africa, pottery manufacture is generally a female occupation.[63] Among the Akan there is no proscription against men making pottery and tobacco pipes, and anthropomorphically decorated pots as well as clay bead molds are made by men (Johnson 1982:212; Rattray 1959:301). However, the potters at Elmina and neighboring settlements observed ethnographically are all women, and production is mostly confined to food bowls and simple cooking pots, though some new forms have been produced in recent decades.[64] The potters are regarded as specialists who usually learn their skills from their mother or a female relative. Clay is dug from naturally exposed banks or shallow pits located within a short distance of the settlement. Although some locations are reportedly used habitually, there appears to be an abundance of suitable material, and potters have relied on several sources at different times. The dry clay is mixed with water, soaked for several days, and then kneaded by hand and foot pounding until it reaches a uniform degree of wetness and plasticity. Larger inclusions are removed by hand, but the clay is neither sifted nor pounded with a pestle, as it sometimes is in other parts of Ghana and West Africa in general. Temper is not intentionally added. The prepared clay is usually worked soon after preparation, often the following day or after a few days at most. This seems more determined by the potters' schedules than any prescribed period for aging the clay.

The tools of the potter are simple—corn cobs, metal scrapers, stones, and a shaped fragment of calabash. These tools are sometimes inherited, but they can easily be fabricated as needed. The clay is placed on a board, which provides a flat working surface as well as a convenient means of moving the pot during manufacture. A small amount of fine beach sand may be placed on the board to prevent the clay from sticking. Vessels are formed by molding, pinching, and dragging: a hollow is pushed into the clay ball and the sides are drawn upward. Slabs or daubs of clay are added as needed. Large pots may be made in two sections and then joined together. A wet corncob is used to smooth the sides, bottom, and rim to a uniform thickness.

At this stage the thickness of the vessel's walls may be substantially greater than desired in the finished form. Thinning the vessel walls by scraping is thus an important aspect of manufacture. After the vessel has partly dried, a ring of metal is used to scrape clay from the interior and exterior. If a carinated bowl or pot is being made, it is at this stage that the carination is added. Although the potters seem to have a remarkable ability to judge the thickness of the vessel walls, this process often produces walls of highly variable thickness. Broken specimens showed as much as a 5-mm (0.2-inch) difference in wall thickness at the bottom, the carination, and the rim. Holes or gouges made during the scraping process and cracks are filled with daubs of wet clay. A piece of wood or a calabash is used to paddle the sides smooth. The surface of the finished vessel, particularly the rim and sides of the vessel above the carination, is lightly burnished with a smooth stone. Groove incising is added to the inside of the rim and on the sides above the carination with a small stick, which is held against the vessel as the board is rotated. Finally the vessel is removed from the board, and the bottom side of the carination and the base is scraped and paddled.

Firing takes place in the open after the pots have dried in the sun for a number of days. The firing site may be on barren ground or, if the ground is damp, on an area specially prepared with a thin layer of sand. The pots are laid on a layer of coconut shell, wood shavings, and grass. Thick layers of the same material completely cover the pots, producing a small mound. The bottom of the pile is lighted in several places simultaneously. Vents are poked into the base of the fire with a palm frond. The pile burns down quickly and more grass is added. This improvised cover may account for slightly higher and uniform firing temperatures than were achieved on Iron Age ceramics.[65] After about half an hour the vessels are removed from the fire in a red-hot state. Some are put aside to cool, and those to be smudged are placed on a pile of dampened grass. More grass is placed on top of the vessels. Because of the intense heat of the pots, the grass may burst into flames, but these are quickly doused with water. After 20 minutes the pots are allowed to cool without any further treatment.[66] This description is comparable to early documentary accounts.[67]

Akan pottery includes a number of specialized forms, such as pots for water storage, cooking, salt production, soup, shea butter, palm wine, *pito* (brewed millet beer), and ritual offerings (Elmina interviews, 1987, 1993; de Marees 1987:52, 68, 77; Jones 1983:244, 253; Tetrault 1998). Some of the Asante vessel forms were quite elaborate, particularly ritual pots. An example (*mogyemogye*) illustrated by Rattray (1959:Figure 252) bears a close resemblance to a Rhenish stoneware jug, including a stylized cipher. Similar elaborate pots have been recovered from ritual contexts dated to the eighteenth and nineteenth centuries. This diversity in vessel forms is not represented in recent production at Elmina, but potters were able to identify the uses of many of the reconstructed vessels from the excavations.

All of the sherds excavated at Elmina were examined macroscopically. Surface treatment, decoration, color, paste, use wear, and form were recorded for each sherd. A sample of randomly selected sherds was thin-sectioned for petrographic analysis and for minor and major elemental analysis using X-ray fluorescence. Whereas the earlier ceramics (circa A.D. 1000–1637) could be characterized in terms of their homogeneity, the later Elmina ceramics are striking in their variability. Even macroscopically, the pottery presents a great deal of variation in temper, paste color, and surface treatment. The pottery is generally sand tempered, but sherds with micaceous and predominately feldspar inclusions are also represented.[68] There is no indication that these were intentionally added to the clay, and they may represent natural constituents. Color was highly variable, some sherds ranging from light brown or tan to brick red and black. Frequently there was substantial variation in the surface colors of individual vessels as a result of firing clouds, with pieces of the same vessels ranging from dark black to red. Cores in the center of vessel walls were also variable between the assemblage as a whole and portions of the same vessel. Some vessels displayed a uniform color in profile, whereas others showed contrasting colors. Such variation is characteristic of the variable firing temperatures resulting from open firing. Humidity, rainfall, wind, fuel, and a pot's position in the firing all affect individual outcomes. There was also substantial variation in the manufacture of the pot, surface treatment, and firing. Some vessels reflected a great deal of sophistication in manufacture. The vessels were well shaped, the sides were uniform in thickness, and the surfaces were lightly burnished. In contrast, other vessels were somewhat irregular in shape, their surface roughly

Figure 4.5. Local
ceramics from
seventeenth- and
eighteenth-century
contexts. (Illustration
by Christopher R.
DeCorse)

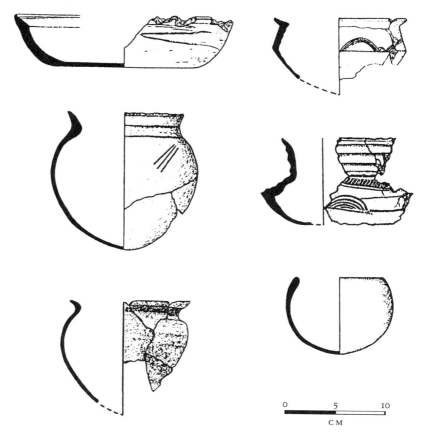

smoothed and unburnished. Such variation was present even among vessels of similar form.

The reason for this heterogeneity is uncertain. It clearly indicates that different clay sources were being utilized, but whether this represents varied exploitation in local clay deposits, varied potting traditions, and/or the import of ceramics from other areas is unclear. Several discrete wares may be represented, but the fragmentary nature of most sherds and the varied archaeological contexts represented make this difficult to evaluate.[69] The collection appears somewhat more variable than assemblages from other post-seventeenth-century sites, such as Efutu, Asebu, Twifo Heman, and the Atweafo pottery from Birim. This variation may be most characteristic of seventeenth- and early eighteenth-century ceramics, perhaps suggesting this was a period of transformation and experimentation in ceramic production.

Emphasis was placed on the reconstruction of vessels and the identification of vessel forms (Figures 4.5 and 4.6). Sherds were sorted into 61 vessel categories. Some of these were broad categories, for example, nondiagnostic body sherds and small, medium, and large pots. Other categories were much more specific, including a variety of pots, bowls, and other vessel forms. Some of the eighteenth- and nineteenth-century forms are indistinguishable from ceramics

Figure 4.6. Local
ceramics recovered
from 1873 floor
contexts. (Illustration
by Christopher R.
DeCorse)

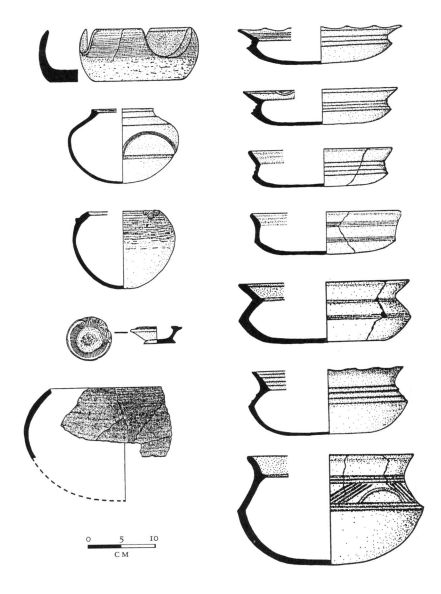

still produced at Elmina and in neighboring areas. Most distinctive are the carinated pots and bowls that dominate the reconstructed forms from 1873 floor contexts.[70] Smudged bowls with carinations and everted rims with incised grooves on the top also have close parallels in other assemblages in Asante, where they appeared earlier.[71] Carination is found on pre-nineteenth-century Asante pottery, but on the coast it becomes frequent only on later pots. These characteristics have been seen as a possible indicator of increasing Asante influence in peripheral Akan areas. The presence of these traits on Elmina pots may correspond to the increasing Asante presence in the town.

The more elaborate vessel forms present in other Akan assemblages are lacking in Elmina pottery.[72] Pedestaled bowls and pots with very restricted necks are uncommon. Applied figurative decorations, which occur on pottery from interior sites, are all but absent in the Elmina collection. Terracotta heads, widely associated with Akan funerary customs, were also absent in the archaeological collections but are referred to in early documentary descriptions of Elmina (but see discussion in Chapter 6). There were also few examples of the hearth pots (*mmukyia*) typical of assemblages from neighboring Fante sites.[73] Ethnographic observations indicate that solid clay hearth stands are more commonly used at Elmina, and these may have been preferred in the past. Uncommon nineteenth-century forms include a single plate and occasional straight-sided bowls with sharp basal angles and completely flat bases.[74] Similar vessels have been noted in surface collections of nineteenth- and twentieth-century artifacts from Efutu and in possible nineteenth-century stratigraphic contexts at Biseasi, 75 km (46.5 miles) northeast of Elmina (Davies 1961a:31). This suggests that these forms are a late innovation. Similarly, pottery grinders, commonly used with a wooden pestle in food preparation today, were absent from the archaeological collection.

The percentage of decorated sherds is much the same throughout the collection, constituting between one-fifth and one-quarter of the total sherd counts, though decoration appears to become less elaborate through time. A tendency toward less decoration has been noted throughout the Akan area, as well as in other parts of West Africa (Bellis 1972:213–214; 1987:42–43; DeCorse 1989c:136; Rattray 1959:300). Decoration is exclusively confined to the area between the shoulder and the neck and on the inside of everted rims. The shell-edge–rocker stamping found on pre-seventeenth-century ceramics is absent. Cord marking and incising occur but are very rare. The primary decorative technique is shallow-groove incising, although stamped or punctate patterns occur rarely and in a variety of different shapes and patterns. Simple stamping, delineated by incised lines or grooves, is most common. Nineteenth-century decoration is almost exclusively confined to groove incising around the shoulders and rims in combination with stamped patterns.

The majority of the ceramics recovered are assumed to be of local manufacture. There is, however, some indication of imports or at least stylistic influences from other areas. Among the more interesting are two distinct types of coal pot. Both suggest potting traditions from other parts of Ghana, and they may provide some clues to the heterogeneous nature of the Elmina settlement. The first type measures approximately 20 cm (7.8 inches) in diameter and 10 cm (3.9 inches) deep. There are three apertures in the sides to allow for sticks to be placed into the fire. Two reconstructible examples were recovered from 1873 floor contexts at Locus B, and the majority of the remaining sherds can be dated to the nineteenth century. Coal pots of this type are not characteristic of the Fante or other Akan groups but are widely found among the Ewe in eastern Ghana and Togo, where virtually identical forms can be seen (Kofi Agorsah, conversation, December 6, 1986; and Merrick Posnansky, conversation, November 2, 1989).[75] A single fragment of a larger coal pot decorated with polychrome decorations of red, white, and black was found at Locus G. No parallels of this vessel form have been located, but the painted decoration suggests that this may have been a vessel produced in northern Ghana.

Smithing, Smelting,
and Casting

Metalworking was well established in West Africa prior to the European arrival, but both iron and copper alloy artifacts were early imports to the coast.[76] The casting of brass objects using imported metal during the pre-European period was limited by the comparatively small amount of material that could be transported across the Sahara. The European trade provided a virtually unlimited source of brass, which encouraged the development of brass working in the coastal area and contributed to a florescence in Akan metal casting (Garrard 1979:39; 1980a:104–105; 1980b:59–63). Much of the brass traded in West Africa was in the form of rods, wire, basins, and bracelets known as manillas. The majority of this material was melted down and recast, and very few examples of early Akan casting have survived (Garrard 1980a, 1989; Ehrlich 1989). Although tons of manillas were sent to Elmina, only two fragments were found in excavations.[77]

Although all of the West African populations encountered by the Europeans were familiar with iron technology, the specific manufacturing traditions represented and their introduction varied a great deal (Kense and Okoro 1993; Miller and van der Merwe 1994; Schmidt 1996). Evidence for pre-European-contact smithing, smelting, and metalworking among the coastal Akan is limited. The earliest indications of iron smelting in Ghana come from sites in the northern forest and savanna margin, which have produced furnaces and slag mounds dating to late in the first millennium B.C. and the early first millennium A.D. In the southern forest and on the coast, the evidence is more limited and of a more recent date. In the Birim Valley, finds of slag seem associated with the first settlement of the region late in the first millennium A.D. The Coconut Grove site, just west of Elmina, excavated during the 2000 field season, produced slag and tuyere fragments in association with large quantities of ceramics and a small assemblage of quartz tools. The site has not yet been dated. However, on the basis of the ceramics present and the complete absence of European trade materials, a date of circa A.D. 1000–1400 is reasonable.

The specific type of iron-smelting furnace used on the coast is poorly documented and dated. An iron-smelting site of uncertain age at Cape Coast suggests that the type of furnace employed on the coast was a small, natural draft, shaft furnace with an aperture for tapping the slag near the base (Penfold 1972; cf. Pole and Posnansky 1973). With some variation, this type of furnace has been identified in other parts of southern Ghana and Togo. On the basis of oral traditions, it has been suggested that the makers of the Cape Coast furnaces were Fante, but the age and cultural identity of the smelters remain uncertain. Slag and tuyere fragments have been recovered from other sites in the Ghanaian hinterland, where limited smelting may have continued until the seventeenth or early eighteenth century.[78] On the coast, however, production may always have been less than in the interior, and local production may have stopped somewhat earlier.

At Elmina, nine pieces of iron slag (1,715.9 g [3.75 pounds]) were excavated, and isolated fragments were recovered from excavations at Bantoma and in surface collections to the west. This material probably dates to circa A.D. 1000–1637.[79] These finds suggest that iron smelting was undertaken in the vicinity at some time in the past, but large slag mounds and furnace remains

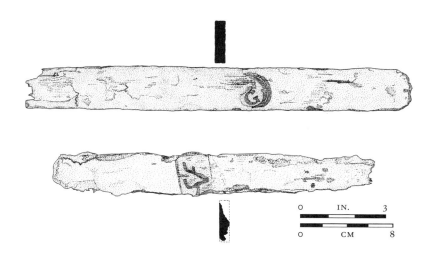

Figure 4.7. Iron bars, with marks, recovered from the wreck of the *Henrieta Marie,* a slave ship that sank off the coast of Florida, United States, in 1701 or 1702. Bars such as these were widely traded in West Africa and fashioned into a wide variety of implements. Although indigenous production of iron in West Africa long predates the European trade, imports increased availability. (Reproduced courtesy of David D. Moore, North Carolina Maritime Museum)

associated with large-scale iron production have not been located.[80] European records are also silent on iron production in central coastal Ghana. There are Portuguese-period references in the mid-sixteenth century to various weapons and implements of iron, but there is no indication that the iron used was smelted locally.[81] Correspondingly, no oral traditions regarding iron smelting have been recorded at Elmina.[82] The coast may have always substantially relied on trade with the interior for raw material. Local production may have already been uncommon by the close of the sixteenth century, by which time iron ingots may have been a principal European trade item (Figure 4.7).[83] Iron bars of variable length were produced in England, Sweden, Spain, France, Belgium, Germany, Denmark, Norway, Ireland, and Siberia for the African trade (Alpern 1995:12).

The European descriptions make it clear that, regardless of the extent of metalworking in the coastal Akan settlements during the preceding centuries, the techniques and methods utilized during the seventeenth century were indigenous. Iron was heated on hearths using skin bellows and worked on anvils of iron or stone:

The blacksmiths in the Fetu country work in a different way from those in Europe. The anvil does not stand firmly on a piece of wood, but lies on the ground and is simply a large piece of iron. The smith's hammer, including the handle, consists of one piece of iron, like a cooper's mallet. Sometimes the blacksmith hammers with the corners, sometimes with the flat of the hammer. The bellows are made out of goatskins and sheepskins, like a pouch, with the raw side of the skin and an elongated vent, to which they attach a handle. In the mouth of the pouch is attached an iron pipe which goes through a mud wall to the window. As long as the blacksmith works the iron in the fire, the bellows are pulled up and down by hand. (Müller in Jones 1983:254)[84]

The advent of the casting of copper alloys and gold on the Akan coast is also uncertain. *Cire perdue,* or the lost-wax casting process, may have spread to the

Figure 4.8. Gold objects from Bantoma (*a, b*) and Elmina (*c–m*). The items in *a–c* were produced using cold hammered gold foil or strips. The beads in *d–g* are flatttened, irregularly shaped lumps of gold or gold alloy with perforations through the short axis. The objects shown in *h–j* were produced using lost wax casting. The filigree beads (*k, l*) and earrings (*m*) date to the late nineteenth (post-1873) or twentieth century. All of the objects are shown at the same scale. The bead illustrated in *h* measures 1.95 by 1.25 cm (0.8 by 0.5 inches). (Photographs by Christopher R. DeCorse)

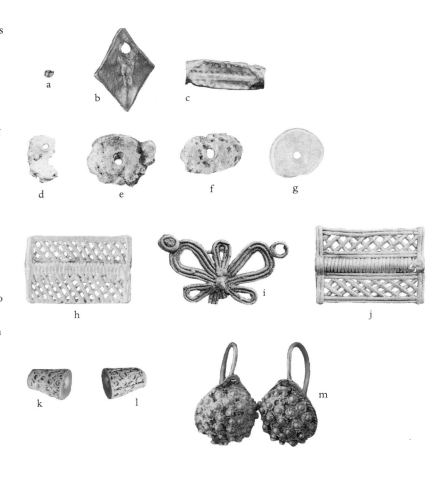

Akan world during the fourteenth or fifteenth century A.D. from the savanna regions to the north.[85] References to worked gold ornaments occur in the earliest descriptions of the coast. Indeed, when the African ruler Caramansa met the Portuguese in 1482, he was said to have been "covered on his legs and arms with bracelets and circlets of gold, on his neck was a collar from which hung some small bells, and twined in his beard some pieces of gold which so weighed down its hairs that the curly ones had become straight" (Hair 1994b:21). Akan metalworkers produced a variety of delicate pieces in copper alloy and gold, and documentary evidence attests to the variety of ornaments worn by the people on the coast (e.g., de Marees 1987:34, 96, 167, 169, 175; Jones 1983:253–254).[86] There is, nevertheless, little indication of when production of these items on the coast actually began or of the specific manufacturing methods involved. As in the case of iron smelting, the paucity of evidence for casting in coastal sites may indicate that much of the production before 1600 was in the coastal hinterland or even farther afield in the interior. Even during the eighteenth and nineteenth centuries, the total number of Akan casters may have been relatively small, perhaps no more than 200, and only a portion of these were located in coastal settlements.[87] The earliest reference to Fante gold workers and brass casting dates to the seventeenth century.[88] The limited archaeological evidence for brass working is of similar or more recent age.[89]

At Elmina, possible archaeological evidence for brass casting or gold working is provided by two crucibles. Both date to the nineteenth century, with one coming from an 1873 floor context. The crucibles are less than 4 cm (1.5 inches) in diameter, glassy, and vitrified. In form they are similar to archaeological examples from other parts of Ghana that have been found associated with brass-casting debris.[90] However, no hearths, smithing furnaces, molds, spew, or nonferrous slag was found at Elmina. The two crucibles lie in stark contrast with the hundreds found at some hinterland sites.

Archaeological data suggest that manufacturing methods other than casting may initially have had a greater importance. A variety of beads, pendants, and earrings were recovered at Elmina, several of which can be closely dated to the seventeenth, eighteenth, and nineteenth centuries (Figure 4.8).[91] Nine gold beads measuring less than 1 mm (0.04 inch) in diameter, probably produced by cold hammering, can likely be dated to the seventeenth century. Beads of this type may have been worn, but they were also used in trade: The tiny perforations were sometimes filled with sand to increase their weight.[92] A similar bead with slightly larger dimensions was recovered from eighteenth-century contexts at Bantoma (Figure 4.8a).[93] Similar cold hammering techniques were also used to make gold chain. An archaeological example from Elmina, dated to the late nineteenth century, has 105 links with a simple loop for the hasp. The workmanship is careful but not overly elaborate. The links and the loop were formed by hammering, cutting, and bending. Some of the joints in the unsoldered links have partly separated.

Thin gold foil or strips were also used to produce objects. A gold ornament from Bantoma consisted of a thin strip of gold or gold alloy folded into a diamond shape measuring 1.8 by 1.2 cm (0.7 by 0.5 inches) (Figure 4.8b).[94] A more elaborate bead, also produced using gold foil, was found in a late eighteenth- or early nineteenth-century context at Locus E (Figure 4.8c). This bead is tubular with a carefully stamped decoration. The gold foil is so thin that it is not surprising that the bead was partly crushed. A bead produced in a similar manner was excavated at the Coconut Grove site. Such artifacts, manufactured using relatively simple techniques, can be contrasted with the better-known cast beads, long associated with the Akan (e.g., Ehrlich 1989). The gold beads described and illustrated by Barbot (1992:494, 527, Plate 43) in the seventeenth century more closely parallel cast, *cire perdue* beads, not the beads described above. Earlier writers say comparatively little about gold working, perhaps because it was less well developed on the coast in the preceding centuries (editors in Barbot 1992:541 n. 37). Cold hammering, drawing, bending, folding, cutting, and stamping may have initially been the predominant methods of working gold, but they were increasingly supplanted by casting technology in the seventeenth century.[95]

Other beads found archaeologically were produced by heating and casting. Four other Elmina beads appear to consist of lumps of gold metal filings that were fused, hammered flat, and drilled (Figure 4.8*d–g*). They vary substantially in color and likely contain admixtures of copper, lead, brass, and gold. These may provide the first examples of the *kacraws*, which were used as a medium of exchange at Elmina and some other portions of the coast. Writing in 1602, Pieter de Marees noted: "They do not use any money or coins to pay each other, and when they buy anything they pay each other with Gold using weights. But if the quantity is so small that it cannot be weighed, they pay each other with small square pieces of Gold, weighing one *aes* or half an *aes*" (1987:65).[96] These objects are said to have been made mostly of "broken, low carat trinkets which had been beaten flat and cut into little pieces" (de Marees 1987: 65 fn. 5).

More elaborate gold and brass ornaments were produced using *cire perdue*. Using this method, a craftsman would shape an object out of wax and carefully cover it with clay. The clay would then be heated and the molten wax poured out, leaving a cavity in which metal could be cast. In some instances, the wax was applied over a clay core. In other cases, casts were made from natural objects such as pods, corn cobs, shells, insects, and crab claws. The simplest example of this kind of manufacture from Elmina is a tubular gold bead (1.05 by 0.03 cm [0.41 by 0.01 inch]) with six gentle convex facets, which was found in a late seventeenth- to eighteenth-century context.[97] Examples of cast gold and copper alloy objects recovered from late eighteenth- and nineteenth-century contexts are more elaborate. The wax threads used to make the models of these pieces were sometimes less than a millimeter (0.04 inch) in diameter, and the objects themselves were very carefully constructed (Figure 4.8*h–j*). These include gold beads of latticework rectangles with cord tubes through the middles.[98] There are also five copper alloy beads from fill deposits containing artifacts of seventeenth- through nineteenth-century age.[99] The beads are flat disks measuring between 1.7 and 1.9 cm (0.66 and 0.74 inch) in diameter. The edges are folded over, and the perforations are made by making two holes in opposite sides of the edge. They are badly corroded, but it is likely that they had open latticework patterns. One example is distinct from the others in its traces of gilt. A thin overlay of gold foil or a thin coating of gold on copper alloy beads has not been reported in earlier contexts, and this technique may be a more recent technological innovation.

Two examples of copper alloy *cire perdue* beads dating to the eighteenth and nineteenth centuries are quite distinct.[100] They are tubular, measuring approximately 2.0 by 0.6 cm (0.78 by 0.23 inch). The beads are not solid—the sides are less than 0.5 mm (0.02 inch) thick—but the ends curve toward the perforations, giving the impression that the beads are more solid. One is decorated by a series of holes around each end, and the other has eight raised lines parallel to the perforation. Both objects were likely produced by wrapping thin wax thread around a clay core. A more elaborate object, produced in a similar way, is a delicate pendant that consists of six conical threadwork projections joined at their bases. A loop and attached chain extend from the juncture of two of these projections. The pendant measures less than 1.2 cm (0.5 inch) across.

Among the most ubiquitous products of the Akan metal casters were brass gold weights (Figure 4.9). As many as 3 million may have been made between

Figure 4.9. Gold weights from Elmina. The weight immediately to the left of the scale indicator is from a set of European nested weights. All of the other pieces were locally produced using *cire perdue,* or lost wax casting. The weights were all recovered from nineteenth-century contexts, but some may have been produced earlier. (Illustration courtesy of Christopher R. DeCorse)

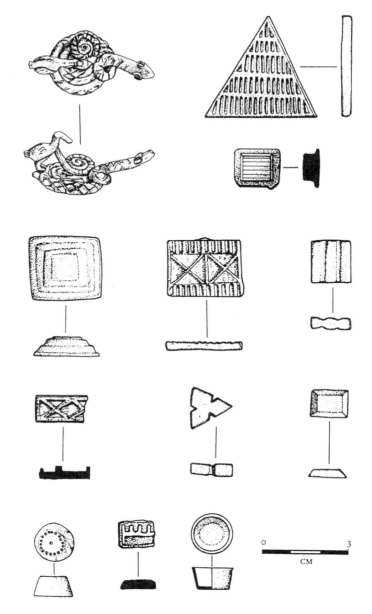

1400 and 1900 in a wide variety of geometric and figurative forms (Garrard 1980a:112). The majority were produced using *cire perdue.* Despite the many thousands that were produced and their importance in the gold trade, few have been recovered from archaeological contexts. Buried hoards have been discovered, but such examples are rare.[101] A typology, based on an extensive examination of private and museum collections, has been developed. This divides the weights into "Early" (circa A.D. 1400–1720) and "Late" (circa A.D. 1700–1900) periods of production (Garrard 1980a:274–321; 1973, 1979).[102] Nevertheless, weights of mixed styles or ages clearly continued in use in the same collections (Garrard 1980a:182).

The stylistically diverse examples from nineteenth-century archaeological contexts at Elmina are indicative of the wide range of weights that remained in use long after their manufacture.[103] Early period weights are represented by a simple square weight and a truncated cone with a punctate decoration on one surface. Other weights are more ornate and analogous to examples identified as Late period weights. The single figurative weight found depicts two snakes and a bird (see Figure 4.9). The smaller snake is biting the bird as it perches atop the larger snake. The complexity of the design and the careful detailing of the figures also place this weight within the Late period. Representations of birds are common in Akan art, but there are no exact parallels to this weight in the published examples. Many proverbs could easily be made up to denote the symbolism of the weight. It may mean something like: "Too much curiosity leads to disaster" or, perhaps, "Don't make rude remarks about the snake until you are out of its reach" (Peggy Appiah, correspondence, November 1989).

Although there are no exact parallels to the Elmina finds, the casting techniques, styles, and decorative inventories represented are comparable to those found in other examples of Akan metalwork. Both the simple, faceted gold bead and the more complex latticework decoration have parallels in jewelry illustrated by Barbot in the seventeenth century (Barbot 1732:Plate 22). All have short cord tubes that are a feature on other early examples of Akan beads. They are also comparable to modern Akan and Baule gold working. There are also similarities to examples recovered from the pirate ship *Whydah,* which sank off Cape Cod, Massachusetts, in 1717 (Ehrlich 1989).[104] Collectively these finds illustrate a great deal of continuity within the Akan casting tradition since the late seventeenth century. In addition to the use of gilt, soldering may be a relatively recent innovation. The only examples date to the late nineteenth century. They include a pair of earrings and two matched beads, all decorated with delicate filigree soldered onto gold or copper alloy plates hammered and cut to shape (Figure 4.8k–m). Metalworking of this type characterizes the style and manufacturing methods used in some of the modern jewelry produced in Ghana and other parts of West Africa, and it is likely an introduced technique.

Other cast brass objects found at Elmina include pieces that may have a non-Akan origin. Most interesting are two pairs of bells, or crotula, one found in rubble fill from circa 1873 and the other in eighteenth-century levels. Stylistically similar objects have been found in ethnographic collections from northern Ghana, particularly the Frafra area (Garrard 1986:511). De Marees (1987:175) illustrated similar ornaments in use during the early seventeenth century. His description may refer to northern slaves, providing a small indication of the ethnic diversity on the coast. The crotula from Elmina may provide indication of trade or trade contacts with northern Ghana or indirect evidence for the presence of people from northern Ghana in the settlement.

Sheet Brass   Ghanaian craftsmen made a wide range of items by cutting, cold hammering, bending, and stamping European sheet brass, rods, and wire. Objects recovered at Elmina include accouterments for the gold trade, such as the spoon (*saawa, atere, atire*), shovel or pan for separating gold dust (*famfa*), scalepan (*nsenia koraa*), and balance (*nsenia dua*) (Figures 4.10 and 4.11).[105] Implements were cut, folded, and beaten into shape and then stamped or incised with simple decorations. The archaeological examples of the scalepans and shovels are engraved with compass designs of concentric circles and intersecting arcs, comparable to many examples found in ethnographic collections. Other items locally fabricated from imported brass include ritual vessels (*forowa*) and fragments of less specialized vessels such as basins. The vast majority of archaeological examples clearly postdate the seventeenth century. At this time the working of imported sheet brass may have become increasingly common among the coastal Akan, with production increasing and forms becoming more diverse and elaborate during the nineteenth century.

Part of the impetus for these developments was undoubtedly the availability of European brass. Rolling mill technology may have been developed on the Continent during the fifteenth century, and it was introduced to Britain by the late seventeenth century, gradually replacing battery-produced sheet brass (see Aitken 1866a:231–232, 310).[106] At Elmina, a boom in the access to brass may have occurred with an increase in the availability of Continental sources following the advent of the Dutch in 1637. The Portuguese did not produce copper or finished wares but rather depended on imports from other areas, particularly Flanders (Herbert 1984:127–140). One seventeenth-century source estimates that, collectively, the Dutch, English, French, and other European countries annu-

Figure 4.10. Spoon and scales locally made with European sheet brass (shown slightly reduced; the scale pans measure approximately 3.3 cm [1.3 inches] in diameter). (Illustration by Christopher R. DeCorse)

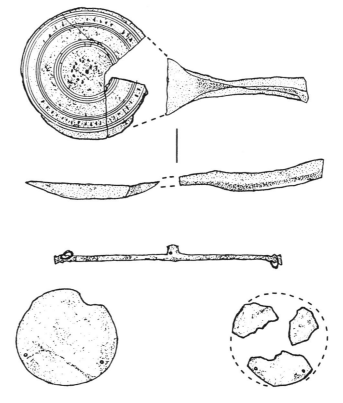

Figure 4.11.
Miscellaneous sheet
brass objects from
Elmina. The figure on
the left is the rim of a
European pan or basin
with a locally incised
decoration. A gold dust
pan (*famfa*) is shown in
the upper right. The
two objects at the lower
right may be part of a
large set of scales. All of
the objects are
nineteenth-century.
(Illustration courtesy of
Christopher R.
DeCorse)

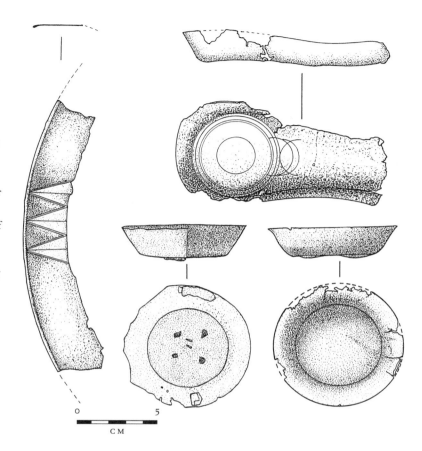

ally shipped 1 million to 1.4 million pounds of copperware to West Africa
(quoted in Herbert 1984:133). English copper and brass became increasingly important as the eighteenth century progressed (Herbert 1984:144–153).

Unfortunately, detailed documentary evidence for both the importation of
sheet brass and its modification by African craftsmen is rare for all periods.[107]
The importation of unmodified brass sheets may have been limited. However,
even in the absence of such items, reworked pieces of European brassware
could have served as raw material for African craftsmen. Sheet brass, in the
form of pans, plates, cups, urinals, kettles, and basins, reached West Africa in
substantial quantities from the earliest years of the European trade (e.g., Alpern
1995:15–16; Craddock and Hook 1995).[108] Although a substantial amount may
also have been melted down by casters, a significant portion may have been
used to make prototypes of the scalepans and sheet-metal vessels ethnographically associated with the coastal Akan. African craftsmen likely flattened
out and cut into appropriate shapes fragments of new and used brassware. This
pattern of reuse is suggested by the patching and joining of different pieces of
brass and also by the distinctive isotopic signatures of lead in different pieces of
brass in the same vessel (Tchakirides 1999).

A particularly interesting category of objects that attests to the local working of imported sheet brass during the early eighteenth century is *forowa*. These are sheet brass containers fastened together with rivets and decorated with repoussé and punch-work designs of animals and geometric forms. They are associated with the coastal Akan, where they functioned in specialized ritual contexts. Christensen, for example, commented: "A common practice formerly, but now rare, is the inclusion with the corpse of a brass vessel (*forowa* or *kuduo*) containing shea butter and gold dust" (1954:71). He further recorded that *forowa* were used "[f]or keeping gold dust, shea butter, and mixture of shea butter, cowrie shells and herbs for magical powers to cure. Owned by an important man and buried with the owner" (Christensen 1954:71).[109] Informants at Elmina indicated that *forowa* filled with gold dust were traditionally placed under the head of the deceased at burial. Archaeological finds and examples on the antiquities market are frequently from grave contexts.

Forowa have been regarded as a late product of the coastal and near-coastal Akan, with most production probably occurring between 1830 and 1930 (Garrard 1979:43; 1980a:186; Ross 1974:49). However, the discovery of several fragmentary *forowa* from burial contexts at Elmina indicates that *forowa* were being produced by the mid-eighteenth century and, further, that their stylistic origins may, in fact, rest with the earlier *kuduo*—cast brass vessels that date back to the origins of Akan casting in the fifteenth century.[110] The earliest *forowa* found at Elmina was associated with the mid-eighteenth-century burial of an adult male.[111] The *forowa* was severely corroded by brass disease and extremely fragile, but portions of the lid, sides, and bottom did survive, and these provide a clear idea of the container's original appearance.[112] The overall form is squat with a flat lid, and it is clearly similar in form and decoration to presumed eighteenth-century examples (Ross 1983). These vessels bear a strong similarity to some *kuduo*.[113] This shape contrasts with *forowa* from late nineteenth-century contexts, which are generally taller, less squat in appearance, and covered by a hammered, dome-shaped lid.[114] Also, like the *kuduo*, the Elmina vessel's lid fits inside the rim. The base was formed by two undecorated sheets that were overlapped and riveted. The bottoms of *forowa* are more commonly made from a single piece of brass, but parallels to the Elmina piece can be seen in museum collections.[115]

Intact *forowa* were recovered from late eighteenth- or early nineteenth-century articulated burials at Locus A and Locus E. Stylistically these pieces appear to be transitional between the flat-lidded, squat forms like the Locus A *forowa* and the dome-lidded examples of the nineteenth century. The Locus E *forowa* are similar in size and dimensions to the late nineteenth-century examples, but the covers are flat. In other respects their decorations and manufacture are similar to other examples.

Decorations on all of the *forowa* are stamped or punched into a plain background and include typical Akan motifs. The foot of the eighteenth-century example had a continuous band of decoration formed by vertical lines. The main decorative elements on both the sides and the top are geometric. However, a 12-petal flowerlike pattern is found on the side (see also Ross 1974:46). In addition, the oblate decorations on the upper edge of the sides may be stylized representations of leather treasury bags or, perhaps, locks. Although it is not clear, the design between these figures may be an oversized key. Symbolically the treasury bag and the lock convey the same measure of security in this context (e.g., Doran Ross, conversation, September 1989). The final figurative motif is a lizard or crocodile found on the lid. These two animals, often prominent on *forowa*, are among the earliest decorative motifs in Akan art (Ross 1974, 1983).

Metalworking

A wide range of artifacts were made by bending, molding, and further modifying imported pieces of copper, copper alloy, and silver (Figure 4.12). European technology for refining and drawing rods, wire, and tubing rapidly advanced during the nineteenth century, and a large quantity of these was exported to West Africa. In discussing the British brass industry in 1866, W. C. Aitken wrote:

A considerable quantity of the brass wire made in Birmingham finds its way to the Gold Coast, to Old Calabar, in the form of what are called "guinea rods," one hundred of which, each three feet in length, of Nos. 4 and 5 gauge in thickness, packed up in deal cases, and being at their destination, sold in exchange for palm oil, &c., are used as the "circulating medium" by the natives, and at the death of the possessor are interred with the body. An influential Birmingham merchant states the orders from that country frequently amount to from five to twenty tons each. Large numbers of rings made of solid brass wire, about seven-sixteenths thick and three-and-a-quarter inches diameter, made of wire, are also sent to the Gold Coast. A smaller size of brass wire (a little thicker than ordinary pin wire) is converted by being wound around spits into spirals like an ordinary check bell spring, and is also exported to the locality named for purposes of ornament and personal decoration. (1866a:319)[116]

Given the simplicity of the manufacturing processes involved, it is difficult to differentiate among some of the items fabricated in Europe, such as the simple rings described above, and items that may have been produced in coastal Ghana. A bundle of rods that may correspond to those described by Aitken was recovered from an 1873 floor context in the Locus B structure. Although such items may have been bartered and served as a "circulating medium" on parts of the coast, as Aitken indicates, it is more likely that many were purchased as raw material and used in the fabrication of products in Africa. As in the case of sheet brass, the availability of copper and copper alloy wire, rods, and bars likely increased during the Dutch period.

Numerous chains, necklace fragments, rings, and earrings were recovered archaeologically, the majority from nineteenth-century contexts.[117] Of all the pieces, only three rings have soldered ends, and these may be imports. A few were flattened by hammering. Others were produced by simply cutting, bending, and stamping wire and rods. The rings and chain links are undecorated, and ornamentation on the bracelets mostly consists of simple geometric punctate designs. In their material and method of manufacture many of these pieces are indistinguishable from bangles still sold in Ghanaian markets. Although expanded production may have resulted from increased accessibility to imported brass between the seventeenth and nineteenth centuries, this type of produc-

Figure. 4.12. European and African copper-alloy, white metal, and iron jewelry from pre-1873, nineteenth-century contexts at Elmina. The bracelet at the upper left is a machine-made brass tube with machine-incised decoration. A manilla, probably cast in Europe, is shown at the upper right. The other artifacts were likely produced locally, using European rods and wires. The two bracelets at the lower right are white metal, and the bracelet at the lower left is iron. All of the other objects are copper or copper alloy. (Illustration courtesy of Christopher R. DeCorse)

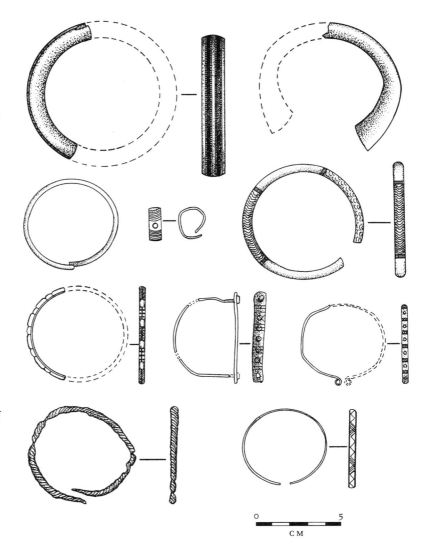

tion likely has a long history. As in the case of cutting, bending, folding, and cold hammering gold and sheet brass, African craftsmen may have long produced rings, bracelets, and necklaces using imported materials.

Bead Production

Bead production may be one of the earliest craft traditions on the Mina coast. These traditions include both the modification and reworking of imported glass beads and the fabrication of local products using European beads and powdered or chipped glass fired in clay molds. Documentary and archaeological data indicate that several different industries of unknown ancestry are represented (Bowdich 1966:268; Connah 1975:167, 170; DeCorse 1989b; Delaroziere 1985:41–44; Dubin 1987; Krieger 1943; Lamb 1976:34; Lui 1974; Nadel 1940; Sinclair 1939; Sordinas 1964, 1965). A variety of shell and stone beads were also produced in Ghana before European contact. Stone beads are characteristic of Late

Figure 4.13. Sandstone
bead abraders found at
Elmina. (Illustration by
Christopher R.
DeCorse)

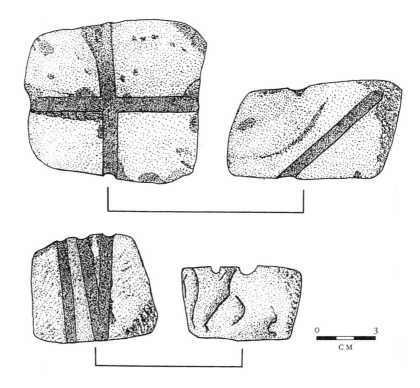

Iron Age and early historic period sites, such as Coconut Grove. It is possible
that some of these finds represent local production. Shell and stone bead manufacture survived in Ghana until the present century, though not in the Central
Region (Lamb 1976; Lui 1974; Shaw 1945; Sordinas 1965; Wild 1937).

An industry based on the polishing or modification of imported glass beads
likely emerged by the sixteenth century. The Portuguese purchased *coris* on the
lower Guinea coast and brought them to Elmina, where they were polished,
drilled, and strung for sale.[118] Writing in the early seventeenth century, de Marees, indicated that the polishing and modification of imported glass beads were
common in coastal Ghana (de Marees 1987:53, 54, 80, 84). Reference to these
practices at Elmina also occurs on a 1629 Dutch map of the Gold Coast (Daaku
and van Dantzig 1966:15).

The earliest historical reference to the actual fabrication of glass beads using
imported glass may be provided by Barbot, who noted that the Elmina Africans
"recast crystal and glass, taking considerable pains" (1992: 381, see also 389).[119]
He may have been referring to fired bead technology ethnographically known
from Asante and Krobo. Modern beads are produced by placing the powdered
glass in a clay mold. A stick or cassava stalk is set into a depression at the bottom of the mold, extending above the top. When the mold is fired in a clay
oven, the stalk burns away leaving a perforation. Stripes, lines, eyes, or other
decorations are made by painstakingly layering glass of different colors in the
mold or by placing previously fired colored glass eyes or lines of powdered glass
along the sides of the mold.

Archaeological insights into African glass bead manufacture and modification are of special interest because little work has been done on their origins and ages, most work having focused on the ethnography of twentieth-century craftsmen.[120] Over 40,000 beads were recovered from Elmina, providing a unique opportunity to examine the temporal distributions of European trade beads as well as locally produced beads of stone, shell, metal, ivory, bone, coral, and glass. Direct evidence of manufacturing, such as molds, wasters, or cullet, was not found at Elmina, but several grooved sandstone blocks that probably served as bead abraders were recovered (Figure 4.13). Similar examples have been found at other Ghanaian coastal sites, such as Ankobra, Sekondi, and Winneba.[121] These stones could have been used for polishing imported glass beads or for grinding local beads of stone, shell, or glass.

Discoveries in the 1873 Locus B floor include what may have been bead stringing materials. Some 962 shell beads were found stored in glass vials. Associated artifacts included unperforated shell beads, a small copper alloy pan, and a bundle of thin copper wires that may have been used for stringing the beads. In addition, many of the European glass beads excavated at Elmina show evidence of local modification, especially grinding on the ends.[122] In other instances, outer layers have been ground away to expose inner layers of different colors. Some of the drawn beads appear to have been cut into shorter lengths. Other beads have been reheated to change their color and opacity. The grinding, reworking, and reheating of beads has been widely reported ethnographically and noted in other collections from West Africa.[123]

Some of the most interesting reworked beads from Elmina are those made by heating glass fragments to the melting point and then perforating them with some type of pointed implement. The majority of these were made from broken European beads, but there are some examples that may have been made from glass bottle fragments. There is a single example of an intact drawn bead with a second hole pushed through, perpendicular to the original perforation. Other bead fragments have drilled perforations.

A variety of African-made beads were found at Elmina, and they include a wide range of manufacturing and decorative effects. Most were made by firing glass chips or powdered glass. All were presumably dependent on imported sources.[124] None of the beads was drawn or wound like those that have been noted in other parts of West Africa. No manufacturing debris was recovered during excavations, and given the current state of research it is not possible to be certain where these beads originated. Some may have been fashioned at Elmina, but there was an active trade both along the West African coast and within the forest hinterland, so beads from other areas could easily be represented. However, it is notable that the distribution of these beads seems confined to Ghana.

The African glass beads from Elmina occurred in early eighteenth- through nineteenth-century contexts. Those made from glass chips are mostly white and blue glass or blue-green glass, but examples with yellow and brick-red glass fragments were also found. The source of glass seems to have been imported glass beads, augmented with bottle glass. Perforations can be seen in some of the glass chips, and the colors are consistent with European trade beads. The perforations in the finished beads are irregularly shaped and noticeably tapered, similar to the holes in the locally perforated fragments of imported beads and glass sherds. After perforation, the beads were generally ground to a disk shape. In most cases the individual glass chips are easily discernible, but in some examples the beads appear to have been turned in the mold while still in the molten state, swirling the chips together and giving the bead a wound appearance. A single example consists of glass chips covering a dark core.[125] Other beads may have been produced by winding viscous glass sherds around a mandrel. Beads similar to these examples have been recovered in seventeenth- or eighteenth-century contexts at New Buipe (Lamb 1978), in northern Ghana, and at Twifo Heman (Bellis 1972:85).[126] Other archaeological examples from Elmina may have been produced by manipulating powdered glass on a mandrel. The perforations are smooth and irregularly shaped. Most of these beads appear to have been light gold in color, but weathering has in some cases made them a yellowish tan. Some of the beads have not properly fused, and they have a powdery, fragile structure, perhaps as a result of a low firing temperature. Unlike modern fired glass beads, the surfaces of beads of all shapes are unground, and some of the shapes clearly could not have been produced in a single-piece clay mold. The decorated beads have inlays of trailed glass and/or fired glass chips of pale blue, navy blue, black, white, and redwood, which seem to have been added or inserted during the firing process.

Ivory Carving

The importance of ivory in West Africa is well established in documentary, ethnographic, and archaeological sources.[127] It was desired prior to the European arrival for use as horns, bracelets, and combs. References to a trade in ivory occur in the earliest Portuguese accounts of coastal Ghana, but there are no documented examples of Portuguese-period ivory artifacts from the Mina coast, and the time of the appearance of these early artifacts is uncertain (Barros 1967:108; de Marees 1987:34, 93, 171; Ross 1992).[128] Writing in the seventeenth century, Müller, in his account of the areas east of Elmina, noted that "people who make ivory trumpets, bracelets, and combs" were among the best-known craftsmen (in Jones 1983:253).

Ivory and bone objects excavated at Elmina are poorly dated, and they provide only limited insight into the origins and development of the craft (Figure 4.14). Notably, however, a sawed-off section of tusk measuring 11.5 by 7.0 by 1.7 cm (4.5 by 2.7 by 0.7 inches) was recovered. Although this is from a disturbed, post-1873, nineteenth-century feature, it provides evidence for ivory working at the site. Several ivory objects were found in post-1873, nineteenth-century features and were clearly not in situ. Fragments of a single bone comb, possibly originally part of a burial, were scattered throughout fill deposits that contained seventeenth-, eighteenth-, and nineteenth-century material. Other finds of ivory at Elmina were from similar contexts.

The ivory finds included three unidentified artifacts, examples of which have not been previously reported in ethnographic, historical, or archaeological literature. All are carefully cut from single pieces of ivory, the biggest measur-

Figure 4.14. Ivory and bone objects from Elmina: (*a–c*) ivory stamps, (*d–e*) ivory bracelet fragments, (*f*) bone comb, (*g–i*) bone artifacts. (Illustrations courtesy of Christopher R. DeCorse)

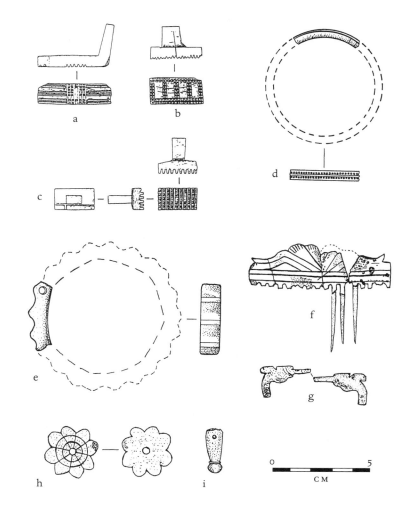

ing 1.0 by 3.2 cm (0.39 by 1.24 inches). The largest flat surface of each piece has been repeatedly sawn at regular intervals, leaving small posts or ridges. Some of these have been broken off to create geometric patterns. A handlelike projection is found on the opposite side of each piece. They were all found in nineteenth-century levels in widely separated parts of the site.

The form of these objects suggests that they may have been some type of stamp, possibly for body decoration. In 1617 the warriors of Asebu and Efutu covered their bodies with paint before going into battle (Jones 1983:95). There are also references to stamped and painted body decoration on women in the Elmina area by the beginning of the seventeenth century (de Marees 1987:37–38, 89).[129] Müller, in describing the Fetu country east of Elmina in 1662–69, noted that ladies would make "tiny crosses, stars, and other elegant figures and marks in red and white" on their foreheads, cheeks, arms, shoulders, and breasts (in Jones 1983:206). Body stamping is still done by Elmina women today, generally in connection with ritual occasions such as the Bakatue Festival. These circular patterns are frequently made using the pod of *Abutilum mauritianum*, known as *nwaha* in Fante (Cofie Odarty, correspondence, February 8, 1987). These pod-stamps are much larger than the ivory objects from Elmina. Wooden stamps collected in the Ivory Coast, which were probably used for a similar purpose, are also greater in size than the ivory objects from Elmina.[130]

Salt Making

Salt production is one of modern Elmina's primary industries, and it has long been assumed important in pre-European trade (see, e.g., Bech and Hyland 1978:21; editors in de Marees 1987:188 fn. 1).[131] Historically, it is an important condiment throughout Africa and has been an important trade item in many parts of West Africa.[132] Foods are frequently heavily salted, and daily intake may be as much as 10 g (0.35 ounce). In the early eighteenth century Asante traders came to Elmina specifically to buy salt (Fynn 1971:6–7). Some evidence of village specialization also occurs in oral histories. Wartemberg notes that the commercial production of salt was specifically the work of the villages bordering the Benya Lagoon, where "[p]its were bored deep in the earth to allow percolation of mineral salt deposits in liquid form, which was collected and boiled until after evaporation, the salt congealed and settled down" (1951:72). Oral testimonies from Elmina, Ampenyi, Brenu Akyinim, and Dutch Komenda also stress the importance of salt production (Fynn 1974b:14–15, 25, 35).[133]

Despite these sources, evidence for early production, for the type of manufacturing techniques employed, and for the extent of the pre-seventeenth-century salt trade is limited. Two different methods of salt production from seawater have traditionally been used in coastal Ghana. The most common method today is the solar evaporation of salt pans, which is currently used commercially in the Benya Lagoon (Figure 4.15). Alternatively, salt can be obtained, and was historically, by boiling seawater in pots. This was done by placing pots over an open fire or cementing a series of large copper cauldrons or local pots into a simple clay oven stoked from below. The seawater evaporated after a few days, leaving a fine salt residue that was so strong and white that it was "not inferior to the best European salt in taste and color" (Jones 1983:244).

Other sources of salt were available and were clearly exploited to a substantial degree in the past. The major source in much of the West African hinterland was geologic salt that was mined or extracted from salty earth through evaporation. The better known of these sources are located in the desert and the Sahel far north of the coast and forest: Mauritania, northern Mali (Teghaza, Taoudenni, Erebeb), southern Algeria (Amadror), and Niger (Bilma, Dirkou Djaba, Teggidda-n-Tesemt) (Alexander 1993:655–656; McDougall 1990). There were, however, other sources, such as Daboya in northern Ghana, where deposits of salt-rich earth may have been exploited by the first millennium A.D.[134] In other areas, for example, the Anlo-Ewe areas of southeastern Ghana, salt was obtained from plants (Greene 1988; Sutton 1981).[135] Scraping salt from the leaves of a certain species and the roots of the mangrove tree was the primary method of obtaining salt until the late seventeenth century.

Prior to the advent of evaporation of lagoonal salt pans, it was likely geologic salt, rather than sea salt, that was the key component of much of the long-distance trans-Saharan trade. Production on the coast by using plants or by boil-

Figure 4.15. Salt pans in the Benya Lagoon. Large-scale production of salt using the evaporation of salt pans was not introduced at Elmina until the twentieth century. (Photograph by Christopher R. DeCorse)

ing seawater was probably initially aimed at local consumption and the imme-diate hinterland (Alexander 1993:656; Daaku 1970; Greene 1988). Salt pans were used on parts of the coast to the east and west of Elmina by the end of the six-teenth century. An anonymous Portuguese report of 1572 notes that salt pans at Accra "should be kept in repair by slave workers managed by whites, and this I understand would be very profitable. . . . [I]t could be even more profitable if the blacks were prohibited from making salt as they do now by boiling sea water" (Teixeira da Mota and Hair 1988:74–75). The 1602 description of salt mak-ing by Pieter de Marees (1987:201) indicates that the best salt ponds were in the Ahanta area, in western Ghana, and Ada, near the Togo border.[136] On the Fante coastland, however, seventeenth- and eighteenth-century salt production was still done by boiling. Describing the Fetu country, Müller states: "[T]he Fetu people conduct great trade in salt, which they know how to boil in their coun-try themselves; for they fill large earthenware pots with the stagnant water which is brought inland when the salty sea overflows and which then settles there. They place the pots on a large fire, let the water become hot and boil it till the brine has completely dried up and turned to salt. Then they tip the salt out in the sun and stir it frequently, till it is dry, fine and good" (in Jones 1983:244).[137] This description is comparable to the method still sometimes used at Elmina. Despite Müller's positive evaluation, it was areas farther to the west that became the principal focus of commercial salt production during the sev-enteenth and eighteenth centuries. African traders from Elmina and other set-tlements west of Accra, as well as the Dutch, purchased salt from Accra and Ningo salt makers (Sutton 1981:44; Feinberg 1969:129; Sundstrom 1965:123, 142; van Dantzig 1978:69, 144–145, 279, 295).

From an archaeological standpoint salt production is difficult to evaluate. No evidence of the specialized ovens has been identified, and fragments of large ceramic vessels and metal vessels may have had other, varied purposes. More evidence is provided by references to the thick vegetation of the Benya Lagoon and the paucity of references to salt pans. As noted in Chapter 2, the origins of the Benya salt pans must date to the late nineteenth and twentieth centuries, because the interior of the Benya Lagoon was covered by brush until after 1873. Prior to this time manufacture would have been dependent on boiling. It may also be reasonable to suggest that in the past the extent of salt production in the Elmina settlement itself may have been limited. The crowded nature of the pre-1873 settlement, including many houses with thatch roofs, would have made it an ill-suited location for extensive salt-boiling ovens. It is, perhaps, more likely that the salt that was traded was produced in neighboring communities. Such specialized "salt-making" villages are shown to the east between Elmina and the Kakum River on the 1629 Dutch map.[138] A Sout Dorp, or "Salt Town," is located on the 1647 Baelarus plan of Elmina, and a village where they obtained salt by boiling seawater is described in eighteenth- and nineteenth-century descriptions of the area (Feinberg 1989:81). As noted, however, the Dutch, at least at times, apparently did not rely on salt from Elmina but obtained it instead from Accra. Although salt may have historically formed a component of the economy, the central Gold Coast was not a major production center compared with some neighboring areas, the real expansion of production occurring at Elmina during the colonial period.

THEY WERE TRADERS . . .

It is illustrative that oral traditions stress the role of trade in Elmina's past. Accounts such as the epigraphs in the chapter opening underscore the settlement as a trading center and the importance of commerce in the livelihood of the people. Many early documentary accounts also attest to the principal role of trade at Elmina (e.g., de Marees 1987:120–125, 158–166, 201; Jones 1983:220–223, 231–233). When the Portuguese arrived on the West African coast, they found a ready market. Although it is reasonable to suggest that demand for commodities such as textiles, brass, and beads was already established as a consequence of pre-European trade, the sea trade drastically increased the volume of goods that were available on the coast and reoriented existing trade routes.[139] Demand for European commodities was met through trade in local commodities. Fish and salt are said to have been important trade items, yet this picture is more a representation of what occurred in the centuries following the arrival of the Europeans than a representation of the situation within the precontact settlement. As has been noted, there is little evidence for substantial marine fishing, salt production, iron manufacture, or brass casting on the central Gold Coast and its immediate hinterland before the fifteenth century. These things became increasingly important as the European coastal trade developed. This is not to suggest that markets and exchange networks did not exist earlier but that such interactions were primarily tied to local, regional consumption.

What the Europeans could readily obtain at Elmina when they first arrived on the coast was gold. From the first years of European contact, it was traded on the Mina coast more easily than in any other part of West Africa (see Garrard 1980b:104). The gold bracelets, rings, and necklaces that bedecked the inhabitants of the Akan coast in the fifteenth century captivated European interest. Gold dust or small, low-carat lumps called *kacraws* became the primary medium of exchange on the coast. At Elmina and in some adjacent areas, *kakaras,* a mixture of brass and copper filings, was also used (see accounts by Bosman 1967:81–82; Jones 1983:250; Sundstrom 1965:55).[140] Gold dust was carefully weighed on scales, and traders necessarily possessed their own sets of weights and weighing equipment (e.g., Garrard 1980b; de Marees 1987:60, 65, 192–195). European coinage did not circulate widely in West Africa until the late nineteenth century, although it was apparently in more common usage at São Tomé by the seventeenth century (Bosman 1967:82; de Marees 1987:65; Garrard 1980b:95–96; Jones 1983:133).[141] Weights, on the other hand, remained an important feature in the Gold Coast trade until the late nineteenth century, when European coinage became more prevalent (Garrard 1980b:301). All of the gold-weighing implements recovered archaeologically would have been typical contents of a weight bag carried by an average person.

The early Portuguese presumption was that the source of gold was to be found locally. Oral traditions further suggest that alluvial gold was readily gathered along the seashore and, after rains, in village streets and ditches.[142] Yet, later Portuguese sources make it clear that only small quantities of gold were recovered in this way, and Dutch sources clearly indicate that gold was obtained from the interior.[143] Small-scale mining, locally called *galamsey,* is still carried out in many of the areas around Elmina and the coastal hinterland, notably at Efutu, Asebu, and Eguafo, and enough gold is extracted to make excavation worthwhile. However, examination of these sites indicates that the majority of the gold collected in this way is clearly from archaeological contexts, particularly burials. The gold artifacts that are recovered are sold for their mineral value. Although some alluvial gold may have been procured in the past, it is far more likely that the greatest amount of the gold traded on the coast was brought from the hinterland. The principal sources were likely the Dormaa, Sefwi, Aowin, and Wasa in the forest north-northwest of Elmina (Garrard 1980b:51). From these areas the gold was traded to the coast, as well as to northern markets such as Begho. Both the Portuguese and the Dutch, though able to obtain gold on the coast, were clearly aware of the interior sources. Outposts were established, albeit unsuccessfully, in the interior in attempts to obtain gold from the inland states.

Elmina's emergence as a mercantile center resulted from its preeminent position in the European trade, a position that guaranteed that many of the ships visiting West Africa would stop there. In 1602 de Marees noted: "Thus they [the Africans] are now beginning to acquire as good a knowledge of the commodities which they are sold as we Dutchmen ourselves have" (de Marees 1987:54).[144] The small European population relied on African or mulatto middlemen, called *makelaers* in Dutch, to conduct much of the trade (Feinberg 1969:128–129). Great care was taken by both Africans and Europeans to examine carefully the goods being traded. European factors at times sought to sell inferior goods. Conversely, Africans sometimes offered low-carat or inferior gold in payment (Bosman 1967:82; de Marees 1987:192–195).

The Europeans experimented in bringing a wide variety of items for which there was demonstrated demand, as well as an array of new items. Even a partial listing of these trade goods is staggering. Such novelties as spectacles, mirrors, keys, and other "knickknacks" did not form a large part of merchants' cargoes, but they illustrate the range of items offered in trade. The townspeople were not passive recipients of European commodities but rather active participants in shaping and structuring trade relations, and the lists of trade materials offered are testament to the ever-widening economic system of which Elmina was part. The archaeological record from Elmina provides an equally dramatic illustration of this. From an archaeological standpoint, the trade materials also provide a critical means of establishing chronological contexts of the deposits excavated. These imported materials and their implications for interpretations of the archaeology and trade at Elmina are the focus of the following chapter.

5

THE EUROPEAN

TRADE

When the Portuguese arrived on the West African coast in the fifteenth century, they found a ready market for commodities such as textiles, brassware, and beads. A trade in these items was already well established as a consequence of the regional and trans-Saharan trade. A portion of the trade did consist of inexpensively produced trinkets and outmoded or used items. But, in fact, the great bulk of trade materials consisted of more practical selections of cloth and metal goods.[1] European merchants tailored their shipments to meet specific demands on particular parts of the coast.[2] During the nineteenth century in particular, these shipments included an increasing number of items specifically produced for African markets. Such artifacts contrast with the view sometimes expressed that the articles the Europeans traded were of little value, defective, or rubbish (see Alpern 1995; Curtin 1975:312).

Among the first European imports were a wide variety of beads. Beads have traditionally been worn around wrists, necks, waists, and ankles by people in many areas. They were exported to Africa in huge quantities, and over 800 type varieties were found at Elmina.[3] Many of these have counterparts in beads used in Europe. Nevertheless, Africans often specified particular colors and types of beads, to the frustration of European traders. Elaborate mosaic beads from Venice are sufficiently associated with Africa that American dealers sometimes advertise them as African trade beads. During the early twentieth century, Czech bead manufacturers fabricated glass cowries, teeth, and imitations of African-made beads specifically for the West African trade (e.g., Lui 1995:42–43).

Many metal objects of personal adornment were also produced specifically for West African markets. Some proved less than suitable. Aitken (1866a:274) relates an attempt to market iron manillas, coppered over by electroplating, which were readily identified as fakes and not accepted in Africa.[4] Other, more suitable products included anklet and armlet rings made from brass tubing. These reportedly had an internal diameter of between 7.1 and 10.3 cm (2.75 and 4 inches), the opening left unsoldered "in order to admit of their being opened the more readily, to allow of their being placed on the arm and leg of the wearer" (Aitken 1866a:320). A bracelet likely representative of this type of manufacture was found at Elmina (see the bracelet in the upper left corner of Figure 4.12). It has an internal diameter of 6.8 cm (2.7 inches). The outside is simply decorated with milling tools.

An even more striking example of production specifically for African markets is brass *forowa,* probably manufactured in Britain.[5] Given the limited distribution of *forowa,* such objects could only have been fabricated with the Akan coast in mind. Hoes of different designs comparable to local examples were also produced. These imports competed with, and sometimes replaced, locally produced goods. Perhaps the most explicit statement of the local perception of this trend is given by J. Sylvanus Wartemberg, the native historian of Elmina's past, who explained that the Elmina pottery industry "suffered a set-back after the British Empire Exhibition of 1925 to which specimens of local production were sent; the immediate effect was a diminution of interest in the local industry as a result of the importation of cheap enamelware imitation of the local specimens, which eclipsed and paralized the industry to some appreciable extent" (1951:72). Although the specific consequences of the British Empire Exhibition of 1925 may be uncertain, the mass production and increased availability of enamelwares in the late nineteenth and early twentieth centuries likely had real impact on the demand for local ceramics.

The complexities of supply and trade patterns over the past five centuries make it difficult to define the role of individual European countries solely on the basis of artifactual assemblages. Nations that maintained forts and trade posts on the West African coast often tried to exclude traders of other nationalities, but these efforts were of limited success, and interlopers conducted a brisk trade. The European power that came closest to enjoying a monopoly was Portugal. By establishing fortified outposts such as Elmina and patrolling the coast, the Portuguese hampered the trade of other European powers in West Africa until the second half of the sixteenth century. Other Europeans were effectively excluded from Elmina until the castle was taken by the Dutch in 1637, yet goods from other locales readily reached the town from neighboring areas, where interlopers were active. Conversely, even after the Portuguese lost their final outpost on the Gold Coast in 1683, they maintained an active presence, trading in Brazilian tobacco (e.g., van Dantzig 1978:9, 152, 235). In the seventeenth century African traders became so bold in trading with unsanctioned non-Dutch traders that the Elmina council "unanimously resolved to write to the Captains of the cruising frigates to hang the very first Negro they could find on board of such a captured interloper ship from the end of the mainyard, and if they find more than one Negro, to let them draw lots for it" (van Dantzig 1978:47–48).[6] Nevertheless, such unsanctioned trade likely became the norm rather than the exception in the seventeenth century. Dutch control of trade, as well as similar efforts on the part of other European nations, was tenuous even in the areas adjacent to their coastal outposts. Because many forts and trade posts on the Gold Coast were in close proximity to one another, goods from different distribution points no doubt circulated freely through the hinterland. In the nineteenth century entire ship cargoes were sometimes smuggled ashore.[7]

Regardless of nationality, traders frequently relied on supplies from other countries, and the products offered by representatives of different nationalities were probably much the same. From the earliest years of the trade, Portugal was dependent on Flemish and Dutch textiles and metal goods, and Venetian beads and Indian cloth remained a staple in trade until the present century (Milo 1961).[8] The Dutch brought Rhenish stoneware, Venetian beads, and an array of Indian cloth. The irregularities of supplies from Europe sometimes forced factors to rely on competitors' goods, even when their respective countries were at war.[9]

Poor archaeological visibility and limited documentation make it difficult to assess the relative importance of different commodities. In some instances the volume of materials traded was vast. One source notes a single order for over 1 million manillas (brass bracelets) in 1548 (cited in Teixeira da Mota and Hair 1988:27).[10] The total amount of Portuguese copper and brass imports—basins, bracelets, and cauldrons—on the coast may have reached between 27.5 and 49.5 t (25 and 45 tons) per year during the Portuguese period (Garrard 1980a:105).[11] Not surprisingly, writers have assessed the trade from varying perspectives. In terms of the percentage of value, cloth and metalware were leading imports. Considering samplings of scattered years in the period 1480–1540, Vogt (1979:76) estimates that by value, cloth sales accounted for about 40 percent of Portuguese trade at Mina, and metal products made up another 37 percent.[12] The sale of slaves and other items accounted for about 10 percent and 13 percent, respectively. Surveying Dutch records for 1725 and 1727, Feinberg (1989:50) identifies five principal categories (cloth, military supplies, alcohol, tobacco, and metalware), which accounted for 75–79 percent of the goods traded during the years surveyed. He further notes that other categories such as beads and trinkets—items that might be recovered archaeologically—played a very small part in the trade, amounting to no more than 2–4 percent of it. The eighteenth century was also characterized by increasing quantities of goods of non-European origin, especially Indian cloth.

Such discussions are germane to an economic assessment of the relative importance of different nations' trade, but resolution of these questions is more easily reached through the documentary record than through archaeological excavation. The variables that contribute to the formation and preservation of the archaeological record include a variety of environmental phenomena, aside from culturally ascribed values. Feinberg's (1989:50) division of materials into "durable" and "nondurable" goods is a case in point.[13] For 1727, he reports that nondurable goods, led by tobacco and alcohol, made up 47 percent of the trade. Tobacco leaves limited traces archaeologically, and the trade in alcohol can be only indirectly and partly inferred through the remains of the containers used in shipment. Cloth, which has minimal archaeological visibility, made up a large portion of the *durable* goods from Europe, Asia, and other parts of West Africa that were discussed by Feinberg. Even more substantial metal artifacts were subject to modification and reuse and are poorly preserved in archaeological contexts.

Such poor visibility renders archaeological evaluation of the trade very incomplete. This can be further illustrated by considering the nineteenth-century American trade. Yankee merchant seamen played a well-documented and key role in the trade among Africa, Europe, and the Americas during the eighteenth and nineteenth centuries. American captains regarded Elmina as one of the principal places for trade on the West African coast and at times gave up calls at other ports in order to reach Elmina before other ships.[14] In nineteenth-century lists, American ships are consistently among the most commonly reported at Elmina, surpassed only by those of English registration. For example, ships calling at Elmina in 1853 included 1 Austrian, 6 Dutch, 6 Hamburgian, 7 Portuguese, 8 Sardinian, 9 French, 15 American, and 22 English (annual report for 1853, quoted in van Dantzig, n.d.:228). In addition there were visits by two American and six French warships.

Despite the documentary evidence attesting to the American presence, few artifacts of American origin were found in excavations. A single sherd of a gray salt-glazed stoneware crock, coated on the inside with the distinctive chocolate brown "Albany" slip, was found at Elmina. This type of ware characterized the products of eastern North American potters of the nineteenth century. Another American product is evidenced by fragments of Perry Davis Vegetable Painkiller bottles. This nostrum was first marketed in Taunton, Massachusetts, in 1840 (Munsey 1970:65).[15] Advertisements claimed that the painkiller could cure cholera, and the product gained steadily in popularity after the 1849 cholera epidemic. During the mid-nineteenth century, hundreds of thousands of bottles were sold annually, and a branch office had to be opened in London to accommodate the extra business. Embossed bottles, like those found at Elmina, were produced after 1854 (Fike 1987:130). These few artifacts give scant indication of the volume of American trade.[16]

The paucity of artifacts of American origin at Elmina, in spite of what was a yearly trade in hundreds of thousands of nineteenth-century dollars, can be explained by the types of materials involved. The trade lists of American merchants are dominated by consumables and raw materials, such as beef, pork, tongues, hams, pickled fish, wine, gin, rum, brandy, sugar, cordials, rice, flour, cornmeal, bread, crackers, butter, tobacco, vinegar, lard, molasses, cheese, tea, pitch, candles, soap, tallow, corks, tar, twine, stationery, paint, nails, lumber, iron hoops, iron bars, lead bars, gun powder, copper rods, and cloth (e.g., Bennett and Brooks 1965:33, 37–42, 282). The few ready-made items, such as leather goods (boots, shoes), furniture, and trunks, are not well represented or readily identifiable as American in the archaeological record. A portion of the goods may also have been for the consumption of the European factors and not the Africans.

Other manufactures traded by American merchants were of European origin. Items such as gunflints, for example, were obtained from European sources (e.g., Bennett and Brooks 1965:41, 116).[17] Similarly, crockery and glassware listed on American trade lists were probably obtained from British or European sources until the last quarter of the nineteenth century, the real growth in American production of these goods taking place after the destruction of Elmina.[18]

The strength of archaeological data lies in two areas. The first is the archaeological and historically documented production ranges of some of the European trade materials, and the second is the information gleaned from the specific archaeological contexts in which the artifacts were found. The dating provided close chronological control for many of the archaeological deposits and associated African artifacts. Archaeological contexts furnish excellent information on some behavior, often more detailed than that found in documentary sources. Materials such as ceramics, glass, pipes, and firearms are notable not simply because of the amount found archaeologically but also because of the insight they afford into local use patterns, foodways, and the impact of the European trade on coastal societies. Others provide glimpses of life in Elmina and suggest both the cultural and social influences that affected Elmina society.

The amount and variety of trade materials recovered at Elmina are unparalleled in excavations at any other West African settlement. The fragments of imported ceramics (6,801), glass (13,906), imported tobacco pipes (3,911), metal artifacts (4,607), small finds (1,421), and the 39,131 European trade beads outnumber artifacts of local manufacture. The wealth of trade items at Elmina contrasts with the paucity of such material found at sites only a few kilometers into the interior. The total amount of trade materials excavated at the Fante capitals of Eguafo, Efutu, and Asebu consists of several dozen tobacco pipes, occasional glass fragments, and a few handfuls of ceramics spanning the sixteenth through the nineteenth centuries.[19]

Some artifacts, although few in number, suggest aspects of influence and change in Elmina society. The more tantalizing of these relate to literacy (Figure 5.1). A European education was undoubtedly regarded as very useful by many Africans, for it facilitated trade (Abraham 1964; Graham 1976). By order of King John III, a school was established at Elmina as early as 1529 to teach reading, writing, and the holy Scriptures to the children. Education was also considered important during the Dutch period. In the 1740s a school at Elmina was established by Jacobus Capitein, an African educated in Holland. At the time of Capitein's death, the school had over 400 male and female students. There is little indication of how successful these early efforts were. As in Europe, before the nineteenth century a cohesive educational system was lacking, so a great deal depended on the work of individuals. Willem Bosman's (1967:121–122) account of the late seventeenth century suggests that for the most part formalized schooling generally did not play a part of the average child's upbringing. During the nineteenth century, schools with European-style curricula became much more common. Many were linked to Basel, Wesleyan, and Catholic missions. Nineteenth-century accounts of Elmina note that many of the African and mulatto merchants spoke several European languages fluently

Figure 5.1. Glass inkwells (shown) and slate pencils from nineteenth-century contexts only hint at the degree of literacy among the Elmina population and the advent of European educational curricula. (Photograph by Christopher R. DeCorse)

because they had been sent to England for their education (e.g., Bennett and Brooks 1965:118). A few were educated at European universities.

Education-related artifacts found at Elmina are few in number. They include 12 slate pencils and 43 writing slate fragments. An additional 77 pieces of slate that were found were unpolished and unruled. They are all small fragments that bear some fine wear scratches, and they can tentatively be included with the pieces of writing slate.[20] To these few artifacts may also be added inkwells and stoneware bottles that could have been used to store ink. These artifacts were all confined to nineteenth-century levels, including some from 1873 floor contexts, providing a meager indication of literacy and the advent of European schooling during this period.

Another indication of change is provided by artifacts related to clothing. European descriptions provide an indication of change in the manner of dress between the fifteenth and the nineteenth centuries. References to clothing in Portuguese accounts point to simple, brief garments (e.g., Barros 1967:117; Blake 1942:73). Pereira, for example, wrote: "The negroes in this country go about naked, save for a loin-cloth or a piece of striped cloth" (1967:121). The "loin-cloth" may have been similar to the undergarments still occasionally worn by men in northern Ghana, whereas the "striped cloth" was probably worn draped over the shoulders in a manner similar to the modern cloth. These articles were supplemented by hats and other garments of bark cloth, leather, and straw (e.g., Brun in Jones 1983:86; Hemmersam in Jones 1983:113; Müller in Jones 1983:205–207; and Towerson 1967:367).

European factors were quick to fill local demand for fabrics. Cloth from other parts of the West African coast and North Africa, as well as used bed linen from Europe, was frequently traded (Alpern 1995; Blake 1942:94, 06, 97, 103, 107, 109, 127, 128, 130). Pieter de Marees (1987:33–39, 62, 66, 88, 98, 167, 179, 217), observing the coast over 100 years after the founding of Elmina Castle, discussed clothing that may have been similar to the caps, mantles, and loincloths worn during the preceding century (see also Jones 1983:205). Simple loincloths and wraps were apparently still the principal dress at this time. However, de Marees (1987:215) also recorded the increasing use of European clothing, particularly by the mulatto population. During the seventeenth and eighteenth centuries there was a demand for a wide range of European clothing including hats, stockings, shoes, coats, breeches, gowns, and even old wigs (see also Blake 1942:98, 131; Jones 1983:205; van Dantzig 1982b:293). Boxes of shoes, boots, hats, and clothing continued to appear in nineteenth-century trade lists (Bennett and Brooks 1965:39, 282). European and American military uniforms were also a very desirable trade item on parts of the coast.[21] This may explain the presence of a set of mid-nineteenth-century U.S. Marine buttons in late nineteenth-century trash deposits. Keys were also traded in large quantities, and they were worn from women's waists as decorative accessories (de Marees 1987:39; Jones 1983:205; Meredith 1967:110). Wealthy men and women could be distinguished by the richness of their dress and their necklaces, rings, and bracelets of gold and precious stone (de Marees 1987:34; Jones 1983:112, 204–205). Although some of these items were locally produced, many were imported.

Archaeology provides limited and indirect indication of the clothing worn at Elmina. No garments were recovered, let alone traces of the bustles that Fante women were said to have worn between the seventeenth and nineteenth centuries.[22] Dress is evidenced by a few buttons, buckles, hooks, and clasps, plus an array of beads, necklaces, bracelets, and pins (possibly for securing shrouds). The majority of the goods were found in nineteenth-century contexts, though many are clearly older. They may be indicative of the increasing popularity of European clothing, but many of the pieces could have originated from Dutch or European military uniforms. The majority of these items need not have functioned on clothing at all. Things such as brass buckles, keys, clasps, and hatpins were reused as gold weights and are present in collections of weighing equipment.[23] The imported cloth and clothing itself may have often been disassembled and rewoven. Burials produced no evidence of European buttons or fasteners, perhaps an indication of continuity in traditional dress in ritual expression. Such absence of clothing would be consistent with documentary and ethnographic descriptions of the use of burial shrouds.

IMPORTED CERAMICS

The variety of imported ceramics at Elmina is impressive, the collection accounting for almost one-fifth of the ceramic vessel sherds recovered and including over four dozen type varieties (Table 5.1).[24] Although a portion of the archaeological assemblage may have originated from the European garrison, the majority is clearly from African contexts. The amount and diversity of ceramics recovered lie in dramatic contrast to the limited documentary evidence for their import. Occasional references occur, but ceramics are generally not singled out as an important trade item, especially before the nineteenth century. Earthenware appears on lists of merchandise brought to the coast by the Dutch at beginning of the seventeenth century (Kea 1982:207–208).[25] Later in the same century the Brandenburg company sold "489 lb. earthenware pots" for a 168 percent profit at the fort Gross Friedrichsburg in Princes Town (Pokesu), Western Region. At least some of these ceramics may have reached

Table 5.1

Trade Ceramics from Elmina

Type Varieties[a]	Date Ranges[b]
PORCELAIN	
English bone china with hand-painted gold luster: tea cups	1820–73
German Meissen or Meissen-style porcelain with underglaze blue decoration	1720–1800
British or European porcelain or porcelanous ware: ointment jars	1830–1910
Chinese porcelain with underglaze blue decoration: plates, saucers, tea ware	1690–1800
Chinese Imari-style porcelain with overglaze enamel: saucer	1720–40
Chinese porcelain with Batavian glaze and underglaze blue decoration: bowls, saucers	1690–1790
Chinese coarse porcelain with underglaze blue decoration: lidded ginger jars	1790–1873
Japanese porcelain with underglaze blue decoration: plate	1670–1700
EARTHENWARE	
Unglazed	
Iberian, Merida, or Merida-type ware	1471–1637
Portuguese red earthenware with inlaid feldspar and punctate decoration	1471–1637
Glazed	
Portuguese buff-paste earthenwares with clear lead glaze	1471–1637
Portuguese buff-paste earthenwares with green (copper oxide) lead glaze	1471–1637
Portuguese red-paste earthenwares with green (copper oxide) lead glaze	1471–1637
Iberian buff-paste earthenware with white slip interior: olive jars	1560–1800
German buff-paste earthenware with clear lead glaze	1700–1800
European or English earthenware with clear lead glaze	1600–1800
Buckley ware	1720–75
Astbury ware with white sprig decoration	1725–55
Jackfield-type ware	1740–1800
Refined redware with luster decoration	1790–1873
"Castleford" molded decoration with blue applique	1820–30
Yellowware, plain and decorated with annular bands of blue and white: chamber pots, bowls, and mugs	1820–73
"Bennington" or Bennington-like ware	1840–73
Refined red-paste earthenware with blue and brown annular bands: mugs	1850–73
Blue-paste ware with clear alkaline glaze: ointment pot	1840–73
Tin-Glazed	
Caparra Blue	1471–1600
Iberian faience, plain and with blue decoration: plates and bowls	1471–1700
Iberian polychrome majolica	1550–1700
Delftware with blue decoration	1600–1800
Delftware, undecorated	1640–1830
Delftware, undecorated: cylindrical ointment pots	1700–1800
Delftware, undecorated: ointment pots with pedestal feet	1730–1830
French faience with polychrome decoration	1750–1800
French tin-glazed: ointment pots with green exterior and white interior glazes	1730–1830
Creamware	
Undecorated, "dark" and "light"	1762–1820
Embossed beaded decoration	1762–1820
Feather edged: plates	1765–1820

Table 5.1 (continued)

Overglaze black transfer printed	1765–1815
Blue shell edged: plates	1770–1820
Green shell edged: plates	1775–1820
Annular decorated	1780–1815
Mocha decorated: mugs	1795–1820

Pearlware

Plain white	1780–1830
Hand-painted blue	1780–1830
Blue and green shell edged	1780–1830
Earthtone annular decorated	1790–1830
Blue transfer printed	1790–1840
Molded decoration	1800–1840
Blue and polychrome hand-painted, thick-line style	1820–40

Whiteware

Undecorated	1820–1900
Blue tranfer printed	1820–73
Underglaze transfer prints in green, red, lavender, purple, blue-gray, brown, and black: plates, bowls, and cups	1828–73
Molded decoration	1820–60
Blue sprigged decoration	1820–73
Hand-painted blue decorated (thick lines) and blue annular decoration	1820–70
Hand-painted polychrome decoration (pink, maroon, light, and dark green, black, blue, yellow, and occasional brown lines), thick-line style	1820–70
Sponge decorated in blue, green, purple, yellow, and red: bowls	1830–73
Finger-painted swirls	1820–60
Blue, black, and light green shell edged	1820–60
Cut-sponge stamped floral and geometric patterns in black, blue, brown, green, maroon, pink, and purple	1845–73
Sponged-stencil decoration in green and yellow with fine-line hand painting	1830–73
Flown blue transfer printed and hand-painted floral decoration	1840–73
Underglaze green transfer print and light green and yellow hand-painted detail	1840–73

STONEWARE

Cologne stoneware with sprig molding: *Krug*	1500–1600
Salt-glazed and brown stoneware: Bellarmine	1550–1700
Rhenish gray stoneware with incised, cobalt blue decoration: *Krüge*	1650–1750
Rhenish gray stoneware with sprig molding, incised combed lines, and blue and purple decoration: *Krüge*	1650–1750
Burslem or Staffordshire stoneware, mottled brown	1700–1810
White salt-glazed stoneware: plates	1740–75
Nassau reddish brown stoneware: cylindrical bottles with small lug handles	1800–1900
American gray salt-glazed stoneware with Albany slip interior: crock or jug	1800–1873
Brown stoneware: bottles for ink, blacking	1820–73
Nassau gray stoneware with debased blue decoration	1850–73
"Bristol" white stoneware: bottles for ink, blacking, and ginger beer	1830–73
Ironstone, plain white	1840–1900

Sources: Work by Noël Hume (1958, 1960, 1967, 1977, 1978); Deagan (1987); Klose (1997); and Majewski and O'Brian (1987) was particularly helpful in defining the ranges of some of the Elmina ceramics. South's (1977a) table of ceramic types found in Anglo-American sites and their date ranges provided a model and substantive information. Other sources consulted include: Abrahams 1996; Baart and Caladro 1987; Baart, Krook, and

Table 5.1 (continued)

Lagerweij 1986; Baker and Harrison 1986; Brain 1979; Fairbanks 1966; Faulkner and Faulkner 1987; Finlayson 1972; Fleming 1923; Goggin 1963; Goggin 1968; Gusset 1984; Herskovits 1978; Hughes 1968a, b; Hurst 1977; Ketchum 1983, 1987; Kirkman 1974; Leibowitz 1985; Lister and Lister 1976, 1987; Lofstrom, Tordoff, and George 1982; Martin 1979; Meurer 1974; Nienhaus 1981; Palmer 1976; Pendery 1999; Price 1982; Quimby 1980; Redman 1978, 1979, 1986; Reineking–Von Bock 1971; Robaker and Robaker 1978; Savage and Newman 1976; South, Skowronek, and Johnson 1988; Sullivan 1986; van der Pijl–Ketel 1982. In addition to published sources, several individuals were kind enough to look at the type collection of the ceramics recovered. I owe special thanks to Ivor and Audrey Noël Hume, Jane Klose, George Miller, Jim Boone, Emlyn Meyers, Terry Majewski, and Jan Baart.

[a]The type varieties listed were all recovered archaeologically at Elmina and are intended to serve as a preliminary catalog of trade ceramics found in Ghana.

[b]The date ranges given are intended not as the period of manufacture but as the possible age of the ceramics recovered at Elmina. Some date ranges have been modified on the basis of the known historical context at Elmina. For example, 1471 denotes the arrival of the Portuguese on the Gold Coast; 1637 is the date of the Dutch takeover of Elmina. Other date ranges reflect the ages of specific finds.

Elmina (A. Jones 1985:78, 112, 114).[26] References remain infrequent during the eighteenth century. In 1770, Liverpool exported 14,524 pieces of earthenware to Africa, not a substantial amount considering the vast area represented (Alpern 1995:27). In contrast, over 800,000 pieces of "earthenware of all sorts," valued at £9,145.00, were declared as imports to the Gold Coast alone from Britain and Ireland between 1827 and 1841.[27] This amount is dwarfed by the trade in such items as arms and ammunition, brass and copper manufactures, spirits and wine, and especially cotton, but it exceeds the declared value of some categories, including jewelry, pewter, and tin manufactures.

The use of imported ceramics within the Elmina settlement may have been limited, as compared with local pottery, prior to the nineteenth century. Documentary references to their use are almost nonexistent. Gramberg's disparaging account of Elmina in 1861 gives some indication of the use of both imported ceramics and glassware. He writes that, in addition to other furnishings of the average African household,

[o]ne may add a pitcher, of which the cover is generally missing or cracked, a few glasses, which are so dirty that no European would ever dare to drink, an old gun (hardly ever missing from the collection), and that is about all there is to be found in a well furnished Negro *salon*. In another cubicle one may find what makes the household complete, such as: a pot containing some offerings for the House-fetish; some European earthenware such as bowls, pitchers and plates, as well as a few pots for keeping provisions. The proper cooking pots are to be found outside. . . . (1861:88–89)

Gramberg contrasted these limited furnishings with those of an African in the employ of the Europeans: "Here one finds a moderator-lamp, there a tea ser-

Figure 5.2. A unique example of sixteenth-century unglazed Portuguese earthenware with inlaid feldspar and incised decoration. Sherd measures 5 cm (1.9 inches) at widest point. (Illustration and photo by Christopher R. DeCorse)

Figure 5.3. Sixteenth-century Iberian faience plate with a cobalt blue decoration. Vessel measures 30.5 cm (11.9 inches) in diameter. (Illustration and photograph by Christopher R. DeCorse)

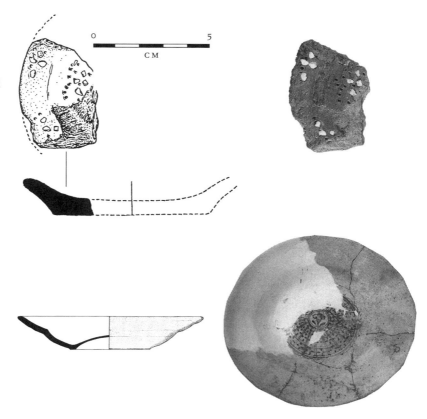

vice, and in another house a curious collection of champagne, wine and beer glasses, or even a pile of old books" (1861:89–90; see also Bennett and Brooks 1965:118).

Archaeologically, imported ceramics were recovered from many different contexts including fill and 1873 floors, consistent with Gramberg's description. However, as noted previously, a significant number of intact ceramics were also recovered from burials. Vessels from the latter include a diversity of type varieties and forms, and this may have been one of the principal uses to which imported ceramics were put.

The majority of imported ceramics found at Elmina dating between the late fifteenth and early seventeenth centuries are Iberian, providing some indication of Portugal's monopoly on the trade. Included are wares of general Iberian tradition, such as pieces of Merida or "Merida-like" wares, lead-glazed earthenwares, and examples of sixteenth- and seventeenth-century tin-glazed earthenwares (Figures 5.2 and 5.3).[28] However, some clearly Portuguese production is present. Most distinctive of these ceramics is a single sherd of unglazed redware, decorated with incising and patterns of inlaid stones. Examples of this type of ceramic have been found at other Portuguese sites, and similar wares are still produced in southern Portugal.[29] Many of the other "Iberian" ceramics may, in fact, be specifically Portuguese. Thick-walled utilitarian storage vessels, as well as delicate bowls, jugs, and cups, are represented.

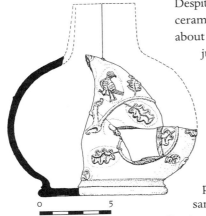

O   5
             C M

Figure 5.4. Rhenish
brown stoneware *Krug,*
circa 1500–1550.
(Illustration by
Christopher R.
DeCorse)

Despite the range of wares and vessel forms found, Portuguese-period ceramics are represented by only about 300 sherds.[30] This constitutes about 6 percent of the imported ceramic vessel sherds recovered and just over 1.1 percent of the total ceramic assemblage.[31] There are also occasional sherds of early German stoneware, such as the early sixteenth-century *Krug* illustrated in Figure 5.4 and pieces of Bellarmine bottles. Germany itself had no direct trade links with Africa until after 1650, thus such wares reached West Africa through the Portuguese or non-German interloper trade.

The small number of ceramic sherds from the Portuguese period may, in part, be a consequence of the comparatively small sample of fifteenth-century deposits. It is, however, also likely indicative of the limited importance of imported ceramics as trade items during this period. In the Americas, small amounts of ceramics were traded and given as gifts to Native Americans by the Spanish, yet they never accounted for a substantial portion of the trade (Lister and Lister 1987:192–197; see also Deagan 1987:20–22, 103; Haring 1964:113). Pottery may have played a similar role in West Africa during the fifteenth and the sixteenth centuries. Although the Portuguese offered novel vessel forms, the relatively low-fired earthenwares may have aroused little African interest in the face of a well-developed indigenous potting tradition. Imported ceramics may have been possessed by relatively few individuals and served in specialized contexts.

The relatively limited trade in ceramics continued with the Dutch during the seventeenth and eighteenth centuries. These periods present an even wider range of wares, including earthenwares, stonewares, and porcelains of European, British, and Chinese manufacture. Yet, some types are represented by isolated examples or only a few sherds, as is the case with Buckley-, Astbury-, and Jackfield-type wares. These are eighteenth-century British ceramics that were imported to North America in significant quantities (see, e.g., Noël Hume 1978:122–124, 132–133). Compared with the amount of nineteenth-century refined, white-paste earthenwares, there was also a comparatively small amount of delftware, which was a major export of Holland during the seventeenth and eighteenth centuries. The vessels that are represented span a range of forms from ointment pots to bowls and plates. Sherds of eighteenth-century European faiences and porcelains are equally uncommon. British ceramics, which characterize late eighteenth- and early nineteenth-century European sites in other world areas, are present in only slightly greater quantity than the European faiences and porcelains. Only 125 pieces of pearlware and 68 creamware sherds were found. Vessel forms range from the earliest blue transfer-printed pearlware cups to floral hand-painted pearlware chamber pots of the early nineteenth century.

Another import of the seventeenth and eighteenth centuries was Chinese porcelain. Although occasional sherds of Chinese wares have been recovered from other archaeological contexts in Ghana and West Africa, such occurrences are rare.[32] The Dutch East India Company maintained an extensive trade with Asia beginning in the early seventeenth century, and returning merchantmen sometimes carried substantial quantities of porcelain.[33] In Europe, Chinese export wares became high-status items, but they seem to have been more widely available in portions of Africa. They make up a substantial portion of assemblages at the South African Cape, where they appear to have served the same function as other imported wares among the European settler population.[34] A single sherd of Chinese porcelain from Elmina may be sixteenth- or early seventeenth-century in age, but the majority are from the Dutch period and probably date to the eighteenth century.[35] There is a single sherd of a Japanese export porcelain dish or plate, which could date to the seventeenth or early eighteenth century. As with other varieties of ceramic, the Elmina Chinese porcelain includes pieces of varied quality and form. The vessels represented include blue decorated saucers, bowls, and ginger jars with simple patterns. However, a single sherd with polychrome decoration in the Imari style and blue decorated pieces with chocolate brown Batavian-glazed exteriors were also found. The latter include an intact saucer with the distinctive chocolate brown Batavian glaze on the exterior, which was excavated from a burial dating to the first half of the eighteenth century (Figure 5.5). A few sherds of Chinese coarse porcelain ginger jars were found in nineteenth-century contexts, but no examples of the gray-paste "Canton" porcelains occur.[36]

The most common imported ceramics of the seventeenth and eighteenth centuries are Rhenish gray stonewares, particularly jugs (*Krüge*). Several reconstructible examples were found in association with burials, and their preponderance may indicate that they were held in particular esteem. Examples of these ceramics have also been recovered from other parts of the coast. They are among the most common European ceramics noted during survey of the Eguafo. The ritual importance of Rhenish stoneware jugs has been noted in other parts of West Africa, particularly the Baule area in the Ivory Coast, where they are frequently found in family treasures (Meurer 1974).[37]

The nineteenth-century ceramic assemblage is different from those of preceding periods. A larger amount and a greater consistency in the forms, varieties, and decorations are represented. There are bowls, cups, mugs, chamber pots, and clearly utilitarian, functional forms represented in whitewares, yellowwares, and stonewares.[38] The assemblage is dominated by whitewares decorated with hand-painted, thick-line floral patterns, colorful bands, and brightly colored sponged decorations. The last type includes a wide variety of cut-sponge-stamped decorations, a technique that became common after about 1845 (Fleming 1923:59, 195; Robacker and Robacker 1978:122). Although many vessel forms are represented, bowls are by far the most common. Ceramics with similar decorations have a wide distribution in Africa. They occur on sites in the Sierra Leone interior and on nineteenth-century sites in South Africa (DeCorse 1980; P. Jeppson, conversation, 1989). In contrast, they appear with less frequency in North American and European sites. Some of these ceramics clearly represent factory overstock, including such novelties as plates com-

0   5
C M

Figure 5.5. An eighteenth-century Chinese porcelain saucer with hand-painted cobalt blue decoration and Batavian glazed exterior. (Photograph by Christopher R. DeCorse)

memorating Greek monarchs. However, the assemblage is more indicative of the tailoring of European manufactures for the African market and the creation of specialized export wares.

Sourcing of these ceramics is difficult. Manufacturer marks are present on only nine pieces of nineteenth-century whiteware. Somewhat surprisingly, all of the marks are English. Aside from a single undecorated piece, the marks are from transfer-printed vessels dating to the middle of the century. The hundreds of pieces of hand-painted and sponge-decorated sherds are unmarked. The output of British and Continental factories was no doubt very similar, and unmarked wares may be impossible to separate. The majority may be British, an indication of the ascendancy of the Staffordshire potteries. However, given the Dutch presence at Elmina, it is reasonable to presume that at least some of the vessels are products of Dutch or Continental factories. Some twentieth-century hand-painted vessels bearing the mark "Societe Ceramique Maestricht Holland" are indistinguishable from unmarked examples from Elmina.

The preceding discussion assumes that most of the ceramics were produced in British or Continental centers. This conclusion is lent only minor support by the exclusion of any American firms from among the few makers' marks. In fact, American ceramic manufacturers of stoneware, buff-paste earthenware, and refined white earthenwares were established during the second half of the nineteenth century. Sponge-decorated pieces comparable to examples from Elmina were also produced in the United States.[39] Because American production did not fully expand until the last decades of the nineteenth century, it is unlikely that American ceramics were reaching West Africa in large quantities prior to Elmina's destruction. However, in light of the absence of marks, the paucity of detailed trade records, and the volume of the American trade at Elmina, an American provenance for some of the ceramics cannot be ruled out.

Nineteenth-century ceramics represented also include a diversity of utilitarian stonewares such as crocks, jugs, and ink bottles. Most common of these ceramics are cylindrical stoneware bottles with small lug handles connecting the abrupt shoulders and short necks. The paste varies from buff yellow to gray, but the majority is a reddish brown. Vessels of this type have a long ancestry in the Rhineland, where they were frequently used as containers for mineral water and sometimes for gin (see Wittop Koning 1976, 1978; Nienhaus 1981).[40] Because of their convenient size and shape, they likely saw a great deal of reuse in Africa. A number of the pieces from Elmina are marked, the only identifiable examples being nineteenth-century emblems from various factories in the duchy of Nassau, Germany.

Cobalt blue decorated gray stonewares produced in the Westerwald district after 1800 are also well represented in the Elmina assemblage. Many of the older factories had closed by this time, and the remaining output was of inferior quality compared with the products of the preceding centuries (Noël Hume 1967). The Westerwald was incorporated into the duchy of Nassau in 1803, and for this reason the later products are sometimes called Nassau ware. At Elmina, pieces of crocks, jars, and occasional mugs were found widely distributed in 1873 debris. These are crudely incised and decorated with quasi-floral motifs.

GLASS

The Elmina trade manifests include numerous references to wine and spirits, and it is likely that the majority of the 14,000 glass fragments from Elmina are from bottles used for shipping these commodities between the seventeenth and nineteenth centuries. Glass was, of course, used for shipping other things, and even the so-called Dutch gin bottles were not necessarily used for gin. For example, oils, syrups, toilet waters, olives, capers, anchovies, and tuna were shipped in bottles during the seventeenth and eighteenth centuries (McNulty 1971:100). However, the prevalence of references to wine and spirits on Gold Coast trade lists makes their use for wine and spirits more likely. The majority were probably imported for trade with the African population, though some of the late nineteenth-century bottle glass recovered probably includes material from the European garrison.[41]

Wine was the predominant beverage imported during the Portuguese period. In the early sixteenth century, Pereira (1967:121) stated that Africans preferred European wine to the local palm wine (also see Vogt 1979:71; Blake 1942:105). During the seventeenth, eighteenth, and nineteenth centuries, gin, rum, and brandy were commonly offered, as well as some wine (Bennett and Brooks 1965:26, 33, 38, 275; Bosman 1967:107, 403; de Marees 1987:41; Müller in Jones 1983:213; van Dantzig 1978:265). Throughout the Fante coastland, Dutch gin remains important both for consumption and for pouring libations or for offerings during rituals. It was not, however, available or widely popular until the seventeenth and eighteenth centuries.[42] Gin—the Dutch *geneva*—or similar drinks were produced earlier, but it was not until the seventeenth and eighteenth centuries that gin became widely available and not until the nineteenth century that production really burgeoned. Throughout much of the seventeenth century brandy, especially French brandy, was the preferred spirit on the Gold Coast.[43] Gin and rum became more popular in the eighteenth century.[44] These imported spirits were used for libations, as welcoming drinks, and as an aperitif in much the way gin is used today. They replaced the use of indigenously brewed millet beers (*pito*), which have relatively low alcohol content.[45]

Early records give little indication of the specific types of containers used in shipping. Some liquor clearly arrived in casks, jugs, and barrels, and this method of shipping was most common throughout the Portuguese period.[46] Even in Europe, bottles did not come into general use for the storage of wine until the eighteenth century. Wine was stored in casks and then decanted into large four-sided bottles for serving (McNulty 1971:99; Noël Hume 1969:62–69), a practice that was likely also at times followed at Elmina. Examples of these types of bottles are represented in the Elmina glass, including an intact specimen dating to the early eighteenth century.[47] In all cases, the bottles lack the pewter caps noted on many European examples. Also represented in the archaeological collection are the brass spigots that were used for dispensing liquor from casks and barrels.

Increasing glass production made the use of glass containers more common beginning in the seventeenth century. The majority (over 75 percent by count) of the archaeological glass from pre-1873 contexts consists of green or olive

Figure 5.6. Case bottle seals from Elmina. The "star" seal (*right*), used in the nineteenth century by the J. H. Henkes Company, was purportedly a brand that became very popular in the Africa trade. Also represented is the *AVDE* seal (*left*) of A. van den Eelaard, the director of a Schiedam distillery between 1851 and 1878. (Photographs by Christopher R. DeCorse)

green sherds from wine, liquor, and case bottles. Although fragmentary and not always diagnostic, most of the sherds were probably from eighteenth- or nineteenth-century bottles produced using various contact molds, including dip molds, two- and three-piece molds, and turn molds. There are, however, also examples of the distinctive free-blown, onion-shaped wine bottles characteristic of the late seventeenth and early eighteenth centuries.

The majority of the bottle glass from Elmina is most likely European and probably Dutch, but positive identification is difficult.[48] Only five or six dozen pieces of bottle glass had embossed marks or carried seals. Many of these were incomplete, and many could not be identified. English, French, Dutch, and American manufacturers are represented (Figure 5.6). The most common marks are seals from the shoulders of case bottles. Identifiable marks include those of the J. H. Henkes Company, founded in the 1820s, which remains one of the more common imported brands of schnapps in Ghana. The company used several distinctive marks including a stork with a worm, a cornflower, and a star. The last occurred without the Henkes name and was purportedly a brand that became very popular in the Africa trade (Peter Vermeulen, correspondence, August 4, 1999). Also represented is the *AVDE* monogram of A. van den Eelaard, the director of a Schiedam distillery between 1851 and 1878.[49] Other marks, postdating 1873, may be British.[50] As noted above, some gin was also likely shipped in distinctive stoneware bottles.

Stylistically most of the wine bottles appear to be of Dutch or Continental origin, including some that could have been associated with the Dutch wine industry in South Africa. That industry was well established by the late seventeenth century, and it would not be surprising if some of its wine was traded at Elmina.[51] Constantia wine was widely exported, and specially embossed bottles were being manufactured by the middle of the seventeenth century. Other liquor and wine bottles are clearly British in form, many postdating 1873. Some are, however, earlier and have forms and finishes typical of eighteenth-century English glass. American glass manufacture also became more established during the second half of the nineteenth century, but a substantial quantity may not have been exported to West Africa before 1873. The notable exceptions are Perry Davis Vegetable Painkiller bottles, probably dating to the mid-nineteenth century. Also absent, or at least unidentified, in the Elmina assemblage is Portuguese glass. The extent and range of output from early Portuguese glass factories is poorly documented. Examples of well-dated Portuguese glass studied are nineteenth-century and have no clear parallels in the Elmina collection.

Aside from wine and spirit bottles, other glass vessel forms are more diverse and occur with far less regularity. They include 31 varieties of pharmaceutical bottles; 8 categories of glassware; 2 types of inkwells; 9 closure types; plate glass; and several other miscellaneous bottle forms. Pharmaceutical vials predominate in pre-1800 forms. Nineteenth-century vessels are more diverse, including a variety of toiletry and medicine bottles, flasks, storage bottles, Vaseline or pomade containers, pickle jars, beer bottles, and soda water bottles in the distinctive "torpedo" shape. Many of these forms are represented only in the post-1873 fill deposits that cover the site and, thus, may be associated with the British garrison.

Bottles can be readily reused, and regardless of their original contents they undoubtedly served secondary functions as containers for palm oil, shea butter, *pito,* or other products. Nineteenth-century glass bottles being reused in this manner can still occasionally be seen in West African markets.[52] There is some evidence for the reuse of glass at Elmina. A cache of nineteenth-century bottles of various forms was recovered from the corner of a structure at Locus F in an 1873 floor context. The empty bottles had been packed upright in the corner of a room, possibly for sale or reuse. A clear example of reuse is also illustrated by a Dutch case bottle recovered from a room in the Locus B structure. The bottle was found within a local water pot in the corner of a room, probably having been placed there to keep the contents cool. The bottle contained wood chips, typically associated with "bitters," a mixture of alcohol flavored with herbs, still produced locally.

A small collection of 200 glassware fragments—tumblers, shot glasses, stemware, bowls, and carafes—was recovered. Glassware is almost unmentioned in documentary sources, though there are occasional references and at least one noting glassware as an item that "must be on board" to pursue the African trade to advantage (Bennett and Brooks 1965:42).[53] Some of the archaeological glass could have been discarded from Elmina Castle and then reused by the African population, perhaps in different functional contexts. For example, Garrard (1980a:178) illustrates a wine glass stem of probable seventeenth-century manufacture in a collection of gold weights from Bondakile, Ghana. As indicated by Gramberg's observations, however, there was some demand for glassware among the African population.

The majority of glassware (over two-thirds) consists of tumbler and stemware fragments of mostly eighteenth- through nineteenth-century age,

Figure 5.7. Excavations at Elmina produced a variety of glassware fragments including the examples of stemware shown here. The glass at the left has a single, elongated teardrop. The two center glasses have cut facets. All were recovered from nineteenth-century contexts. Examples of glasses with air twist stems, as well as a variety of tumblers, decanters, and glassware, were also found. (Illustration by Christopher R. DeCorse)

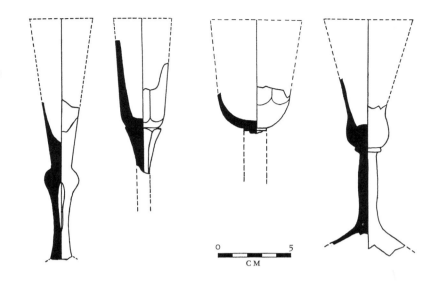

the stemware accounting for about half the number of examples as the tumblers. A few pieces of potentially earlier age are represented. In contrast with the demand for ceramics, a dramatic increase in the local demand for glassware does not appear to have characterized the nineteenth century, as indicated by both documentary sources and the archaeological record. An increased diversity of forms is represented, but there is not a significantly greater quantity of glassware from nineteenth-century deposits (Figure 5.7). Glassware is, as yet, unreported from other Central Region African sites prior to late nineteenth- or twentieth-century contexts.

The tumblers are, for the most part, undecorated with simple tapered bodies. The fragmentary sherds cannot be reconstructed, but at least some of the eighteenth-century examples are free blown with pontil-marked bases, comparable to dated examples of the late eighteenth and early nineteenth centuries from Britain, Europe, and the Americas (see, e.g., Noël Hume 1969:24; O. Jones 1985:35).[54] The decorated examples of tumblers and shot glasses mostly date to the nineteenth century and may, in fact, postdate the town's destruction. They are press molded with tapered sides, the decoration consisting of vertical lines and, in some instances, a star pattern on the base.

The stemware is highly variable in terms of form and decoration. It is of note that stemware, though socially and aesthetically superior to tumblers, was not necessarily much more costly.[55] A diversity of forms were produced in Europe during the seventeenth through the nineteenth centuries. Many were associated with particular wines or liquors, but the lack of contemporary illustration makes the identification of specific forms impossible (O. Jones 1985:38–39). There is, in any case, no reason to suppose that stemware was necessarily used in comparable ways on the Gold Coast. The Elmina stemware is difficult to source and date stylistically on the basis of the fragmentary pieces recovered, and more work needs to be done. The archaeological assemblage includes pieces of good-quality glass decorated with cut flutes, knops, air-twist stems, and bubbles of air within the stem, which are comparable to English products of the eighteenth century (e.g., Bickerton 1986; cf. Ffooks 1969). Yet, Continental sources, particularly Holland or Belgium, cannot be ruled out. There are others, however, that may represent Bohemian products of the mid-nineteenth century. These are lighter soda glass and lack ornamentation aside from single-knop stems.

The relative paucity of glassware leads to the question of what containers were used for drinking. Calabashes, gourds, and ceramic vessels could have been used. These containers would have been complemented by copper, brass, and pewter imports. Unfortunately, these categories of artifacts are poorly represented archaeologically. Some small ceramic vessels are represented, but they are in relatively small numbers.

TOBACCO PIPES AND SMOKING

Tobacco is an American cultigen that was likely introduced to coastal Ghana by the Portuguese.[56] Although there is evidence for the use of pipes and the smoking of *Datura* and hemp prior to European contact in other portions of Africa, no such evidence exists for coastal Ghana. Both indirect documentary information and archaeological information point to an introduction of tobacco smoking in the early seventeenth century, and, hence, both locally produced and imported pipes found archaeologically date to that period or later. Hemmersam's description (circa 1639–45; in Jones 1983:117, 244, 255) is particularly important because it indicates that tobacco was already widely accessible just two years after the Dutch takeover. Regardless of the ultimate source of introduction to coastal Ghana—whether through the European coastal trade or through traders moving south from the West African Sahel—the use of tobacco was probably known at Elmina during the Portuguese period (pre-1637). The word *kaschot,* which Hemmersam (in Jones 1983:117) used for locally made pipes, may have a Portuguese etymology (cf. Walker 1973). It is doubtful that tobacco was introduced prior to 1600, because it is not mentioned by de Marees in 1602 or by any earlier writer, nor are there sixteenth-century references to tobacco from other parts of the West African coast. This would place the timing of the introduction to Elmina and vicinity during the first decades of the seventeenth century, a date consistent with other parts of the West African coast: Sierra Leone, circa 1607; Senegambia, 1620; Congo, 1612; and Accra, 1640. Significantly, there is an earlier date—1594, from Timbuktu—in the West African Sahel.

A Portuguese-period introduction is lent further support by pipes from pre-1637 archaeological contexts. A total of almost 4,000 European pipe fragments of seventeenth- to nineteenth-century age were recovered from Elmina. European tobacco pipes are important, for their bowl forms, manufacturers' marks, stem diameters, and stem-bore diameters have all been shown to be useful chronological indicators (Figure 5.8) (Atkinson and Oswald 1972; Harrington 1954; Oswald 1975; Walker 1977). Several can be dated to early seventeenth-century Portuguese contexts on the basis of bore diameters, decoration, and stratigraphic

Figure 5.8. European white clay tobacco pipes. The nineteenth-century pipe at the upper left shows use wear or secondary modification at the end of the stem. All of the other pipes display typical Dutch marks of the eighteenth century. (Illustration by Christopher R. DeCorse)

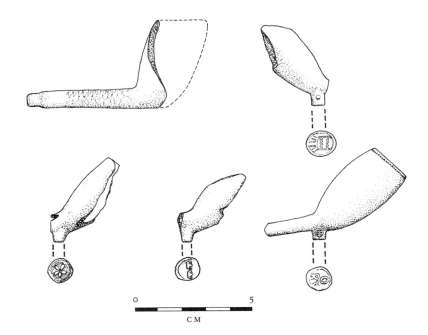

context. All are stem fragments, and most lack any kind of adornment. The few decorations are limited to rouletted, denticulate lines around the stem and fleur-de-lis stamps. The latter appeared in the second quarter of the seventeenth century and remained popular until after 1700 (Noël Hume 1978:305; Potgieter and Abrahams 1984:45). In addition to their presence at Elmina, European pipes securely dated to the seventeenth century have been identified only at nearby Asebu (Nunoo 1957:17; Walker 1975:184). Seventeenth-century pipes from other sites are typically examples of locally produced forms.

The majority of the Elmina pipes are likely Dutch manufactures. In this context it is useful to point out that a Portuguese-period introduction of tobacco to Elmina does not preclude the presence of tobacco in the trade inventories of the earliest Dutch merchants to reach the coast. The Dutch pipe industry was founded by English craftsmen who fled to Holland during the first two decades of the seventeenth century. By 1641, the trade was flourishing, and Gouda makers dominated the market. It is of note that this growth of the pipe-making industry conveniently corresponded with the Dutch expansion in West Africa. Pipes, and possibly tobacco, were very likely among the first products offered for sale at the newly established Dutch outposts on the Gold Coast. By 1640 there were Dutch forts and trading lodges at Elmina, Mori, Anomabu, and Shama, and lodges were established at Axim, Sekondi, and Accra during the following decade.

It is, perhaps, more than coincidental that Dutch pipes dominate the assemblages of eighteenth-century imported pipes found throughout coastal Ghana.[57] The majority of pre-1873 makers' marks present on pipes recovered at Elmina are Dutch. These include over 80 different manufacturer marks.[58] Many of the pipes bear the shield of Gouda on the sides of the foot frequently used on Dutch pipes after 1740. The bowl shapes, surface finish, and stem decorations are also indicative of a Dutch origin.

British marks predating 1873 include a *TD* mark similar to eighteenth-century examples from North America and two nineteenth-century stems with names stamped parallel to the bore (Walker 1966, 1975:183). It seems likely that the majority of pipes reaching Elmina prior to the nineteenth century were Dutch. However, after 1800 an increasing number of pipes were left unmarked, and attribution is more difficult. During this period Continental, British, and American bowls also became more similar in form in the later part of the century, adding to the difficulty in distinguishing their origins. The decline of the Gouda pipe industry may have left the market open for the manufactures of other countries, and a larger proportion of non-Dutch pipes may be present in the nineteenth-century collections (Calvocoressi 1975a:195). Certainly by the end of the century the situation had dramatically changed. British marks predominate in collections at Elmina as well as in other parts of British West Africa, dating to the late nineteenth and twentieth centuries. A similar prevalence of French pipes is found on sites of similar age in Francophone West Africa, such as Senegal. These imports included pipes specifically produced for the African trade; they contained the names of trading firms on the coast and involved specific forms, such as elbow-bend, socket-stem pipes, duplicating African styles.[59]

Bowls and bowl fragments are typically far less common than stem fragments in archaeological contexts, and this pattern is consistent with the pipe assemblage from Elmina. Work by Harrington and others on English pipes in the Americas demonstrated that stem-bore diameters progressively decreased in a regular, patterned manner and could be used as a dating tool. Stem-bore-diameter dating has subsequently proven particularly useful on eighteenth-century Anglo-American sites. Unfortunately, the majority of the Elmina pipes are Dutch, and the mean bore diameters of these pipes are more variable over time. Harrington (1954) specifically excluded Dutch pipes in his seminal study of bore diameters, and stem-bore dating has proven impractical in applications at Dutch sites. In well-dated eighteenth-century archaeological contexts, they have been shown to yield erroneous dates when compared with English pipes from the same deposits (Walker 1965).[60]

The bores of the Elmina pipes, measured using both $\frac{4}{64}$-inch to $\frac{9}{64}$-inch drill bits and metric drill bits of 1.5, 1.7, 2.0, 2.2, 2.5, 2.7, 3.0, 3.2, and 3.5 mm, were of little use in dating deposits. Problems in assessing the validity of age attributions on the basis of bore-diameter measurements were further complicated by the large amount of fill at Elmina, which often combined pipes of potentially different ages. In addition, the sample of pipe stems from individual stratigraphic contexts was too small to make any meaningful evaluations.[61]

Several accounts describe local tobacco pipes in the central Gold Coast. Hemmersam refers to bowls that were "so big that half one's hand goes in when one puts in tobacco. The stems are the length of an arm" (in Jones 1983:117). Similarly, another source described pipes with bowls "the size of a fist" (Müller in

Jones 1983:244), and another reported that the African pipes had stone or earthen bowls so large "they cram in two or three handfuls of Tobacco" (Bosman 1967:306). Despite these references to what are clearly non-European pipes, there is little evidence for local pipe production in the Elmina area. The introduction of tobacco at Elmina may have been characterized by an early reliance on imported pipes.

Locally produced tobacco pipes have a wide distribution in West Africa (e.g., Daget and Ligers 1962; Philips 1983; Shaw 1960; Shinnie and Kense 1989:145–170). They were generally made of fired clay with a female socket to receive a long reed stem. Ceramic production within the Akan area is predominantly a female activity, but the making of figurative pipes is restricted to men (Rattray 1959:301). Local pipes have been widely reported in Ghana. Surveying 1,500 examples from Accra and Shai, Paul Ozanne (1962, 1964b) developed a typology ranging from circa 1640 to 1750. This has proven useful in ordering pipes from other sites in Ghana. It is, however, helpful to keep in mind that the typology was initially based on surface material from a relatively restricted area of southern Ghana, and comparison with areas farther afield should be made with caution. Examples of local pipes from Accra and Shai are larger than European tobacco pipes of the seventeenth and eighteenth centuries but are not so large as to cover "half one's hand." It is possible that some early European writers were describing pipes that cannot be directly integrated into Ozanne's typology.

The dozen examples of local pipes recovered archaeologically at Elmina vary substantially in form, decoration, and manufacturing technique and hence may represent several different sources. The closest parallels can be found in a collection from the Akan hinterland and more northern areas. Two of the Elmina pipe fragments were found in the nineteenth-century rubble fill containing artifacts of seventeenth- through nineteenth-century age. Given the poor context of these two finds and their fragmentary nature, their age(s) and place(s) of manufacture are uncertain. One of the pipes is represented by a bowl fragment too small to equate with a specific form. The other is probably the worn base of an Ozanne "Group" or "Type" 2. Ozanne notes these as having a wide distribution in Ghana, with finds from the Northern and Western regions in addition to Accra and Shai. In his typology of the last two areas, Ozanne places the appearance of Type 2a at circa 1655–60 and that of Type 2b before 1677. Type 2b is characterized by a loop between the bowl and the stem and "is typical of coastal areas [of Ghana], occurring as far west as Essiama" (Ozanne 1962:54), a settlement located approximately 100 km (62 miles) west of Elmina.

Fragments of two other pipes were recovered from earlier contexts. One was partly reconstructed from several fragments. It was associated with a burial probably dating between 1740 and 1750.[62] The base, which has proven a useful typological feature, is unfortunately missing. The decoration, size, and general form of the reconstructed pipe suggest that it falls within the same tradition as Ozanne's Northern Type 2a. This attribution is further suggested by the paste and the thick, blood-red slip that covers the exterior (Ozanne 1964b:28; see also Shinnie and Ozanne 1962:94–98).

Figure 5.9. African tobacco pipe in the shape of a snail from an 1873 floor context (shown slightly reduced; object's maximum length is 5.9 cm [2.35 inches]). The style closely parallels pipes produced in Asante during the nineteenth century. (Illustration courtesy of Christopher R. DeCorse)

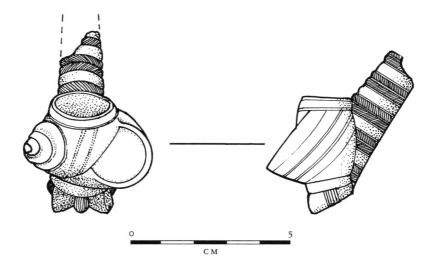

Another pipe, represented by a single burnt bowl sherd, was found in an unstratified fill layer containing European ceramics of the seventeenth and eighteenth centuries. The most recent artifact in the deposit was a single piece of blue transfer-printed pearlware manufactured between 1790 and 1840. The fragment indicates a very thick-walled (6.5 mm [0.25 inch]) and large bowl. A few stem and bowl fragments of similar thickness were noted in surface-collected material from other coastal sites.[63] These sherds may represent earlier forms that might well have been able to hold "two or three" handfuls of tobacco.

The most interesting pipe excavated was found on the floor of a structure destroyed in 1873.[64] The bowl forms a careful representation of a snail shell (Figure 5.9). The bowl is not perfectly circular, the axis perpendicular to the stem measuring slightly greater in length. The pipe has a gray paste with a dark gray-black surface. Its general dimensions are similar to examples of Ozanne's Type 3 pipes, which appeared in Accra between 1688 and 1697 (Ozanne 1964b:31–32; see also Davies 1955:Figure 27; Ozanne 1962:57). The incised decoration and quatrefoil basal spurs are also stylistically similar. Ozanne further recorded the prevalence of Type 3 pipes on eighteenth- and nineteenth-century sites in the Asante region and noted similar forms from as far afield as Mali. Figurative pipes, such as the Elmina snail pipe, may have appeared as variants within this group during the late eighteenth or early nineteenth century. Pipes with a variety of human and animal forms are known from West Africa, but again the closest parallels to the Elmina pipe are from the Asante region (Rohrer 1947:Plates 2, 4; Valentin 1976). Other examples have not been recovered from stratigraphic contexts, and the earliest documentary references date to the nineteenth century (Bowdich 1966; Freeman 1898:114, 123–124). The Elmina pipe is almost identical to examples collected ethnographically in the Asante region. The origin of the latter may therefore also have been away from the coast in the same center of production.

FIREARMS

The first Europeans to arrive in West Africa carried firearms. Matchlocks, along with examples of helms and breastplates, can be seen on representations of sixteenth-century Portuguese soldiers on Benin brasses (see, e.g., Ben-Amos 1980:26). Guns may also have reached the West African Sahel via the trans-Saharan trade during the fifteenth century, and it has been suggested that they played a key role in the ascendancy of some West African states.[65] The importance of firearms in the expansion of coastal and forest states such as Asante and their impact on various other aspects of African history have received extensive attention from historians. On the Gold Coast, Africans' first major use of firearms in a conflict may have been when the Etsi invaded Asebu in 1629 (Kea 1971:189).[66] Firearms have, however, not been well reported in archaeological contexts. A side plate of a percussion or flintlock rifle found at Efutu and a goose-necked cock from excavations at Bui are two of the few examples of gun parts recovered archaeologically in Ghana.[67]

At Elmina, African access to firearms may have been limited prior to the late sixteenth century. The Portuguese garrison at Elmina did maintain an armory of *arcabuses*, as well as crossbows, suits of armor, lances, and halberds (de Marees 1987:220; Vogt 1979:331, 125). The papal ban on the trading of firearms to non-Christians was lifted in 1481 to allow the Portuguese to offer them to African allies. However, although weapons were issued to African allies of the Portuguese in case of attack, there is no indication of the use or trade in firearms prior to the sixteenth century.[68] In any case, these early weapons were not very efficient, and the damp climate and poor storage facilities on the West African coast probably rendered them even less useful.[69] The crossbow, in fact, remained the primary personal armament of the Europeans at Elmina until the sixteenth century, when it was supplemented by the smooth-bore musket. Even so, crossbows and half-pikes remained an integral part of the European armory in West Africa until the early seventeenth century (Hemmersam in Jones 1983:132; Vogt 1979:45, 155–157, 192). Helmets, javelins, swords, shields, spears, and iron-tipped arrows also continued in African use until the end of the century (Brun in Jones 1983:92; de Marees 1987:88–93; Kea 1982:157; Müller in Jones 1983:193–197). At the time of the Dutch takeover in 1637, the Portuguese were forced to abandon a mixed assortment of crossbows, pikes, axes, and personal weaponry, as well as 10 casks of musket balls and 300 packages of gunflints (Vogt 1979:192).

If trade in firearms had been limited, it burgeoned during the seventeenth century. De Marees, writing in 1602, noted: "They [the Africans] also buy many firelocks and are beginning to learn to handle them very well" (1987:92, see also 220). The trade in firearms might not, however, have really expanded until the second half of the century. Trade lists in a mid-seventeenth-century manuscript present a conspicuous absence of firearms (Jones 1995:16; see also Daaku 1970:149–150; Kea 1971:189).[70] This may reflect a Dutch ban on the sale of firearms between the 1610s and the 1650s. Local demand, increasing competition, and interloper trade contributed to the growth in the trade of firearms. By the mid-seventeenth century on, they were widely available, and there is no question that European traders of the seventeenth, eighteenth, and nineteenth centuries maintained an extensive trade. Guns, powder, bullet lead, and flints all figure prominently in European trade lists (e.g., Bosman 1967:184–185; A. Jones 1985:115; Kea 1982:207–208; Müller in Jones 1983:193; van Dantzig 1978:82, 264–265).[71] It has been estimated that 20,000 firearms a year were being brought to the West African coast by the beginning of the eighteenth century (Alpern 1995:19).

The firearms traded on the West African coast were typically of poor quality or antiquated, and documentary sources frequently refer to demand for new as well as *old* firearms. This had important consequences, given rapid innovation in European firearm technology. In Europe, more efficient firing mechanisms, including the wheel lock and snaphance, appeared in the first half of the sixteenth century, and the flintlock, which set the pattern of weapons until after 1800, appeared in the early seventeenth century. With the advent of the flintlock and the corresponding industrial capability for inexpensive mass production, firearms became both more efficient and affordable. These improved mechanisms quickly replaced the less efficient matchlock. The "French-lock," developed in the early seventeenth century, was in general use by most of the Western world by the end of the century (Wilkinson 1977:50). Later, in the early nineteenth century, a variety of percussion-firing weapons were developed, and they quickly replaced the flintlock throughout Europe.

Innovations in European firearm technology were not reflected in the firearms available in West Africa. Matchlocks were still in use until the 1670s (Müller in Jones 1983:193), and flintlocks were still in widespread use at the time of Elmina's destruction.[72] A British military report of June 18, 1873, states that arms captured from the Asante outside Elmina were "old flint-lock muskets," at least one of which had a Tower of London proof mark (*British Parliamentary Papers* 1970a:454; see also Allen 1874:51–52). During the late nineteenth and early twentieth centuries, colonial governments restricted the use of firearms. As a result, percussion caps were not widely adopted in some areas until the 1940s. West Africa remained a major consumer of gunflints produced in Brandon, England, until the 1960s (Seymour de Lotbiniere, conversation, September 12, 1984). Lock mechanisms made by West African blacksmiths during the present century differ little from flintlock and percussion cap patterns of the eighteenth century. Local African blacksmiths probably made some parts to effect repairs during the earliest years of the firearm trade, but the manufacture of complete weapons likely began far more recently because barrels could not be fabricated locally.[73] Production of percussion cap and flintlock guns, locally made using imported pipe, probably did not begin until the present century.

The Elmina excavation provided some indication of the firearms in use until 1873. The only relatively complete weapon recovered archaeologically was a brass-barreled pistol found on the floor of a building destroyed in 1873 (Figure 5.10). The weapon was certainly "old-fashioned" by the late nineteenth century. The incising of the brass hardware gives the gun an Arabesque appearance, but it is more likely a trade piece produced in southern Europe. It is eighteenth-century in style with a faceted brass barrel and engraved fittings. These parts

Figure 5.10. Parts of a brass-barreled pistol recovered from an 1873 floor at Locus B. The image in the lower left is a radiograph of the iron firing mechanism. (Radiograph reproduced courtesy of Daniel Ball; illustrations by Christopher R. DeCorse)

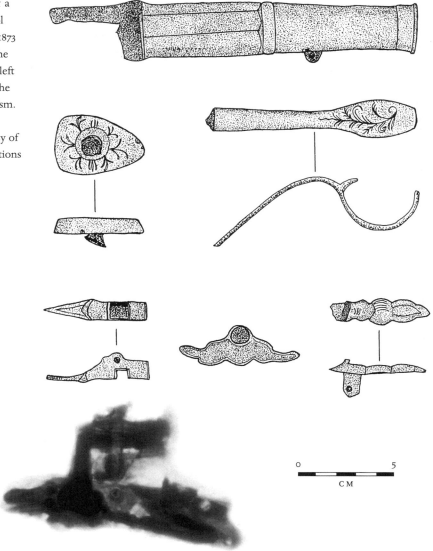

and a radiograph of the firing mechanism show it to be comparable in style to Spanish pieces of the second half of the eighteenth century (see Wilkinson 1977:53).

More common in the excavated material were examples of brass hardware from European muskets. These include 6 butt plates, 13 ram pipes, and 1 side plate. All were recovered from nineteenth-century contexts. Ram pipes held the ramrod used with muzzle-loading guns. Such brass fittings would have been standard accouterments on trade pieces (see, e.g., Hamilton 1980). None was found in association with other gun parts. These items provide poor indication of the trade in firearms. In fact, they may have equally served in a functional context not envisioned by their manufacturers: a variety of brass furniture from firearms can be seen in gold weight collections (see Garrard 1983b).

Figure 5.11. Firearm-related artifacts: (*a*) French, English, and Belgian gunflints; (*b*) brass ram pipes; (*c*) drawn and coiled brass .450 Martini-Henry cartridges; (*d*) iron bullet mold. (Illustration by Christopher R. Decorse)

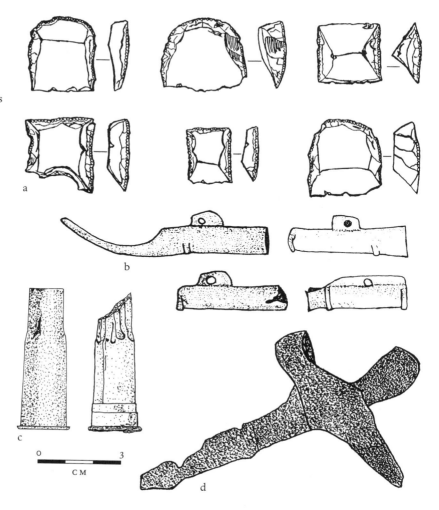

The most ubiquitous type of find associated with the use of firearms was gunflints, and these are not necessarily related to the use of firearms all at. Firing wears flints down rapidly, and they could generally be used only 30–40 times before misfires became more likely and a replacement was needed (Wilkinson 1977:57).[74] Elmina flints show hard use, with some worn down to a third or even a fourth of their original size. The majority have distinctive battered edges or a distinctive **U**-shaped wear pattern, indicating use or reuse as strike-a-lights. This activity may have been the primary use of imported gunflints. Gunflints are useful indicators of source and time period, for various innovations in the method of manufacture were introduced. Several different types of flints were recovered, reflecting the sources used by the Dutch. The Netherlands possessed no indigenous industry and so was dependent on foreign sources (see de Lotbiniere 1980:62; 1984).[75] The one exception is the brief Dutch occupation of Belgium and the flint sources around Mons in the early nineteenth century.

Over 100 flints were found at Elmina, all associated with the Dutch or British periods of occupation (Figure 5.11). They include 29 French and 63 English. All those that are complete enough to determine their original form are indicative of the more formalized flints that replaced earlier, less systematic cottage-production flints beginning in the second half of the seventeenth century.[76]

The remaining three flints may be Dutch products from Mons, Belgium (Figure 5.11). The history of this industry has not been well documented, and it appears to have been of limited importance compared with the French and English traditions. There do not appear to be any examples reported from any other African sites or from sites in North America. The examples from Elmina are in excellent condition. They were all recovered from 1873 rubble and so could date to the period of the Dutch occupation of Belgium. In form they are similar to the French platform, exhibiting a rounding of one edge. The Belgian examples, however, are thicker and more crudely executed (de Lotbiniere 1984:208–209). They also are made from the speckled-gray Spiennes flint, not the more honey-colored French flint or the gray-black of the English pieces.

No examples of locally produced flints were found in the Elmina excavations or located in other archaeological sites in Ghana. However, local flints can be purchased in northern Ghana, particularly the area around Nalierigu. The flints are crudely formed out of a variety of lithic sources, including light gray or yellow cherts. They approximate European flints in form and size, but the flaking technique is very irregular. These local flints continued to be used as strike-a-lights until recent times and have been noted for sale with strike-a-lights. The history of these industries is unknown. They may have developed, or at least experienced a resurgence, as a result of declining European flint imports during the twentieth century.[77]

Few pieces of lead shot were found in excavations. Lead appears on trade manifests as early as 1540 and is commonly listed in later accounts (Bennett and Brooks 1965:41; Meredith 1967:69; van Dantzig 1978:77). In the early seventeenth century, de Marees (1987:106) noted that lead sheathing was often stolen from ships. It is likely, especially in the earlier cases, that some of this was used to make net weights, melted down by smiths, or used for other purposes. However, the presence of two bullet molds at Elmina indicates that at least some shot was being made at the site. Cast slugs may, in fact, provide only a partial indication of the ammunition used. Rather than depend on imported metal sources, Elimina residents probably found alternatives. Scrap metal, glass, and stone are still used for ammunition by hunters in parts of West Africa. These objects were probably also utilized in the past.

A wide variety of infinitely more efficient cartridge guns were developed during the second half of the nineteenth century and were quickly adopted by the European military, including regiments that served in West Africa. Collectively, however, they present a list of items *not* traded on the coast. The Martini-Henry rifle joined the Snider as an official firearm of the British military between 1871 and 1888. Different British military accounts of the defeat of an Asante force of between 2,000 and 3,000 outside Elmina on June 13, 1873, reported on the efficacy of the Snider (*British Parliamentary Papers* 1970a:453, 458). An estimated 200 Asante were killed, but only 2 British soldiers were killed and 7 wounded.

Examples of 577 Snider coiled-brass cartridges, as well as Snider shells crimped to fit the smaller 577–450 Martini-Henry, and later drawn-brass 577–450 cartridges were found in post-1873 destruction deposits.[78] The Martini-Henry rifle did not see overseas service until 1875, thus 577–450 cartridges used with these weapons would have to postdate 1875. However, the Gatling gun was in service during the Elmina conflict, and this also fired similar cartridges. Exploded pistol cartridges were also recovered. These were probably ammunition for Spencer or Remington sidearms, used by the British military (Logan 1959:70–72, 93, 144, 145). Almost without question, all of the cartridges recovered archaeologically were used by British troops and not the African population.

The European arsenal also included artillery pieces.[79] Throughout the Dutch period, Elmina Castle was regarded as one of the best-fortified places on the coast (see, e.g., Nathan 1904:15).[80] In 1802 the armament included 84 cannons, plus a number of mortars and howitzers. Brass guns were preferred because they withstood the climate better. Apparently the Dutch weapons were not in working condition, or at least not adapted to British ammunition, by 1873. In a report on Elmina's defenses following the bombardment, Captain Crease noted only 11 artillery pieces in serviceable condition at the castle.[81] Nevertheless, this limited arsenal included the most up-to-date breech-loading, rifled cannon, as well as one Gatling gun and "plenty" of nine-pound rockets. It was, however, noted that the last were without firing troughs. Guns at the out forts were mostly six-pounders. These were described as being "suitable for firing case shot with light charges, or a spherical shell, could they be obtained" (*British Parliamentary Papers* 1970b:360–361). During the bombardment of Elmina, these were supplemented by light guns in the boats from the British warships *Argus, Barracouta, Decoy, Druid,* and *Seagull,* which were anchored in the Benya Lagoon (*British Parliamentary Papers* 1970ba:457).

Cannon fuses, balls, and shell fragments (remnants of hollow projectiles that had been filled with gunpowder) were found in 1873 floor contexts and in debris dating to the town's destruction. During the bombardment, the British apparently relied on the more outmoded guns; all of the projectiles recovered are spherical. No evidence of Hale rockets was found, nor pieces from antipersonnel charges such as grapeshot, canister shot, and case shot (Dickey and George 1980:15–16), though it is possible that some of the small iron balls recovered were from the last. The projectiles are fairly concentrated in the center of the peninsula, particularly at Locus B.

IT IS THE WHITEMAN WHO SELLS SCISSORS . . .

The trade materials found at Elmina are an unambiguous indicator of the expansion of Europe into the non-Western world that began in the second half of the fifteenth century. Their presence and the precision with which many of these artifacts can be dated are a hallmark of the archaeological record of the past 500 years. Worldwide, ceramics, beads, metal goods, glass, and other materials represent a widespread and rapid expansion of culture contacts and interactions unparalleled in scope in preceding ages. It is possible to pick up identical sherds of nineteenth-century refined white-paste earthenware produced at the same Staffordshire pottery at such disparate locales as coastal Ghana, California, Jamaica, and India. This is a great benefit for archaeologists, who can use them to delineate contact spheres, trace expanding trade connections, and establish regional chronologies.

It is, however, more difficult to assess to what extent the European trade materials at Elmina are a measure of European influence on African epistemology and belief systems: the worldview of the Elmina people. Although archaeologists at times have equated particular artifacts or a specific artifact assemblage with ethnographically perceived cultures, such an interpretation is challenging and must be evaluated within individual historical, cultural, and archaeological contexts. The trade materials found at Elmina are not a trope for the European influence on Elmina culture, nor are they simply an expression of an Elmina cultural ideal. Rather, they are representative of all the complexities of contact, misunderstanding, reinterpretation, and economic structures that came together in the meeting of very different cultural groups.

6

CULTURE CONTACT, CONTINUITY, AND CHANGE

But the houses inhabited by natives in the service of the Europeans begin to show another appearance; one finds there are more paintings, the mirror tends to be bigger and often has a gilt frame. Here one finds a moderator-lamp, there is a tea-service, and in another house a curious collection of champagne, wine and beer glasses, or even a pile of old books. The master *uses* these things, the servant merely shows them off, for most of these articles cannot be used [by the servant]. Even if this phenomenon is caused by the mere urge to imitate, it does undeniably prove that we could, if we paid a little more attention to them and were more interested in their development, also cause them to imitate us in *moral respect.*

J. S. G. GRAMBERG,
Schetsen van Afrika's Westkust

❖

[Traditional societies] view themselves as primitive, for their ideal would be to remain in the state in which the gods or ancestors created them at the origin of time. Of course this is an illusion, and they can no more escape history than other societies."

CLAUDE LÉVI-STRAUSS, IN C. LÉVI-STRAUSS AND D. ERIBON, *Conversations with Claude Lévi-Strauss*

Gramberg's observations of nineteenth-century Elmina are illuminating. They inform us on the European attitude, which, by the late nineteenth century, was one of comfortable superiority. The comments are also interesting because of the inferences presented concerning material inventory and culture change.[1] To Gramberg, African use of imported trade goods was simply an imitation of European behavior and yet, perhaps, an avenue for changing their nonmaterial beliefs and epistemologies. As examined in the opening chapter, however, the implications of technological innovation and acceptance of trade materials in cross-cultural context are ambiguous. Trade lists and archaeological data of fifteenth-through nineteenth-century age document a dramatic increase in the amount and variety of imported goods that attest to the European Industrial Revolution and Elmina's inclusion in a world economy. There was also extensive change in subsistence strategies and in house construction, as well as in other classes of material culture that point to transformations in African patterns of consumption, behavior, and beliefs. Elmina, originally a small settlement subservient to neighboring states, emerged as an independent polity with concomitant changes in sociopolitical institutions. The society viewed at Elmina by Azambuja in 1482 was dramatically different from that witnessed by the British almost 400 years later. Despite the obvious role of the European trade in these changes, it is germane to examine how they were shaped by African objectives and beliefs, as opposed to European, and the ways in which the archaeological record may be representative of them. Externally induced transformations were internally orchestrated, and local conditions and concerns mitigated the contexts in which artifacts functioned. The data available indicate that the Elmina people exhibited a great deal of continuity with an African, largely Akan, cultural tradition.[2]

PERSPECTIVES OF CHANGE AND CONTINUITY

The historical context of the influences and consequences of African-European interactions is a critical consideration when examining the archaeological record of the past 500 years. Although European trade materials are comparatively limited in many post-fifteenth-century African sites of the Ghanaian coast and hinterland, there are nevertheless significant changes represented in other aspects of the archaeological record.[3] The timing and nature of these transformations suggest they are related to the advent of the Europeans on the coast and the subsequent changes that unfolded. Studies of local ceramics and settlement patterns from throughout southern Ghana have noted dramatic differences between assemblages dating after the later seventeenth century and those from earlier time periods. These observations were first noted on the basis of surface material from Accra and Shai but were later documented stratigraphically in other portions of the coast (Ozanne 1962, 1963, 1964a).[4] Data from Elmina and adjacent sites in the Central Region reflect similar transformations. The ceramics and settlement patterns seem to indicate a great deal of continuity from the early first millennium A.D. until the seventeenth century. Ceramics postdating this time period are different in style, form, and decorative inventory and may also represent different manufacturing methods. In addition, there is increasing evidence for urbanization and, indirectly, for the elaboration of sociopolitical complexity, as exemplified by Elmina but present in other areas as well.

The marked changes represented are indicative of transformations throughout the entire coast and hinterland. Although migration and limited population movement occurred, it is unlikely that the changes observed archaeologically represent complete depopulation or population replacement. The specific ethnic and sociopolitical affiliations of the early settlers of Elmina remain uncertain; the salient consideration, though, is the cultural similarity among the African populations represented and their cultural dissimilarity to Europeans. Linguistic studies and written accounts equally suggest that Akan speakers dominated the central Ghana coast at the end of the fifteenth century, and the distribution of ethnolinguistic groups remained much the same over the past 500 years. Rather than representing replacement populations, the changes in the archaeological record are representative of an ongoing system of change within an indigenous African population.[5] The rate or tempo of these changes is greater than those in earlier periods, incidentally supporting interpretations that the European expansion into Africa—including the emergence of the Atlantic slave trade—marked a radical break in the history of Africa.[6]

These transformations and their material expression cannot, however, simply be reduced to the European presence. The distinctive historical context of African-European interactions in coastal Ghana makes this of particular concern in evaluating transformations in this region. However, reasons for change may be traced to a variety of pressures arising after the fourteenth century, including the introduction of new diseases, changing economic relations, and additional factors resulting from the arrival of the Europeans, but also to other variables, including influences from the Sahel and North Africa (Bellis 1987:49).

In areas of the interior forest, savanna, and Sahel, the factors that influenced change and the ways in which history unfolded were distinct from those of the coast. More germane to the current discussion is the point that the culturally coded structure of these settings also varied, presenting different perspectives, solutions, and consequences in different cultural contexts. The tensions between external demands and internal response have been typical of contact settings throughout human history. Contrasting these varied historical and cultural contexts provides a means of explicating the specific features and patterns observed archaeologically.[7]

Elmina's special position vis-à-vis the Europeans afforded the town a unique intermediary position between the coastal frontier and the interior. In this respect, the town offers a way of investigating the historical specifics in a particular setting, the form and varieties of consequences represented, and the distinctive local conditions that prevailed—the ways in which events and the history of Elmina were indigenously articulated and locally structured. The variety of source material available on Elmina—written, oral, and archaeological—collectively suggests a great deal of perpetuity in certain aspects of religious beliefs, behavior, and material culture. These range from expressions of the most cognitive, extrasomatic aspects of the cultural system to the more basal or superficial. Early Portuguese accounts describing the initial meeting of Caramansa and Azambuja are illustrative: "Hither the king came, and before him a great noise of trumpets, bells and horns, which are their instruments, and he was accompanied by an endless number of blacks, some with bows and arrows, and others with assegais and shields; and the principal persons were attended behind by naked page-boys, with seats of wood, like chairs (cadeiras), to sit upon" (Rui de Pina, translated in Hair 1994b:20).[8] This description is of interest at multiple levels. The weapons, the musical instruments, and the kingly procession itself are consistent with later descriptions of ceremonies at Elmina and adjacent parts of the coast down to the present day (de Marees 1987:33–35; Hair 1994b:83–84 nn. 145, 146, 148; Wartemberg 1951:98–99; and miscellaneous accounts translated by Jones [1983:33, 113, 168, 186, 196]).[9]

Locally configured features can be seen in various aspects of the archaeological record and the behavioral patterns implied. It was, for example, noted that the many dwellings of multistoried, flat-roofed, stone construction were among the most visible material indicators of change and a distinctive aspect of the Elmina settlement.[10] These construction methods illustrate a unique aspect of Elmina, probably originating in the latter half of the seventeenth century with African artisans trained by the Dutch. Yet at least some of the buildings located archaeologically appear to have conformed to African ideals of the use of space. The linear arrangement of small rooms around a central courtyard is comparable to traditional house construction throughout the Akan area. Its multiplicity of function seems to have changed little between the earliest descriptions and the present.

African foodways can be considered from a similar perspective. Although some individuals at Elmina may have adopted European mannerisms in certain contexts, for the most part food preparation and consumption practices proba-

Figure 6.1. Women cooking over a clay hearth. (Reproduced courtesy of the Illustrated London News Picture Library [vol. 63, no. 1790, December 13, 1873])

bly remained much the same. Mixed stews and soups, often eaten with the hand or a spoon, are still typical of dishes prepared today (Figure 6.1). Early documentary accounts of West Africa also refer to the use of the hand in consumption (e.g., de Marees 1987:43; Müller in Jones 1983:211). Archaeologically, this pattern is shown by the prevalence of both imported and locally produced bowls in the ceramic assemblage and the shattered, fragmentary nature of the bone recovered. The social context in which food was consumed has also likely remained much the same. Although individual servings and restaurants are increasingly common, people still gather in a circle on low stools, the cooked food then being placed on the ground in the middle (Figure 6.2).[11]

RITUAL AND WORLDVIEW

The preceding features suggest continuities, but they are less expressive of the most cognitive cultural aspects, such as religion, cosmology, and worldview. Continuity and change in these areas are difficult to assess precisely because of their sacred nature. European visitors to coastal Ghana did not witness the full extent and variety of ritual activity, and those events that were observed were generally not described in detail in written accounts. To what extent these limited references present an accurate perception of African religious beliefs is questionable, a case in point being the Elmina Bakatue ritual discussed below. There are, however, indications of continuity in ritual expression and the underlying epistemologies over the past 500 years. Reasons for this consistency rest with both the African cultural context and the nature of the contact setting.

Figure 6.2. Modern Ghanaian dishes include a variety of soups and stews that may be served and eaten communally. (Photograph by Christopher R. DeCorse)

The comparatively small European population in coastal Ghana and the economic context of African-European interactions were examined in the preceding chapters. The Europeans' primary interest was in trade, and interactions unfolded mostly within this framework. They did, however, make some efforts to alter African beliefs.[12] Beginning with the earliest Portuguese visits, there were attempts to convert the local population to Christianity. Indeed, Portuguese expansion into West Africa was sanctioned by papal decrees, and the Portuguese crown identified their Elmina "vassals"—the people of the town—as Christian.[13] Priests served at the garrison, and several churches or chapels were built in Elmina, the earliest dating back to the founding of Castelo de São Jorge da Mina (Hemmersam in Jones 1983:118; Teixeira da Mota and Hair 1988:93 n. 54). There were also chapels established in neighboring areas, and sources note the conversion of some Africans, among the most notable being the baptism of the people and chief of Efutu in 1503 (Teixeira da Mota and Hair 1988:9).[14] Occasional references suggest that the majority of the Elmina population was Christian, but these were likely gross exaggerations. There were isolated instances of Christian converts who recanted their beliefs and were tried by the church and imprisoned in Lisbon, but despite these occasional efforts missionary activity was limited and the results ambiguous.[15] Proselytizing during the Dutch period was equally, if not more, erratic. Services were held in the principal forts for servants of the European companies, but there is little indication of efforts to serve the African population. Willem Bosman (1967:154), the chief factor at Elmina in the late seventeenth century and a key figure in Elmina-Dutch relations, disparaged the possibility of converting the Africans to Christianity.[16] There never seems to have been a substantial congregation of local converts, and there were no large-scale conversions.[17] This situation can be contrasted with the large number of converts and the more ready acceptance of Christianity in other parts of the western and central African coasts.[18]

The retention of traditional beliefs, selective acceptance of some aspects of Christianity, and syncretism in religious practices are commonly referred to in descriptions of the Gold Coast. Indeed, the continuation of African beliefs and maintenance of offerings, rituals, and religious structures often incomprehensible to European viewers were seen as characteristic. The lack of success in converting the Africans was explained by the African temperament and their tendency to return to their traditional beliefs. Africans, at least in some cases, did not view conversion to Christianity as antithetical to continuation of

Figure 6.3. De Marees (1602:Plate 5) described local religious practices. (Reproduced courtesy of the Rare Books Division, the New York Public Library, Astor, Lenox and Tilden Foundations)

African religious life. There are numerous allusions to Christian converts relapsing to or maintaining clearly non-Christian practices (Figure 6.3).

Akan religious beliefs exist at varying levels of conceptualization.[19] They include a concept of a supreme deity and sole creator of the world, *onyame,* who may be venerated in household shrines but who is generally considered to have withdrawn from the daily affairs of humans (e.g., Bosman 1967:146–147).[20] Expressions of supernatural power are most frequently and powerfully manifest in levels of embodiment below that of *onyame.* Among these are *ɔbosom,* supernatural powers that dwell in rocks, rivers, groves, and other natural features that are their point of origin.[21] They are alternatively anthropomorphized as spirits, children, or servants. They may also possess human beings, and they express their desires through an *ɔkɔmfɔ,* or medium. Also of great importance are *asaman,* the spirits of the ancestors. The *asaman* are thought to behave in human ways, needing food and drink and expressing feelings. They are propitiated though offerings and libations, and their help is sought in daily affairs. *Asuman,* in contrast, are man-made objects of worship that are the embodiment and means of accessing supernatural power. They include household shrines, amulets, charms, and anything that might serve as a repository for the efficacious aspect of spiritual power. The *asuman* are especially important because of their physical nature, which often made them the feature of Akan cosmology most readily apparent to European observers. They were variously referred to as idols, fetishes, and gris-gris and often viewed as the principal component of Akan religion.[22]

These supernatural powers have been pervasive in Akan life and have manifested in a variety of physical expressions, including sacred locations, groves, personal amulets, and household and community shrines. Wartemberg (1951:104, 157), referring to *ɔbosom,* comments that there were 77 tutelary deities who dwelled in Elmina.[23] This did not include the wide number of *asuman* and *asaman* that have been part of the town's religious life. Continuities in these religious beliefs and the historical responses they engendered illustrate the in-

Figure 6.4. The Bakatue, the ritual opening of the Benya Lagoon, today includes a procession of the "king," or ɔhen, and other royals through the town. The public aspect of the ritual culminates with a festival of chiefs at the old town site. (Photograph by Christopher R. DeCorse)

digenous structuring of some aspects of the contact setting. An example, again, comes from Portuguese descriptions of the founding of Castelo de São Jorge da Mina, the construction of which disturbed the place of an ɔbosom. João de Barros reported: "[W]hen the masons began to break up some rocks overlooking the sea, near the place selected for the foundations of the fort, the blacks, not being able to tolerate such an injury as was being done to that *sacred spot* which they worshipped as God, rose up in a fury . . ." (translated by Hair 1994b:32; emphasis added).[24] Azambuja subsequently sent presents to the African "king and his knights," which appeased them, and work continued. The sacred place and the African reaction are consistent with later sources. Such features may be marked with small shrines, but in many instances there is little physical indication of their existence, and Europeans frequently disturbed them.[25] Müller, who was a more astute observer than many Europeans, describes accidentally sitting on a large rock that was dedicated to the Africans' *fitiso,* or fetish, a European gloss for a variety of African religious expressions (in Jones 1983:160).

Accounts of more complex ceremonies also exist. These demonstrate both similarities and differences between the ritual practices of Elmina and those of neighboring Akan groups. Although the ritual practices of Elmina share underlying concepts with neighboring coastal Akan communities, the distinctive features of the locally expressed supernatural powers result in manifestations and ceremonies that are slightly different in their particulars. The Bakatue, one of the principal festivals of Elmina, illustrates this point.[26] The festival is now well known and generally held each year in June or July, marking the admission of the new harvest to market and the symbolic opening of the fishing season (Figure 6.4). The focus is the ɔbosom of the Benya Lagoon.[27] It is, perhaps, notable that the ritual culmination is cast-net fishing in the lagoon, not fishing for offshore marine resources. As discussed, archaeological evidence suggests that the exploitation of the lagoonal resources may have been of prime importance in the early history of Elmina. During the Bakatue Festival, the Benya ɔkɔmfɔ moves in ritual procession from the Benya shrine to the water's edge, where he casts a net into the lagoon. The number and variety of fish caught are said to be indicative of the coming season. Following these rituals the Bakatue concludes with boating displays on the lagoon and a durbar, or meeting of the chiefs, on the old town site.[28]

The Bakatue is representative of the tensions between change and continuity. On one hand it may be indicative of conservatism in ritual practice; on the other, an indicator of transformation in other aspects of Elmina society. A likely reference to a similar ritual occurs in de Marees's 1602 account, one of the earliest detailed descriptions of the coast. He describes a ritual practiced to ensure a plentiful catch of fish that culminated with an elaborate ceremony at the water's edge (de Marees 1987:68–69, 170). Despite this reference, the documentary record provides frustratingly little mention of the Bakatue before the mid-nineteenth century, when it is first referred to by its current name.[29] The lack of earlier documentary references can perhaps be partly explained by the general lack of detail provided in European accounts.[30] This problem may have been exacerbated by the absence of a public component in the ceremony prior to the nineteenth century. Even today the majority of the ritual is not public.[31]

The appearance of references to the Bakatue in the Dutch records of the mid-nineteenth century may be connected with the increasing importance of certain political offices, particularly the *ɔmanhen,* and a corresponding growth in related public components of the ceremonies (see Yarak 1993).[32] In fact, the current role of the *ɔmanhen* in the ritual is limited, the objective of the procession by the *ɔmanhen* and prominent lineage members to the Benya primarily being to witness the ritual casting of the net by the Benya *ɔkɔmfɔ* and to open festival display on the lagoon. The durbar of chiefs at the old town site on the Elmina peninsula that ends the Bakatue festivities is of recent origin; the more private rituals that take place focus on the northern side of the lagoon near the Benya shrine and at the place where the net is cast by the *ɔkɔmfɔ.* The public festival aspects of rituals have, in general, become increasingly important in Ghana during the present century.[33] Rituals paying obeisance to the Benya *ɔbosom* may be quite ancient, with some elements changing to afford increased recognition of the *ɔmanhen* and the more general participation of Elmina and non-Elmina people.

Ritual practices noted ethnohistorically are represented in artifacts, features, and site patterning. Particularly prominent, for example, are groves and burial grounds, which can often be distinguished by their virgin, uncleared forest. Bosman, for example, noted: "Almost every village has a small appropriate grove, where the authorities frequently repair to make their offerings; either for the public good, or for themselves. These groves are esteemed sacred, no person presuming to defile them, pluck, cut, or break off any branches of trees; who, besides the accustomed punishment, is not willing to lay himself under an universal malediction" (1967:153; cf. van Dantzig 1977:250–251). Bosman goes on to describe how he attempted to have the Africans cut down one such grove near the fort at Sekondi during a conflict with a neighboring polity to improve the line of fire, but "that was as effective as knocking on a dead man's door: none was willing to undertake that" (van Dantzig 1977:250). Many such groves, still in use, can be found throughout the Central Region (see Chouin 1998b).[34]

Asuman, the man-made embodiments of supernatural power, can also be located archaeologically. The characteristics and archaeological contexts of several categories of ceramic vessel forms found at Elmina suggest they were placed, and perhaps intentionally manufactured for use, in these contexts. Excavated features include vessels found beneath living floors in seventeenth- and

Figure 6.5. A libation pot and a photograph of a similar pot in situ at a chief's house at Egyaa. Examples of such vessels occur in nineteenth-century archaeological contexts at Elmina. (Photograph reproduced courtesy of Tara L. Tetrault, University of Maryland; illustration by Christopher R. DeCorse)

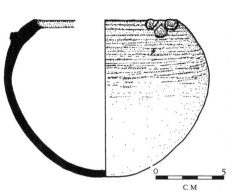

eighteenth-century contexts, close to house foundations. All contained chicken bones and had been placed upside down on the bedrock on which the foundations rested.[35] Their placement accords with ethnographic accounts that indicate that offerings were made when a house was constructed.[36] Pots of similar size, roughly smoothed, and with everted rims can still be purchased in Elmina, Cape Coast, Accra, Kumasi, and other locations throughout Ghana. Their function is often given as "pots for medicine," and they are likely often purchased for *asuman*.[37]

The form, decoration, and surface attributes of two other categories of ceramic vessels also suggest that they served ritual functions. One is a simple direct-rim pot with three sets of three knobs on the exterior of the rim. The surface of the pot is even but unsmoothed and unburnished, the somewhat rough surface texture and decorative attributes contrasting with vessels used in food consumption. Their use seems quite distinct from the vessels described above. They were identified by informants as pots specifically used as receptacles for libations, liquid offerings usually consisting of gin, schnapps, or locally distilled *akpeteshie*.[38] Vessels of this kind are still produced and have been observed in use as places of libation within a family compound, the pots often being set in the ground or placed in a clay or cement pedestal outside the room with the household shrine at the house of an *ɔkɔmfɔ,* or chief (Figure 6.5).[39] Libations may be made as individual supplications to the ancestors by an individual or an *ɔkɔmfɔ*. While a person pours the libations, he or she may make invocations to the ancestors for the health, safe travel, and well-being of the village, clan, or family. Each family member might pour a libation in remembrance of his or her ancestors.[40]

Another category of ritual vessel also seems to have been used primarily for offerings or libations. These differ from the libation pots described above in that

Figure 6.6. Local pottery cups from Eguafo. Many examples of these vessels have intentionally roughened interior surfaces, possibly suggesting a specialized function. The maximum diameters of the vessels range from 9.7 to 6.1 cm (3.8 to 2.4 inches). (Photograph by Douglas Pippin)

they were used as containers for libations or offerings that were poured out or possibly left at a sacred spot, rather than serving as a fixed receptacle into which libations were poured (Figure 6.6).[41] They are stylistically very distinct from other vessels, being characteristically small, ranging from nearly 10 cm (3.9 inches) in diameter to as little as 6 cm (2.3 inches). They are roughly conical in shape, with the apex at the base and the rims slightly everted. They are usually decorated with roughly incised arches or swags. They are called *pokwa,* which translates simply as "cup," a term that equally applies to vessels with other characteristics and made from other materials. The vessels described here, however, are clay. Virtually identical artifacts have a wide distribution within the Akan area and are particularly numerous in parts of Asante, where their function may have been entirely utilitarian.[42] On the coast, however, some of the vessels described are distinct in having interior surfaces that were intentionally incised and gouged during manufacture. This roughening of the interior surface, readily distinguishes them from other ceramics and identifies and maybe denotes a special ritual function. Informants suggested that these vessels were specifically used to pour libations, and archaeological contexts suggest they were used at a separate location, such as a shrine or grove, and left there. No modern examples of this type of vessel have been noted for sale during fieldwork.

The practice of using specialized pots for offerings is referred to in documentary sources, and the practice may long predate the European arrival. De Marees provides an illustration of one such context from the early seventeenth century: "Whenever they hear it calling [a bird that represents their *Fetisso*], they bring it *Millie* to eat and Pots of water to drink. . . . This is why one finds at some Road-junctions and Bushes in the open country a lot of Pots and other food . . ." (1987:70–71). A possible archaeological example of such a ritual context is provided by excavations at Komenda, located some 15 km (9.3 miles) west of Elmina (Calvocoressi 1975b).[43] The site was accidentally discovered and unfortunately largely destroyed prior to archaeological excavation in 1968 and

Figure 6.7. Jean Barbot's illustration of ritual objects from the Gold Coast, shown here as it appears in his original French manuscript, depicts an elongated object with a face at the top resting on what is described as a reed-basket. Barbot's accompanying discussions of ritual practices, like those in most early descriptions of the coast, are brief, at times contradictory, and frequently reflect limited understanding of indigenous religious practices. (British Crown copyright photograph, reproduced by permission of the British Library, Department of Manuscripts [Add. 28788, folio 39v])

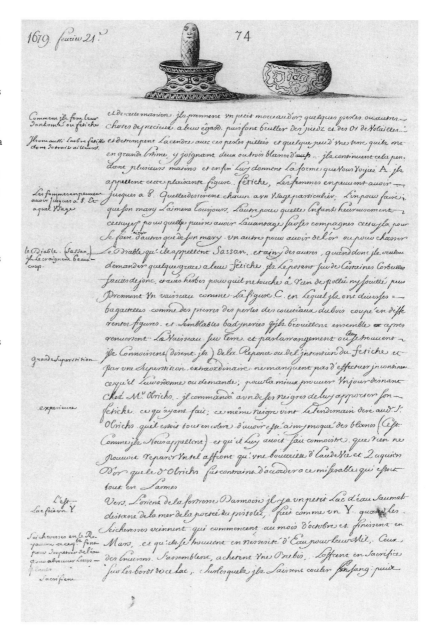

1969, but a large assemblage of local ceramics (over 200 kg [440 pounds]) was recovered. There were no surface indications, cultural contexts having been located beneath approximately 1 m (39 inches) of water-laid deposits. The area had been adjacent to or within the Susu Lagoon and would, therefore, have been a logical place for the propitiation of an *ɔbosom*. The site was situated approximately 1.5 km (0.9 miles) from British and Dutch trade posts dating to the late seventeenth and early eighteenth centuries.[44] The pottery was spread over an area of about 20–25 m² (215–270 square feet). The ceramics, which formed the vast majority of the assemblage, are characterized by "one immediately striking feature: almost all the pots were miniatures" (Calvocoressi 1975b: 155–160). The largest measurable pots were all less than 15 by 15 cm (5.9 by 5.9 inches) in height and diameter, with the peak frequencies being between 6 and 7 cm (2.3 and 2.7 inches) in height and 7 and 8 cm (2.7 and 3.1 inches) in diameter. No European artifacts or oral traditions were associated with the site. Nonceramic artifacts consisted of stone beads. In form, decoration, and surface treatment the pots have the closest parallels in Central Region ceramics that have been dated to circa A.D. 1000–1700.[45]

Shrines and places of offering often have limited archaeological visibility, and the identification of sites outside settlements, such as Komenda, are particularly difficult. Historical and ethnographic accounts also indicate that shrines are relatively small and highly variable in appearance and composition; the very features that distinguish them make them difficult to discern archaeologically. Household shrines might consist of special areas or platforms with a variety of objects and figures set on them, but might alternatively consist of a basket that could be readily moved or carried with the owner (e.g., Bosman 1967:150–151; de Marees 1987:69, 70; Gramberg 1861:89–90; Hemmersam in Jones 1983:108; Müller in Jones 1983:162–163). The Benya shrine includes a small thatched building, but the principal aspect viewed publicly during the Bakatue rituals consists solely of a low, featureless earthen mound, perhaps 15 cm (5.9 inches) high and 0.5 m (19.7 inches) across. This is normally covered with the shell of a sea turtle but is uncovered during the Bakatue rituals. *Asafo* shrines, which are a striking feature of modern coastal Akan settlements, are not explicitly referenced prior to the present century.[46] The places of offerings and ritual space associated with the companies were, undoubtedly, present earlier but in less clearly represented forms. Even today some *asafo* shrines may be marked by a simple post. A shrine identified during survey work consisted simply of a stick and palm-frond framework over the jawbone of a whale. Other shrines noted ethnographically and historically are equally variable in form, at times including pots, various natural materials, and anthropomorphic figures: "Generally [in making their fetishes] they take them from one of the elements, from forests, rocks, animals, birds, plants, herbs or from a compound, for instance of moistened earth with tallow and feathers, the whole object being covered on top with a small piece of linen" (Barbot 1992:578; see also de Marees 1987:66–70) (Figure 6.7).[47] Materials such as these are poorly perceived archaeologically.

A single shrine was identified during excavations at Elmina. This was found in the southwest corner of the Locus A structure. As noted, this building was occupied until the town's destruction, and its construction and the associated archaeological materials are primarily nineteenth-century, though much earlier contexts are represented. The shrine dates to the building's nineteenth-century occupation. Its presence is notable, for the building as it appeared in 1873 did not conform to traditional construction in either form or use of space, in contrast with some of the other structures discussed. The room in which the shrine was located opened to the building's exterior and was used as a kitchen or cooking area in 1873. The shrine itself, however, dated to an earlier nineteenth-century floor context that had been covered with fill and a more re-cent floor. It consisted of a low clay platform, measuring approximately 1.5 by 2 m (4.9 by 6.6 feet) and 15–20 cm (5.9–7.8 inches) high. Embedded in the plat-form and centered on the western side of it adjacent to the wall was a tortoise shell resting on its back with an upright iron key inserted at the end.[48] No other artifacts or features were found, associated artifacts perhaps having been re-moved prior to the renovation of the structure or having been made of mate-rials not preserved archaeologically. The form and context would indicate that this was a household shrine.[49]

Burials and the mortuary rituals they represent can also be characterized in terms of their non-European aspects. Because the funerary complex involves various artifacts and features, as well as the burial itself, it provides one of the best loci for the archaeological definition of *worldview*.[50] Documentary sources on Elmina and Akan burial practices prior to the nineteenth century are lim-ited. Ethnohistorical and archaeological data from Elmina attest to the preva-lence of burial beneath the house and the placement of grave goods, such as *forowa*, with the deceased.[51] Yet, although pre-nineteenth-century documen-tary references to burial can be found, they are far from prevalent and offer frus-tratingly little information on the specific manner of interment, the location of the burials, and the sociocultural practices represented. Twentieth-century Akan mortuary rituals preceding the burial, the actual interment, and subse-quent obsequies express multiple influences, including age, gender, religion, social status, and wealth, as well as a diversity of sociocultural affiliations such as patrilineal, matrilineal, and agnatic kin ties and, among the Fante, *asafo* mem-bership.[52] These are not dichotomous, bounded categories, and their relative significance may have changed through time. Notably, these distinctive Akan mortuary practices were not related to the more "traditional" or less "accul-turated" members of society. There are instances of individuals or merchants of some social prominence being buried within the house.[53] Funeral rituals are complex, festive occasions, which in the case of important individuals may span several years. They interrupt the ordinary functions of the community: "[N]ormal time gives way to sacred time, and ordinary occupations give way to ritual tasks, depending on each person's relationship to the deceased" (Voll-brecht 1978:xix).[54] The actual location, placement, and detail of the interments are highly variable. The variable, multipatterned nature of the burials is one of the principal characteristics of the funerary complex. European burial customs are, of course, also multivalent in the sociocultural phenomena represented, and burial patterns vary; and European mortuary ritual has also changed through time. These patterns, these changes, and the underlying cultural con-structs represented are, however, different from those of the Akan.

In lieu of a coffin, a specially prepared cloth or mat was used to wrap the body in the customary Akan practice prior to the late nineteenth century.[55] Bur-ial within the house continued at Elmina, despite European prohibitions (Fig-ure 6.8). In fact, chiefs might still be buried within the house today. Specially designated burial areas outside settlements have also been used in the past and

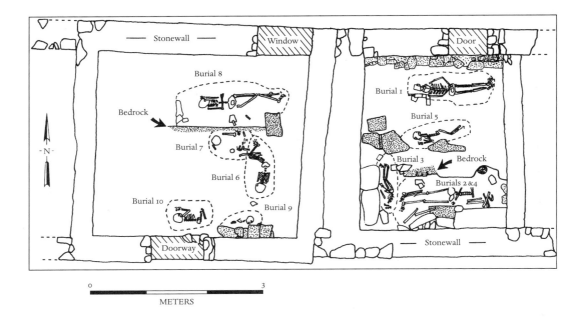

Figure 6.8. A section of the Locus A excavations showing the location of nineteenth-century subfloor burials. All of these features postdate the house's construction. (Illustration by Christopher R. DeCorse)

the present.[56] Yet, burial features also distinguish these from European patterns. Aside from the obvious lack of fences and associated Judeo-Christian symbolism and markers, Akan burial grounds are traditionally unmarked or marked in ways distinct from European practices, the area intentionally left unaltered and natural. The method of interment may also readily differentiate African burials. De Marees, for example, notes: "[T]he Grave-digger makes a Grave about four foot deep. Then [the corpse] is laid in it, and they lay many wooden sticks over the Grave, close together . . . and then earth is laid over it and built up like a coffin or square wall" (1987:181). This type of grave is comparable to burials observed ethnographically.[57] The above-ground covering may now be made of cement, sometimes with a vertical headstone, but more frequently it consists of a simple mound of earth. As the sticks over the grave shaft decompose, they collapse, leaving a depression that gradually fills with sediment, leaving little surface indication of the grave's presence. Burials within houses were typically shallow hollows, sometimes clay lined. Later interments, both within the house and in burial grounds, often disturb earlier graves.[58] These features can be viewed as aspects of a distinct "Akan" mortuary pattern. The more salient point, however, is the degree to which they are indicative of nonmaterial beliefs and rituals distinct from those of Europeans. These are complex and multifaceted and are only dimly perceived archaeologically.

The funerary complex may reflect more continuity than change, but Elmina worldview and its physical expression were by no means static. One characteristic of the burials was the presence of grave goods, which archaeological and documentary data indicate were a feature of coastal Akan mortuary ritual by the early seventeenth century. The custom, however, likely predates European contact.[59] The practice is well documented in Elmina as well in adjacent areas. De Marees observed: "All his [the deceased's] goods, such as his cloths, weapons, Pots, Pans, Stools, Spades and similar chattels which he has used during his lifetime, are brought to the Grave, buried with him and put around [the body in] the Grave, so as to serve him in the other World in the same way as they did during his life on this earth" (1987:182). Their function is more complex, however, perhaps also reflecting some aspects of the rituals completed at the grave site and vessels used in preparing the body for burial.[60]

Although the use of locally produced clay pots in *asuman* may represent a conservative aspect of ritual practice, the function of some European ceramics was clearly transformed to meet new roles, the use of imported trade materials in burials being among the most notable examples. Trade ceramics, including Chinese porcelain plates, Rhenish stoneware *Krüge*, creamware and whiteware mugs, and whiteware ointment jars, as well as pewter tankards, European clay pipes, jewelry, and a wide variety of glass beads, were found in more burials than local ceramics were. Indeed, imported ceramics were far more common in undisturbed, articulated Elmina burials. Interviews at Elmina suggest that such non-African artifacts served in ritual contexts analogous to *forowa* or *kuduo*, sometimes having been used as containers for gold dust and shea butter and as grave offerings.[61] On the other hand, archaeological data provided no indication of the placement of skulls of enemies or sacrificial victims in graves—practices that are frequently noted in documentary accounts.[62] Unfortunately, full evaluation of change and continuity in mortuary ritual among the coastal Akan is constrained by the lack of information on pre-European-contact practices.[63]

The genesis, use, and historical context of terracotta figurines perhaps illustrate the most dramatic material indicator of change in Akan mortuary rituals during the past five centuries (Figure 6.9). These figures are commonly said to represent the deceased and are placed in burial areas outside town, where they are the focus of funerary rituals for up to a year following the original burial. These customs and the archaeological context of the figurines and associated pottery are documented in twentieth-century ethnographies.[64] Documentary sources provide no indication of this custom prior to the seventeenth century, and archaeological data from the Akan area similarly suggest contexts of seventeenth- through twentieth-century age for this practice. Associated ceramics with various anthropomorphic and figurative adornment appear to be of similar age. The earliest documentary reference is found in de Marees's 1602 work, where he describes their use at the grave of a king: "[A]ll his Nobles who used to serve him are modelled from life in earth, painted and put in a row all around the Grave, side by side" (1987:184–185).[65]

The dating and distribution of these sites are of particular interest because they suggest a connection between the emergence of a figurative terracotta tradition in mortuary ritual and the changes that took place during the post-European-contact period. Although no terracottas were found at Elmina, their presence is indicated by Barbot's seventeenth-century account, which discusses some features that are distinct from the customs recorded ethnographically.[66] Barbot notes:

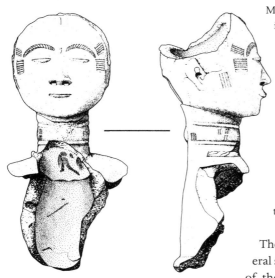

Figure 6.9. Akan terracotta sculpture recovered from excavations at Twifo Heman. The figure measures 36.2 cm (14.1 inches) in height. (Reproduced courtesy of James O. Bellis [1982])

Mausoleums . . . [are built for important individuals and] in addition, they are accustomed to decorate these with a large number of clay busts representing men and women, designed in a fairly jolly manner. These busts are painted in various colours and garnished all over with coral and fetishes. At Mina, on the road leading from the castle to the garden, I saw several such mausoleums, for *brafos* and officers, including one for a relative of the king of Fetu, which had between 35 and 40 of these busts, displayed on the posts and in a semi-circle in the midst of the fetishes. All around them were several pots of palm wine and meat, together with leaves and branches from fetish trees. (1992:595–596)[67]

The accounts by de Marees and Barbot present general similarities to ethnographically described contexts of the terracottas in their grave settings, associated grave goods, and accompanying rituals, suggesting that the customs represented are analogous to some of those described ethnographically for the terracottas. The documentary sources, however, also include several distinctive features. Most notably they suggest that the figures are not representative of the deceased but rather the nobles who served him in life.[68] Both sources also mention that the figures were painted and dressed with various adornments—features dissimilar to more recently described practices. Placement of the figures on the graves or in discrete areas of the burial ground also seems to have varied.[69]

Early documentary references to terracottas may be indicative of the writers' limited understanding of the phenomena they witnessed. However, the observations are suggestive of variation in ritual contexts represented, change through time, and the material culture concerned. Painting or slip decoration of any kind is not typical of ceramics from southern Ghana, though red slip is a distinctive characteristic of some terracotta figurines and the associated ceramics.[70] The use of paint suggests innovation, perhaps both stimulated and facilitated by coastal European trade posts.[71] It is possible that European observers of the seventeenth century were describing an innovation in the funerary complex that was still relatively new, having arisen on the Akan coast or in the hinterland in the century following European contact. Stylistic change, as well as change in the terracottas' symbolic role, is also represented during more recent periods.[72] While there may be a link between the European presence and the appearance of the terracottas, there can be no doubt of the non-European, locally constituted contexts in which they functioned.

Other archaeological materials also suggest practices and epistemologies distinct from those of Europeans. For example, human teeth with drilled holes for stringing were found in several eighteenth- and nineteenth-century contexts. These may relate to divination practices referred to in seventeenth-century accounts. Müller commented that to question their oracles, some people "have cords into which are woven the teeth of dead people. With such teeth they have rules which depend on whether they end up straight or crooked, below or on top, when the cord is twisted" (in Jones 1983:166).[73] Other categories of ceramics and artifacts recovered during archaeological work at Elmina may also have served in ritual contexts. There is, however, no archaeological, historical, or ethnographic information to provide a context. In particular, the range of ceramics associated with the funerary complex is undocumented.

Figure 6.10. Photograph of a nineteenth-century brick tomb at Locus A. The tomb postdates the destruction of the town. The contents of the tomb had been removed in the late nineteenth or early twentieth century. (Photograph by Christopher R. DeCorse)

At Elmina, indications of changing values appear more prominently in the nineteenth century, after the advent of colonial rule. This period of time saw different sources and manifestations of change. Imported products, including manufactures specifically made for the African trade, became much more readily available. During this period, European involvement in African affairs was also much more overt. These influences included a very direct role in the selection of leaders and the structuring of the political hierarchy. British, American, and European missionaries were devout evangelists who firmly believed Africans would benefit from European-Christian beliefs. These well-intentioned individuals helped shape perceptions of Africa and influenced public policy. Their efforts were both facilitated and strengthened by a coincidence with a period of increasingly direct European political intervention. There is some indication of this in the material record, as evidenced by the increasing frequency of houses conforming to European floor plans and the neoclassical features of the surviving nineteenth-century buildings. Discrete burial areas, coffins, and masonry tombs were now the norm (Figure 6.10).[74] Even more telling is the gradual disuse and destruction of formerly sacred groves. Such transformations may be indicative of an increasing tempo in the changes that occurred in coastal Ghana. Yet, even so, such changes cannot be divorced from their distinctive local context and indigenously articulated expression.

PERSPECTIVES OF EUROPEAN-INDIGENE INTERACTIONS

Studies of European-indigene interaction tend to emphasize the impact of European contact, focusing on discontinuity within the indigenous culture rather than on its resilience. There is no question that tremendous European influence was felt in some areas, and many of its related transformations are manifest at Elmina. Although culture contact has been a pervasive and ever-present aspect of human interactions, Europe's expansion into the non-Western world that began in the fifteenth century initiated an era of encounters among dramatically different societies unparalleled in previous ages. From an archaeological perspective, such interactions are manifest in fairly dramatic changes in the artifact inventory, in technological innovations, and in the modification of settlement patterns in coastal Ghana. Yet the preceding data, which only hint at the complexity of underlying belief systems, have been used to illustrate resilience in African worldview. The focus, however, is not on the continuities within specific indigenous rituals, ceremonies, and practices—evidence of immutable symbolic meanings and function in the epistemology of the coastal Akan—but rather on what the combination of these traits indicates: that the indigenous, local structuring of belief provides a context for understanding the history of African-European interactions and its archaeological manifestations. Methodologically, the Elmina data are evidence of a *combination* of behavioral patterns that argue for cultural continuities and an indigenous means of conceptualization throughout the period under study. Rather than indicating drastic replacement and modification of African culture, the Elmina data reflect the adaptation of some European features and additions to the indigenous material inventory.

Although extensive comparative data on Akan culture of the pre-European-contact period are lacking, the absence of clearly European cultural patterns in the Elmina data is perhaps the most significant point. Organizations such as the *asafo,* with their pseudomilitary regalia and activities, bear superficial similarity to the European features, but their origins, underlying structure, and cultural expression could occur only among the coastal Akan. In a similar fashion, the use of European trade goods in burial contexts, the creation of *forowa,* and the use of terracotta heads cannot be considered outside the cultural and historical settings in which they functioned.

Culture process results not in dichotomous phenomena characterized solely by either change or continuity but rather in phenomena that involve both. The evidence at Elmina demonstrates this, and such tension is inherent in all cultures (see Kent 1983; Mizoguchi 1993; Whitley et al. 1999). When viewed from this perspective, change and continuity in Elmina society are equally essential to the interpretation of the historical and archaeological reconstruction of the consequences of African-European interaction. These observations have immediate relevance to archaeological interpretation. The richness of the documentary and ethnographic records illustrates the grand historical themes of which Elmina was part and the complex, multivalent nature of the changes that occurred. Change in African culture did not occur at a relentless fixed rate, nor did change in the artifact inventory and the way in which artifacts functioned proceed in an externally ordered way. The archaeological data are testament to the varied and tenuous ways in which nonmaterial beliefs are conveyed by their material traces.[75]

NOTES

INTRODUCTION

1. For some of the translated and annotated sources utilized, see Baesjou 1979a; Barbot 1992; Blake 1942; de Marees 1987; Hair 1994b; Jones 1983, 1985; Teixeira da Mota and Hair 1988; van Dantzig 1978. Other important translations include Barros 1967; Bosman 1967; and Pereira 1967. The 1967 English translation of Bosman is used here in conjunction with the translations and annotations by van Dantzig (1975, 1976, 1977, 1982b).

2. Ballong-Wen-Mewuda (1984, 1993), Blake (1977), Hair (1994b), and Vogt (1979) have concentrated on the Portuguese period, and Baesjou (1979a), Feinberg (1969, 1989), Brukum (1985), and Yarak (1990) have focused on Elmina during the Dutch period. Works by Agbodeka (1971), Chouin (1998a), Coombs (1963), Daaku (1970), Delaunay (1994), Kea (1982), Fynn (1971), McCaskie (1995), Porter (1974), Reynolds (1974), Wilks (1993), and others allow Elmina to be placed within the broader context of Gold Coast history.

3. For reviews and critiques of source material, see comments in Blake 1987; Fage 1980, 1987, 1992; Hair 1994a, b:1–2, 46–47 nn. 15 and 16; Heintze and Jones 1987; Jones 1986, 1987, 1990; and Teixeira da Mota and Hair 1988.

4. Pereira was the Portuguese commander of São Jorge da Mina during 1520–22, and Bosman served the Dutch West India Company circa 1688–1702, primarily at Elmina, Komenda, and Axim, and eventually reached the rank of chief merchant (Jones 1986:227, 231).

5. The interest generated by the Asante War of 1873–74 led to the publication of accounts by individuals who had served on the coast earlier (Gordon 1874; Whitford 1877).

6. This refers to the stylistic and technical aspects of the drawings, as well as the actual inspiration or sources of the images represented. Whereas some drawing were completed by visitors to West Africa, others were created in Europe. When evaluated in historical context they may, nonetheless, provide important information. See Iselin 1994 for a review of the illustrations that accompany de Marees's (1987) work.

7. It may be that such identification would be possible in some contexts. The Ghana National Archives at Cape Coast include an account of a carved stone with a Dutch inscription dated 1782, discovered in October 1944 by a military officer "whilst on a digging fatigue. . . . This was found embedded amongst the foundations of a ruined building in the middle of the land now in use as this Unit's parade ground" (Document 267, letter from the commandant, Trades Training School to the Provincial Commissioner Office, October 28, 1944). In further correspondence (Documents 270 and 271), it is noted that the stone had the inscription "Dit Huysis gebouwt Door I. W. N. 1782," which was translated as "This house is built by I. W. N. in 1782." On November 7, 1944, the military officer sent

another letter to the provincial officer with "a rough sketch giving approximate dimensions of location of the find of carved stone" (Document 274). Unfortunately, such inscriptions were likely uncommon in the town, and no similar finds were made during archaeological work. I am indebted to Gérard Chouin for providing this reference.

8. Oral traditions are here considered to be recollections of the past that are commonly known within a particular culture and have been passed down for at least a few generations. Oral histories, on the other hand, are considered to be memories, reminiscences, or eyewitness accounts from an individual's lifetime (e.g., Henige 1982; Miller 1980; Vansina 1985).

9. The concern in the present discussion is the specific information about the town that might aid in archaeological interpretation. However, it is also useful to consider the way in which oral traditions are created and how interpretations of the past may serve to reify contemporary views. See discussions and references in Miller 1980 and Vansina 1985 for general considerations in evaluating oral traditions and histories. Wartemberg (1951) and Meyerowitz (1952a:70–73; 1952b, 1974) each drew heavily on oral traditions and histories in their reconstructions of Elmina and coast society. Fynn (1974b) also presents brief comments relevant to Elmina as well as to other coastal states. Useful review and evaluation of oral traditions relating to migration and the early settlement of the West African coast and Elmina in light of documentary sources are provided by Hair (1967b, 1994b:45 n. 7).

10. I conducted interviews during the 1985–87, 1990, 1993, 1997, 1998, and 2000 field seasons. Work specifically focusing on the local ceramic industry was undertaken by Tetrault (1998), Bourque (1997) examined butchering practices, and Cook's ongoing research concentrates on fishing (DeCorse 1998a).

11. Hair (1994b:45 n. 7) rightfully refers to Wartemberg's work as a commendable "pioneering local history," but its numerous factual errors make it of little use in reconstructing Elmina's early past. Hair goes on to comment that "[t]he author conflates personal knowledge of present-day customs and received traditions with historical material derived at third-hand from printed sources, and fills gaps with literary invention." Wartemberg, however, becomes a much more useful source when he discusses oral histories or his own observations, for example, contemporary ritual and the development of salt pans in the Benya Lagoon. The earliest published suggestion that Caramansa represents a corruption of the Akan name Kwamina Ansa appears to be in Ellis 1893:18; see discussion in Hair 1994b:55–56 n. 37.

12. This tradition, collected by Meyerowitz (1952a) and Wartemberg (1951:86–87), is also found in documentary references dating back to the seventeenth century. In his description of the Gold Coast of circa 1639–45, Hemmersam provides an account of a pre-Portuguese, French outpost, in which he identifies the location as the northeast battery of Elmina Castle and describes the massacre of the French garrison (Jones 1983:130). The specifics of the demise of the garrison, however, seem derivative of an account of a conflict between the Portuguese and the Africans recorded in earlier sources (Brun in Jones 1983:83–84, 130; de Marees 1987:91–92). Mauny (1950) and Monod (1963) provide critiques of the historical basis for the claim, and Calvocoressi (1968, 1977) also briefly discusses the origins of the tradition and the archaeological work he undertook at the supposed site of the French lodge as described to Meyerowitz. Villault de Bellefond (1669) popularized the idea of early Norman traders, which undoubtedly influenced later accounts, but the tradition would appear to have started earlier. It is of interest to note that memory of Calvocoressi's work itself seems to be entering the oral traditions of Elmina. Stories collected during my research identified the site of the early "French" lodge and further recounted how a white man had come there to excavate all of the gold.

13. Although Lawrence (1963) remains a principal source on the history and construction of the European outposts in West Africa, his key role in the restoration work of 11 of the most important of these monuments has been left sadly undetailed.

14. Archaeological investigations of European interactions with the indigenous populations of Africa are far less developed than those of portions of the Americas. For reviews of work in West Africa, see Posnansky and DeCorse 1986; and DeCorse 1996, 1997. The most extensive research

15. See references in DeCorse 1992b, 1993; and Bredwa-Mensah 1996.

16. These publications include a variety of guide-books with brief discussions and limited references. For example, see: Anquandah 1999; Cave 1961; Ephson 1970; Fage 1959; Flight 1968; Hyland 1971; van Dantzig and Priddy 1971; and Varley 1952. The single work dealing solely with the archaeology is the interesting, but exceedingly brief, report on the excavations undertaken in the slave barracoons of Cape Coast Castle (Simmonds 1973).

17. Merrick Posnansky, then head of the Department of Archaeology at the University of Ghana, Legon, advocated the importance of work examining archaeological perceptions of African-European interactions in the 1960s and 1970s. The most important result of this interest was the Coastal Survey (Golden 1969). Excavations were also undertaken at the site of Fort Ruychaver (Posnansky and van Dantzig 1976).

18. Davies (1976:109) carried out a limited surface survey of the old town site. He noted the presence of stone foundations and made a small surface collection of Dutch brick, local ceramics, and imported pottery. In addition to his own observations, Davies cites a report by Raymond Mauny of grooves in the bedrock along the shoreline west of the castle and miscellaneous finds in the Ghana National Museum, in Accra.

19. Work by Golden (1969) primarily focused on European forts and associated African settlements known through documentary records. Davies's (1976) important pioneering research identified many sites, some of which were relocated during the present work, but the areas covered by these preliminary surveys were not examined systematically.

20. The information on the archaeology of adjacent areas is explored in Chapter 1. The Komenda site, excavated by Calvocoressi (1975b), is discussed in detail in Chapter 6.

1. HISTORICAL BACKGROUND

1. The account by André Bernáldez, dated to circa 1515, is one of the earliest Spanish sources on Mina. For a detailed survey of European sources on the founding of Castelo de São Jorge da Mina, see Hair 1994b. The actual wealth derived from Castelo de São Jorge da Mina was already limited by the third decade of the sixteenth century, but the perception of the wealth of Mina continued both within and outside Portugal (see note 8 below).

The Portuguese used the expression *a mina de ouro,* or "the mine of gold," after their arrival on this portion of the coast in the 1470s. For use of the name "Mina" and its variations, see Hair 1994b:43–44 n. 3. This area is somewhat smaller than the Gold Coast, which encompassed the coast and immediate hinterland between Half Assini in modern Ivory Coast and the Volta River in eastern Ghana. The names make reference to the fact that gold could be readily traded on the coast; in fact, the majority of the actual gold deposits were in the interior.

For convenience, the name "Elmina" is used at times anachronistically throughout the book to refer to the African settlement located south of the Benya Lagoon on the Elmina peninsula. This name, in fact, emerged in Dutch and German sources only in the mid-seventeenth century, becoming the most commonly used variant by the end of the seventeenth century (Hair 1994b:44 n. 4; A. Jones 1985:14; Vogt 1979:192). Hair (1994b:44 n. 4) suggests that the name likely resulted from confusion over references to Mina in Portuguese, Italian, and Spanish sources, the possible sequence being: da Mina, de la Mina, della or dela Mina, del Mina, del Mina, d'el Mina, d'Elmina. French and English sources do not use the name "Elmina" until well into the eighteenth century.

The settlement's pre-European-contact African name is uncertain. The "Village of Two Parts" (Aldea das Duas Partes) is mentioned by Eustache de la Fosse in 1479 and by both Pina and Barros in describing the foundation of Castelo de São Jorge da Mina (Hair 1994b:4, 16; 1974). While it is possible this is the corruption of a local name, it is more likely a European reference to a distinctive physical characteristic of the settlement. The possible meaning of this term is explored in Chapter 2. Occasional references are made to Dondou, Dana, or Oddena (Blake 1942:45, 47). "Elmina" and "Edina" are the names used locally today, though some traditions favor the "Anomee" (Wartemberg 1951:15).

2. There were a number of earlier Portuguese out-posts in North Africa, most notably at Qsar es-Seghir, which has been the focus of intensive ar-chaeological research (Redman 1986).

3. As a result of the Eurocentric nature of the West African documentary record, modern historical studies have been viewed as interpretations in-herently "European and imperialistic in scope and organization" (Vogt 1979:xi), which histori-ans of Africa must view "through European eyes, and must infer—not directly from unmedi-ated African sources—how its people lived" (Rodney 1970:viii). It is illustrative that the eth-nicity and position of Caramansa, the African leader who met with Portuguese at the founding of Castelo de São Jorge da Mina, are unknown (Hair 1994b:55 n. 37).

4. Much of the previous work on the post-European-contact-period sites in coastal Ghana has focused the European sites themselves. See references and reviews in DeCorse 1992b, 1993, 1996. On other parts of the coast, Kelly's (1997a, b) work at Savi in coastal Benin provides impor-tant parallels and contrasts with Elmina. In Ghana, there have been important excavations at a number of Late Iron Age or early historic pe-riod sites at Begho (Posnansky 1987), Banda (Stahl 1999), Daboya (Shinnie and Kense 1989), Dawu (Shaw 1961), New Buipe (York 1973), Sekondi (Davies 1956), Bono-Manso (Effah-Gyamfi 1985), and Twifo Heman in the Birim Valley (Kiyaga-Mulindwa 1982).

5. These are the details of everyday life that Deetz (1996) calls "small things forgotten." They pro-vide ancillary information that often escapes the written record, but their significance transcends particularistic minutiae to the interpretation of the broader issues (e.g., Beaudry 1988; Lightfoot 1995; Little 1994; Vansina 1995:397–398).

6. See Young 1993:49–54 for a useful examination of the Portuguese seaborne empire in comparative perspective.

7. This discussion and subsequent ones stress the relations between West Africa and Europe that are most relevant to developments at Elmina. It is, however, important to remember that the same time period also saw varied and dynamic inter- and intraregional interactions throughout the coast, forest, savanna, Sahel, and North Africa. In southern and eastern Africa there were interactions with societies of the Indian Ocean and Asia, as well as with Europe. On the East African coast, limited contacts with the classical civilizations to the north as well as with Asia began in the first millennium A.D. Western Euro-pean contact with East Africa began in the six-teenth century and culminated with partition into German, Portuguese, and British colonies in the late nineteenth century.

8. The actual amount of gold realized and its value in the overall trade are open to question, but it was nonetheless a motivation (Teixeira da Mota and Hair 1988:26–33).

9. There is a vast literature on the slave trade, its size, and the impact on African populations. Sub-stantive and readable overviews are provided by Eltis and Richardson (1997); Hair (1989); Inikori (1982); Manning (1990); and Thornton (1992). Es-timations of the numbers of enslaved Africans brought from West Africa have varied. A range of 12 million to over 15 million is taken from reviews by Lovejoy (1989) and Inikori (1976a, b). Also see other discussions in the *Journal of African History* 17, no. 4 (1976). The European-based Atlantic trade is most relevant to Elmina, but the oriental or Islamic slave trade with North Africa was of critical importance in developments in other parts of West Africa. Its origins began with the spread of Islam across North Africa in the late first millennium A.D., and it peaked during the first half of the nineteenth century.

10. For general discussions and examples see Austen 1987; Curtin 1975; Dike 1966; Gemery and Hogen-dorn 1979; Henige and McCaskie 1990; Hopkins 1973; Polanyi 1966; and Wallerstein 1986. For stud-ies specifically examining economic transforma-tions in coastal Ghana see Daaku 1970; Kea 1982; Priestley 1969; and Reynolds 1974.

11. It is notable that the examination of Africa's rela-tions with Europe was critical to Wallerstein's (1976a:4) formulation of the world-system model.

12. For examples of archaeological perspectives of world-system theory in both capitalist and pre-capitalist settings, see contributions and refer-ences in Chase-Dunn and Hall 1991; and Cusick 1998. Friedman's (1991) study of the lower Congo, western central Africa, attempts to link the processes of the world system with local transformations.

13. Boahen's (1991) survey of African perspectives on

colonialism is a succinct and readable account of the social, technological, and cultural developments that were occurring in Africa on the eve on colonial conquest.

14. Sahlins notes: "I have seen among theoreticians of 'the world-system,' for example, the proposition that since the hinterland societies anthropologists habitually study are open to radical change externally imposed by Western capitalist expansion, the assumption that these societies work on some autonomous cultural-logic cannot be entertained. This is a confusion between an open system and a lack of system. And it leaves us unable to account for the diversity of local responses to the world system—persisting, moreover, in its wake" (1985:viii). Cultural belief systems may be conservative, but this does not imply stasis (e.g., Lévi-Strauss and Eribon 1991:125; Sahlins 1991). With regard to Ghana, McCaskie (1995) provides an excellent illustration of the ways in which the history of the Asante state at once shaped and was shaped by the cultural context in which it unfolded.

15. A survey of data from different parts of the coast suggests that Africans had an admirable understanding of at least some of the nuances of European social, political, and ethnic divisions (Curtin 1972).

16. No single source can provide a comprehensive review of the cultural and sociopolitical diversity represented. Murdock 1959 still provides a useful overview of the linguistic and cultural diversity. Several edited volumes survey West African historical and sociopolitical developments, including Ajayi and Crowder 1976, 1984; the *Cambridge History of Africa* (Gray 1975; Flin 1976; Oliver 1977), McIntosh 1999; the UNESCO-sponsored *General History of Africa* (Niane 1988; Ajayi 1989); and Shaw et al. 1993.

17. This issue is highlighted by comments by Jan Vansina (1995) in the provocatively titled article "Historians, Are Archaeologists Your Siblings?" Also see comments by Robertshaw (1999) and Thornton (1999). The perceived disjuncture in the aims and objectives of history and archaeology is not unique to studies of the African past. It is an issue that has been explicitly confronted in the origins and growth of historical archaeology in the Americas, and it remains of fundamental concern today (e.g., Beaudry

1988; Deagan 1982; Little 1994; Rogers and Wilson 1993; Schuyler 1978).

18. These are only simple glosses of what are often dramatically different perspectives of underlying epistemologies (Robertshaw 1999; cf. Connah 1987:12–20; Jones 1988; Kelly 1997b; Miller 1980:1–59; Schmidt 1990; Stahl 1993a; Vansina 1985, 1995). This is perhaps most vividly illustrated by the very limited use, in practice, that most historians of Africa have made of archaeology—their data sets, and hence their interests, lying elsewhere. Some of the most truly interdisciplinary projects have focused on ethnoarchaeological research, a notable example being that of Schmidt (1978), one of the few Africanist archaeologists who have received training in oral historiography. The more significant issue here, however, is that Schmidt framed his research in terms of questions that would necessitate the use of archaeology as well as other source material. For most researchers, anthropological, archaeological, and historical research has more often than not focused on questions that can be evaluated through the use of individual categories of source material.

19. Many of these populations are virtually unmentioned in documentary sources or oral traditions until the late nineteenth or the twentieth century. This vast topic has received limited attention, but there has been important work, some of which promises to change how historians as well as archaeologists perceive the past (e.g., DeCorse 2000b; MacEachern 1993).

20. See Colton 1942, Cowgill 1993:555, and Watson 1995 for differing perspectives on this point in historical perspective.

21. Thomas (1991) provides an excellent examination of such entanglements in terms of anthropological examinations of exchange. However, the broader point that material culture is contextualized and given new meaning in different cultural settings is of general relevance.

22. For varying impacts of the Atlantic slave trade on African societies see DeCorse 1991, 2000b; Eltis and Richardson 1997; Inikori 1982; and Manning 1990. Van Dantzig (1982a) contrasts the situation on different parts of the Gold Coast with other areas of West Africa.

23. Here and in subsequent discussions, the term *coast* is used in the sense of the lands immediately adjacent to the seashore. As will be seen,

historically these areas have been characterized by subsistence practices distinct from those in forested hinterlands behind the coast. The term *coast* is, however, sometimes used in a much broader sense, including all of the land between the ocean and the interior savanna (e.g., Manning 1990:41–46).

24. On the Gold Coast, the Portuguese sent missions to the interior, but detailed accounts either do not survive or provide very limited information (Teixeira da Mota and Hair 1988:9, 41–42 n. 24; Vogt 1979:82–87). During the seventeenth and eighteenth centuries the Dutch also established links with the polities of the interior, but these clearly were not sustained (Feinberg 1969:6–7; 1989:129–132). In the seventeenth century, the Dutch attempt to establish a fort on the Ankobra River ended after only a short time, when the factor blew himself up (Posnansky and van Dantzig 1976). The earliest Dutch emissary to Kumasi was van Nyendael, who departed for the interior in late 1701 and returned to Elmina in October 1702. Unfortunately he died nine days after his return, without reporting on his mission. His letters from Kumasi were also lost (van Dantzig 1980b:133–140).

25. Curtin's (1961, 1998) surveys of death rates, expressed per 1,000 of British personnel during the early nineteenth century, are illustrative. Surveying Dutch West India Company data on eighteenth-century Elmina, Feinberg (1974:363) calculated a death rate of between 188 and 242 per 1,000. Feinberg also reviews the data on which Curtin based his estimates and suggests that death rates for West Africa should be revised downward. Commenting on the records between 1719 and 1760 for Dutch West India Company personnel on the Gold Coast, he notes that on average less than one European in five died annually (Feinberg 1989:37–38). The rates are still striking, however, when considering the comparatively lower death rates in British military personnel during the late nineteenth and early twentieth centuries (see Headrick 1981:69–71). In any case, estimates of deaths per 1,000 are misleading, for they suggest a larger European presence than there actually was. The European complement of specific Gold Coast forts, missions, and expeditions frequently consisted of only a few men. Deaths, therefore, had immediate impact on the management and functioning of the Europeans on the coast. Samuel Brun (in Jones 1983:79), a surgeon at Dutch Fort Nassau between 1617 and 1620, recounts that a major purpose of the yearly supply ship was to bring replacements (see also Isert 1992:158). Disease sometimes left smaller garrisons without any European staff (e.g., van Dantzig 1978:199–200).

26. Map by George Cox (London, 1853), in my collection.

27. The polities of central coastal Ghana, generally labeled states, in fact lack characteristics such as non-kin-based, highly institutionalized bureaucracies that extend power and authority over large territories that are often used by anthropologists to delineate state-level societies (e.g., Eisenstadt et al. 1988; Fortes and Evans-Pritchard 1940; Lonsdale 1981; McIntosh 1999; Service 1971). The territories covered by the individual Fante states are quite limited. In this respect, the Fante illustrate the complex issues confronted in such general classificatory schemata, a point well illustrated in recent reviews of complexity from Africanist perspectives. With regard to coastal Ghana, the issue is sometimes side-stepped by using the more general term *polity*. In the present volume, the term *state* is consistent with current and historical usage in Ghana.

28. During the eighteenth century, the new *ɔhen* was brought to the castle to be recognized by the Dutch director general, but there is no indication that a proffered candidate was ever denied (Feinberg 1989:101).

29. The king also noted that they should be treated well because "they are Christians and have received the water of baptism" (Blake 1942:133). As will be discussed in Chapter 6, the degree to which the town's inhabitants actually converted to Christianity is open to question.

30. For discussion of the limited European authority on the coast, see Blake 1942:44–45; Brukum 1985:40; Daaku 1970:24, 33–34; Feinberg 1969:158; Priestly 1969:8–9; van Dantzig 1980a:8–9; and Yarak 1986b. Brukum quotes a 1752 reference that states: "in Africa we are only tenants of the soil we hold at the goodwill of the natives" (1985:68). More to the point, there was no legal basis for European authority (e.g., Hailey 1938:465–480). This view was clearly not the same as that held by Europeans in the late nineteenth century.

31. Perhaps the most dramatic illustrations are the small numbers of imported artifacts recovered from excavations at capitals of neighboring Fante states (Nunoo 1957; Agorsah 1975, 1993). Test excavations at Eguafo in 1993 recovered no trade materials, though some imported ceramics, glass, beads, and metalware have been found in disturbed contexts (DeCorse 1998a).

32. In this description de la Fosse provides the earliest description of the "Village of Two Parts." For a discussion of the spatial implications of the Village of Two Parts, see Chapter 2.

33. Also see comments in Vogt 1979:20. Sixteenth-century descriptions refer to the small size of towns along the coast, further noting the difficulty in identifying places to trade, as illustrated in William Towerson's accounts of the 1550s (Blake 1942:375–392, 399–404).

34. Recent excavations at Brenu Akyinim produced pottery to a depth of over 1 m (39 inches). Two sherds from depths of 0.85 m (33.46 inches) and 1.15 m (45.27 inches) in Test Unit 2 produced thermoluminescence dates of A.D. 1112 ± 276 and 1109 ± 146. If the two sherds represent the same occupation, the mean occupation based on these dates would be 1110 ± 129 (James K. Feathers, reports, September 19, 1995, and April 27, 1997). Survey work identified several coastal sites between the village of Brenu Akyinim and Cape Coast. There has not been a comprehensive survey of the Central Region. However, preliminary surveys were undertaken by Golden (1969), Davies (1976), and as part of the Central Region Project in 1993, 1997, 1998, and 2000 (DeCorse 1998a). Pottery stylistically similar to that found at Brenu Akyinim was recovered from excavations at Coconut Grove, Eguafo, and Elmina, as well as from a variety of surface contexts. Larger settlements with rich organic midden deposits are represented at such sites as Efutu, Eguafo, and Asebu (Agorsah 1975, 1993; Davies 1976; DeCorse 1998a; Nunoo 1957).

35. This spelling of the name "Brenu Akyinim" is used by the people of the modern village and is the version closest to the Fante etymology, which is linked to the production of salt. The spelling on the 1:50,000 topographic map is "Breni Akyim." Other alternative spellings sometimes used are "Brenu Achimen" and "Brenu Akyienmu."

36. Ozanne (1963), surveying sites in the Accra and Shai, to the east of Elmina, observed a transition to more nucleated settlements between the late fifteenth and seventeenth centuries. The Sekondi site, located 40 km (24.8 miles) west of Elmina in the Ahanta area, is the most thoroughly investigated Portuguese-period contact site in coastal Ghana (Davies 1956, 1961b). However, the chronology of the site may be problematic, and the dates of some of the archaeological features may actually be somewhat later than suggested.

37. The general conclusions are presented in Hair 1967a, and a substantive review of the linguistic data can be found in other articles (Hair 1967b, 1968, 1969). Hair studied the names of ethnolinguistic units, their boundaries, and vocabularies along the entire coast. He concludes: "[T]he history of the units defined in this study, in the centuries considered, is clear, and is not one of migration, or of fundamental change in the particulars studied: with very few exceptions, our ethnolinguistic units *stayed put*, topographically, over the centuries" (Hair 1967b:265–266). Blake (1942:52–54) reached similar conclusions earlier, primarily on the basis of documentary references. Such evaluations are facilitated in coastal Ghana by the availability of information beginning with the first years of the European arrival and continuing more abundantly than many other regions in the following centuries.

38. Cf. Alexandre 1972; Greenberg 1966: 6–41; Manoukian 1964; Murdock 1959:252–259. The principal Akan linguistic groups include the Asante, Fante, Bron, Akwapim, Akyem, Agona, Kwahu, and Wasa. For examination of the archaeological implications of these divisions, see contributions by Kropp Dakubu and Posnansky in Ehret and Posnansky 1982.

39. Also see Chapter 6 and discussion, comments, and references in Christensen 1954:1; Chukwukere 1978; Effah-Gyamfi 1979; Kiyaga-Mulindwa 1980; Murdock 1959:253; Rattray 1959; Schildkrout 1987; Warren 1973; and Wilks 1993. McCaskie (1995) provides an excellent examination of the Asante state and society, placed in its cultural and historical context. Although most ethnographers and historians would agree that Akan language groups are characterized by a high degree of cultural similarity, there is disagreement as to the specific characteristics that

constitute "Akan" culture. Much of this disagreement rests on definitional parameters, but the picture could also be clarified by additional ethnographic and ethnohistorical research outside Asante.

40. For discussion of the *ntɔrɔ* and Akan kinship, see Denteh 1967; Fortes 1970; Gyekye 1987; and McCaskie 1995.

41. Several archaeological studies have examined the genesis of Akan culture and the expansion of the Asante state (Posnansky 1973; Effah-Gyamfi 1979, 1985; Stahl 1992). Also see contributions by Merrick Posnansky, Peter Shinnie, Francois Kense, and James Bellis in Schildkrout 1987. The results of Peter Shinnie's long-term project on early Asante settlements is currently in preparation. Preliminary results and the project objectives are outlined in Shinnie and Vivian 1991.

42. This Akanization of the ceramic inventory does not, however, seem to be represented in northern Ghana (Kense 1987).

43. These issues are more fully examined in Chapter 6.

44. Although the Luis Teixeira map was not published until 1602, it was derived from information collected from earlier Portuguese missions to the interior, particularly between the years 1570 and 1573. The course of the Upper Volta River is also shown fairly accurately. The 1629 map or versions of it were incorporated into a number of later works, including those of Barbot and Dapper, perhaps indicating more continuity in specific names than was actually the case (Jones 1986:223–224).

45. Agorsah (1993) conducted test excavations at Efutu in the 1970s. I made brief visits to Efutu, Eguafo, and other settlements in the Central Region between 1985 and 1987. Test excavations at Eguafo were conducted by Singleton as part of the Central Region Project in 1993 (DeCorse 1998a). The excavations extended over 2 m (6.5 feet) deep and did not reach sterile soil. Thermoluminescence dates on two pottery sherds from the lower levels of the excavation dated to A.D. 1238 ± 77 and A.D. 1325 ± 67. Historical research on the Fetu state has been the focus of work by Deffontaine (1993, 1996), and Chouin (1998a) has provided a detailed study of seventeenth-century Eguafo. Preliminary archaeological surveys of Eguafo were completed by Gérard

Chouin and Samuel Spiers as part of the Central Region Project (DeCorse 1998a). These materials have not been thoroughly studied, but imported material from excavations, unstratified surface collections, and modern gold-mining activities dates between the sixteenth and the nineteenth centuries. Chouin and Spiers are currently planning more intensive work at Eguafo.

46. There were connections between Africa and medieval Europe, but the sparse documentary record of these links only serves to underscore the limited firsthand knowledge Europeans had of areas south of the Sahara.

47. For a general review of the literature on early European maritime technology, see Smith 1993.

48. The official Portuguese accounts place 1471 as the date of arrival (see Pereira 1967:118; Hair 1994b). Evidence for earlier voyages is cartographic (Cortesão and Teixeira da Mota 1960:xxxi; de Oliveira Marques 1972:135).

49. This remained a concern. Writing in the early seventeenth century, de Marees (1987:214) also emphasized the need for a base to unload and gather merchandise.

50. Portuguese perceptions of the advantages of the site are reconstructions rather than documented fact, because the actual Portuguese accounts are limited and somewhat contradictory (Hair 1994b:177). All the attributes noted here were probably important, but the paramount concern was likely an African settlement and the associated trade opportunities. Shama was probably the only other possibility considered.

51. See Hair 1994b for an authoritative review of the relevant documentary sources. Lawrence (1963:103–179) surveys the physical traces of the Portuguese structure. Although some recent writers, including van Dantzig (1980a), have described the castle as Dutch in appearance, this is more in reference to buildings, rooms, and detail work added to the Portuguese structure. In fact, Elmina presents a good example of fifteenth- to sixteenth-century Portuguese military architecture. Many of the structures in Portugal, including Castelo de São Jorge in Lisbon, are more representative of other periods or have been extensively altered by later modifications and restorations.

52. Papal decrees were invoked to support the primacy of Portugal's claims during the war with

Castile between 1474 and 1478, and in later years, political pressure from Lisbon successfully halted preparations for both French and English voyages to Guinea. Although he does not deal with the *regimentos* concerning Mina, da Silva Rego (1959) provides a useful overview of royal ordinances relevant to Portuguese colonization in the sixteenth century.

53. Whether or not European prisoners were actually executed at Elmina is open to question (Teixeira da Mota and Hair 1988:11).

54. See Teixeira da Mota and Hair 1988:28–33 for translation and critique of available sources.

55. The reference to "no winter or summer of navigation" may refer to the general mastery of the knowledge of the currents and winds that had been closely guarded by the Portuguese.

56. As Young (1993:49–54) has pointed out, inefficiencies of the Portuguese seaborne empire can be traced to its origins, which took shape in the absence of any colonial administrative or bureaucratic models.

57. Paul Hair (1990) has pointed out that the union of Portugal and Spain created the first empire on which the sun never set.

58. The first efforts by interlopers to establish trade posts in West Africa were made during the 1550s (Blake 1977:155; Teixeira da Mota and Hair 1988). References to Dutch settlements in the Senegambia occur in the 1590s, where a number of fortified trade posts were later established between Cape Verde and the Gambia during the first half of the seventeenth century (e.g., Thilmans 1968:18; Wood 1967). The French maintained small factories on the Island of Gorée by 1606. The island was purchased by the Dutch in 1617, and the forts of Nassau and Orange were constructed.

59. The English negotiated to locate forts on the Gold Coast in the 1550s, but these efforts were unsuccessful (Blake 1977:155; Teixeira da Mota and Hair 1988).

60. Vogt (1979:184) also describes in some detail how the new Portuguese governor literally had to "fight his way to his post" in 1632, but the archival source is not indicated.

61. The estimate of the attacking force is of interest, because the Dutch presumably had an accurate count of their own troops and thus, by comparison, a good sense of the number of African soldiers. On the other hand, a humiliated Portuguese force might have exaggerated the number of the attacking forces. Further, Vogt does not indicate the archival sources he is drawing on. For discussion of the agreement between the Dutch and Eguafo, see Chouin 1998a:48–51.

62. Surveying the Portuguese position, Vogt comments: "By 1600 the Dutch were far better equipped to conduct a successful trade in Mina than were the Portuguese. First and most obvious, they possessed the necessary ships with which to trade. . . . Equally important the Dutch controlled the source of much of the metal and cloth commodities which the Portuguese had customarily brought to trade at in Mina" (1979:146).

63. The Portuguese were fully aware of the Dutch threat. A Portuguese writer commented: "They [the Dutch] have goods on board which are imitated in [the northern Netherlands] and are better than the Indian; the Netherlanders cause us great damage" (quoted in Feinberg 1989:30). Similar observations were made at other times: "As a Portuguese agent at Antwerp sadly complained in 1561, the English were going 'to Mina,' not only to build a castle but also to sell more cheaply than the Portuguese; and the English themselves noted that at times they were outsold by the French" (Teixeira da Mota and Hair 1988:23; see also Vogt 1979:144–193). Referring to the early seventeenth century, Vogt writes: "In fact, prices of trade goods on the Mina coast were so depressed by Dutch imports by this time that reasonable profits were no longer possible" (1979:168–169).

64. Van Dantzig (1980a:vii) estimates that there were 60 forts and castles constructed over three centuries, but by 1800 only 30 or so of these were functional.

65. The French briefly maintained trade posts at Assini, Apenyi, Anomabu, Komenda, Saltpond, and Takoradi.

66. There has long been consensus that this change occurred in the second half of the century. However, more recent analyses have revised the numbers of slaves exported and the relative amount of gold (Elbl 1997; van den Boogaart 1992; cf. Bean 1974; Eltis 1994; van Dantzig 1980b:144–157).

67. Wallerstein states: "Ashanti (and its analogs) thus became part of the periphery of the capitalist

world economy not by *producing* slaves but by raiding them from areas outside this world-economy" (1986:106).

68. The most thorough archaeological examination of the potential consequences of slave raiding in the Gold Coast hinterland is provided by David Kiyaga-Mulindwa (1978, 1982), who notes the appearance of fortified settlements and changes in ceramic assemblages in the Birim Valley.

69. For references to *panyarring* see: Brun (in Jones 1983:88–89); Müller (in Jones 1983:189–190); Priestley 1969:152; and Römer 1989:148–149.

70. Also see comments by Jones (1983:113 n. 65). Elmina oral testimonies collected by John Fynn (1974b:15, 39) give some account of the slave trade but are limited in context and detail.

71. Examples of the disruptions to trade caused by slave raiding and related conflicts on the Gold Coast are provided in documents translated by van Dantzig (e.g., 1978:82, 355–359).

72. For references and discussion of Elmina in the St. John revolt, see Westergaard 1917:144; Oldendorp 1987:397–400; Pope 1969:121–136; and Kea 1996.

73. Surveying the transitions in West Africa during the nineteenth century, Wallerstein notes: "Even the British withdrew from Ouidah (Whydah), and several times contemplated abandoning all their West African forts. That they never actually took this step, however, was due solely to the protests of the merchants, who realized—if some British civil servants did not—that it was Britain, as the dominant world commercial and industrial power, which stood to reap the greatest benefit from the new situation" (1986:15). The development and expansion of British steamship service and the palm oil trade is usefully surveyed by Lynn (1989).

74. Trade was briefly given over to the machinations of private trading companies between 1774 and 1776 and in 1782.

75. See discussions and references in Coombs 1963; Cruickshank 1853; and Reynolds 1974. Many of the relevant contemporary documents are usefully abstracted in Crooks 1923; and Metcalfe 1964. Correspondence relating to the transfers of 1872 can be found in the *British Parliamentary Papers* (1970a, b).

76. During the nineteenth century Dutch revenues continued to decline, the situation of the Dutch having been not unlike that of the Portuguese three centuries earlier. In 1848 Bouët-Willaumez commented: "Although amongst the products, which are exchanged by the Dutch merchants, a great number comes from national factories, but many more products from English factories enter also their market; in conclusion I must say, that is really an extravagant luxury to have all those cannon and thick walls, soldiers and arms, to protect a trade of minutious quantities of gold and very small amounts of trade goods" (translation courtesy of Albert van Dantzig, January 17, 1989). Henige (1973:226) discusses the 1850 Elmina letter in the context of Elmina oral traditions.

77. Other towns formally under Dutch authority also resisted British authority following the exchange, including Butre.

78. The earliest attempts at estimating the entire population of Ghana were made in the 1840s (de Graft-Johnson 1969), but detailed information is not available until the twentieth century. These difficulties are true of Africa in general (Johnson 1977a).

79. The limitations of such compilations of diverse data need to be underscored at the onset. The information presented reflects varied degrees of accuracy, none very good. Presentation here in Table 1.1 serves to underscore the limited information available and to illustrate the relative difference in the size of the settlement suggested by the early and the late estimates. The Europeans had only limited knowledge of the settlement's composition and of African residential customs. The ambiguous meaning of *households* is examined by Fage (1980). It might be expected that estimates of the numbers of militiamen would be more accurate because they fought with European forces in several instances, but such numbers might have been intentionally embellished or distorted for a number of reasons. A critique of the material presented in Kea 1982:39, the conclusions derived from it, and the general problems with charts of this kind can be found in Jones 1990:125–128.

Table 1.1

Estimates of the Elmina Settlement's Size, as Expressed in Numbers of Canoes, Houses, Households, Families, Militiamen, and Population, Sixteenth through Nineteenth Centuries

Year	Fishing Canoes	Houses/ Households/Families	Militiamen	Population
c. 1578			500–600	
1606			130	
1621		300 (*vizinhos*)	200	3,000–4,000
1625			900	
1630s			800	
1631		800 (*habitatori*)		
c. 1640	300–400			
c. 1650	400–500		2,000	
1670			8,000	
c. 1680	400–500	1,200 (houses)	6,000+	
1682				15,000–20,000
1688	300		4,000	
1695			5,000–6,000	
1700			50 (?)	
1700–1800				12,000–16,000
1702			1,000	
1709		"Many thousands of houses"	3,000	
1737			4,000	
1739–40			5,000	
1782			3,000	
c. 1820				12,000–15,000
1859				18,000–20,000
c. 1866				19,000

Sources: The estimates are based on published figures by various contemporary and modern writers. The figures for 1578 and 1606 are from Vogt 1979:125, 155, who describes a conflict with Efutu and a land battle with the Dutch, but the archival sources being drawn on are not specified. By way of comparison, a 1572 Portuguese document described the villages of the "King of Cumane" and the "King of Afuto" as being no more than "one hundred huts or shacks" (Teixeira da Mota and Hair 1988:74). The 1630s population estimate of 800 militiamen is given by Vogt (1979:184) without elaboration. Figures for the 1621–1709 period are drawn from the discussion and chart in Kea 1982:39. The figures for 1621 and 1682 are estimates by Kea, who states, "Information pertaining to Elmina indicates that between 1621 and 1682 the port's population increased from around 3,000 or 4,000 to perhaps 15,000 or 20,000." He also notes that the population may have declined dramatically in the last two decades of the seventeenth century because of a smallpox epidemic and military conflicts. The estimates for circa 1680 are taken from Barbot 1992:373, 381. Feinberg (1989:83–85), who also appraises the population estimates given by Kea, surveys sources for the eighteenth century. The 1700–1800 estimates are Feinberg's, who suggests that the population of Elmina was between 12,000 and 16,000 during much of the eighteenth century. The figure for circa 1820 is based on estimates given by Yarak (1990:48). Referring to the 1820s, he comments that a variety of sources can be used to place Elmina's population between 12,000 and 15,000. Census data on Elmina and surrounding communities for 1859 and circa 1866 were compiled by Baesjou (1979a:214–224).

Note: Empty cells indicate no available data.

80. Johnson (1977b) briefly considers the potential of this approach for the Accra region. Although animals may still be found on the coast, some accounts suggest they were far more prevalent in the past. Note, for example, Bosman's (1967:317–322) description of an elephant in the "garden of Elmina." For a review of animal resources on the coast, see Chapter 4.

81. Wartemberg (1951:14) estimates that Elmina's population was 25,000 before 1852, but no source is given.

82. Oral traditions and documentary sources are replete with references to conflicts and population dislocations (e.g., Meyerowitz 1952a:81–83; 1974:87–93).

83. Estimates of natural population increase are highly speculative without a great deal more information on male to female ratios, survivorship of females to reproductive age, and infant death rates. Natural growth rates for well-fed, stable populations could be estimated at as much as 3–3.5 percent per year, doubling roughly every 30 years (Hassan 1981:139–140). Such figures, however, provide an idealized maximum and are not indicative of the situation at Elmina, which was subject to epidemics, high infant death rates, and warfare.

84. For brief discussions and references to Akani in the sixteenth century, see Ballong-Wen-Mewuda 1984:114–116; Hair 1994b:51–52 n. 28; Texeira da Mota and Hair 1988:64; and Vogt 1979:82–87. Terray (1995:139) clearly shows that the meaning of this term changed with time. In the first half of the seventeenth century, it seems to have designated several states at the confluence of the Pra and Offin rivers (including Assin, Adanse, and future states such as Denkyira and Asante). By the second half of the seventeenth century, the states of Adanse, Denkyira, and Asante appear, and the appellation "Akani" becomes the synonym of "Assini." Generally speaking, "Akani" may be a gloss for traders coming from the western banks of the Pra and Offin rivers up to the eastern borders of Akyem (Terray 1995:139). For nineteenth-century estimates of Asante in Elmina, see Baesjou 1979a; and Yarak 1986a, 1990. I am very grateful to Gérard Chouin for comments on this section.

85. For discussion of the Mande trade at Elmina see Hair 1994b:53 n. 33; cf. Sutton 1981; and Wilks 1962, 1982, 1993.

86. See Feinberg's (1989:82) discussion of outsiders at Elmina. Regarding quarters within the settlement, see Chapters 2 and 3; Barbot 1732:156; Daaku and van Dantzig 1966:15; and Nathan 1904:31.

87. Yarak (1989) provides a very useful review of the evidence for African-European slaveowners at Elmina and the distinctive roles and rights that slaves had in Gold Coast society. For a general overview of slavery in Africa, see Lovejoy 1983; and Manning 1990.

88. On the other hand, a 1523 account suggests slaves could be purchased in the town (Blake 1942:133–134 document 49).

89. Actual records are unavailable for some periods, but the total number of slaves brought to Elmina may be somewhat lower than the estimate of 300 slaves per year suggested by Vogt (1973a:453).

90. Other contemporary accounts are presented in Blake 1942:59–60; and de Marees 1987:48, 176. For comments on the slave trade to Elmina during the Portuguese period, see Ballong-Wen-Mewuda 1984:303–304; Birmingham 1970:4–5; Rodney 1969; and Vogt 1973a, 1979:46, 57–58, 71–72, 230 n. 35. The sale of slaves by garrison personnel may have been an important source of private income (Vogt 1974).

91. Alternatively, Vogt (1979:46) notes a 1529 regimento as providing for 16 slaves, 10 males and 6 females who were supervised by the factor and used for duty within the fortress.

92. For other contemporary references to slaves, see de Marees 1987:113; Hemmersam (in Jones 1983:113); Müller (in Jones 1983:198); and van Dantzig 1978:84, 138, 278–288.

93. Meredith's estimate refers only to company slaves and not privately held slaves in the settlement. There is no way to evaluate the reliability of Meredith's estimate.

94. There are some references to the townspeople's trade in slaves. An early seventeenth-century account describes how an African merchant with many slaves might sell a disobedient slave to the Portuguese for shipment to Brazil (Hemmersam, in Jones 1983:113). In 1739 the townspeople requested "the restoration of the old custom by which they were allowed to try to sell elsewhere all those slaves who were brought to the forts but who were not accepted by the Noble Company" (letter from M. Hoesen and J. Bontan, commissioners for Director General Des Bordes, September 2, 1739, translated in van Dantzig 1978:346).

95. A 1702 document translated by van Dantzig (1978:84) discusses the intention to purchase 250 slaves at Ouidah for use in cultivating cotton at Shama, Butre, and Axim.

96. Barbot (1992:396) mentions the village of "Aquaffou" north of Cape Coast with a slave market that specialized in slaves for this purpose.

97. There is some indication that the captive Africans shipped to the Americas were cognizant of the differences between slavery in Africa and in the Americas. Michael Hemmersam, describing the sale of captives to the sugar plantations of Brazil, wrote: "There have also been some who realized [what was happening to them], and who, before being led away or sold into the country, abstained from food and drink, and thus died. Several offered to place three or four slaves in their stead, in order that they themselves might be set free, just so that they might not enter such bondage so far from their country" (in Jones 1983:114).

98. Such relations were, however, reckoned only through the matrilineage. Offspring from a wife who was a slave became members of their father's *abusua*. Christensen notes, "The Fanti say that slave ancestry is indicated by the fact that a person gives only one descent line, either paternal or maternal, and ignores the other" (1954:38). The children of slaves were also slaves. Slave ancestry is sometimes discreetly alluded to in oral traditions.

99. Hair (1994a) further observes that some such personages may not have been identified in the records, and thus the actual population of Europeans at Elmina may have been somewhat larger than the recorded lists indicate.

100. In 1675 it was suggested that 120 men, in addition to those needed for trade and to man the ships, would be adequate to staff the forts and trade posts in times of peace (letter from Heerman Abramsz, dated April 1675, translated in van Dantzig 1978:19). On the other hand, in 1689 the directors of the Dutch West India Company indicated that the Dutch staff on the coast should number about 350, with 200 of these located at Elmina (document translated in van Dantzig 1978:48–49). The number actually employed was generally lower. A French travel account of 1671 estimates that there were 120 soldiers in the Elmina garrison (Chouin, n.d.-b), and Barbot de-

scribes a garrison of "100 whitemen, not counting blacks in the company's pay" (1992:380). A list of 1702 reports only 238 individuals serving on the coast, 94 based at Elmina (enclosure in letter from W. de la Palma, dated June 26, 1702, translated in van Dantzig 1978:84–85).

101. Feinberg (1989:86) notes examples of two senior Dutch officials at Elmina drawn from the "higher ranks of Dutch society," one of whom may have served on the coast because he was disappointed in love. On the other hand, in the 1840s the Dutch director general was described as "a man of about thirty, who came out in 1832, as a clerk" (Hawthorne 1845:136).

102. See contemporary accounts in Bosman 1967:142; and de Marees 1987:36, 217. Miscegenation also characterizes some frontier-colonial populations in the Americas where small numbers of European females were represented (e.g., Deagan 1983; Lightfoot, Martinez, and Schiff 1998).

103. Feinberg (1989:89) notes that he was able to find references to only seven marriages recognized by Dutch law.

104. The Dutch director general was assisted by a council made up of important officials on the coast, including merchants, factors, the bookkeeper-general, and the commander of the garrison (Feinberg 1989:31–36; van Dantzig 1978:3–4).

105. Although the mulattos were at times afforded high status, in some ways they appear to have remained an anomalous group. Along with other Africans and Native Americans they were generally not allowed to join religious orders, and they were not given West India Company employment until the 1740s (Boxer 1972:42; Feinberg 1969:124). Bosman had a poor opinion of them, saying, "I can only tell you whatever is in its own Nature worst in the Europeans and Negroes is united in them or, to be short, they are altogether Whores and Crooks of one and the same kind" (1967:141–141; cf. van Dantzig 1976:122). Similar views are expressed by other Europeans of the period (Howison 1834:153; Smith 1967:213; Thompson 1937:53–55). For discussion of the complexities of Africans and mulattos in the Dutch world, see Blakely 1993.

106. Jan Neizer traded extensively in slaves, and he rented the Dutch fort at Apam to serve as a barracoon when it was not otherwise in use (Brukum 1985:167).

107. A contemporary account is provided by de Marees (1987:220).

108. It should be noted, however, that the equable relations that characterize European-African interaction at Elmina contrast with Portuguese policy in adjacent areas of the Gold Coast, where they did not hesitate to use force (Blake 1942:43–47).

109. Links with Eguafo are commemorated in Elmina rituals.

110. This observation was repeated by Olfert Dapper, who wrote, "[A]nciently the village of the mine had two masters, one half dependent on the King of Guaffo [Eguafo] and the other half upon that of Fetu" (translated in Feinberg 1969:13). Dapper's source, however, was the 1629 map.

111. The paucity of early documentary sources makes it impossible to evaluate the veracity of either the oral histories or the seventeenth-century written sources. The Portuguese and the Dutch at Elmina gave gifts to both kings at various times (Blake 1942:44–45; Fynn 1974b:4; Meyerowitz 1952a:70–73; 1974:76–80; Yarak 1986b). The meaning of these gifts, however, cannot immediately be equated with political rights in the fifteenth century.

112. The evolution of Elmina sociopolitical institutions, as interpreted through oral histories and documentary sources, is succinctly reviewed by Henige (1974). Some oral traditions provide king lists that extend back before the founding of Castelo de São Jorge da Mina and include Caramansa (Kwamina Ansa) as the ɔhen ruling at the time of the castle's foundation (Meyerowitz 1952a:73; Wartemberg 1951:87). These, however, were heavily influenced by late nineteenth- and early twentieth-century European historiography.

113. Henige (1974:504), in fact, suggests that Caramansa can be considered as no more than "a prominent personage in the Elmina area." However, as Hair (1994b:55–56 n. 37) points out, he is referred to as a king or prince in Portuguese sources, and he was clearly "the most prominent personage locally." Hair also provides a useful discussion of the references to Caramansa as well as the possible etymology of the name. Also see Hair 1966:18; cf. Ballong-Wen-Mewuda 1984:95, 462, 465.

114. The reference to the town as an independent republic mostly governed by the Portuguese is drawn from a 1629 map of the coast drawn by an anonymous Dutch cartographer (Daaku 1970:183–184).

115. In Akan, ɔhene (pl. ahene) is the term for "chief "or "ruler." Lesser village chiefs owe allegiance to the ɔmanhen, or "paramount king," the term now used for the executive and administrative head of the Edina state.

116. The selection process for an ɔmanhen prior to the twentieth century is difficult to trace, for this is not well described in documentary sources. The role of the members of Enyampa Asafo is in contrast with other Akan office succession that is typically selected by families (mmusua). At Elmina, family membership is a criterion secondary to that of the asafo membership: The candidate for ɔmanhen must be a member of either the Anona or Nsona clans. As Feinberg (1970b) points out, a major consequence of this is that there is no Elmina "royal family." It has been suggested that the patrilineal aspect of the ɔmanhen office may reflect non-Fante, or even non-Akan, influences (Henige 1974:510; Feinberg 1970b). In any case, it is likely indicative of the unique historical setting in which the Edina state emerged. Dispute over the lines of succession and patrilineal inheritance is an issue in other coastal Fante states, as well as at Elmina (Chouin 1996, 1998a:65–73).

117. Asafo: literally sa, "war," and fo, "people." The asafo organization may have originated among the coastal Akan and then spread to interior Akan, Ewe, and Ga groups.

118. The asafo are the focus of an ongoing research project by the University of Ghana, Legon, and the Norwegian University of Science and Technology (e.g., Hernaes 1998).

119. This point can, in part, be illustrated by the Europeans' apparent lack of understanding of what the asafo system was. A French visitor to Elmina in 1670s described how the "Negroes who are in the village below the fortress took their arms and came three or four hundred in number with their unfurled flag to have a drill at the castle. I thought that they were doing that on his orders but he [the Dutch governor general] told it was at their own initiative, that they were crazy people who assembled at every moment, day and night" (Chouin, n.d.-b). I am grateful to Gérard Chouin for drawing this source to my attention and providing a translation.

120. Some sources suggest that the military organization of the Asante was based on the lineage system prior to 1700, after which date the king of Asante instituted a system whereby organization crosscut lineages (Busia cited in Christensen 1954:107).

121. Examining Eguafo, Chouin (1998a:129–141) notes the emergence of military associations that can be compared to *asafo* in the second half of the seventeenth century.

122. The 10 *asafo* companies were: Ankobia, Akyimfo, Nkodwofo, Wombir, Abesi, Alatabanfo, Enyampafo, Brofonkowa, Maworefo, Akrampufo (Feinberg 1969:81; cf. Amissah 1975:10). The names and spellings of the different companies vary.

123. Several Asante missions were sent to Elmina (e.g., Baesjou 1979a).

124. A letter from O'Reilly, acting civil commandant, to Goldsworthy, colonial secretary, Cape Coast, states, "I believe it is highly probable that the Ashantees do come to the outlying villages such as Brainoo Akrim, Ampenney, Asiaman & Broninboomah all of which are full of Elmina people who formerly lived in the bombarded portion of the town of Elmina" (Ghana National Archives, Accra, letter dated August 1, 1873, Elmina, ADM 23/1/36, page 280). I thank Gérard Chouin for this reference.

2. THE ELMINA SETTLEMENT

1. Leveling of the town site began within a year of the bombardment. Stanley observed: "The ruins that have disfigured the neighborhood of the Castle of St. George since the destruction of the native town last June, by launches and boats of the English fleet, are being removed by convict labour, and a wide embankment is being constructed along the right bank of the Beyah [i.e., the Benya Lagoon]" (1874:85). However, archaeological data suggest that filling and leveling of the site continued in some parts of the peninsula for the next decade.

2. The works of each of these authors have been translated and published in works of varying quality (Jones 1986, 1987, 1994).

3. Also see annotations in Barbot 1992:458.

4. A map inserted after page 500 in the *British Parliamentary Papers* 1970a shows the vegetation in the Elmina area in 1873. Although not detailed, the Elmina area is shown as "Forest of large trees. no undergrowth," and the interior of the Benya Lagoon is "Dense brush & scrub."

5. All documentary evidence indicates that settlement north of the Benya was quite limited until the nineteenth century. The majority of the old standing buildings in the present town, north of the Benya, are clearly nineteenth-century (Bech and Hyland 1978; Hyland 1970). It has, however, been suggested that the early village was divided on either side of the Benya Lagoon. This is linked to the claims of the Eguafo and Fetu polities over Elmina (see discussion in note 10 below).

6. A version of the same event by João de Barros and a slightly different version of Pina are given in Hair 1994b:33–34.

7. Both Barros and Pina use the name "Aldea das Duas Partes." Pina states: "[H]e [Azambuja] arrived near the village, which was called das Duas Partes" (translated in Blake 1942:72; see also Hair 1994b:16).

8. The most clearly discerned archaeological example of divisions within a settlement from the Akan area is provided by the site of Begho, which had four quarters 1–2 km (0.6–1.2 miles) from one another. Oral histories suggest these may have represented areas occupied by the Akan-speaking Bron; Muslim Mande merchants; artisans; and the Nyaho, a mixed settlement (Posnansky 1987:17–20). Also see Farrar 1996.

9. Viewed from the east and northeast, the mouth of the Benya and the discrete settlements on each side are difficult to discern.

10. The earliest references to a division of the Elmina settlement between Fetu and Eguafo date to the early seventeenth century, almost 150 years after the founding of the castle. More recent writers, however, have commonly linked the Fetu-Eguafo claims with the fifteenth-century references to the Village of Two Parts, further accepting that these parts were divided by the Benya Lagoon. Van Dantzig states: "As the town straddled the Benya, which formed the border between the Eguafo and the Fetu states, there was no strong leadership . . ." (1980a:9). Also see Burton 1863:63; Crone 1937:109; Blake 1942:44; Ward 1958:70; Ballong-Wen-Mewuda 1984:76, 95–106; and van Dantzig 1990:207.

11. Wilks (1962:339; 1982; 1993:4–8) discusses the presence of Mande traders at Elmina, and van

Dantzig suggests that Elmina's two parts consisted of "a largely Mande trading town situated
on the rocky tip of the Elmina peninsula and an
Akan fishing and salt-making village farther to
the west, where fisherman could safely land their
canoes on the beach" (1990:207). The evidence of
a Mande presence at Elmina is critically ap-
praised by Hair (1994b:53–54 n. 33, 55–56 n. 37).
The Portuguese were certainly familiar with the
kingdom of Mali, and Portuguese missions were
dispatched in 1487, 1488, and 1534, but these were
from the Gambia River, not Elmina (see comments by Hair in Jobson 1999:7). An emissary
was also sent to Mali in the 1490s (Teixeira da
Mota cited in Hair 1994b:51 n. 28), and this may
also have been from the Gambia (Paul Hair, correspondence, January 22, 2000).

　　As will be discussed in Chapter 4, evidence for
salt production and an extensive marine fishing
industry and interior trade during the fifteenth
century is also limited.

12. Garrard (1980b:25) and Hair (1994b:55) suggest
that the term *mansa* was brought by African interpreters who accompanied the Portuguese.
See Hair 1966 for a useful review of interpreters
in African-European interactions between 1440
and 1560.

13. Some indication of the limited land available for
settlement is suggested by early illustrations. In
particular, 1671 French plans show the shoreline
extending very close to the northeast, north, and
northwest walls of the castle. This view is consistent with archaeological evidence. The illustrations are in the collections of the Centre des
Archives d'Outre-Mer, Aix-en-Provence, France:
Dépôt des Fortifications des Colonies, Côtes
d'Afrique, "Les plans des deux forts qui sont à
Saint George de la Mine" (XIII/24pfb/83), and
"Le plan du chasteau de Saint George de la
Mine" (XIII/24pfb/84), par Gimosac (de Gémosat), 1671. One of the group, including a close-
up of the castle, is published in Roussier
1935:Plate VI. I thank Gérard Chouin for bringing
these illustrations to my attention.

14. The wall is also shown very clearly in different
versions of plans of Elmina Castle done in 1637
(Lawrence 1963:Plate 7; Vogt 1979:174).
Ulsheimer's view of Elmina circa 1603 also
seems to show a wall at this point (reproduced in
Jones 1983:22).

15. A 1572 Portuguese document states that the
Elmina Christians "should have their dwellings in
one place, in that area which is closest to the
fortress" (Teixeira da Mota and Hair 1988:78).
This statement is made within a discussion of
Christian instruction and cannot necessarily be
taken to mean that there were not already
houses of both Christians and non-Christians
close to the fort.

16. The nature of the Portuguese-African interactions during this initial period remains unclear.
Portuguese accounts refer to conflict, but the inhabitants are reportedly appeased with gifts. Yet,
whereas Barros reports that the inhabitants "consented easily and without offense" to the destruction of some of their houses, the following passage reports that the Africans forbade the
Portuguese to draw water and "they began to
need water urgently" (see discussion in Hair
1994b:36–37). This would seem to suggest continued tensions. Barros goes on to note that because
of the many "thefts and ill-deeds" of the people,
"Diogo de Azambuja thought it necessary to
burn their village, after which, as between this
punishment and the benefits they for the most
part gained, peace and security were maintained"
(in Hair 1994b:36). A 1531 account further notes
that the inhabitants of the town actually started
to move away (Blake 1942:135–136). The text of
the document, however, discusses the undesirability of this situation and the need for the
Africans to be "defended, protected and instructed, and not banished." There were also periodic conflicts during the Dutch period, most
notably in 1739–40 (Feinberg 1989:145–151).

17. Vogt (1979:191) also states that the Africans fled to
the castle during the 1637 Dutch attack. This
practice continued during the following centuries. In fact, even during the conflict with the
Asante following the 1873 bombardment of
Elmina, women and children, as well as people
loyal to the British, were given refuge in the
castle (*British Parliamentary Papers* 1970a:474).

18. Vogt (1979:99) indicates that the wall was built
during the major renovations initiated in 1540s,
which continued for most of the century, but no
further details are provided. The references he
cites are from Lawrence 1963:62, 108, which discuss the castle's defenses, not the peninsula wall.

19. Barbot describes "a strong rock-stone wall, in

which is a gate, defended by some iron guns and a large ditch" (translated in Feinberg 1989:93). This account is an expanded version of Dapper's, with the reference to a rock wall and a large ditch having been added (Barbot 1992:375). Alternatively, Müller (in Jones 1983:142) refers to a "remarkably deep ditch hewn out of hard rock." Feinberg (1989:80) suggests that the wall was clay rather than stone. This is possible, but in any case the wall almost certainly took advantage of the natural contour of the bedrock.

Lawrence's (1963:129) suggestion that the peninsula wall was located near the "huge pits, quarried deep in the rock, almost half a mile from the castle" is unlikely. Even in the late nineteenth century these pits, remnants of stone quarrying undertaken through the twentieth century, would have been well beyond the maximum extent of the settlement. The wall was located much closer to the castle.

20. It is of marginal note that if the plans are reduced so the peninsula is of similar dimensions, the wall shown in the 1637 plan is approximately in the area suggested, with the areas of standing water just to the west. This likely means very little, however, because the plans are clearly rife with inaccuracies. The scaled-down plans, in fact, show Ft. St. Jago in widely different positions.

21. For additional published illustrations of Elmina, see Bech and Hyland 1978; Lawrence 1963; Pezzoli and Brena 1990; and Roussier 1935.

22. A single large building of distinctive shape shown on the northern edge of the peninsula settlement may have been an attempt to locate a specific building, but this is speculative.

23. References to the wall disappear, but allusions to the chapel that had been located near the wall continue. A 1709 account notes an "old Portuguese Chapel" in use as a guardhouse at the end of the African settlement (Balme Library, Furley Collection, Gold Coast Tribal States Notebooks, 1707–15, N58). De Marrée (1818) also does not discuss the wall but does mention the remains of a Portuguese chapel, "perhaps named St. Joris church" (translated in Feinberg 1969:115–116). De Marrée (1818, 2:10) then described passing this point and *continuing* for another 500 steps to the end of the village. Also see 1702 and 1764 references in Feinberg 1989:93 n. 13. Lawrence (1963:114) doubts de Marrée's com-

ments because the building would have been long robbed for stone and all vestiges removed. However, the presence of traces of the church in the early nineteenth century may have been made more likely by the continued use of the church as a guardhouse.

24. Some earlier illustrations do show dwellings in this area. Ulsheimer's plan of circa 1602, which appears to show a wall between the castle and the foreshore, also seems to illustrate houses southeast of the castle (reproduced in Jones 1983:22). Buildings are also illustrated in this area in the 1671 French plan (Roussier 1935:Plate VI). If structures were located in this area before the seventeenth century, they were likely impermanent structures connected with the European garrison, not part of the African town.

25. Feinberg notes: "Another term used [by the Dutch] for part of the village was the 'fisherman's village,' which undoubtedly was located near the river but exactly where is not known" (1969:112–113). It would also seem possible that the site southeast of the castle could have been intended.

26. The garden may have included a summerhouse. This is referred to by Barbot (1992:388), who describes a "large, round, open and curious summerhouse, with a cupola-roof, several steps leading up to it," though he may have been confusing Elmina with Frederiksborg. Lawrence, without reference, notes: "An engraving of 1704 represents it [the summerhouse] as a little classical building, which apparently consisted of a raised wooden platform, a circle of wooden arches and a dome of thatch" (1963:148).

27. A careful description is given by de Marrée (see Feinberg 1969:117).

28. The bridge apparently had not been constructed by 1645, when Hemmersam left the coast (see Jones 1983:131). However, it does appear on a French plan of 1671, which shows a break in the middle (Roussier 1935:Plate VI). In 1744 William Smith noted "a beautiful Draw-Bridge, after the *Dutch* fashion" (1967:131). Wartemberg recounts a tradition that relates that Nana Ebu II objected to the bridge's construction because the ɔmanhen had "never traveled from his seat nor crossed a bridge" (1951:71). He adds that the bridge was built "in the teeth of opposition" by the eminent Dutch engineer Jacobus Ruhle. However, as dis-

cussed, the office of *ɔmanhen* appeared at a substantially later date, and Ebu II does not appear
in lineages until the twentieth century (Henige
1974:502). The tradition, hence, may be an invention or a conflation with a more recent event.
The drawbridge was no doubt more appropriate
than the fixed span bridge that served the town
during much of the later twentieth century and
did not allow enough clearance for fishing boats
to pass beneath it at flood tide. This problem has
been remedied by a new bridge constructed in
the 1990s.

29. Lawrence (1963:164–165), surveying late eighteenth-century illustrations, suggests that the
bridge was moved "some eighty feet upstream"
at this time. This seems very unlikely, for this
would have placed the bridge in an area that was
substantially wider and bordered on each side by
sandy, sloping foreshores. It is more likely that
the "move" reflects a discrepancy in the plans. In
fact, nineteenth-century illustrations seem to
show the bridge in roughly the same position as
earlier drawings. For example, note an 1806 ren-
dering by Webster for the duke of Clarence, reproduced in Bech and Hyland 1978:28.

30. A 1730 document notes the construction of a
stone wall that ran "about half the length of the
Castle" (van Dantzig 1978:246).

31. See the 1671 French plan (Roussier 1935:Plate VI).

32. Also see comments by Feinberg (1979) and Jones
(1980) concerning the originality of some of
Smith's observations. Smith was sent to West
Africa by the Royal African Company to complete maps and plans of Royal African Company
forts and settlements and to collect information
on the major rivers. His observations on the key
in the Benya Lagoon seem to be his own.

33. De Marrée (1818) describes a walk through this
area and identifies the owners of the houses by
name (translated in Feinberg 1969:115–116; see
also Bech and Hyland 1978; Hyland 1970; van
den Nieuwenhof 1991).

34. A British report of 1873 notes "a small village of
mud huts, occupied by Javamen pensioners"
(*British Parliamentary Papers* 1970b:359; see also
van Dantzig 1980a:76).

35. Documents dated August 18, 1818, in the Algemeen Rijkarchief (NBKG 374, fol. 64), The
Hague, indicate that officials had sometime earlier founded a *societeit,* or clubhouse, in the gar-

den house of Johan Neizer but that Neizer was
claiming it back, so an attempt was being made to
locate a new site, which was eventually found at
the corner of High and Marblestone streets (Albert van Dantzig, correspondence, January 17,
1989). There are other references to places for re-
laxation at various locations during the early
nineteenth century. De Marrée (1818) notes "a
very good building" built by General Bartels as a
"pleasure house" and also the "remainder of a
building, formerly having served for an inn, provided with a billiard, where the officials delighted
outside of business times" (in Feinberg 1969:117).

36. Vogt (1979:149, 190) notes that the dismantling of
the chapel may have also been linked to hostilities
with the king of Efutu, whose conversion to
Christianity was the raison d'être for its construction. Although this is possible, the reason remains
speculative.

37. During the Dutch period, this weakness was also
commented on by Barbot, who found it amazing
that the Dutch director general did not realize
that "if this redoubt [Coenraadsburg] were once
captured, it would mean the loss of Mina"
(1992:380).

38. A detailed description of the forts is given in a report by J. Fred Crease, September 8, 1873 (*British
Parliamentary Papers* 1970b:359–362). The dating
and appearance of the redoubts are also discussed
by Lawrence (1963:80–82) and van Dantzig
(1980a:17).

39. A British report of June 5, 1873, notes: "In each redoubt there are guns in good and serviceable
order, but no shelter to protect the men from the
sun or rain, or I would station a corporal's guard
in each of them" (*British Parliamentary Papers*
1970a:473).

40. Lawrence dates the tower to the last decade of
the eighteenth century on the basis of de Marrée's (1818) reference to the "flag tower" and on
limited stylistic grounds from the brickwork. The
tower appears on the 1829 plan, but not the plan
of 1799, which, unfortunately, does not include
the area where the tower is located.

41. On the basis of the documents, it is difficult to determine the positions of Waakzaamheid and the
later Veersche Schans, or Fort de Veer. De Marrée
(1818) describes Waakzaamheid as having been
"about five hundred footsteps higher up, westwards from the village (translated in Feinberg

1969:115), and an 1873 British report places Fort de Veer "some 400 yards" from the ruins of the old town (*British Parliamentary Papers* 1970b:361). These statements would seem to accord nicely, but only if the size of the settlement in 1817 and the early 1870s was the same and if the distances given were accurate. In fact, the settlement was likely substantially larger in 1873 and the later fort located much farther west.

42. The 1799 plan and eighteenth-century Dutch references label Cattoenbergh as "Galgen Berg" and Coebergh as "Krabben" or "Crabben Berg." Galgen Berg can be translated as "Gallows Hill," and Krabben, the plural of *crab,* would mean "Crabs Hill."

43. For discussion of similar interpretive difficulties in a colonial North American context, see Yentsch 1994.

44. The term *bron* is used by various historical and modern writers to refer to divisions within coastal towns. The word's origin is the Akan *borɔŋ* (pl. *mborɔŋ*), literally meaning "street" or "lane" (Christaller 1881:41; McCaskie 1995:276).

45. For example, Vogt states: "Sale of personal clothing by crew members was permitted on a limited scale and all such transactions had to be made through the intermediary of the factor of the post. Direct bartering between the crews and the Africans was strictly forbidden" (1979:34). Ordinary members of the garrison were also to buy hens only from traders calling at the fort or from "specially entrusted individuals" who were searched on their return (Hair 1994b:71 n. 97; see also Ballong-Wen-Mewuda 1984; Birmingham 1970:2).

46. In a memorandum by Heerman Abramsz, translated in van Dantzig 1978:19–20. Writing somewhat later, Barbot (1992:512, 514 n. 9) noted that the market or parade grounds of Elmina and Cape Coast were paved with stone.

47. In a 1739 report by M. Hoesen and J. Bontan, translated in van Dantzig 1978:345. It may or not be significant that this regulation was adopted during the directorship of Director General Martinus de Bordes, who behaved in an unusual manner and may have been mentally ill (Feinberg 1989:88).

48. A suggestion of the square's varying function is given by Barbot (1992:514 n. 9), who uses both the term *parade-ground* and the term *market* in differ-

ent versions of his work. Barbot was almost certainly referring to the square in front of the Elmina Castle; however, he gives no clear indication of the location. It is possible that the space was both market and parade ground, with a formal portion (paved with stone) adjacent to a market. It is this same area that is today the site of the meeting of chiefs, which culminates the Bakatue Festival.

49. Algemeen Rijksarchief, NBKG 362. I am indebted to Adam Jones for this reference and translation (correspondence, June 11, 1987). At Cape Coast the English appear to have had somewhat more success in alternating the plan of the African settlement, "opening up a few good streets" and creating a parade ground opposite the principal entrance (Cruickshank 1853, 1:23–24).

50. For varying interpretations, discussions, and references see Busia 1951; Firman-Sellars 1996; McCaskie 1995; and Wilks 1993.

51. Algemeen Rijksarchief, NBKG 318, certificate by W. Butler. I am grateful to Albert van Dantzig for this reference and translation (correspondence, January 17, 1989).

52. Algemeen Rijksarchief, NBKG 239, note by N. Somerus, March 16, 1736. I am indebted to Adam Jones for this reference and translation (correspondence, April 8, 1987).

53. See also Algemeen Rijksarchief, NBKG 301, folio 135 (Albert van Dantzig, correspondence, January 17, 1989).

54. Complexities of ownership are illustrated by continuing disputes over house ownership.

55. Lawrence (1963:105) notes that a "spring" was discovered during the building of the castle. This is not elaborated on, and no other mention of a spring on the site appears in the records. The 1647 plan shows several wells, including one at the tip of the peninsula—an area of exposed bedrock. Even if wells could be dug (there are some deep pockets of soil), the quality of the water cannot have been very good. The only other reference to a water source on the peninsula itself is a "rainwater pit" built under the direction of Director General J. Valkenburgh in the mid-seventeenth century (noted in Feinberg 1989:94 n. 24). This, or similar structures, may explain the "wells" or "pits" shown on the 1647 plan.

56. These drainages may have been adequate to

meet the needs of Elmina between the fifteenth and the early seventeenth centuries but may have been insufficient as the population expanded or during times of drought. Wartemberg (1951:15) records that the original location of the African settlement was selected because of the availability of drinking water, the immigrants having exclaimed "Be enya," "I have found," when they discovered the Anwin (Annwew), which, according to Wartemberg, is synonymous with *anno-mansa,* or "inexhaustible water supply." The name "Be enya" was later mistakenly applied to the lagoon.

57. The source described by Hemmersam might be the same one the Elmina people prohibited the Portuguese from reaching in 1482 (Blake 1942:77). Also note the 1510 reference quoted in Hair 1994b:90 n. 185.

58. A detailed description of the water system was given by Phillips in 1732 (quoted by the editors in Barbot 1992:405).

59. Similar seventeenth-century descriptions of house construction are provided by Brun (1611–20) (in Jones 1983:86), Hemmersam (1639–45) (in Jones 1983:108), Müller (1662–69) (in Jones 1983:201), Zur Eich (1659–69) (in Jones 1983:262), and Oettinger (1692–93) (in A. Jones 1985:185).

60. Compare an account by Ulsheimer, who notes, "[T]heir houses are mere huts and not large, being made merely of reeds, and so small that they can hardly do anything in them except sleep" (in Jones 1983:33).

61. Also see descriptions in Bennett and Brooks 1965:118; Bosman 1967:42–43; de Marrée 1818:10; Hawthorne 1845:137; Hutton 1821:54–55; and Meredith 1967:83. Stone was traditionally used on some parts of the coast for foundations or low walls, for example, in the Krobo hills. These were, however, much smaller structures than the multistoried, course stone dwellings found at Elmina.

62. Freeman stated: "Elmina is the only West African town in which I have seen native houses built of stone (I do not consider houses built in the European style by workmen trained by Europeans, 'native houses'), and here the natives evidently learned the art from Dutch settlers" (1898:125).

63. Ballong-Wen-Mewuda (1984:206, 229, 300–301) notes provisions for four masons in 1495–99 pe-

riod, two in 1514 and 1529, four in 1600, 1603–8, and one in 1632.

64. Also see Vogt 1979:166–167, 171 for references to Portuguese masons. Wartemberg (1951:25) notes the Elmina people as being quick to learn from the Portuguese, and he notes local traditions crediting the Elmina as having been skilled stone workers, suggesting that stone masonry was learned early in the Portuguese period. As noted, however, both the archaeological and historical data suggest a later introduction.

65. In particular, note accounts by Brun (in Jones 1983:85), Hemmersam (in Jones 1983:108), and de Marees (1987). These writers mention architecture and refer to Elmina but make no mention of stone buildings. Discussing the early years of the Dutch occupation, Hemmersam (in Jones 1983:127) notes that masons, presumably European, were sent from Elmina to undertake repairs at the old Portuguese fort at Shama, west of Elmina. On other parts of the Gold Coast, European masons were still used in the early eighteenth century (e.g., Hair 1994b:73 n. 106).

66. A document dated September 2, 1739, reported a number of complaints from the townspeople, including the fact that "[t]he Donko slaves, when they go to quarry stones, deprive the women in the market of their bread, cloth, and *kakeraas*" (translated by van Dantzig 1978:345). The last refers to a mixture of brass filings that circulated as currency. Although the site of the quarry is not described, it was likely at the western margin of the peninsula (see Chapter 3).

67. This and all other English translations of quotations from Gramberg 1861, which was published in Dutch, are courtesy of Albert van Dantzig.

68. Examples of thatch roofs on stone two-storied dwellings can still be seen at Anomabu, east of Elmina. Today the majority of houses in the coastal towns are roofed with tin sheets.

69. An 1874 description of Cape Coast notes: "Flat roofs are used with every house" (*Daily News* Special Correspondent 1874:40; see also Gordon 1874:4). The account also indicates the erosion of the walls by the rains. The houses of the poorer people had thatch roofs.

70. In one unique eighteenth-century instance, the hall in Elmina Castle was roofed with lead sheeting. There is at least one example of African timber and clay construction being used on a Euro-

pean structure on the coast: the early nineteenth-century Danish plantation house at Daccubie (DeCorse 1993).

71. Copies of photographs taken circa 1888–89 can be seen in the collections of the Military Museum in Kumasi, Ghana, and also at the Koninklijk Instituut voor Taal-, Land- en Volkenkunde, University of Leiden, document H 449 (Adam Jones, correspondence, March 6, 1989). Yarak (1995) notes that daguerreotypes were made of Elmina as early as 1840. In addition, the nineteenth-century European merchant Hubertus Bartels was a photographer (van den Nieuwenhof 1991:51, 102), yet no examples of images predating the town's 1873 destruction have been located. A wonderful collection of photos from 1890 is being published by Michel Doortmont (n.d.).

72. See discussions of churches within the castle in Lawrence 1963:127; and Hair 1994b:92–93. The principal church during the later Portuguese period was in the castle's main courtyard. There was also a chapel located adjacent to the burial ground in the northwest corner of the riverside yard by the time of the Dutch takeover, for it appears on the 1637 and 1647 plans as well as in Hemmersam's description of the 1640s (in Jones 1983:130). During the Dutch period the church in the courtyard was converted into the House of Trade, and a Dutch Reformed church was built on the east side of the inner courtyard (Lawrence 1963:142–43).

73. The conversion of the king of Efutu "on the eve of Santyago" is discussed in a 1503 document translated by Blake (1942:95–96). The construction of a chapel is discussed, but it is in the village Efutu. Vogt (1979:55, 149) suggests that this event was linked to the chapel on St. Jago Hill. De Marees (1987:219) relates the dismantling of the chapel to the 1596 Dutch attempt to capture Elmina.

74. Balme Library, Furley Collection, Gold Coast Tribal States Notebooks, 1707–15, N58.

75. See discussion in Chapter 6. Understanding of the full extent of variation in African mortuary practices is far from complete, and there are no convenient surveys of the data that are available. Documentary records provide only limited information, and most descriptions are provided by twentieth-century ethnographies. Archaeological data are also limited. The diversity in specific mortuary patterns and interment practices at Elmina is also illustrated in other African contexts. Recognition of the complexity of African burial practice and the cultural diversity represented need to be carefully considered when examining burial practices among populations in the African diaspora.

76. Interviews with Nana Kojo Nquandoh, Peter King Badu Prah, and Decosta Vroom, Elmina, Ghana, 1986–87. Other people also mentioned finding bones and artifacts in this area.

77. Literally, "the bush of the *asaman*," or spirits of the ancestors. See discussion in Chapter 6.

78. It is not evidenced by the documents, but it is possible that the criminals executed on Cattoenbergh (Galgen Berg) were buried there. Fort Coenraadsburg served as a prison for condemned prisoners during the colonial period, and burials may also have been placed there.

79. Note van Dantzig 1980a:86 for some observations on European burial practices at Elmina and on the Gold Coast in general.

80. The year 1806 appears on a plaque on the large central monument of the "new" Dutch cemetery. Lawrence (1963:167), citing de Marrée 1818, notes a cemetery near the shore of the bay inaugurated in 1802, so the one located on the north side of the St. Jago Hill must date later than this. The central monument was not a tomb but rather was used for the storage of bodies prior to burial. It was opened and found empty by Albert van Dantzig in the 1970s (van Dantzig, conversation, January 7, 1989).

81. I am indebted to Michel Doortmont for drawing my attention to the possible existence of this cemetery.

82. When the swamplands were initially dredged and reclaimed to make salt pans is not clear. Limited clearing was undertaken in the nineteenth century to improve fields of fire. Note the references to brush clearing in *British Parliamentary Papers* 1970a:445, 449; 1970b:331, 361. Wartemberg states: "The reclamation of the swampy areas and the extension of the embankment was the work of Mr. Baxter, an Engineer appointed by the English Government" (1951:71). Reclamation for what purpose is not made clear, but salt production seems likely. Wartemberg (1951:72) further notes that a small experimental steam plant was in-

stalled on the lagoon in 1930. Removal of the mangroves during the late nineteenth and twentieth centuries accords well with archaeological data (see Chapter 3).

83. See reviews of relevant legislation in Bech and Hyland 1978:105–107; Kankpeyeng 1996; and Nunoo 1972. The Ghana Museums and Monuments Board was broadly inclusive in what it was willing to consider designating a historic monument, including nineteenth-century houses in coastal towns, the residences of chiefs, mosques, and shrines. Unfortunately, it has been primarily the major forts and castles that have been studied and afforded protection. This is, however, a result of financial constraints and not a policy decision.

84. Note the structures shown west of the castle in Groll 1968:Plate 9. A photograph taken by Doran Ross in 1974 shows two small, wooden-frame structures in this area (Geary and Nicolls 1992:17). The presence of buildings in this area was also noted by informants at Elmina in 1990.

85. A pile of tombstone fragments from this operation was long stacked on the east bastion of Fort Coenraadsburg. Other fragments were recovered from fill layers during the 1986 excavations.

86. The work undertaken is probably best called renovation or reconstruction rather than restoration. Modern plumbing and facilities have been added, and the peaked roofs have been done with Dutch-style terracotta tiles. Although the latter make the buildings more attractive, many of the Dutch-period roofs would have been flat. Study of the structures' complex history of construction and renovation work has not been undertaken.

3. THE ARCHAEOLOGY OF AN AFRICAN TOWN

1. Symbols representing *sankofa* (or *sonkofa*) appear widely in Akan art. The proverb may be graphically represented by heart-shaped designs found on Adinkra cloth or calabashes, or it may be represented three dimensionally as a backward-looking bird.

2. A notable exception is the site of Qsar es-Seghir, Morocco, which was first a medieval Islamic city and then a Portuguese stronghold between 1458 and 1550 (Redman 1986). As a Portuguese settlement it is very distinct from the African settle-

ment at Elmina. Of course, the presence of modern settlement does not preclude the presence of archaeological deposits, and, in fact, finds have been exposed at both Cape Coast and Christiansborg castles. However, locating and excavating such finds are much more difficult.

3. The late Nana Kofi Condua V, ɔmanhen of the Edina traditional area, and other elders poured libations for a second time on July 31, 1990, at the beginning of the 1990 field season, and elders have poured libations at the start of each field season at Elmina, as well as at all other sites where excavations have taken place. In the case of survey, traditional leaders are always met with before work begins.

4. Although this assessment proved incorrect, when I began work in Ghana in 1985, Elmina was only one of three sites that I asked the Ghana National Museums and Monuments Board for permission to excavate. The other sites were the Danish plantation of Daccubie, near Accra, which was excavated in 1987 (DeCorse 1993), and Butre, in the Eastern Region, where excavations began in 1993.

5. See discussion in Chapter 2. The principal wards in the eighteenth century were the Ankobia, Akim, Encodjo, Apendjafoe, Abesi, Allade, and Enyampa. On the basis of documentary reconstruction of the possible location of the wards and the archaeologically defined margins of the town, the areas exposed at Loci A, B, C, and D might have included Ankobia, Akim, and/or Encodjo. Areas farther west, as far as Locus G, may have included Allade and/or Enyampa. The area southeast of the castle (Locus E) was possibly Apendjafoe (Feinberg 1989:106).

6. These have been compiled and revised into the Central Region Project Field Manual (DeCorse 2000a). Some of the recording and procedures are being modified to meet demands at sites other than Elmina.

7. Most areas were examined multiple times. Because of development and increased activity on portions of the site, there were sometimes dramatic differences in the deposits exposed and the material present on the surface at different times.

8. Initially, mapping was completed using a compass, hand level, and tapes. Distances were then checked in 1987 with an electronic range finding transit and found to be less than 10 cm (3.9

inches) off over 400 m (437 yards). I extend thanks to Diederik Six and Arjen Joustra, who made the transit available.

9. Trash accumulated very rapidly. Test excavations at Locus D in 1986 showed only limited amounts of modern refuse. However, when excavation resumed in 1990, two weeks were spent removing modern rubbish to expose foundations that had earlier been visible on the surface. Subsequent excavation showed that thick deposits of modern trash extended to more than a meter in depth, even over those areas that had been tested in 1986. In 1997 and 1998 mounds of trash, mostly immediately on the ocean edge of the site, towered above the foundations.

10. In particular, the area immediately behind (east of) the Quayson and Bridge houses was tested in 1997 and 2000. The excavations farthest to the east revealed over 2 m (6.5 feet) of twentieth-century trash and waterlogged deposits. Excavations immediately behind Bridge House revealed nineteenth-century foundations resting on beach sand.

11. Surface collections were made at the sites of the redoubts Beekestein, Veersche Schans, and Cattoenbergh (Fort Java) in 1993 and 1997. At Beekestein and Cattoenbergh all of the visible pre-nineteenth-century material was collected. The Veersche Schans site, which has a complex history predating the redoubt, has an extensive scatter of material. However, it has been the focus of intensive archaeological excavation; therefore, only a few diagnostic artifacts were collected to supplement the excavated material.

12. In fact, even 3-mm (⅛-inch) wire mesh is inappropriate for the recovery of many artifacts, such as very small beads. Emphasis was consistently placed on finding all material in place.

13. The Ghana Museums and Monuments Board graciously made Ft. St. Jago available as a field camp during the 1985–87, 1990, and 1993 field seasons. Space in private houses and hotels was rented during the 1997, 1998, and 2000 field seasons.

14. I completed the analysis of the imported material, small finds, and beads with help from Edward Carr in 1997. Analysis of the metal artifacts, shell, building material, and local pottery was completed by Bossman Murey, Seth Danquah, Jackie Becker, and John Ako Okoro under my supervision. A preliminary analysis of the faunal re-

mains from the 1985–87 and 1990 seasons was made by Bourque (1997).

15. Material from the 1986 and 1987 fieldwork was left at the Department of Archaeology, University of Ghana, and artifacts from the 1990, 1993, 1997, 1998, and 2000 field seasons were deposited at West African Historical Museum curation facilities in Cape Coast. Although this obviated the need for shipping large amounts of material to the United States and ensured the prompt completion of analysis, it has made the reexamination and illustration of some material more difficult.

16. Mean ceramic dating was developed by Stanley South (1977a) on the basis of his work on historical sites in eastern North America.

17. In addition to these phases, a limited amount of Late Stone Age material is also represented (see note 47 below).

18. Large sections were burned accidentally or during conflict. For example, following the Elmina-Dutch conflict of 1739 the town was described as being completely in ashes (Feinberg 1969:114, 180). An account in the Algemeen Rijksarchief (NBKG 362), The Hague, reports that fires destroyed a total of 90 houses during March and April 1837 (Adam Jones, correspondence, July 11, 1987).

19. Following Schiffer, we could refer to these deposits as de facto refuse: "*De facto* refuse consists of the tools, facilities, structures, and other cultural materials that, although still usable (or reusable), are left behind when an activity area is abandoned" (1987:89). On the other hand: "Artifacts discarded at their locations of use are termed primary refuse; those discarded elsewhere are known as secondary refuse" (Schiffer 1987:58). Schiffer suggests that "the larger the population of an activity area [e.g., a settlement], and the greater the intensity of occupation, the larger the ratio of secondary to primary refuse produced" (1987:59).

20. Such potential archaeological deposits, constantly washed by the sea, are difficult to locate and recover. Carmel Schrire (1996:107–110), who excavated the Dutch station Oudepost I on the South African coast, noted an instance of discovering a midden deposit, fortuitously exposed by the sea, long after she had completed excavation of the site.

21. Toilet facilities remain a concern at Elmina. Here, as in much of the coastal region, indoor plumbing and latrines are uncommon, and people from throughout the town often go to toilet along the shoreline and on the shore during high tide. Much of the oceanfront along the town site has long been used for this purpose. It continues to be used in this manner today, though there have been efforts to prevent this. There are also public latrine facilities in the town, but these are limited.

22. See discussion in Chapter 6. The burials, some including brick tombs and coffins, could be clearly differentiated from the older features that they cut into.

23. Photographs and oral histories indicate the parade ground was kept cleanly swept by the Ghana police. The grassy area in between the parade ground and the road was marked by white curbstones, and the pedestrian traffic prohibited.

24. This disposal pattern is distinct from those found archaeologically in some eighteenth-century European-American sites, where sheet middens adjacent to doorways, in depressions, and in public streets can often be associated with particular households (e.g., Deagan 1983; South 1977a). The density of the Elmina site makes it more analogous to situations in larger cities and towns, where association of refuse deposits with specific households is impossible.

25. Walking surveys of this area were conducted in 1986–87 and 1990. No artifacts were collected, apart from the mid-eighteenth-century fragment of a delftware bowl. This was the only clearly pre-nineteenth-century artifact noted. The other diagnostic material included 33 tobacco pipe fragments of possible eighteenth- to nineteenth-century age and imported ceramics and glass dating to the nineteenth and twentieth centuries. A more comprehensive surface collection was undertaken as part of the Central Region Development Commission work in 1992 (Anquandah 1992, 1993). A total of 186 artifacts were collected at that time including: 5 fragments of burnt daub, 9 fragments of mammal bone; 21 shells (primarily *Arca senilis*); 5 fragments of glass; 50 pieces of imported ceramics; 67 tobacco pipe fragments; four glass beads; 1 clay tile fragment; and 2 pieces of human bone. The majority of the material (129 artifacts) came from the area east of the fort.

26. It is further suggested that the foundation traces noted may relate to a summerhouse built in the castle's garden during the late seventeenth century by the Dutch. However, the documentary source cited for a garden house in this area is Barbot 1732, and Barbot may have confused Elmina and Frederiksborg in this passage (editors in Barbot 1992:388 n. 26). The archaeological evidence for the plan and age of the foundations recovered is also limited.

27. Anquandah (1992:44; 1993:16) suggests that bricks and tile fragments from these excavations represent the remains of the Portuguese chapel dismantled in the late sixteenth century. This supposition, however, requires more study. The chapel's presumed presence is based on the discovery of red bricks, measuring 21 by 10 by 6 cm (8.2 by 3.9 by 2.3 inches), and red ceramic roof tiles that are identified as Portuguese. Construction material was imported by the Portuguese, and some of this material may have included brick or tile used in the chapel or in the later Portuguese redoubt on St. Jago Hill. However, similar materials were imported by the Dutch, and a wide variety of red bricks were recovered from Dutch-period levels at the Elmina town site. Dutch sites in Amsterdam and elsewhere include bricks of similar dimensions to those excavated at Fort St. Jago.

28. Both documentary evidence and archaeological information indicate that settlement around the redoubts was limited until the late nineteenth and twentieth centuries. Because the purpose of the redoubts was to protect the town, they had been situated at the outer limits of the settlement.

29. See discussion in Chapter 2. Fort Nagtglas was not manned by the British during the conflict of 1873, by which time it was already collapsing. In his report on the defenses, J. Fred Crease stated: "Bearing in mind the distance of this fort from the town, and the expense which would have to be undergone to put it in such repair as would render it habitable, necessitates the draining of the wet ditch, as well as the entire rebuilding of one of its faces. I cannot recommend its being occupied" (*British Parliamentary Papers* 1970b:106). A single, almost completely buried cannon that may be from this redoubt was recorded just north of the Edina tranditional council offices.

30. Surveys of Beekestein in 1990 and 1997 located small amounts of artifacts of probable nineteenth-century age. These were, however, clearly from disturbed contexts and, aside from possibly confirming the nineteenth-century occupation of the redoubt, they were of limited value.

31. This collection was undertaken with the help of George Sackey, then curator for the Ghana Museums and Monuments Board, and student volunteers from the Foundation for Field Research during July 1990. The site was visited again during the 1997 field season. In each instance all of the diagnostic surface material observed was collected, making a total artifact count of 193.

32. They are now in disrepair, and one has completely collapsed.

33. I am grateful to Michel Doortmont for pointing this out to me. The channel passes across the northern side of Trafalgar Square, crosses Buitenrust Lane, and then turns south toward the lagoon. This area was the location of the Ruhle and Neizer plantations in the nineteenth century.

34. The original shoreline appears to have been much closer to Liverpool Street and the back (eastern) side of the houses along the street. Oral histories and documentary sources suggest that this area was used as a burial ground, but, although the site was repeatedly surveyed, no archaeological material predating the twentieth century has been identified. Test excavations revealed only thick deposits of twentieth-century fill and trash. It is possible that early archaeological deposits lie buried beneath the roadway or the nineteenth-century buildings.

35. During the 1997 field season, 10 test units, 1 by 1 m, were spaced across the area between the castle and the shore. The lack of any cultural features and the waterlogged nature of the deposits support the interpretation that the eighteenth- and nineteenth-century *fisherkrom* was confined to the portion of the peninsula south of the castle and the area of bedrock exposure immediately to the southeast.

36. Collapse of portions of the wall on two occasions and construction of the new bridge provided an opportunity to examine the wall's exposed foundations to a depth of 1 m (3.3 feet) below ebb tide level. This suggests that at least portions of the wall were likely contemporaneous with the previous fixed span bridge. The 2–3 m (3.3–9.8 feet) behind the wall consisted of stone rubble. A single British pipe of late nineteenth- or early twentieth-century age was found in the rubble, suggesting a *terminus post quem* for recent repair, if not the wall's initial construction. It is possible that the pre-nineteenth-century sea walls were located closer to the riverside yard beneath the present roadway (cf. note 37 below).

37. A document of 1730 discusses the house of the *tapoeijer* Andries, which was "located near the bridge" and was razed to make room for two storehouses and a stone wall that ran "about half the length of the Castle" (van Dantzig 1978:246). Although the description is somewhat ambiguous, it suggests that the house was located north-northwest of the castle, between the castle and the bridge.

38. Housing for police officers was located adjacent to the northeast corner of the castle, and cement-block garages were constructed north of the riverside yard. The garages and most of the housing were demolished as part of renovation work in the 1990s.

39. The wall, built to protect the archaeological site in part, is located south of the road along the north side of the peninsula opposite the fish market. It then cuts south across the peninsula in two places to delineate an area for a market. This project was not monitored by archaeologists, but a contractor reported that "the excavations for the wall revealed that the foundations of the houses [representing the old settlement] were about six inches from the ground [surface] and that, the entire length of the wall's foundations passed over archaeological finds" (letter to Kwesi Agbley from Ato Austin, chairman of the Central Region Development Commission, November 21, 1990). Examination of back dirt adjacent to the wall in 1993, 1997, and 1998 revealed limited archaeological material, including a few pipe stem fragments and several nineteenth-century European beads. No artifacts in the back dirt were clearly pre-nineteenth-century. Archaeological testing in 1997 revealed substantial archaeological deposits throughout adjacent areas, and the contractor's observations are not surprising. It is, however, unlikely that the contractor observed foundations along the entire length of the wall. Excavation indicates that much of the area

north of Locus F was waterlogged and filled by refuse during the late nineteenth century.

40. The State Fishing Corporation building dates to the late 1960s or 1970s. Oral histories noted that the foundations of these buildings had been intentionally incorporated into the later building in order to preserve them.

41. K. R. Miller of the Department of Weapons, Equipment and Vehicles, National Army Museum, Chelsea, London, notes: "As the cannon is in such a poor state of preservation it is only possible to give a very general identification of type. . . . As the cannon is of iron this may well indicate a naval origin. Most ships of the early nineteenth century carried small iron cannons with a bore of 1¾–2 inches as close range weapons. They were normally mounted on a swivel to give a wide radius of action and could easily have been demounted from a ship and used in fortifications. I do not think the cannon is an early weapon which probably indicates [given its context at Elmina] that it was used by the Dutch" (correspondence, April 25, 1996).

42. See discussion in Chapter 2. As noted below, this area also appears to have been previously used as a burial area, and this also may account for the fact that the foundations were not extended deeper. However, evidence from many other contexts suggests that burials were frequently disturbed by construction. Additional excavations of Locus G were planned for the 1997 field season, but increasing settlement complicated access to this site. A large number of dwellings were erected without the consent of the Edina traditional council, and it was suggested that excavation could be undertaken. This was not, however, considered practical.

43. In September 1873, J. Fred Crease noted: "The ground in front of this fort [Veersche Schans] is tolerably clear, but the space (some 400 yards) between it and the ruins of the Dutch town, is covered thickly with brush and cactus, and being, moreover, full of water, holes, rocks, and half-sunken quarries, is altogether impenetrable to European troops" (*British Parliamentary Papers* 1970b:361). He is certainly describing the quarry area. Oral histories suggest that the quarry had been in use for centuries (Elmina interviews, 1986, 1990; Calvocoressi 1977:118), but stone could also have been obtained from bedrock

outcrops nearer the town, such as the location of the old Portuguese town wall. A possible 1739 reference to the quarry is translated in van Dantzig 1978:345.

44. The areas around the redoubt and the shore 2 km (1.2 miles) to the west were systematically surveyed in 1986, 1987, 1997, and 1998, and brief visits were made on a number of other occasions. Surface material was only noted, not collected. Iron Age material in this area was first reported by Oliver Davies (1976:77), who described a shell midden on the northern (lagoon) side of the peninsula. A shell scatter that may represent this site was relocated in 1993. Paul Ozanne also collected Late Iron Age ceramics from clay pits between Pehi (Pershie) and Bantoma, approximately 1.5 km (0.9 miles) west of Bantoma (Department of Archaeology, University of Ghana, Catalog No. 61.249-254).

45. A particularly dense concentration of material near the Coconut Grove Beach Resort was tested in June and July 2000. The material excavated included a large assemblage of local ceramics, stone beads, tuyere fragments, and a limited number of flaked quartz tools, but no European trade materials.

46. Ceramics of this type have been found at a number of sites and, typically, are not associated with European trade materials. Similar ceramics have thermoluminescence dates of A.D. 1012 ± 124 and 887 ± 104 at Elmina and A.D. 1112 ± 276 and 1109 ± 146 at Brenu Akyinim (James K. Feathers, reports, September 19, 1995, and April 27, 1997). No charcoal or organic deposits suitable for carbon 14 dating were recovered. Central Region Project excavations at Eguafo in 2000 recovered similar ceramics, and a small number of associated trade materials of probable fifteenth- to seventeenth-century age.

47. Evidence of Stone Age occupation at Elmina is limited. Material from excavations consisted of one quartz flake and two groundstone celts. These may, in fact, not necessarily represent a Stone Age occupation, for these artifacts continue to occur in Iron Age assemblages. They are still ritually important and can be purchased in markets. At the Bantoma excavations, Calvocoressi found a single quartz flake, and isolated flakes were also noted on the surface west of Bantoma.

48. The single outlying European artifact was an intact nineteenth-century bottle. This was found approximately 10 m (33 feet) from the shoreline in an upright position with only the mouth visible above the ground. It was firmly stuck in the ground, and at the time of discovery it appeared to have been only recently exposed by erosion. None of the inhabitants of the nearby compound was aware of the bottle or its possible reason for being there. No other archaeological materials were found in the vicinity, and no pre-twentieth-century material was found for another 200 m (219 yards) to the east.

49. Calvocoressi's archaeological work clearly demonstrated the presence of burials at the site, and it is likely that burials are located in adjacent areas. The exposed burials south of the redoubt were first noted during the 1990 survey. More bone was exposed in 1993. Unfortunately, there was no time to undertake excavations. Since then the burials have been heavily impacted by the construction of pigsties. The burials did not appear articulated.

50. References to pre-Portuguese visits by French merchants from Dieppe and Rouen have a long and interesting history. Although no substantive documentary evidence has been produced to support this claim, various writers down to the present century have accepted the idea (see discussion in the Introduction). Oral histories relating to an early French presence at Elmina were collected by Meyerowitz (1952a:70–73) and during the present research.

51. The report on the excavation provides descriptions of the orientation and archaeological context of the burials. The ages of some of the individuals are noted (e.g., "probably adult male"; "a child aged between six and seven years"; etc.), but detailed analyses of the skeletal material were not undertaken. The skeletal remains were reburied by the excavator (Calvocoressi 1977:121; and correspondence, February 24, 1990).

52. See discussion in Chapter 2. An early African settlement could have been located in the quarry area, but all vestiges have, of course, been obliterated.

    The distance between the parade ground and the site of Veersche Schans is over 1,500 m (0.9 mile) and, thus, well beyond a "bowshot": "The ordinary MILITARY CROSSBOW of the fifteenth century, with a thick steel bow, was able, if elevated to 45°, to propel its bolt from 370 to 380 yards [338–347 meters]"; the range of the English longbow was somewhat less than 275 m (300 yards) (Payne-Gallwey 1995:20). On the other hand, distances of over 700 m (766 yards) have been obtained with Turkish crossbows (Payne-Gallwey 1995:26–30).

53. The reference to the vale is given in Hair 1994b:18–19. It seems less likely that the vale was located farther away, among the hills north of the Benya Lagoon and some distance from the most likely landing places, but this is an alternative.

54. The problems of delineating timber and clay structures archaeologically in West Africa are examined by Agorsah (1985) and McIntosh (1976, 1977).

55. The foundations of this structure extend over the shoreline east of Locus D in Figure 3.14.

56. Many of the most prominent of the surviving nineteenth-century buildings were, in fact, built by European merchants or government officials. Van den Nieuwenhof (1991:35–51) sees the establishment of European manor houses outside the castle as closely connected with the emergence of a mulatto class and the development of closer links between the African community and the Europeans during the nineteenth century. Although expansion of the settlement is clearly a nineteenth-century phenomenon, there is ample evidence for a mulatto class and closer interpersonal relationships with the Europeans back to the Portuguese period.

57. The Dutch merchant Hubertus Varlet Sr., who probably designed the Viala houses, possessed Dutch journals for the promotion of architecture (van den Nieuwenhof 1991:55–56). Bech and Hyland state that the Conduah House on the north side of Trafalgar Square "represents a popular development of the old Basel Mission House type of plan" more commonly found in the Eastern Region (1978:56).

58. Characterizing the dichotomy between Elmina's European-style manor houses and others of more typically African arrangement as formal versus less formal, or conscious versus unconscious, or popular versus vernacular may actually misconstrue the point being made. In fact, the cultural beliefs that direct and guide house con-

struction in African cultures may dictate very specific arrangements of rooms consistent with African sociocultural relations, beliefs, and epistemologies. See, for example, Agorsah's (1983a, b) discussion of "local rule models" among the Nchumuru or discussions of cultural constructs of African architecture in Denyer 1978:118; David 1971; and Prussin 1995.

59. In Fante, the courtyard is called *gyase*, literally "beneath or behind the hearth." It is usually surrounded by small, closed rooms (*nampon*; sing., *dampon*). For examples of compounds, see Agorsah 1983a, b, 1986; Farrar 1988, 1996; and Fletcher 1975.

60. Plans of several Fante houses illustrating these features have been completed but not yet published. For the Guan area see Agorsah 1983, 1986:31. Merrick Posnansky (conversation, November 11, 1986), who has conducted a long-term ethnoarchaeological project at the site of Begho in Brong-Ahafo, also noted similar arrangements. Rooms used as shrines may also be used for sleeping quarters.

61. In the 1820s, George Howland noted: "The houses of the native Fantees are all well built of stone and plastered on the outside. (The native town is near the walls of the Castle. Many of their houses are large and commodious built of stone plastered and whitewashed on the outside.)" (Bennett and Brooks 1965:118).

62. The ready supply of quarriable rock was likely one of the reasons for the Portuguese selection of the site for the castle (Blake 1942:72). The best evidence for the rocky nature of the peninsula is the archaeological data, but some indication is provided by documentary sources. In 1679 Dutch director general Heerman Abramsz commented that the paving of the market was necessary because it was difficult to walk on the uneven rock (van Dantzig 1978:19).

63. This sandstone occurs in several bands in the Central Region. The stone's properties proved very problematic from a preservation standpoint. Once exposed, excavated stone cracked and crumbled, and stone walls collapsed. For this reason the exposed foundations were reburied after excavation.

64. Even in instances where fort walls were constructed with unmortared stone or fill, they often have mortared, and frequently plastered, facing stone. However, there is no detailed information on the forts' construction, and study is complicated by more recent restoration work.

65. These imports were noted in Brun's account of his voyage in 1617 (in Jones 1983:79). The shipment noted by Brun may be somewhat anomalous: Brun, as well as the shipment of building supplies, was destined for Fort Nassau, Mori, the first non-Portuguese trade post established on the coast. Because of the concern to complete the fortification quickly, it was built using a large quantity of Dutch brick and, apparently, imported mortar as well. When the Dutch position became more secure, they may have relied on local shell.

66. The same source also indicates that a mixture of mud with a glaze of palm oil could be used as mortar. Several sources indicate that shell mortar, and in some instances brick, was being produced locally for use on European forts in the late seventeenth century (Davies 1957:241; A. Jones 1985:75 n. 3, 93, 148). In 1874 shell was still the principal source of lime on the coast (Gordon 1874:4). Lawrence (1963), and possibly other restoration workers, intentionally added shell to the mortar to give it a more authentic appearance. Because detailed records of restoration work were not kept, it is difficult to differentiate between original construction and reconstruction. The unrestored, early nineteenth-century Danish plantation house of Daccubie, outside Accra, included shell mortar that would have had to be imported from the coast (DeCorse 1993). The collection of shell could have impacted the visibility of Iron Age and early historic period sites, of which shell is a major component. The gathering of shell for use as mortar was done at other European outposts in West Africa. A striking feature of the small English fort on Bunce Island, off the coast of Sierra Leone, is the presence of a massive pile of shell, apparently gathered to make lime for fortifications that were never completed.

67. Jan Baart, Stedelijk Beheer, Amsterdam, correspondence, May 6, 1996. Redman (1986) reports similar roughly cut, cobbled flooring at the site of Qsar es-Seghir, Morocco, which was a Portuguese settlement from 1458 to 1550.

68. It is possible that some floors were dug out and then refilled, but there is no evidence for this.

Building walls and profiles of excavated floors show no traces or footprints of earlier, partly removed floors: They do show multiple floors placed on top of one another. Removal of earlier floors would also be inconsistent with traditional building customs, which typically include regular replastering and reflooring.

69. See discussion of evidence for indigenous metalworking technology in Chapter 4. There are examples of brass or copper alloy window hinges from the coast. One was located during the 1993 mapping of an early European structure at Biriwa, east of Cape Coast. This could have been imported or locally formed out of imported sheet metal.

70. The fragments of burnt daub recovered, probably from portions of roofs, measured 20–30 cm (7.8–11.7 inches) thick, with impressions of supporting poles 3–8 cm (1.2–3.1 inches) in diameter.

71. The Dutch were known to have changed the gabled roofs of the Portuguese structures to flat roofs soon after they occupied the castle. Tiles were also ground up to make *tarras.*

72. Ceramic barrel tiles, or *tejas,* were imported in large quantities to the Americas by the Spanish during the early years of colonization. They were, notably, made by masons rather than potters and were among the first items locally produced at Spanish colonial sites, where they occur in contexts of sixteenth- through nineteenth-century age (Deagan 1987:124–126). Although the Portuguese brought masons to the Gold Coast, there is no archaeological or documentary evidence that they produced tiles. This may be a consequence of the limited size of the Portuguese settlement at Elmina compared with the Spanish colonies of the Americas. Portuguese documents make occasional reference to the importation of tiles. The contexts of the references suggest these were for use on the fortress. See a 1557 document translated by Teixeira da Mota and Hair (1988:63).

73. A tile from Fort Ruychaver (Dutch 1654–59), in the Western Region, included a foraminiferad-bearing chert probably belonging to the Cretaceous period. Such cherts are unknown in Ghana but common in the alluvial clays of Holland (Posnansky and van Dantzig 1976:12). The tiles recovered at Elmina were all fragmentary, and none could be reconstructed in its entirety. The

size estimates and drawings are based on virtually indistinguishable, but more complete, tiles recovered at Fort Ruychaver.

74. A small concentration of daub was found adhering to the stone floor in this area, but no clear traces of a wall.

75. This includes the courtyard area along the southern side of the building, which was likely unroofed. The structure may have extended farther to the north in areas that were unexcavated.

76. Features of this kind, commonly found in some African American contexts, appear to be largely unknown in West Africa, and there are no archaeological examples relevant to the period of the Atlantic slave trade.

77. Preliminary analysis of the skeletal material was undertaken at the University of Ghana. The material was labeled, and a preliminary catalog was prepared. Since 1990, all of the human skeletal material has been brought to the United States for study with the permission of the Ghana Museums and Monuments Board. It is the focus of ongoing work under the supervision of Owen Lovejoy, at Kent State University, Ohio.

78. Few of the burials located archaeologically were intact, which makes it difficult to date them precisely. The archaeological evidence that is available suggests that the burials predate 1900. However, the use of this part of the peninsula may have continued into the twentieth century. Several informants noted that the old town site was used as a burial area, but they could not provide specific information, perhaps an indication that the practice had stopped well before recent memory. One of the late nineteenth-century brick tombs was exposed at the surface, which may have served as a reminder of the site's use for this purpose.

It is possible that some of the post-1873 burials are European and associated with the British use of the site. However, the archaeological associations (i.e., extensive waist beads, jewelry, etc.) of the more intact burials suggest they are African. Further analysis of the skeletal remains may provide more information.

79. The fact that some of the coffin hardware occurred in fill contexts east of Locus B raises the possibility that this is not associated with African burials but rather with the old Dutch cemetery located just south of the castle entrance, dis-

turbed by the grading of the parade ground in the 1960s. Isolated fragments of human bone were also found in this area. However, the style of the coffin hardware was more consistent with the nineteenth century, by which time this burial area was no longer in use.

80. Aitken, in fact, suggests that coffin furniture manufacture in Birmingham gave rise to the stamped-brass foundry trade, "the manipulatory processes in the production of coffin-furniture in thin rolled lead, block-tin, or Britannia metal, suggesting the employment of similar methods in the treatment of brass" (1866b:704).

4. SUBSISTENCE, CRAFT SPECIALIZATION, AND TRADE

1. Müller, quoted in the initial opening epigraph, then comments on each of these professions. It is interesting that he makes the observation that young people choose their own means of sustenance. In fact, ethnographic observations indicate that many occupations identify certain families: e.g., potters train their daughters as potters; a fisherman's sons go to sea (e.g., Bosman 1967:123). Müller may have been contrasting the situation on the Gold Coast with the more formalized apprenticeship system of seventeenth-century Europe. The second opening epigraph, quoted from Fynn, was a response by an Elmina elder to the question "What was the main occupation of your ancestors, before the arrival of the whiteman?" (Fynn 1974b:14).

2. These data will be presented in more detail elsewhere. Several publications on the project are planned on individual artifact categories. See DeCorse 1989b for a preliminary discussion of the Elmina beads.

3. See reviews by Anquandah (1993) and Stahl (1993b). The evidence for the origins and development of food production in West Africa as a whole remains very incomplete. From the sites of Kintampo and Ntereso, evidence for animal husbandry consists of sheep/goat bone and clay figurines that may represent cattle, sheep, or goat. There is little direct evidence for the use of domesticated plants.

4. Further, appropriate recovery methods have not been employed to address subsistence, and the data that are available have generally not been recorded or synthesized in ways that facilitate comparison. Important exceptions within the relevant study area are studies by Bellis (1972, 1982) and Kiyaga-Mulindwa (1978, 1982).

5. A pocket of charred palm kernels was found at Sekondi (Davies 1956:56–57, 69). Their age is uncertain but they were found in a sealed stratigraphic context that clearly postdates Late Iron Age shell middens. At Elmina several palm kernels were found in twentieth-century contexts.

6. Carney (1996) makes the interesting observation that enslaved Africans from rice-growing regions were specifically brought to the rice-growing regions of the Americas because of their expertise. The intensive rice-growing areas of West Africa are somewhat more limited geographically than she suggests and actually concentrate on the upper Guinea Coast and hinterland.

7. For a discussion of shellfish consumption as an important and sustainable subsistence strategy, see Deith 1988; Erlandson 1988; and Moseley and Feldman 1988.

8. Shell from the Phase I component excavated at the Veersche Schans site, Bantoma, consisted entirely of *Arca senilis* (Calvocoressi 1977:120). An assemblage that is probably of comparable age was excavated at Sekondi. It includes a greater variety of species than reported from Bantoma, but *Arca senilis* predominates (Davies 1956:67). The species noted at Sekondi include: *Arca senilis, Balanus tintinnabulum, Bursa pustulosa, Cantharus viverratus, Cardium costatum* (rare), *C. rigens* (rare), *Conus* sp. (rare), *Cymbium* sp., *Cypraea stercoraria, C. zonata, Fissurella nubecula, Haliotis tuberculata* (rare), *Littorina angulifera, Murex* sp., *Mytilus perna, Natica* sp., *Nerita* sp., *Olivancillaria hiatula* (rare), *Ostrea cucullata, O. denticulata* (two specimens), *O. tulipa, Pachymelania fusca* var. *quadriseriata, Patella safiana, Pinna rudis* (very rare), *Semifusus morio* (rare), *Siphonaria grisea, Strombus bubonius* (rare), *Tagelus angulatus, Thais haemastoma, T. nodosa*, and *Tympanotonus fuscatus* var. *radula*. Some of the specimens were noted as having been clearly killed by marine predators. Davies further suggests that the Sekondi shells may have functioned in a ritual context: "Shells and fish-bones were sometimes found with the burials, but especially in large heaps near by. These may have been domestic middens, but are more likely to indicate ritual meals" (1961b:98). In

fact, the former supposition may be more likely. The size of the Sekondi middens is consistent with the thin shell scatters that characterize the precontact period along much of the coast.

Arca senilis shell is also characteristic of the mollusk remains found at Elmina, which, like the collection from Sekondi, include both lagoonal and marine species. Shell middens or thin scatters of *Arca* shell have been noted throughout the Central Region and other parts of the coast. The middens, on the whole, are small, generally covering no more than a few square meters and less than 0.5 m (1.6 feet) deep. Their size can be contrasted with areas such as the Senegambia, where shell middens of considerable extent and several meters deep dot some areas of the coast (e.g., Linares de Sapir 1971; Descamps, Thilmans, and Thommeret 1974; Descamps et al. 1977). The ages of some of these middens, spanning the late first millennium B.C. through the fourteenth or fifteenth century A.D., are comparable to some of those in coastal Ghana.

9. *Arca* spp. may be unattached or attached to the substrate by a byssus passing anywhere between the valves.

10. Portuguese accounts of the fifteenth and sixteenth centuries deal exclusively with imported sea shells or *conchas* (*Cyrpraea moneta*), which were used as a medium of exchange, not as a food source (e.g., Hair 1994b:48, 68, 89, 96, 114, 116). References to shellfish can be found in Dutch accounts of the seventeenth and eighteenth centuries (de Marees 1987:124; Jones 1983:238–239, 296, 297). The 1629 Dutch map discusses the people of Little Incassa and how "these sow and mow—but (they) fish also mostly oystershell from a river" (Daaku 1970:182). However, the text goes on to discuss how this shell was burned for lime. Although it seems likely that these oysters were also used for food, this is not made clear in the text. Müller gives an extended discussion of little oysters that grew on the trees in the Benya Lagoon, which he notes were seldom offered for sale. He says: "In the mouth of the aforementioned river stand many short lime and orange trees. When the tide comes in, they are inundated, so that they stand under the water. During that time these little oysters, which the rising sea brings with it, attach themselves in large numbers to the trees and remain hanging on them. After the sea has receded, they are to be seen there and plucked off by hand. . . . Thus anyone fond of gathering oysters can immediately enjoy a dish of fresh ones. He has only to take the oysters from the tree and can also use the juice of the limes on the tree. In the same way I have before now actually collected mussels from a tree which lies in the harbour below Friederichs-Berg" (in Jones 1983:238–239). Jones (1983:239 fn. 442) cites a similar account from 1694 by Otto Friedrich von der Groeben. Oysters and mussels make up a minor portion of the shell recovered archaeologically, suggesting either that they were not abundant locally or that the African population exploited these species to a limited degree. Alternatively, it is possible that Müller was not actually referring to either the blue mussel or the oyster but to other species that attach to the substrate by a byssus, such as *Arca*. Müller's account provides another indication of the vegetation that covered the Benya Lagoon until the late nineteenth century: today no trees are found in this area. Even in the seventeenth century it seems likely that mangroves would have been more common than orange and lime trees.

11. Excavated shell was cleaned, sorted by species, counted, and weighed. For the sake of expediency, large amounts were weighed and the number of individuals estimated on the basis of mean weights for different species.

12. Much of the shell occurred as isolated fragments or in small concentrations that may represent disturbed midden deposits redeposited in fill.

13. Mollusk shells from St. Jago, mostly consisting of *Arca senilis*, include 21 from surface contexts and 248 from excavations (Anquandah 1992, 1993), the majority coming from test trenches inside the fort. Anquandah further suggests that these remains indicate that "mollusca played an important role in the diet of the African military personnel who were deployed in the outer walks during the seventeenth and eighteenth century" (1992:42).

14. Shell naturally washed onto beaches and shell used in mortar is infrequent in the archaeological assemblage. Comparative collections from Central Region beaches indicate that the majority of the species represented archaeologically could have been readily found washed up onto the lit-

toral, but few of the archaeological examples showed evidence of water polishing or traces left by marine predators, such as sponge and starfish. A few of the species represented prefer deep-water habitats, and it seems unlikely that they were commonly gathered for food. These typically occur as isolated finds along the seashore and are uncommon archaeologically. Beginning in the seventeenth century, shell was widely gathered for the manufacture of mortar, and its inclusion in building debris accounts for its distribution in parts of the site. However, such shell, identifiable by traces of mortar, constitutes only a minute portion of the assemblage.

15. It has, for example, been suggested that smoked fish from the coast was an important trade item with the interior (e.g., Anquandah 1982:70; Fynn 1974a:vi; 1974b:x, 14; 1974c:vi, 11; Hair 1994b:53 fnn. 32, 33; van Dantzig 1990:206).

16. At Bantoma, Calvocoressi (1977:130) recovered significant amounts of shell, but the only faunal remains consisted of a single fragment of long bone from an animal the size of a sheep or a goat from a Phase 2 context. Surface material from Late Iron Age–early historic period sites and test excavations at Brenu Akyinim in 1993 (DeCorse 1998a) recovered no faunal remains but plenty of mollusk shell. With regard to adjacent parts of the coast outside the Akan area, Davies commented that at Sekondi "[t]he number of fish-vertebrae does not suggest that fish was an important article of diet at the site. The largest fish found were not too large to have been trapped in a lagoon, and are no proof of sea-fishing" (1956:68). *Arca senilis* shell characterizes sites of comparable age on the Accra plains (Anquandah 1982:115–116). It is possible that the paucity of fish bone in archaeological contexts is partly the result of preservation and foodways. Smaller fish bones may be pulverized in food preparation and consumption. Yet this would also result in higher fragmentation, increasing the minimum number of individuals identified (Bourque 1997:33). Future archaeological fieldwork by the Central Region Project will specifically be undertaken to examine this issue.

17. Preserved watercraft from West African archaeological contexts are rare. A wooden canoe excavated in northern Nigeria has produced carbon 14 dates of 7264 ± 55 B.P. and 7670 ± 110 B.P. mak-

ing it one of the earliest dugouts in the world (Breunig 1996). The canoe measures 8.4 m (27.5 feet) long with a maximum height and breadth of around 0.5 m (19.7 inches). De Marees (1987:116–119) describes canoes and fishing practices in some detail. He attributes the introduction of sailing technology to the Portuguese, and his illustration depicts a canoe with a European configuration of stays supporting a mast with sails made from mats of straw. However, as Greg Cook (correspondence, September 24, 1999) observes, the use of bark sails does not appear to have parallels in Iberian or Basque sailing technology, and the depiction of European-style rigging may have been artistic license.

18. Shark centra were found from Locus B, which was located well away from Elmina Castle and was clearly within the African settlement. They are certainly seventeenth-century in age, possibly earlier.

19. Fishermen throughout the Central Region still do not go to sea on Tuesdays. See Brun in Jones 1983:86 for another historical reference. It is also of note that the Bakatue ritual culminates on a Tuesday (see Chapter 6). In the interior, there are similar days where people are forbidden to farm, but the actual day varies from town to town.

20. The nets seem to have been gill nets or special nets with hooks (de Marees 1987:120, 123–124). The former technique is still occasionally used, which was observed by Greg Cook (correspondence, September 24, 1999), but procures a limited number of fish compared with seine nets.

21. In 1850, the canoes used by the fishermen on the coast were described as having been no more than 10 or 12 feet in length (*Colburn's United Service Magazine* 1850:75). In the seventeenth century, De Marees (1987:118) describes the fishing canoes as having been 16 feet long and 1½–2 feet wide (4.9 m long and 0.5–0.6 m wide). He further notes that they had larger canoes, one "as big as a Sloop" that was 35 feet (10.7 m) long, 5 feet (1.5 m) wide, and 3 feet (0.9 m) deep. These were clearly as large as the canoes typically used for fishing during the twentieth century, but de Marees (1987:118) indicates that these were not typical but special and used by the Africans for warfare and for transporting oxen. The practicality of the last is raised by van Dantzig and Jones (de Marees 1987:118 fn. 6), but large canoes can carry an im-

pressive amount of cargo. The catch from a large seine net (or the cargo from a ship) could easily weigh more than an ox, which presumably would have been hobbled for transport. While mounting a cannon and a carriage in a canoe would clearly have been unfeasible, a small swivel cannon could have been mounted in the prow.

Larger canoes were more common on other parts of the coast, particularly from the Ahanta area to the west, where some of the canoes for Elmina were obtained. This may have been due to a greater availability of suitable trees in that area (Barbot 1992:528–529; Bosman 1967:129; de Marees 1987:118; Jones 1983:254). Today trees for the construction of canoes are brought to Elmina on flatbed trucks from Brong-Ahafo.

22. De Marees (1987:123) provides the best early reference to the gathering of lobsters, crabs, and other creatures along the shore. He also describes and illustrates the use of several traps and the cast net, which are today primarily used in freshwater or lagoons.

23. Gordon, describing the mid-nineteenth century, states, "The net most frequently used is the circular form, thrown by hand . . ." (1874:45).

24. Lawson suggests: "Until the beginning of the twentieth century the main methods of fishing seem to have undergone very little improvement consisting of simple lines and small cast nets which were used both from the shore and also from canoes" (1968:90). She further suggests that while seine and ali nets may have been introduced in the second half of the nineteenth century, their use did not become widespread in Ghana until the development of the colonial government Fisheries Department in the 1940s. As part of the Central Region Project, Greg Cook's ongoing work on fishing may provide additional insight into this issue (DeCorse 1998a).

25. They are similar in form to examples from late eighteenth- and nineteenth-century European trade sites in North America, though the American examples are more typically made of iron (e.g., Karklins 1981:150–151; Noble 1973:247–248; Stone 1974:244–245). I am grateful to Olga Klimko for her comments on fishhooks and for drawing several references to my attention. Eight of the nine Elmina examples have round wire shafts, but the ninth is square in profile. Six of the eight intact hooks have barbs, all on the side facing the shank.

26. Documentary references to the importation of premade lead weights appear to be absent. Lead was imported in bars weighing 1.4–1.8 kg (3–4 pounds) each (Alpern 1995:14). Lead was also brought in the form of musket balls, which could have been hammered flat to make net weights. Africans also removed the lead plating of ships, which could have been used for weights and musket balls or in metal casting.

27. At Sekondi, in the Western Region, a single bone was tentatively identified as *Bos* (Davies 1956:69). River turtle (Tryonichidae sp.) was also represented, but the other bones, representing small, medium, and large mammals, were too fragmentary to identify as domesticated or undomesticated.

28. The Locus B data show an absence of these species before the nineteenth century but many finds in 1800–1873 contexts (Bourque 1997:45–46). This may represent a general trend, but the greater quantity of nineteenth-century material, as well as the varying contexts represented, must also be considered. The number of fish remains is also greater for the nineteenth century.

29. A review of the introduction of European crops into West Africa can be found in Alpern 1992 (see also Lewicki 1974; Miracle 1965, 1972). As Alpern discusses, the routes of introduction were highly varied. Some Asian species were already present in the Mediterranean world before the European expansion into sub-Saharan Africa.

30. Contary to this observation, McCaskie states that "all of our evidence indicates that the technological and other factors of production remained constant throughout the precolonial period. . . . [T]he core crop association was characterized by very long-term invariability and consequent stability" (1995:26–27). His broader point, however, is continuity in the basic reliance on high-yielding bulk foodstuffs such as yam, plantain, and cassava, whether indigenous or introduced. In fact, he points out variation in the importance of crops such as corn (American *Zea maize*) and cocoyam (*Colocasia esculenta*) during the nineteenth and twentieth centuries. Corn may have had an earlier and more lasting role among the coastal Akan.

31. There is a paucity of documentary references for the Portuguese period, but this is more likely a reflection of the limitations of the sources avail-

able rather than a lack of introductions. De Marees's (1987:158–166) description is notable as one of the earliest. In 1602 he noted the presence of many introduced crops already on the coast. Also note the discussion of tobacco in Chapter 5 below.

32. For early documentary references see de Marees 1987:40 and observations by Brun (in Jones 1983:85), Hemmersam (in Jones 1983:111), and Ulsheimer (in Jones 1983:29).

33. Kea (1982:59–60) suggests that mixed forest and mixed bush farming, as well as methods of land clearing that characterize later periods, expanded along the coastal zone during this period. As noted, concrete evidence is limited, but the picture that is emerging of low population densities on the coast during the pre-European-contact period indicates that such a transformation is reasonable.

34. Posnansky (1984b) reported that during the drought and economic crisis of 1982–83 the people of Begho collected more of the plants and wild foods they had traditionally collected, and they also exploited several new varieties of wild plants that were identified as edible through observation and experimentation.

35. For wild fauna on the Gold Coast, see descriptions in Barbot 1992; Bosman 1967; de Marees 1987; and Jones 1983:124–127, 240–243. Vogt notes that "Portuguese gunners could secure a variety of wild game from the nearby riverbanks and especially to the west, towards Axim" (1979:71). However, the documentary evidence for this is limited (see comments by Hair 1994b:71).

36. This observation is important because the excavation is of significant size and the faunal remains were analyzed. The species found include antelope (*Cephalophus niger, C. maxwelli, Dendrohyrax* sp.), wild pig (*Potomochoerus proms*), forest hog (*Hylochoerus meiner tshangeni*), monkey (*Colobus* sp.), class Aves, and crocodile.

37. The majority of documentary references to spears and bows and arrows point to their use in warfare, perhaps an indication that snares and traps played a more central role in obtaining game (e.g., Jones 1983:34, 88, 92, 95, 107, 116, 159, 186, 193–196, 254). The role of firearms during the Portuguese period was probably limited by both their accessibility and their efficiency (see Chapter 5 discussion). In 1637, the Portuguese garri-

son's armaments still consisted primarily of crossbows. Writing in the seventeenth century, Müller notes that dogs were not used in hunting: "Wild animals in this country are therefore shot with a musket or caught with snares and nets" (in Jones 1983:240).

38. Elephants can still be occasionally found near Elmina, particularly to the northeast in Kakum National Park.

39. See Chapter 6. Chickens are still commonly used in ritual offerings, and chicken bones were found in offering pots beneath house floors. See observations by Hemmersam (in Jones 1983:122). A tortoise shell was found in a shrine at Locus B (see Chapter 6). Sea turtle shells also figure prominently in current ritual use.

40. Some snail shell may be unrelated to comsumption; however, some clearly is food related.

41. Bone from other collections is also very fragmentary. Bellis (1972:84) notes that only half of the faunal remains examined from Twifo Heman were identifiable.

42. Data on butchering are currently available only for Locus B (Bourque 1997:24–25). A significant portion (almost half) of the marks represented are from post-1873 fill and, hence, could represent discard from either the garrison or the town. Occasional specimens bear evidence of burning or charring (Bourque 1997:22, 27–30). This may be more indicative of trash burning and discard than food preparation. Gnaw marks may also be indicative of the depositional context.

43. In addition to beef, pork, ham, mackerel, salmon, and codfish, foodstuffs that were sold by American traders at Elmina include flour, cornmeal, rice, crackers, breads, lard, cheese, butter, sugar, and tea. Some American-preserved meats are still imported today, particularly turkey tails and pig feet.

44. It is possible that differences in form and shape of the depression may be used to infer what foods were ground. There have, however, been no quantitative studies of West African grinding implements.

45. These seventeenth-century accounts suggest that the grinding slabs were primarily used for pulverizing corn. Müller noted: "If one wants to have fresh bread, the grain is not taken to the mill, about which people in this country know nothing: it is ground by hand the previous evening.

Handfuls of it are dropped on a stone not unlike the grindstones which the millers in this country use. . . . This stone slopes downwards in front, but at the back it stretches a foot above the ground. The person who grinds the *milie,* be she a free woman or a bondswoman (men are not used for this at all, or very seldom), stands behind the stone; in front of it is placed a dish or large calabash, into which the ground milie is to fall, and at the side is put a pot, with which to sprinkle the grain. Then another lump of stone, about a foot long, is taken in one's hand and in this way the grain is finely ground" (in Jones 1983:207–208). The grain would have been first pounded using a wooden mortar and pestle to separate the chaff (Jones 1983:197). Ceramic grinders (bowls with incised interior surfaces for grinding) with small wooden pestles, which are commonly used today, are not represented archaeologically.

46. Seventeen pestles and eight grinding slabs were discovered in the Elmina excavations.

47. At Elmina, the single deposit that can probably be directly related to the European garrison is the Portuguese-period midden in the lower levels of Locus E. Although the castle's moats would also seem a promising site for middens, test excavations there have produced little material. They may, in fact, have been cleaned out during restoration earlier in the century. Excavations at St. Jago produced bones of cattle, chicken, and caprids, in addition to marine and freshwater mollusks. As Anquandah (1992:42) points out, this may relate to the African soldiers manning the garrison.

Information on European subsistence from other parts of the coast is also limited. Paleobotanical remains from the early nineteenth-century Danish plantation site of Daccubie consisted of one palm kernal, a mango pit, two bones from a small antelope, one fragment of sheep/goat, two land snail shells, and one marine shell, probably *Arca* sp. A single grinding stone was also found. The majority of the other artifacts consist of African pottery, especially bowls (see DeCorse 1993). The seventeenth-century Dutch site of Fort Ruychaver produced several fragments of Dutch roofing tiles, 61 sherds of local pottery, and a grinding stone.

48. An anonymous report on Mina in 1572 advocates the breeding of local cattle and the use of some local foods so "the whites would not have to rely on food sent from Portugal, other than a certain amount of flour and wine" (Teixeira da Mota and Hair 1988:76). The same account further suggests that European foods were consistently in short supply: "What kills individuals here would kill them in the healthiest part of Spain—a shortage of the foodstuffs from their native land, for there cannot be a substitute for these, and a shortage of local foodstuffs, these being unobtainable" (Teixeira da Mota and Hair 1988:80).

49. Reconstructions have been made, but these are extrapolations of much later sources (e.g., Ballong-Wen-Mewuda 1993).

50. Kea (1982), who examines transformations in specialization and the division of labor within coastal Ghana, observes that there is some evidence that individual coastal towns increasingly specialized in different types of production. Also note observations by Daaku (1970).

51. Colors ranged between Munsell color hue values of 5YR 5/6 or 5/8 (yellowish red) and 10YR 5/4–5/8 (yellowish brown).

52. Of the 4,346 sherds excavated at Brenu Akyinim, 17 were noted with large pebble inclusions, and micaceous temper was present in 65 examples.

53. The Brenu Akyinim site may present a skewed perspective of the ceramic inventory because the assemblage consists primarily of very fragmentary eroded sherds. The Coconut Grove site, excavated in 2000, produced a large assemblage including many more conjoinable sherds. However, analysis of this collection has not been completed.

54. For example, Davies (1955) examines a probable eighteenth-century assemblage from the village of Mampongtin, 14 km (9 miles) northeast of Kumasi. However, Brian Vivian notes that the ware types, decorations, and forms represented have earlier antecedents and are well represented in assemblages excavated by the Asante Research Project (Vivian, conversation, February 16, 2000; see Shinnie and Vivian 1991).

55. The description of pottery manufacture is based on interviews and observations at Elmina and in neighboring areas. Initial work was conducted in 1986 by myself, followed with work by Tara L. Tetrault (1998). For other descriptions of pottery manufacture among the Akan, see Rattray

1959:303; Bellis 1972:154–164; Crossland 1973:105–125; and Johnson 1982.

56. The gritty orange Iron Age ceramics are consistently found stratigraphically beneath local ceramics associated with European imports. Sherds of Iron Age ceramics occur in later assemblages at Elmina and Eguafo but in statistically insignificant amounts. The sherds are fragmentary, worn, and may represent artifacts from redeposited midden soil.

57. Sherds from the lower levels of Brenu Akyinim produced ages of A.D. 1112 ± 276 and A.D. 1109 ± 146. If these sherds represent the same occupation, the mean date based on these estimations would be A.D. 1110 ± 129. Dates from the lower levels of excavations at Elmina and Eguafo, respectively, range between A.D. 887 ± 104 and A.D. 1012 ± 124, and between A.D. 1238 ± 77 and A.D. 1325 ± 67. These dates will be evaluated in light of future work.

58. The chronological framework for the Birim finds was based on several carbon 14 dates, tentatively correlated with oral traditions. Carbon 14 dates of A.D. 1465 ± 65 and A.D. 1540 were associated with the later earthworks period, whereas dates of A.D.1540 ± 80 and 1740 ± 110 were associated with postearthworks, Atweafo settlement (Kiyaga-Mulindwa 1978:97, 100, 102, 186–189, 191; Kiyaga-Mulindwa 1982). Kiyaga-Mulindwa suggests that the apparent overlap in the traditions is, in fact, not representative of the archaeological and historical situation but rather a result of the limitations of the carbon 14 dates obtained. With these limitations and differences in interpretation in mind, the timing of the transition in pottery styles during the early historic period is consistent with the chronology proposed for the early coastal ceramics.

59. The illustration of typical Atweafo ware shown in Kiyaga-Mulindwa 1978:131 parallels the many post-European-contact ceramics from Elmina, whereas some of the "earthworks ware" (Kiyaga-Mulindwa 1978:135) is indistinguishable from Late Iron Age–early historic period ceramics on the coast.

60. Bellis suggests that in addition to the impact of the slave trade, reasons for change may be traced to the effects of new diseases, changes in economic relations, and other factors connected with the advent of the Europeans, as well as influences from the West African Sahel.

61. A sample of 22,637 sherds was analyzed. This consisted of all of the local ceramics recovered from the 1985–86, 1990, and 1993 excavations, plus sherds from the 1997 excavations dating from 1873 floor contexts or earlier.

62. The majority of these assemblages have not been published in detail, and they provide only brief descriptions and limited illustrations of representative forms. Nevertheless, they provide useful comparative material with the Elmina finds. Collections at the Ghana National Museum, the Department of Archaeology of the University of Ghana, and the West African Historical Museum at Cape Coast were also examined.

63. Rattray discusses an Asante oral tradition that states that a woman named Denta became barren as a result of having made figurative pots: "From that time onwards, it is stated, women ceased to make highly ornamented designs in pottery" (1959:301).

64. Tetrault (1998) documented the production of pottery braziers at the village of Pomadze. These are similar to metal examples and are a ceramic form unrepresented archaeologically. Sadly, the last active Elmina potters passed away since my research at Elmina began.

65. Unfortunately there is little information available on the relative firing temperatures of different types of fuel used in open firing. James Amoah, cited in Bellis 1972:156, estimates that the temperatures of 600°–700°C are reached under these firing conditions. Rice (1987:156) notes that temperatures in open firings generally range between 600° and 850°C but with considerable variation. Amoah (Bellis 1972:156) also notes that it was customary to have three layers of pots, separated by layers of fuel. During ethnographic observations at Elmina, a relatively small number of pots were fired at a time, generally no more than one or two dozen, arranged in one or two layers.

66. Smudging is the only ethnographically observed Akan method of blackening pots. However, Bellis (1972:159) reported sherds blackened with graphite at Twifo Heman. In addition, both the interiors and exteriors of pots recently produced east of Elmina are at times painted black with an oil-based enamel, but this is unusual, clearly not

traditional, and not very practical, for the paint wears off quickly. Slips and painted decoration are generally absent on Akan pottery, but they are characteristic of some of the potting traditions in the north. The main exception among the coastal Akan is hearth pots, or *mmukyia* (sing., *bukyia*), which sometimes have a thick red slip.

67. Müller provides the first relatively detailed description of pottery production on the central Gold Coast: "The potters do not work on lathes, but shape a pot with their hands in the form and manner they want, out of previously prepared clay. They then make a large fire around the pots, till they are sufficiently hardened and, after several days, are completely dried out by the heat of the sun" (in Jones 1983:255). In fact, the pots would have been dried in the sun prior to firing, not after. Müller does not elaborate on the preparation of the clay.

68. Twenty-one sherds with micaceous inclusions are represented, two of which occurred in nineteenth-century levels.

69. The majority of the sherds proved to be nondescript body fragments. The pottery was recovered from diverse contexts including burials, living floors, and fill layers. How these factors affected attribute distributions is uncertain. If sherds from mixed contexts, poorly dated layers, and disturbed deposits are omitted, 8,303 sherds remain. Only 2,559 of these were from prenineteenth-century contexts. Thus, although the assemblage provided a number of well-dated examples, observations that can be made are limited.

70. Examples of pottery bowls purchased at Elmina by the crew of the United States survey vessel *Eclipse* in 1898 and now in the collections of the Smithsonian Institution, National Museum of Natural History, are virtually identical with those still produced in Elmina.

71. One of the best-described collections from Asante is from the seventeenth- to early eighteenth-century assemblage from Mampongtin (Davies 1955). Some of the forms and rim decorations at Elmina are indistinguishable from Mampongtin examples (Davies 1955:Figures 16, 17). More recently, excavations have been undertaken at a series of very important sites associated with early Asante oral traditions (Shinnie and Vivian 1991).

72. This disparity may in part result from the archaeological contexts sampled at Elmina. For examples of more elaborate forms, see Davies 1967:310–313; Bellis 1982, 1987; Kiyaga-Mulindwa 1982; and Rattray 1959:Figure 234.

73. Note the discussion of *mmukyia* from the site of Twifo Heman, 60 km (37.2 miles) north of Elmina, in Bellis 1972:162–164. A large number of *mmukyia* were also found in excavations at the Fante site of Eguafo. In addition to their distinctive shape and the thick walls, *mmukyia* are typically covered with a red slip and fire reddened.

74. Only three such sherds were found at Elmina, and these may all be from the same vessel. Some early vessel forms have relatively flat bases, but they lack the very straight sides and abrupt basal angle that characterize these later forms.

75. Cooking in the Akan area is more commonly done with special hearth pots or clay hearths.

76. For overviews of the origins of metal technology in West Africa, see Holl 1993; Kense and Okoro 1993; McIntosh 1994; Miller and van der Merwe 1994; and Schmidt 1996. Furnace types, the amount of iron produced, and the quality of the output varied substantially in different regions. The earlier dates for the advent of iron technology in northern Ghana are consistent with the general pattern of earlier urbanization and technological innovation in the savanna and forest-savanna ecotone. Some of the earliest evidence for metallurgy in West Africa comes from sites in Niger and Mauritania dating to the first millennium B.C., and sophisticated brass and bronze castings were being produced in southern Nigeria before European contact. In contrast, evidence for iron production in Sierra Leone doesn't appear until late in the first millennium A.D., and it continues to occur with Late Stone Age tools until the thirteenth century A.D. There may have been a similar pattern in parts of the West African coast, including coastal Ghana.

77. An early sixteenth-century Portuguese *regimento* directed that a stock of 100,000 manillas be maintained (Hair 1994b:89). In fact, sales exceeded that number in some years. Sales of manillas and brass basins at Axim and Elmina in the early sixteenth century may have amounted to 41 t (45 tons) of metal per year (Garrard 1980a:70; see also Vogt 1973a, 1979:8, 14, 147, 153).

78. Surveying collections in the Ghana National Museum and published sources, Pole (Pole and Posnansky 1973:264) notes the occurrence of tuyeres or pipes for slag tapping at Achimota, Legon, Akwatia, Abiriw, Kokobin, Akwamufie, Twifo Heman, and Dixcove. At Twifo Heman, Bellis (1972:71) reported evidence of iron smelting at Site 1, which may date to the seventeenth century.

79. At Bantoma, slag occurred in Phase 2 and 3 contexts (Calvocoressi 1977:130).

80. The size of some of the interior sites is staggering. In the Bassar region in Togo, for example, there are massive slag mounds and banks of furnaces dating between the fourteenth and the early nineteenth centuries, representative of an industry that may have equaled or surpassed that of ancient Meroe in the Nile Valley (de Barros 1988).

81. In his first voyage to Guinea, William Towerson reported: "[A]nd their darts were all of yron, faire and sharpe . . ." (Blake 1942:378).

82. With regard to his work at Bantoma, Calvocoressi (1977:130) noted that the local inhabitants had no memory of smelting. In interviews on traditional economy, Fynn's respondents only mentioned farming, fishing, salt production, gold panning, and trade (Fynn 1974b:14–15, 25, 35–36, 39, 49–50, 62, 72–73). During my interviews and conversations at Elmina over the past 15 years, no informants have been able to provide any specific information on smelting, though some stated that in the past smiths knew how to obtain "metal," including gold, from stone.

83. Vogt, without attributing the source, notes: "Whereas *manilhas* had been the chief item of trade in 1500, a century later they had been replaced by iron ingots" (1979:147). By 1602 iron ingots were clearly being traded and were carefully examined (e.g., de Marees 1987:56). Hair (1994b:2–3) suggests that gold was plentiful and easily worked and thus readily exchanged for iron. The dimensions of the iron bars traded are generally unspecified, and no examples have survived in West African contexts. Bars recovered from the *Henrietta Marie,* a slave ship that sank off the coast of Florida in 1701 or 1702, may illustrate some of the shapes that were used (Moore 1989).

84. Bosman similarly notes: "Their chief Handicraft, with which they are best acquainted being the Smithery; for with their sorry Tools they can make all sorts of War-Arms that they want, Guns only excepted; as well as whatever is required in their Agriculture and House-keeping. They have no Notion of Steel and yet they make their Sables and all cutting Instruments: Their principal tools are a kind of hard Stone instead of an Anvil, a pair of Tongues, and a small pair of Bellows, with three or more Pipes; which they blow very strong and are an Invention of their own. These are most of their Arts, besides that of making *Fetische's;* which I have informed you of . . ." (1967:128). These smithing techniques are typical of those used in much of West Africa.

85. For a detailed discussion see Garrard 1980a, b, 1989. The actual chemical composition of the artifacts found archeologically have not been determined. The term *copper alloy* is used to indicate this uncertainty. In the majority of cases the source material was likely imported brass objects and vessels, but casters likely relied on whatever materials they could obtain. The same uncertainty is true regarding the chemical composition of the "gold" objects. For an excellent overview of copper and copper alloys in precolonial Africa, see Herbert 1984.

86. Garrard cites a Dutch account of 1654, translated in the Furley Collection at the Balme Library, University of Ghana, which notes: "[I]n the afternoon came the Braffo of Fantyn's three wives to dance here, well dressed up in their fashion, each having a peruque on her head, hung full of gold, a gold ring (of the thickness of an arm) round the neck, three gold rings on the arms and also on the legs" (Garrard 1980a:107).

87. Garrard further suggests that "the entire goldweight output of the fifteenth century could have been comfortably achieved by 25 goldsmiths, and that of the sixteenth century by a hundred at the most" (1980b:67).

88. De Marees suggests that knowledge of metallurgy on the coast was limited and that some practices were introduced by the Portuguese. Referring to the production of *kacraws* at Elmina (see note 96 below), he comments: "In other places, where the Portuguese are not known, the Blacks do not use this kind of coin, but sell their Gold just as it comes out of the earth; for they do not have as much knowledge of how to smelt or work Gold as the Blacks who trade with the Portuguese" (1987:65). Yet de Marees seems to some-

what contradict himself later on, describing the "remarkably beautiful gold Chains and other ornaments, such as Rings" produced by the people of Senya Beraku, located east of Elmina. This settlement was the site of English and Dutch rivalry beginning in the late seventeenth century, but it was not a focus of early Portuguese trade. Bosman observed: "[T]heir most artful Works are the fine Gold and Silver Hat-bands which they make for us; the Thread and Contexture of which is so fine, that I question whether *European* Artists would not be put to it to imitate them: And indeed if they could, and were no better paid than the *Negroes,* they would be obliged to live on dry bread" (1967:128–129).

By the later nineteenth century, jewelry was said to be the principal manufacture at Cape Coast (Allen 1874:17–18). This account is interesting, for it includes a description of rings with the 12 signs of the zodiac, which were of imported design and perhaps intentionally made for sale to Europeans.

89. Excavations at Asebu, Efutu, Eguafo, Twifo Heman, and the Birim Valley sites produced no evidence of manufacture, though some brass and gold objects were recovered (Agorsah 1975, 1993; Bellis 1972; DeCorse 1998a; Kiyaga-Mulindwa 1978; Nunoo 1957). Evidence from some other Ghanaian sites is substantial, including hundreds of crucibles as well as spew and mold fragments. The site of Dawu, in the Akwapim, west of the Akan area, produced 288 crucible fragments and 318 fragments of molds used in *cire perdue* casting. The finds probably date to the early seventeenth century (Shaw 1961:59–62). The finds at Begho, possibly dating somewhat earlier than Dawu, included "well over 500 crucibles and several small brass smiths' furnaces" (Posnansky 1977:297).

90. The paste, color, and vitrified appearance are identical to crucibles from Dawu (Shaw 1961:59–62) and Begho (Posnansky 1977:297), but the two Elmina examples are at the smaller end of the size range: the Dawu specimens are 3.8–6.4 cm (1.5–2.5 inches) tall with internal lip diameters of 4.6–6.9 cm (1.8–2.7 inches).

91. Few examples of Akan gold have been recovered from archaeological contexts. Bellis (1972:61–63) excavated three pieces of gold jewelry at Twifo Heman. Agorsah (1993:181) recovered a simple gold ring and a gold disk from Efutu. Other arti-

facts have been reported from poorly known mining contexts. Several objects were found during mining at Eguafo in 1993 and donated by the miner to the West African Historical Museum. One of the most interesting pieces is a delicate set of shackles, barely more than a centimeter (less than half an inch) long. Garrard (1989) provides a thoroughly illustrated survey of the jewelry and ornaments of Ghana and Ivory Coast. Also see Ehrlich 1989.

92. For a seventeenth-century reference to this usage, see Müller in Jones 1983:250.

93. Calvocoressi (1977:130) notes that this bead has a specific gravity of slightly over 5 and may have a high copper admixture. However, no copper was indicated when the bead was tested with ammonia.

94. The diamond-shaped pendant from Bantoma has a specific gravity of approximately 16.5, suggesting a high gold content (Calvocoressi 1977:130). This bead was found in a Phase 2 burial, attached to a skull.

95. The bead from the Coconut Grove site may be particularly interesting in this context. The majority of the material recovered at the site represents a pre-European-contact occupation, and no imported trade materials were found in the excavation levels where the bead was found. Charcoal samples associated with the bead have not yet been dated.

96. De Marees goes on to suggest that this practice was introduced by the Portuguese. Van Dantzig and Jones (in de Marees 1987:65 fn. 5) note that the Akan word *kakra* means "little."

97. The bead was associated with a disturbed burial beneath the Locus B structure. It may have been attached to, or within, a European beaded bag.

98. Two of these gold beads are from Locus E, one from a late eighteenth-century context and the other from the nineteenth century. Another late eighteenth-century context at Locus E produced a bow-shaped copper alloy pendant almost 2 cm (0.7 inch) across. Cord tubes were also found on one of the gold beads excavated at Twifo Heman (Bellis 1972:252).

99. It is unfortunate that the archaeological context could not be more clearly dated. All five beads are very similar in style and, though not found in direct association, may have originated from the same, presumably disturbed, feature. The pre-

dominance of a variety of nineteenth-century material and the gilt suggests that they date to the nineteenth century, but their age remains uncertain.

100. One is well dated to circa 1740–50 by associated European trade goods. The other was recovered from nineteenth-century rubble that contained artifacts spanning the sixteenth through the seventeenth centuries.

101. A small geometric weight was recovered from a late seventeenth-century context at Twifo Heman (Bellis 1972:73–74). Geometric weights have also been recovered during recent excavations at Eguafo (DeCorse 1998a).

102. Timothy Garrard's exhaustive study used the relative amount of wear and patination to distinguish weights of the Early and Late periods. Although subjective, Garrard validated his observations through the examination of 200 comparatively well-dated European nested weights of seventeenth- to nineteenth-century age from Akan weight collections.

103. All of the weights excavated at Elmina were found associated with nineteenth-century European trade material. Four were found in fill layers containing a mixture of seventeenth-through nineteenth-century material overlying the site. A single weight came from below the floor of room C, Locus B, and so predates the 1873 destruction of the town. However, the seventeenth-century material in this unit was disturbed by a nineteenth-century feature, and the exact association of the weight could not be determined. The other four weights were found in the sandy midden soil on the floor of the long corridor (room B) bordering the eastern side of Locus B. The deposits where the gold weights were located probably date to between 1820 and 1873.

104. The artifacts from the *Whydah* consisted of 76 fragmentary pieces that were probably traded as scrap on the Gold Coast.

105. See Garrard 1980a:178–188 for a detailed description of the weighing kit, or *futuo*.

106. Jan Baart, surveying archaeological material from the Netherlands, commented: "Although we have not yet analyzed it thoroughly we believe most of the brass objects we have found so far dating to 16th/17th century were made from rolled sheet brass. The records show the majority of these objects were imported from Germany (Nuremberg, Aachen, etc.). However, finds of other brass objects of the same period were made out of battered sheet brass. So both techniques must have been in practice during the 16/17th century" (correspondence, June 12, 1989). Rolling mills were in use in Britain by the late seventeenth century, but battery mills continued to predominate for the next 100 years (Day 1973:35–36; Hamilton 1967:343–344).

107. Sheet brass tools, possibly of local manufacture, are sometimes referred to in documentary accounts. However, in many cases imported items or tools made of other materials may be referred to. For example, at least some of the spoons used in weighing gold dust were made of wood, not just sheet brass (Garrard 1980a:184). Garrard notes that de Marees's 1602 descriptions of scalepans suggest they were deeper than the scales of flat sheet brass commonly found in collections, and the earlier examples may have been cast (Garrard 1980a:186).

108. It has been suggested that the expansion of the British brass industry based on rolled brass technology during the late eighteenth and early nineteenth centuries and the resulting increase in the availability of sheet brass contributed to expanding production of *forowa* and sheet brass objects in West Africa (Garrard 1979:43; Ross 1974:45; 1983:54). The emergence of Britain as a major producer and exporter of brass in the nineteenth century no doubt increased the availability of sheet brass, particularly in areas of British trade, but other sources were available earlier.

109. Ross (1974:42) suggests that the scarcity of public references to *forowa* may indicate that "they were rarely used in the public displays more readily available to field workers."

110. Ross (1983), drawing on museum collections, was the first to suggest the possible link between *forowa* and the *kuduo* and the possibility that *forowa* production predated the nineteenth century. The archaeological data on the age and the stylistic evolution of the *forowa* are consistent with Ross's observations.

111. The bones were not articulated, and the interment was one of several eighteenth-century burials intruding into sixteenth-century deposits underneath the Locus A structure. The age of the burial was established by associated European to-

bacco pipes, glass, and ceramics. The most recent finds could date no later than 1750. The *forowa* was found with two other brass vessels. The largest one appeared to have been a basin approximately 30 cm (11.7 inches) in diameter. It was very poorly preserved and was little more than a green, copper oxide stain in the soil. The other vessel was a well-preserved European (probably Dutch) tobacco box. It has a flat lid with traces of engraving and is similar to examples of seventeenth- to eighteenth-century age. Other associated finds included fragments of a large, red-slipped, local tobacco pipe.

112. The *forowa* was block lifted and returned to the conservation lab at the University of Ghana, Legon. Much of the unexcavated portion of the *forowa* had completely deteriorated, but a detailed reconstruction was possible from the surviving fragments.

113. Phillips (1996:434–435) illustrates two *kuduo,* one dated to the nineteenth century and the other of possible eighteenth- or nineteenth-century age, that bear a great deal of similarity in the dimensions and general appearance of the eighteenth-century Elmina *forowa*. Stylistically, there is a substantial amount of variation in *kuduo* forms.

114. Machine-made and decorated, European examples of *forowa* that are similar in form are likely also nineteenth-century in age.

115. An example can be found in the Fowler Museum of Cultural History, University of California, Los Angeles. I thank Doran Ross for going through some of the museum collections with me.

116. Aitken (1866a:319–321) further discusses exports to West Africa.

117. Portions of 13 necklace chains, 14 bracelets, and 14 rings were excavated at Elmina.

118. The origins and characteristics of *coris* (also referred to as *accary, akori, aigris,* and *aggrey*) have been a subject of a great deal of speculation. European writers provide frustratingly little information and a variety of conflicting descriptions. With reference to the early Portuguese trade at Elmina, John Vogt (1973a:462; 1979:70) considers *coris* to refer to a type of stone bead. However, it seems equally likely that glass beads were being referred to. Other writers have alternatively hypothesized that *coris* were made of glass, coral, stone, or iron slag. Positive identification of the "original akori bead" remains difficult (see

DeCorse 1989b:44; cf. Davison 1970; Fage 1962; Kalous 1966, 1979; Landewijk 1970; Mauny 1949, 1958). It seems likely that whatever the original meaning, the term became more generalized through usage and came to be applied to a variety of both local and imported products.

119. Although Barbot's account was published in the eighteenth century, he was actually describing the last quarter of the seventeenth century.

120. Beads of many different materials have been recovered from West African sites ranging in age from the Late Stone Age to the historic period. They are among the most widely distributed and ubiquitous finds in West African archaeological sites. Despite their prevalence, they have for a number of reasons been regarded as poor chronological indicators in West African archaeology (DeCorse 1989b; Lamb and York 1972). However, a preliminary analysis of the Elmina collection indicates that both European and local glass beads may have more dating potential than was previously thought.

A limited amount of information on the African bead industry has been provided by previous archaeological and documentary research. Possible archaeological evidence for local bead manufacture has been found at sites in Ghana, Mali, and Nigeria. Possible wasters from the manufacture of drawn beads at the Begho excavations have been recovered, which, on the basis of radiocarbon determinations, are believed to date to the seventeenth or early eighteenth century (Merrick Posnansky, conversation, September 23, 1999). Earlier evidence for the reworking of beads comes from Ife, Nigeria, where wasters dated between the eighth and twelfth centuries were recovered (Willett 1977:16–22).

121. Similar grooves sometimes appear in the distinctive Kintampo "terracotta cigars," but their function is uncertain.

122. Some beads were undoubtedly ground in Europe prior before shipment to Africa. For example, some mosaic beads, probably dating to the mid-twentieth century, were roughly ground by a power grinder on the ends and sides. Facets were also ground during earlier periods.

123. European beads collected in Ghana, now deposited in the Corning Museum of Glass, also have a high percentage of beads with ground surfaces. For discussion of the heat alteration

of beads, see Davison et al. 1971:654; and Sordinas 1964.

124. There is a tenuous hypothesis that silica slag from iron smelting could have been used for the manufacture of beads (Landewijk 1970:96; cf. Kalous 1979).

125. Gray or black cores are a characteristic associated with a distinctive type of powdered glass bead commonly referred to as *bodom* (Dubin 1987:123; Lamb 1976).

126. The beads recovered from Twifo Heman are described as European wound beads (Bellis 1972:85), but they do not have parallels in European assemblages.

127. An excellent review of the use of ivory in Africa and early Euro-African ivories is provided by Ross (1992).

128. The earliest archaeological examples from southern Ghana date to the seventeenth and eighteenth centuries (Bellis 1972; Shaw 1961). Substantially earlier finds have been made in the Ghanaian interior and in other parts of West Africa. Ivory objects dating early in the second millennium A.D. have been excavated at Begho (Posnansky 1987). Ivory artifacts of pre-fifteenth-century age have also been found at Daboya and New Buipe (Shinnie and Kense 1989; York 1973).

Carvers in some areas were noted for their work and incorporated many European features. The production of these elaborate, distinctive pieces was, however, likely far less than the production of items such as bracelets, combs, and horns, which were used locally. One possible example of an ivory object carved by Elmina craftsmen is the "Dutch Baton of Authority," which was originally made for Admiral de Ruyter, who recaptured the Dutch forts on the coast during the Anglo-Dutch war of 1664–65. A copy of the baton was long displayed in the West African Historical Museum, Cape Coast (the original is said to be in the Rijksmuseum, Amsterdam). The original, according to the description in Cape Coast, was made by Elmina craftsmen in ivory and gold and presented to the admiral by the chief and elders of Elmina early in 1665. The reproduced baton is approximately 35 cm (9.8 inches) long, consisting of an ivory shaft with matched gold caps at either end. Although well made, the baton does not incorporate any clearly Akan stylistic elements.

129. It is of note that European brass letter seals occur with some frequency in gold weight collections from the Ivory Coast and Ghana (Garrard 1983b:71). These at one time may have served their intended function and been in common use on the coast. It is conceivable that Elmina's ivory objects are a local functional equivalent. At present, however, there is no documentary evidence that European seals, or any kind of local seal, were used by the coastal Akan.

130. I am very grateful to the late Philip Ravenhill for observations on the stamps used in the Ivory Coast.

131. Noting the paucity of direct evidence, Anquandah (1982:70) postulates that the trade in salt and fish was a key aspect of coastal society beginning in the Middle Iron Age. For oral testimonies concerning salt production at Elmina, see Fynn 1974b:14–15.

132. Alexander (1993) points out the importance of salt in the human diet and its role in Africa as a means of accruing wealth and tribute and as a preservative. Latham (1979:196) notes that a person doing heavy work in a hot climate may lose 15 g (0.5 ounce) of sodium chloride in body sweat, and urinary excretion ranges from 1 to 30 g (0.035 to 1.05 ounces) daily. It is, however, further pointed out that salt (consumed as an additive to food) is generally not necessary because sufficient amounts can be obtained through other foods. Intake is, of course, variable, but dishes in Ghana frequently are heavily spiced with salt and pepper, and some individuals will liberally sprinkle salt on their food.

133. Salt production is noted as not being important at Simbew (Fynn 1974b:62).

134. Excavations at Daboya have revealed occupation deposits spanning three millennia (Shinnie and Kense 1989). Ethnohistorical information indicates that Daboya was important in the local salt trade. Deposits of salt-rich earth can be seen exposed on the banks of the Black Volta at Daboya (Ben Kankpeyeng, e-mail, September 11, 2000).

135. Greene (1988:71) draws attention to an 1819 description by Bowdich that indicates that people north of the Anlo in the Volta Basin were still relying on plants for salt in the nineteenth century. The use of salty plant ashes was also common in Cameroon and Burkina Faso (Alexander 1993:656).

136. Jones and van Dantzig (in de Marees 1987:201 fn. 2) suggest that production in the Ahanta area is limited because there are few lagoons and rainfall is heavy. Sutton states: "The coast west of Accra has a much higher rainfall, and therefore the salinity in any standing water is too low for salt making. Lagoons rarely dry out naturally, and therefore techniques of boiling sea water were more common" (1981:44). However, this observation seems belied by de Marees's reference to salt pans in the Ahanta area, west of Elmina, and by the booming salt production in Benya Lagoon today.

137. Bosman also describes production by boiling seawater, and also discusses the use of local pots or copper cauldrons that were "all cemented together with Clay as if they had been done by a Brick-layer; and under the mentioned Pots is something like a Furnace of Fire" (1967:309).

138. The 1629 map shows several salt-making villages on the coast between Axim and Accra (Daaku and van Dantzig 1966). I am grateful to Adam Jones for drawing my attention to the Baelarus plan. Also see discussion in Hair 1994b:53, 79.

139. Note, for example, discussions and references in Bovill 1958; DeCorse 1989b; Garrard 1980a:6–33; Levtzion and Hopkins 1981; Silverman 1983a, b. Some items clearly reached West Africa in substantial quantities via the trans-Saharan trade. For example, over 150,000 glass beads were recovered from the site of Igbo Ukwu, in Nigeria. Because of the number of beads as well as the presence of manillas, some researchers argued that the site had to postdate European contact, yet calibrated carbon 14 dates place the site in the ninth or tenth century A.D. One of the most exciting archaeological discoveries is the caravan found in the Sahara by Monod (1969), which included camel loads of brass rods.

140. Dutch West India Company employees were paid with it, but it was not always accepted (Feinberg 1970a:360–361).

141. Only 23 European coins and tokens of eighteenth- through nineteenth-century age were recovered from archaeological contexts at Elmina. These include Dutch guilders, English pennies, and several unidentified European currencies. Five were drilled with holes, suggesting they may have been strung in necklaces, a practice still common in many parts of Ghana. In other cases, European coins may have been used as weights (Garrard 1980b:181). British three pence coins dating to 1873 were found in the nineteenth-century fill layers covering the site. Thousands of these coins were brought to the Gold Coast to pay workers during the Asante War of 1873–74 (*British Parliamentary Papers* 1970b:353–354). For an overview of various indigenous and European currencies in Africa, see Rivallain 1994.

142. A number of Elmina informants claimed that gold was found on the ground in the past, though, at least in some instances, finished artifacts such as chains were being referred to (see Fynn 1974a:62).

143. Hair, who provides a succinct examination of this topic, observes: "[I]t is not clear whether the references to gold extraction on the coast are all original and some seem exaggerated (e.g., 500 slaves searching for gold)" (1994b:51). Notably, the principal Dutch writer of the early seventeenth century refers only to gold coming from the interior (de Marees 1987:188–191).

144. European trade goods sent to Africa have been variously portrayed as worthless or confined entirely to luxury goods (e.g., Garrard 1980b:71–98; Rodney 1983:111; Thornton 1992:44–45). This is not born out by a survey of trade lists and archaeological materials, which include a host of products of practical day-to-day value. This observation does not negate arguments about the economic impact and socioeconomic consequences of the European trade. The crux of these interpretations concerns the economic relations that the trade engendered.

5. THE EUROPEAN TRADE

1. An attempt to list the vast diversity of items noted in European cargo manifests, bills of lading, and accounts of the coast for over four centuries was undertaken by Alpern (1995). Despite the title, the work clearly includes items that were traded for things other than slaves. Alpern (1995) notes what appears to be a steady increase in the variety of goods offered by the Dutch on the Gold Coast: 92 items were inventoried in 1645, 150 by the end of the century, and 218 in 1728. On the other hand, Kea (1982:207–208) notes two dozen categories of goods in the cargoes of more than 200 Dutch ships that traded

on the coast between 1593 and 1607. Feinberg (1989:49), surveying Dutch West India Company records on the Gold Coast for 1727, notes the availability of 70 different commodities, including 139 separate items. Although perhaps serving to illustrate a general trend, there is a great deal of variation in the kind of information represented, and such figures can serve as only crude indicators of the diversity of items offered. The relative value of increasing European trade in West Africa during the seventeenth century is discussed in van den Boogaart 1992.

2. For example, note differences in the lists of "goods suitable for barter" on different parts of the coast provided by Adams (1822:104, 109, 113, 115, 116–117) and Jones (1995).

3. A report on the Elmina beads will be published separately. Analysis is not complete, but preliminary data indicate that they may be useful temporal indicators (DeCorse 1989b).

4. A pile of these manillas could supposedly still be seen on the shore of a river in Africa. Aitken provides a useful account of the British trade in manillas, noting that they were produced in Birmingham by casting and "exported to the Spanish settlements on the New and Old Calabar, and the Bonny Rivers in Africa" (Nigeria). He adds that they were also produced by the Bristol house of Harfords and the Cheadle Company: "cast of a metal composed of copper with a very large proportion of lead as an alloy, and hardened by arsenic" (Aitken 1866a:274). The newly cast manillas were "shaken" in a revolving barrel "in order to remove the sand from the exterior, and to give an approximate degree of brightness." Aitken goes on to discuss the detail with which manillas were examined in Africa. Because the manillas were likely destined to be melted down by Akan metal smiths, it is not surprising that the electroplating over iron bracelets was quickly discovered.

5. These examples are clearly machine made with stamped patterns. One can be seen in the Fowler Museum of Cultural History, UCLA. The collections of the British Museum include a *forowa* marked "Birmingham 1926," which is probably a unique example (Ross 1974). See Chapter 4 for a discussion of the production of *forowa* in Ghana.

6. There is no evidence of this threat ever having been put into practice, and there are examples of

Africans trading with the vessels of other countries within sight of the castle (e.g., van Dantzig 1978:43). Barbot (1992:378–379, 385) describes how people surrounded his brigantine while it was anchored at Elmina, despite the fact that he had driven them off at the behest of the Dutch director general.

7. An American trader described this situation in 1810: "The merchants & companies concerned in the African trade in England have attempted & in part succeeded in excluding neutrals from the settlements on the coast, but this can never be carried wholly into effect while the native trade is allowed which can be carried on so near the factories as to smuggle whole cargoes into them if necessary" (Bennett and Brooks 1965:32).

8. For references to Portuguese reliance on Flemish metalwares and Indian cloth, see Vogt 1979:73–74, 146; Elbl 1986; and Alpern 1995. Limited documentary evidence indicates the Venetian origin of trade beads (e.g., de Marees 1987:34, 53, 80), but generally the varied names that traders gave to beads make it difficult to determine their origin. More conclusive is the evidence of the beads themselves.

9. Van Dantzig (1978:245, 318, 319, 333) includes several eighteenth-century instances of Dutch, French, and Portuguese exchanges. For Dutch trade at Príncipe and São Tomé, see the text and annotations on Lübelfing's voyage of 1599–1600 in Jones 1983:17. In the nineteenth century, Dutch and Danish factories on the Gold Coast reportedly depended on American supplies (Bennett and Brooks 1965:41).

10. Garrard (1980a:105) estimates that 1.5 million manillas may have been supplied to the Elmina trade, an estimate that would seem low in light of the preceding citation. Vogt notes that "the factor of the Guinea and Mina House [Portugal] for the three years of 1494 through 1497, indicates that the equivalent of about 71,000 *manhilas* was received annually for shipment to west Africa with perhaps as many as 80 percent of these items earmarked for Mina" (1979:76).

11. The implications for this are further underscored by Garrard's observation that the quantity of metal reaching the Akan area via the trans-Saharan trade was 1.8 or 2.7 t (2 or 3 tons) per year at the most.

12. A more detailed breakdown of the Portuguese

trade between 1529 and 1531 is provided in Ballong-Wen-Mewuda (1984:412–418). Expressed as
percentages of gold received, these data suggest
slightly lesser proportions of cloth and metal
goods and a larger revenue from slaves.

13. Curtin (1975:326), examining eighteenth-century
data from the Senegambia, organizes trade items
from a completely different perspective, dividing
them into these categories: raw material (iron
bars); consumer goods (metals, textiles, coral);
and nonproductive goods (e.g., alcohol); see also
Feinberg 1989:50 for comparison with the Gold
Coast.

14. Writing in 1809, Samuel Swan said: "I get under
weigh [way] from here tomorrow, shall touch at
monserado [Liberia], thence direct to Elmina.
Tho a conciderable intermediate trade to great
advantage may be made I think my grand object
is to get to the Mines before Capt Davis, who will
carry with him a large quantity of rum & Tobacco, & I should rather even run back as far as
Cape Three points than loose the first chance at
Elmina" (Bennett and Brooks 1965:26). See also
Bennett and Brooks 1965:279 for a similar account
in 1843.

15. Painkiller bottles could have been produced in
both the United States and England.

16. American trade on the coast expanded tremendously during the nineteenth century. The period
after the War of 1812 and the start of the Civil
War was a period "characterized by the steady
growth of American commerce to a position of
considerable significance" (Bennett and Brooks
1965:v).

17. Neither of these accounts cited here suggests
that Americans traded in large numbers of flints.

18. The bark *Reaper* carried seven tierces (casks) and
11 boxes of pottery in 1843 (Bennett and Brooks
1965:282), but ceramics are not mentioned in
other accounts, or only small amounts are indicated (Bennett and Brooks 1965:42, 116).

19. See Agorsah 1975, 1993, for Efutu and Nunoo 1957
for a discussion of the Asebu material. Test excavations and surface collections were made at
Eguafo by Theresa Singleton and myself in 1993,
and Samuel Spiers and Gérard Chouin surveyed
the site in 1998 as part of the Central Region Project. Additional mapping and test excavation
were undertaken by Spiers in 2000.

20. As noted earlier, during the nineteenth century

some of the wealthier merchant houses in
Elmina may have had slate roofs. However, the
small number of dispersed slate fragments here
are not associated with a particular structure.
Even if they originally served as roofing material,
the slates may have been reused as writing
tablets.

21. In 1834 a local ruler in Nigeria listed the top five
European trade goods, in descending order, as
cowries, red cloth, red glass beads, soldiers' jack-
ets, and, finally, romals (handkerchiefs) and ban-
dannas (cited in Alpern 1995:40). On the Gold
Coast several nineteenth-century illustrations depict Africans wearing what appear to be military
uniforms, and there are descriptions of the Asante
soldiers wearing pieces of military uniforms.

22. The use of bustles by women was first mentioned by Müller in 1673 (in Jones 1983:205), and
references continue through the nineteenth century (Bennett and Brooks 1965:118; Meredith
1967:108).

23. Garrard (1983b) reviews pseudoweights of European origin.

24. There may be greater consistency in wares
brought to European tradeposts occupied for
shorter time spans by a single European power. A
preliminary survey of Bunce Island, Sierra
Leone, site of an English factory in the seventeenth and eighteenth centuries, suggests a
greater preponderance of English wares. This is
also true of some of the pre-nineteenth-century
European sites in other world areas, for example,
British, French, or Spanish colonial sites in the
Americas.

25. Kea further notes: "All of these goods were
brought from Europe and were retailed at the
ports of Assini, Takoradi, Little Komenda, Cape
Coast, Mouri, Kormantse, Great Bereku (or Sanya
Beraku), and Small Accra" (1982:208). At this time
Elmina was still controlled by the Portuguese. Notably, ceramics are not mentioned in other descriptions of the early seventeenth-century trade
(e.g., Brun in Jones 1983; de Marees 1987).

26. An itemized list of sales for Gross Friedrichsburg for 1683 (A. Jones 1985:72) notes the sale of
two earthenware pots (*diggels*) weighing "6 lbs."
to the "Mina Negroes" Jacobje Herman and
Pieter Claassen. If these were the same kind of
pots and the same units of measurement as used
in the previously cited list, the "489 lbs." of

earthenware pots would have amounted to 163 vessels. The use of the term *earthenware* suggests that these pots may have been utilitarian wares, possibly lead glazed. In other instances, stoneware jugs (*kannen*) are clearly indicated (A. Jones 1985:124, 139).

27. These statistics were compiled from figures in the *British Parliamentary Papers* (Reynolds 1974:185).

28. I am especially indebted to Emlen Myers, James L. Boone, and Jan Baart for helping me with the identification of these ceramics. For examples of Portuguese ceramics from other African contexts, see Redman 1986; and Kirkman 1974. Both of these sites are actually Portuguese, and the assemblages recovered include a greater diversity of forms than is represented at Elmina. However, some of the ceramics illustrated are virtually identical with examples from Elmina. At Elmina, Portuguese ceramics could be readily dated on the basis of the known date of the Portuguese arrival on the coast and their stratigraphic contexts, which clearly predated Dutch-period trade materials. In reality, however, the production range of these ceramics extends earlier and continues later than indicated by the archaeological contexts at Elmina.

29. Examples of probable Portuguese feldspar-inlaid ceramics have also been found in Spanish colonial sites in the Americas (Fairbanks 1966; Deagan 1987:41–43). Production of similar wares began in the Americas, possibly during the seventeenth century. The production range of these ceramics is, however, greater than the sixteenth- and seventeenth-century contexts represented in American sites. It occurs at Qsar es-Seghir, which was Portuguese from 1458 to 1550 (Redman 1986:192), and it is still readily found in Lisbon tourist markets.

30. In contrast with later ceramics, it is possible that a greater proportion of these Portuguese wares were associated with the European garrison. The count, totaling 314, includes sherds from the midden deposits below Locus E that clearly derived from the castle (see discussion in Chapter 3). Others may have been associated with Portuguese burials on the peninsula. However, many of the sherds and a variety of forms are from African contexts. A single sherd of Portuguese lead-glazed earthenware was recovered during surface survey of the site of Eguafo.

31. The figures are meant to provide only a crude indication of the amount of ceramics represented. The great diversity in the size and nature of the archaeological deposits makes simple comparison of different contexts of little value.

32. A single sherd of probable seventeenth-century age was excavated by Posnansky at Begho (Anquandah 1982:95). Farther north, Insoll (1995) reported a sherd of sixteenth- to seventeenth-century Chinese stoneware from the site of Gao in Mali. Two dozen sherds or intact vessels of Chinese porcelain were recovered at Elmina, including both coarse and refined wares.

33. This is illustrated by some spectacular assemblages from shipwrecks (e.g., Klose 1992; van der Pijl-Ketel 1982; Werz and Klose 1994). A superb review of the Chinese porcelain trade and a survey of porcelains from South African sites are provided by Klose (1997).

34. Klose (1997) and Abrahams (1996) discuss porcelain, as well as other categories of imported ceramics, with regard to their archaeological and documentary visibility in Cape Town, South Africa. While the size of the collection from Elmina is small, the forms and wares represented, as well as the sherd count itself, clearly indicate that porcelain was of less significance as a trade item at Elmina than it was with the settler population in South Africa.

35. The piece of possibly sixteenth- or early seventeenth-century age is a bowl with an underglaze blue decoration and a Ming dynasty mark on the bottom. In contrast with other pieces of porcelain recovered, this piece is water worn. Although not from a sixteenth-century context, the sherd was recovered from an area that produced other artifacts of likely sixteenth- or early seventeenth-century age. I thank Jane Klose for her help in identifying the Elmina porcelains.

36. Canton porcelains, named after the port from which they were exported, are common on North American sites of the late eighteenth and early nineteenth centuries (Noël Hume 1978: 262–263).

37. I observed a variety of nineteenth-century European stonewares being used in this way in the Ivory Coast in 1987.

38. The term *yellowware* is used here to refer to a yellow-paste ware with a clear alkaline glaze. It occurs most commonly in utilitarian forms, particularly mixing bowls with annular bands of

blue and white, but mugs, pitchers, and plates were also produced. Also represented in nineteenth-century contexts are a handful of examples of European porcelains.

39. For published examples of American pieces showing decorations (not necessarily forms) represented at Elmina, see Ketchum 1983:122–123, 147, 155, 157, 178–179, 181–182, 213–217, 220–221, 235, 261; 1987; and Leibowitz 1985.

40. These vessels show a great deal of consistency in form. More squat, round-sided vessels were produced, but those represented at Elmina are the cylindrical examples described. This form is more characteristic of the nineteenth century. The color of these vessels is more variable. The exteriors of most are red or yellowish red (Munsell 2.5 YR 4/6 to 5 YR 4/6), but some examples are yellower (Munsell 7.5 YR 6/6–8 to 10 YR 7/6–8). Stoneware bottles of this kind were used for gin by the A. van Hoboken Company, Rotterdam, during the nineteenth century (Pettit 1980).

41. Glass is virtually absent from clearly dated Portuguese-period deposits, either those in the town or those associated with the castle. Post-1873 British deposits covering the site do include substantial quantities of glass. The remainder of the assemblage is from the town.

42. One story has it that gin was accidentally discovered by a professor of medicine at the University of Leiden, Holland, in the mid-seventeenth century (Munsey 1970:84). Also see McNulty 1971:99–100.

43. Müller's description of the Fetu country, 1662–69 (in Jones 1983:213), reported that French brandy was the only brandy that tasted good to the local Africans and that spirits distilled from grain, presumably including gin, were despised. He furthermore adds that rum, brought by the English, would not be taken into their mouths. Also see de Marees 1987:41; and Alpern 1995:24–26.

44. Different spirits were associated with the trade of different nations. Gin was associated with the Dutch, whereas rum was more commonly traded by the British and the Americans (Alpern 1995:25). In some cases the entire cargo of American ships consisted of rum. In 1756, for example, the brigantine *Marigold* carried 37,465 liters (9,900 gallons) of rum to Africa. In contrast, during the eighteenth century, rum has been estimated to have made up 3–7 percent of the British trade by

value (Alpern 1995:25). See accounts of the American trade in Bennett and Brooks 1965.

45. Although today *pito* is associated with northern Ghana, in the past it was also produced and consumed on the coast (Müller in Jones 1983:210–211).

46. Descriptions often do not mention the kind of container involved, but the terms or prices make it clear that glass bottles were the mode of shipment (see, e.g., Ballong-Wen-Mewuda 1984:425; Birmingham 1970:5; Blake 1942:86, 102, 105; Pereira 1967:121; Vogt 1979:75). Also see general comments in Alpern 1995:24.

47. European examples are more characteristic of the seventeenth century.

48. Though occurring earlier on wine bottles, seals did not become common on case bottles until the nineteenth century. Sophisticated chemical and physical analyses to identify sources are complicated, expensive, and not entirely successful (Frank 1982).

49. I am very grateful to Peter A. R. Vermeulen for help in identifying the *AVDE* mark.

50. Unidentified marks from probable British-period contexts are *BR, VR,* and an *S* within a diamond.

51. See Abrahams 1987:11–13 for a discussion of the Constantia wine industry. The Netherlands did not produce wine, and, hence, substantial quantities were imported from the Rhineland, France, Italy, Spain, Portugal, Greece, and the Canary Islands (McNulty 1971:98).

52. Nineteenth-century case bottles are the most common form. Their occurrence in markets in Liberia and Sierra Leone in the late 1970s was relatively common. Although they are less common now, I noted old bottles still in use in Freetown, Sierra Leone, in 1993 and Accra in 1986.

53. Note also the quotation from Gramberg 1861:88–89 in the preceding discussion on ceramics. On the other hand, some exhaustive lists of trade items fail to mention glassware (e.g., Bennett and Brooks 1965:37–40).

54. A reconstructed example was excavated at the Danish plantation house of Daccubie, occupied 1808–11 (DeCorse 1993:166).

55. Olive Jones (1985:38), discussing British military glass, states that wineglasses cost less than tumblers. More recently, however, she has indicated that this statement should be qualified. The cost of vessels was influenced by a variety of factors, including excise duty that was paid by weight.

Wine glasses sometimes cost more, sometimes less, depending on the duty, as well as other variables (Olive Jones, correspondence, July 27, 1999).

56. Several writers have proffered theories of the introduction of pipes and smoking to Ghana and West Africa (Alpern 1992; Lebeuf 1962; Mauny 1954; Ozanne 1969; Philips 1983; Shaw 1960). Although there is a general consensus concerning Portuguese introduction along the coast, the case is circumstantial, based on prima facie evidence. Philips (1983) suggests that the French or even the English were more likely intermediaries than the Portuguese, but this seems less tenable in most areas.

Work by Ozanne (1969) is particularly important because he undertook a detailed study of material from archaeological contexts in Ghana. Surveying European and Arabic sources, oral traditions, and archaeological data, he postulated that smoking spread from Accra throughout southern Ghana, but he noted an apparent "lag" in this area compared with upper Guinea and the Congo. He also stated that evidence from portions of the Gold Coast was even later: "[A]t Asebu, for instance, close to Elmina, the first archaeological signs of smoking are European pipes of the mid-seventeenth century, locally-made pipes not appearing until 1660–80, and then, apparently, under the inspiration of Accra designs" (Ozanne 1969:38). He explained the gap in the Elmina area, despite the early presence of the Portuguese, as a result of unfavorable growing conditions and the nature of African-Portuguese relations. He stated: "[T]he Portuguese settlement at Elmina, and those at Shama and Axim, were of a very different type from those of the Congo and Upper Guinea. There were far fewer people, all tightly concentrated within the forts, on uneasy terms with the local people, and in frequent contact by sea with Cape Verde, whence supplies of American tobacco could regularly be bought" (Ozanne 1969:38).

While the data from Elmina do not negate these general conclusions, some modification can be made with regard to the history of smoking in the Elmina area. Its introduction here was probably at about the same time as in adjacent areas but may have been characterized by an early reliance on imported pipes. In contrast with Ozanne's comments regarding the poor conditions for growing tobacco in the Elmina area, Wartemberg (1951:73) suggests that it has long been cultivated in the vicinity. In addition, Ozanne's reference to the regular supply of Elmina via Cape Verde does not agree with the documentary accounts of the poor supply of the Portuguese garrison during the late sixteenth and early seventeenth centuries (de Marees 1987:212–217; Vogt 1979:114, 157).

57. This observation is based on the study of collections in the Department of Archaeology, University of Ghana. Also see Calvocoressi 1975a.

58. These include marks on both the feet and the stems of fragmentary pipes, and hence in some instances the same pipe may be represented twice.

59. Eluyemi (1975) reports pipes stamped LAGOS STORES, a Liverpool firm, from archaeological contexts in Nigeria. Examples of elbow-bend, socket-stem pipes made in imitation of African forms are prevalent on late nineteenth- to early twentieth-century sites in Senegal. Specific forms for the African trade have not yet been reported from Ghana. The pipes that have been found are consistent with examples produced for the domestic market. The late nineteenth century corresponded with the dramatic expansion of European merchant houses in West Africa and a continued expansion of the volume of trade. See Newbury 1978 for a review of the growth and development of the Niger Company during this period.

60. Huey noted a lack of consistency in the bore diameters of pipes recovered from sealed stratigraphic contexts at the Dutch Fort Orange in Albany, New York. He reported that in the majority of instances the pipes overestimated the age of the archaeological deposits. He suggested that "the pipes of one or more popular Dutch makers did not follow the pattern, remaining large in size thereby altering the averages" (Huey 1988:579). Curves establishing dates based on the ratio of stem bores, bowl sizes, and shape have not been fully tested. In South Africa, Schrire had promising results measuring bores using metric increments. Pipes from the sites of Oudepost I have been used to establish the chronology of stratigraphic layers (Schrire et al. 1990).

61. Sample size is an important consideration. Ivor Noël Hume (1978:300), in examining a collection of approximately 12,000 pipe-stem fragments of known age, concluded that assemblages of over

900 are needed to obtain a statistically representative sample. Smaller samples can be utilized, but a single stem is clearly not sufficient for dating purposes, and stems, bowl forms, and marks are best used in conjunction with one another. At Elmina, the number of pipes for individual stratigraphic levels was generally quite small.

62. This was the pipe found with the eighteenth-century *forowa* described in Chapter 4. Other associated artifacts included a Rhenish stoneware jug, beads, and three brass vessels.

63. These are now in the collections of the Department of Archaeology, University of Ghana.

64. It was associated with a small, unique local pottery vessel that, like the pipe, has no parallels in the assemblage. The pottery vessel may have been used to store tobacco.

65. For references and varying perspectives see Fischer and Rowland 1971; Headrick 1981; Kea 1971; Mbaeyi 1973; Richards 1980; and Tenkorang 1968. Although interpretations of their role vary, it seems clear that firearms were important expressions of the military power in such African states as Asante, Dahomey, Sokoto, and Samory, and in the relations of these states with neighboring polities during the nineteenth century.

66. Firearms did, however, clearly play a role in coastal politics before this. In 1578 a Portuguese and Elmina force defeated a reportedly larger force from Efutu with the help of two cannons and guns (Vogt 1979:125).

67. The Efutu piece is in the collections of the Ghana National Museum, Accra, and the one from Bui, in the Department of Archaeology, University of Ghana.

68. Surveying the fifteenth- and sixteenth-century sources, Hair (1994b:53–54 n. 33) states that it is highly unlikely that any guns were sold, further noting that firearms at this time had limited military value. A 1572 Portuguese report on Mina suggests that it would be a good idea to "forbid them [the Africans] the use of all Spanish weapons" (Teixeira da Mota and Hair 1988:84). See Müller (in Jones 1983:193) for a seventeenth-century comment regarding the limited trade in firearms during the Portuguese period. It has been suggested that Mande traders were eager to trade for firearms from the Portuguese (Wilks 1962:339), but there is no evidence for this (Hair 1994b:53–54).

69. This observation must be qualified. In fact, firearms were of great importance in European military conflicts during the first half of the sixteenth century. However, as Noël Hume (1992:204–205) observes, this was contingent on the enemy playing by the rules. The early matchlocks weighed 4.5–5.4 kg (10–12 pounds), were cumbersome to load, and had to be supported by a U-shaped staff when aiming. Given these limitations "a nimble Indian with a good eye could get off half a dozen well-aimed arrows while a musketeer was getting himself ready to fire one reasonably well-aimed ball a distance of about thirty yards" (Noël Hume 1992:204). A similar situation was likely true in West Africa.

70. The Portuguese position may have changed, because the Dutch governor at Mori received requests for firearms from Asebu after its enemies had reportedly received firearms from the Portuguese (Kea 1971:189).

71. Also see the general review in Alpern 1995:18–22.

72. A French account of 1671 notes the matchlock as the predominant firearm used by the Africans and also notes the locally produced matches as superior to the European ones (see Chouin, n.d.-b). By this same point in time the English Board of Ordnance was likely the single largest buyer of English flints (de Lotbiniere 1980:56).

73. Blacksmiths throughout West Africa make black-powder guns, or did until recently. Most examples are percussion cap rifles, but flintlocks and pistols can also be found. The weapons typically have unrifled barrels, usually made from water pipe, but there are also examples made from other materials, such as a tubular piece taken from the steering column of a Landrover. Local manufacture of entire firearms was probably limited until pipe or similar material became widely available during the present century.

74. There are some differences of opinion on this. A twentieth-century American flint knapper, Frank Galinat, suggests that a single flint could have been used to fire a flintlock 350 times (Clark 1983). However, contemporary accounts suggest a far lower number, with as few as 30 shots considered the ideal (Skertchly 1879:40).

75. North American archaeologists sometimes refer to "Dutch" gunflints (e.g., Witthoft 1966), but these are English wedge-type flints.

76. The best available surveys of the development of

gunflint manufacture during the seventeenth and eighteenth centuries are provided by de Lotbiniere (1980, 1984).

77. Twelve pieces of what may have been English ballast flint were found in the Elmina excavations, but none of this flint shows evidence of flaking. Indigenous gunflint industries have been reported elsewhere in Africa (Clark 1963, 1984; Phillipson 1969).

78. I am very grateful to K. R. Miller, of the National Army Museum, Royal Hospital Road, London, for helping with the identification of the slugs and cartridges.

79. Cannons were imported to the West African coast as gifts or in trade with coastal states beginning in the late seventeenth century (Alpern 1995:21), and they may have occasionally served as strategic weapons on the Gold Coast: Two *gotelingen* (small cannons used aboard ships) were among the armaments lent to Asebu in 1629 (Kea 1971:189).

80. The castle's armaments are also reviewed by Lawrence (1963:161–163, 166).

81. An account of the armaments is given by J. Fred Crease in September 1873 (*British Parliamentary Papers* 1970b:360–361).

6. CULTURE CONTACT, CONTINUITY, AND CHANGE

1. Similar comments were made almost 150 years earlier by Müller, who notes: "Distinguished people, particularly those who have contact with the Whites, possess more utensils, far more precious. There are some among them who are in this respect not inferior, indeed far superior, to many of us. One sees in their houses silver drinking vessels, silver spoons, pewter dishes and bowls, precious table-knives, tables and benches, fine tablecloths and napkins, serviettes etc." (in Jones 1983:202).

2. A complete review of Akan cosmology is not intended. The discussion and examples provided are intended to illustrate some practices, continuities in their underlying conceptual framework, and the ways in which some of these may be presented archaeologically. Fuller discussion of Akan (primarily Asante) religion and rituals may be found in Busia 1951; Christensen 1954; McCaskie 1995; Manoukian 1964; Rattray 1959;

Vollbrecht 1978; Warren 1973, 1990; Wartemberg 1951:150–159; and Wilks 1993. Chukwukere (1978) provides useful discussion of some of the distinctive aspects Fante cosmology as compared with other Akan groups. Early descriptions of religion on the central Gold Coast are provided by Bosman (1967); Barbot (1992); de Marees (1987); and Müller (in Jones 1983:158–181).

It has been suggested that by the seventeenth century the Elmina people regarded themselves as *culturally,* as well as politically, distinct from the surrounding African population (Feinberg 1969:iii; 1970b). Although the degree of Elmina's political independence is well documented, evidence for a distinct culture in any meaningful sense is not supported by historical or ethnographic data. As Feinberg (1970b:23) and Fynn (1974b:vi) have indicated, the distinctive political situation is not a sufficient criterion to delineate a separate cultural group. Although there is some variation, there is generally a high degree of cultural homogeneity within the Akan language family, including the Elmina (Christensen 1954:1; Dolphyne and Kropp Dakubu 1988:50–51; Murdock 1959:253). Feinberg notes that Elmina's close relationship with the Dutch, hostility with the neighboring Fante population, and close ties with Asante served to isolate Elmina from the surrounding African population and led to the creation of a distinctive identity.

3. The range of trade goods recovered from Elmina contrasts with the small number found in other sites of the post-European-contact period (e.g., Bellis 1972; Davies 1955, 1956; Nunoo 1957; Shaw 1961).

4. In addition to the present research, work by Bellis (1987) and Kiyaga-Mulindwa (1982) demonstrated these transformations stratigraphically as well as on the basis of surface material. Although a seventeenth-century age for these transformations is reasonable, chronological control for some contexts, particularly the surface-collected material, is limited. In addition, there is no reason to suppose that change occurred instantaneously in all areas.

5. Although there may not have been substantial population replacement at the regional level, individual sites, in some instances, do appear to have had temporally discrete occupations (see Kiyaga-Mulindwa 1982). For a review of the liter-

ature relevant to archaeological interpretations of abandonment, see Cameron and Tomka 1996.

6. The consequences of the Atlantic trade—the slave trade in particular—have been viewed from varying perspectives, and at times this complex issue has been reduced to a gross simplification of "whether the export slave trade had great influence on African life and Atlantic life" or "whether it had small influence" (Manning 1990:14). As Manning (1990:12–18) points out, the question is not so easily addressed.

7. Holl (2000), for example, contrasts different historical processes and archaeological patterns for the southern and northern portions of the Cameroons during the period circa 1500–1900. For discussion of the varying nature of the consequences on the Gold Coast in comparative perspective, see van Dantzig 1982a.

8. The version of the meeting given by João de Barros is somewhat more elaborate but basically the same: "Those who among them were considered nobles had, as a token of their nobility, two pages following them, one of whom carried a round wooden seat for them to sit on when they cared to rest, and the other carried a battle shield" (in Hair 1994b:20).

9. It is interesting to note that Barros's account states: "Caramansa took the hand of Dioga de Azambuja, and releasing it snapped his fingers . . ." (in Hair 1994b:21). This practice is also mentioned in later accounts and is still used in greetings today. For a seventeenth-century description, see Müller in Jones 1983:155.

The references to chairs or round wooden seats carried by page boys for the use of the more prominent African nobels are also of note. Stools and chairs are important symbols of status in many parts of Africa, including the Akan area. For example, see a 1555 reference by William Towerson published in Blake 1942:378. Also see de Marees 1987:34, 96, 167–168, and miscellaneous accounts translated by Jones (1983:168, 182, 186.) Barbot (1992:Plate 47) illustrates both round and square stools. Today the stool carriers of an officeholder are called nkonŋwasoafoɔ in Twi (see McCaskie 1995:291–292).

10. This unique aspect of the town was commented on by many European visitors who contrasted the stone buildings with the timber and clay (wattle and daub) construction found in neigh-

boring areas (e.g., Bosman 1967:43; Brun in Jones 1983:85–86; de Marees 1987:75; Müller in Jones 1983:201–202; van Dantzig 1975:205).

11. A seventeenth-century description is given by Müller (in Jones 1983:211).

12. There may have been limited Islamic influence on the coast associated with northern traders (see Chapter 2), but the religious practices and rituals described in pre-nineteenth-century accounts principally relate to indigenous African beliefs. De Marees (1987:73) notes that they circumcised their children "following the law of Mohammed," but this and other features are equally representative of local customs. See the comment by van Dantzig and Jones (in de Marees 1987:73 fn. 15).

13. For example, see a 1523 letter from King John III to the governor of Elmina (Blake 1942:133 document 49; cf. Blake 1942:33; Pereira 1967:120–121; Vogt 1979:185).

14. Supposedly the chief, his family, and 1,000 members of his tribe received holy baptism from the Portuguese clergy. The meeting between the chief and the royal chaplain reportedly took place within site of the castle, perhaps on St. Jago Hill.

15. Vogt (1979:55–56) discusses the example of a female Elmina slave named Grace who had received the holy Sacrament and been baptized many years before but who was accused of fetish worship. When brought before the priest at Elmina, she was unable to say the Ave, and the subsequent search of her house revealed a dozen fetish images. She was tried in Lisbon and condemned to "perpetual incarceration in the prison of the Holy Office" (Vogt 1979:56). For other examples and general discussion of the limited nature of Portuguese missionary activity, see Blake 1942, 1977; Boxer 1972; and Hair 1994b.

16. See also Brooks 1962:76; Cruickshank 1853, 1:183–184; de Marees 1987:72–74; Thompson 1937. Barbot makes similar comments. After making the general observation that all of the Africans live in "an abominable state of idolatry and profound ignorance," he notes the mulattos as being somewhat better, but "even these are very indifferent new Christians, as they call themselves, their religion being mix'd with much Pagan superstition. The great concern of the Dutch on this coast, as well as of all other Europeans, set-

tled on trading there, is the gold, and not the welfare of those souls: for by their lewd loose lives, many who live among these poor wretches rather harden them in their wickedness, than turn them from it" (Barbot 1992:389). An exception was Müller, who, when sent as a chaplain for the Danish garrison at Frederiksborg, made some effort to convert the Africans he met (Jones 1983:134). In fact, evangelists seem to have had equally poor success in influencing the behavior of the Europeans in the garrison. Hemmersam, writing in the early seventeenth century, noted that a Dutch preacher had come to Mori, where he admonished the garrison staff to be moderate in their eating and drinking, but they made fun of him and he returned home (in Jones 1983:80; also see Howison 1834:152).

17. The conversion of the chief of Efutu and his followers was the notable exception. The implications and consequences of this conversion are difficult to assess, but the change does not seem to have been lasting. De Marees (1987:66–74), describing the religious beliefs of the people of the Fetu (Efutu) area in 1602, suggested there were not many Christians, aside from a few who pretended to be Christian because they were acquainted with Christians. Although he advocated conversion, he concluded, "But it seems that God has not seen fit to call them into our Christian faith . . ." (74). Hemmersam, who also viewed the Fetu country in the first half of the seventeenth century, noted the numerous attempts to convert the Africans, yet "[w]hen they attended mass, they took the paternoster in their hands, but afterward they lived in as heathen a manner as before, for there is no foundation to be laid in them" (in Jones 1983:118; see also Müller's account in Jones 1983:176). The chapel on St. Jago Hill (if this was, in fact, the location) was replaced with a defensive redoubt in the sixteenth century.

18. For example, in the early seventeenth century, Brun noted: "The Spaniards have converted the people [of the Congo] to the Christian faith, as the natives themselves testify" (in Jones 1983:61). Almost all of the people in portions of that area were reportedly Christian, attending mass twice a day, despite the efforts of the Dutch to counteract Catholic missionary activity (statement by van de Broecke, referenced in Jones 1983:61 n. 94).

19. Akan religion and its particular expressions have been described in different and, at times, contradictory ways. It has, for example, been variously termed polytheism, fetishism, ancestor worship, and animism. The following discussion is principally based on ethnographic information. For expanded discussion, see Christaller 1881; McCaskie 1995; Rattray 1959; and Wartemburg 1951. However, parallels for the concepts and terms described are also mentioned in many historical sources for the coast. Most early European accounts describe African religious practice from narrow, deprecating perspectives and provide only limited detail. A few Europeans, however, were keen observers who, while critical of indigenous local practices, attempted to learn about African beliefs. Some of the more detailed descriptions are presented in Barbot 1992:577–582; Bosman 1967:145–161; de Marees 1987; and by Müller in Jones 1983:138–259.

20. The concept of a withdrawn God, as it is sometimes described, is prevalent throughout West Africa. McCaskie (1995:104–105) observes that among the Asante the reason for the creator's withdrawal is always linked to some human folly or crime. He further notes: "In the eighteenth and nineteenth centuries *onyame* had neither priestly servitors nor temples devoted to his worship" (McCaskie 1995:107). There also appears to be no evidence for these features among the coastal Akan. However, as discussed here, some aspects of the Akan religious life may not have been perceived by early European visitors. European visitors may not have recognized simple *nyame dua* shrines, constructed out of tree trunks with a bowl on top, for what they were (for illustration see McCaskie 1995:110). Lack of evidence in this case may not necessarily indicate that such features did not exist.

21. *Ɔbosom* are divided into categories based on places of origin, for example, the water, sky, or forest (McCaskie 1995:108–111). Early European accounts make some allusion to *ɔbosom:* "There are some Mountains where Thunder and lightning often occur. . . . Consequently they regard many Mountains as their Gods . . ." (de Marees 1987:71, also 84; see also Barbot 1992:579; Bosman 1967:148; Connolly 1897:150; Müller in Jones 1983:160, 164).

22. For seventeenth- to nineteenth-century refer-

ences, see Allen 1874:53–54; Barbot 1992:578; Bosman 1967:147–153, 221–222; Connolly 1897:149–153; Duncan 1847:25–26; de Marees 1987:66–74, 77; Howison 1834:76; Müller in Jones 1983:162, 209; and Thompson 1937:51–53.

23. I have not been able to establish the number of *ɔbosom* in Elmina independent of Wartemberg. Though people often refer to 77 deities, the number is actually a trope for "many."

24. See also the version of event by Pina (in Hair 1994b:32).

25. *Ɔbosom* associated with rocks by the sea are referred to in other accounts of the coast (Bosman 1967:147; see also Müller in Jones 1983:160).

26. The other important yearly festival in Elmina is Bronya, held on the first Thursday in January each year: "It is a day of remembrance of all souls departed from the earthly life . . ." (Wartemberg 1951:105–107, quotation on 106; see also Fynn 1974b:11–12). Other ceremonies, such as those relating to the enstoolment of *ɔmanhen* or *asafohene,* are held on an irregular basis as needed.

27. The Bakatue is typically held in June or July (see note 30 below). Similar rituals are held in neighboring coastal towns, most notably Cape Coast, though some are not as elaborate as the Bakatue. In addition to the differences in the names, location, and specifics of the rituals, the Bakatue is different from these in actually being a *symbolic* opening of the lagoon, which, in fact, is an estuary that is never closed off from the sea. In neighboring areas, sandbars typically block the outlets of lagoons during the dry season and are ritually dug out.

28. The term *durbar,* often used in Ghanaian English and patois to refer to a meeting of chiefs, is a gloss for the public aspect of a wide variety of ceremonies and rituals. The term originated in India, where it refers to an official reception or audience.

29. The Bakatue may be referred to in a 1716 journal examined by Feinberg (1969:135). Yarak (1993) notes that he has found no clear reference to the Bakatue in the daily journals of the Dutch governor in 1847. After this date references occur in 1850–59, 1861–62, 1866–67, and 1869–70. In each of these cases the ceremony was held on a Tuesday in July, except for 1859, when it was held on Tuesday, August 2. During this century, the Bakatue is said to have been traditionally held on the last Tuesday of June or the first Tuesday of July (Wartemberg 1951:101–102).

30. It is, nevertheless, surprising that references to the Bakatue are not found in the more detailed descriptions of the coast. Bosman (1967:145–161), for example, does not mention it in his examination of Gold Coast religion, yet his discussion of religion is framed around description of more general concepts rather than particular details. He may, in fact, be referring to a ritual similar to the Bakatue when he discusses "general religious exercises" that are carried out, in conjunction with which the "priests" might order "ridiculous commands and instructions" that must be obeyed (van Dantzig 1977:250; cf. Bosman 1967:153). In particular he notes: "When their Fishery is at low Ebb, they make Offerings to the Sea: but this generally happens about *August* or *September,* when Experience tells them that a vast Quantity of Fish is commonly taken, yet this is always believed an Effect of the offering" (Bosman 1967:153). The timing given is roughly consistent with the Bakatue, and August and September are months when the catch is often plentiful. Bosman's comments would also seem to suggest that such rituals were carried out on a regular basis. Bosman was critical of African religious beliefs, and he clearly cast his description in such a way as to make them appear frivolous.

31. This point was made clear to me in 1986 when I attended the Bakatue rituals adjacent to the Benya shrine prior to the Bakatue Festival. Activities began on the evening of June 30 and continued through the early morning of July 1. The ceremonies were attended by relatively few people, yet these activities were themselves a "public" culmination of ritual preparations that had begun almost two months earlier.

32. In addition to the *edenahen,* increasing importance of the *asafo,* such as the Ankobia, may also be represented. Like the *edenahen,* the principal roles of the prominent lineage members and the *asafo* companies in the current Bakatue celebrations are in the public festival and processional aspects of the ceremony.

33. This is an interesting area of study that should be explored in more detail. Within the last decade this has become a very conscious effort, with the Ghana government's push for "cultural tourism"

(see discussion of some aspects of this in Bruner 1996). Cultural arts and activities have been highlighted in government-sponsored fairs such as Indutech and Panafest.

34. Chouin is currently expanding his study of sacred groves as part of the Central Region Project.

35. Four examples were found archaeologically at Elmina. The pots are small, the largest measuring less than 18 cm (7 inches) in diameter. In other respects, they differ substantially. The surfaces of two are roughly smoothed and unburnished, and they have simple everted rims. The third vessel is globular in shape with a simple direct rim and smoothed surfaces. The final example is carinated and has shallow-groove decoration. Another larger pot, also interpreted as an offering, was found in recent, twentieth-century fill levels at Locus A.

   Examples that have been noted in markets were consistent in their small size and were typically globular with a small everted rim. The surfaces were unburnished and often not as well evened or smoothed compared with other vessels. The slightly uneven, rough surface may be one of the characteristics that distinguish their ritual purpose (see also libation pots and offering pots discussed below). However, as noted, some archaeological examples have other characteristics.

36. Müller (in Jones 1983:161) may have been referring to a similar practice when he noted the burial of iron or wood for protection.

37. In West African vernacular and creole English, *medicine* is often used in a sense analogous to *charms,* or ritual objects imbued with supernatural power. It is sometimes said that such pots are used by the "old men" to "cook" medicine. This may be literally true in that some *asuman* may involve the boiling of ingredients, but it may not imply that the preparation is to be drunk in the manner of taking medicine (see de Marees 1987:68). The pots are sold empty as pots, and the sellers make no prescriptions for use.

38. Gin, schnapps, and *akpeteshie* are the typical libations used today, but, as discussed in the text, other imported drinks, palm wine, and locally brewed beers were used in the past. Libations are typically poured onto the ground or into the libation pot. At times, however, some of a libation may be taken into the mouth and expelled through the teeth. This may be a more typical practice of the ɔkɔmfɔ. Both pouring and spitting libations through the teeth are referred to in early documentary sources (e.g., de Marees 1987:42–43, 68, 69; Hemmersam, in Jones 1983:117).

39. Sherds from two of these pots, not associated with features, were found during excavations. Informants associated the vessels with offerings to the ancestors (*asamaŋ*). The pot, fixed in a pedestal, is called *akɔr,* which is a shortened version of ɔkoryɔ. The meaning of this can be translated as "we are all together." Elmina potters recognized the form of the libation pots, and vessels of this type may have been produced at Elmina in the past. Examples are still produced east of Elmina and can be purchased at stands along the coast road and in Elmina. Their use was documented in many areas of the Central Region: Interviews relevant to their use were undertaken in 1986–87, 1993, and 2000 in Elmina, Asebu, Biriwa, Efutu, and Egyaa by myself, and in 1996 at Elmina, Amisakrom, Egyaa, and Pomadze in 1996 by Tetrault (1998). Examples of the pots in ritual use were photographed and drawn in several villages. Tetrault noted that depressions in the courtyard surface can be used for a similar purpose. In many instances, libations are poured directly onto the ground.

40. A wide variety of offerings and libations are described in documentary accounts, and some may represent similar practices. For example, de Marees observed a chief's compound where, at the front gate, two pots had been dug into the ground. These contained fresh water, which was changed every day; this may have been "done for their *Fetisso,* in order that he may drink it" (de Marees 1987:77; see accounts in de Marees 1987:42–43, 68; and Jones 1983: 117, 161, 163). Wartemberg (1951:153) also describes a libation pot in connection with the Ntona shrine, which he sees as an illustration of how the worship of the "true [Christian–Roman Catholic] God deteriorated with the lapse of years" following the departure of the Portuguese from Elmina.

41. Only one example, from a nineteenth-century fill context, was recovered at Elmina. However, archaeological survey and surface collections provided other examples, particularly in Eguafo and

Cape Coast. Interviews relevant to their use were undertaken in 1986–87, 1993, and 2000 in Elmina and Cape Coast by myself, and in 1996 at Amisakrom, Eguafo, and Egyaa by Tetrault (1998).

42. Brian Vivian (conversation, February 16, 2000) reports that vessels of this form are very common in sites in Asante and do not seem associated with ritual usage. The interior surfaces of these vessels, however, are typically not roughened in the same manner as the examples described here.

43. Komenda is located at 5°03′ N, 1°29′45″ W.

44. For a discussion of the neighboring European outposts, see Lawrence 1963:288–291; and van Dantzig 1980a:41–44.

45. Calvocoressi (1975b:164) is correct in pointing out that, although the artifact inventory would seem to suggest a context of the pre-European-contact period, the absence of European materials may not be surprising given the specialized nature of the site. Similarly, the 1993 test excavations at Eguafo produced no imported material, though at least portions of the deposit likely postdate the seventeenth century. The vessel forms represented at the Komenda site provide more insight into their probable age.

46. For illustration of *asafo* shrines and associated regalia, see Cole and Ross 1977:170–199.

47. Unfortunately, documentary descriptions often are not overly detailed, making it difficult to ascertain specific forms. Barbot provides somewhat more detailed descriptions as well as an illustration: "The fetish I had taken from this black (*nègre*) was in the shape of a Bologne sausage and was composed of glassware, beads, herbs, clay, burnt feathers, tallow, and threads of bark from the fetish tree, all pounded and kneaded together. At one end of the figure was a sort of human face, as you can see" (1992:580, 586–587 n. 18). De Marees's (1987:66) illustrations of "idolatrous beliefs and idols" seem to represent amorphous shapes without any human features. However, it is possible that he was alluding to anthropomorphic figures in a household shrine when he observed that when a person dies his closest friends "sit down in the corner of their house, taking all his *Fetissos* or relics, and put them near him in proper order, his greatest God in the middle and the other small ones next to it, all nicely arranged" (de Marees 1987:69).

48. The provisional identification of the tortoise is *Kinixys* sp. De Marees (1987:133) illustrates a tortoise.

49. It is, however, of interest to note the shrine's use of a carapace, which gave it superficial similarities to aspects of the Benya shrine. A key is the symbol of the Ankobia, an *asafo* company that has a principal role in the Bakatue procession, and the Ankobia is one of the *asafo* companies that may have been located in the area of town designated Locus A. Also of interest is the potential association of the shrine with the possible site of the early Portuguese church.

50. Yet the features represented in burials are polysemic and also are important indicators of other phenomena such as social organization, which remains a principal focus of mortuary studies (Carr 1995).

51. Archaeological data indicate that *forowa* (brass ritual vessels) were being produced by the mid-eighteenth century, but the earliest documentary reference is substantially later. See discussion in Chapter 4.

52. The Akan term for all funeral observances is *eyiye*. For detailed discussion of the Asante funerary complex, see Rattray 1959; see also Dei 1989; Field 1948:138–150; Manoukian 1964:53–54; and Vollbrecht 1978. These ethnographic descriptions closely accord with many aspects of twentieth-century Elmina rituals, but the latter have not been recorded or observed in detail (e.g., Wartemberg 1951:126–128). Descriptions of Fante funeral rituals may be found in Christensen 1954:67–74; Chukwukere 1981; and Ffoulkes 1909. Gilbert's (1988) examination of the funeral of a wealthy man in a southeastern Akan town provides vivid illustration of the varied and complex concerns that come together in a funeral, as well as the general importance of funerals in Akan life.

53. Hyland (1970:39) reports that Madam Bartles, a prominent mulatto trader during the mid-nineteenth century and one-time owner of the Viala House on Liverpool Street, was buried in her house, as was a son who died in infancy.

54. Also see Gilbert 1988: "Funerals are the most important social and ritual event in the life of an Akwapim person, Christian or non-Christian; other *rites de passage* are of minor importance. People return from their farms and work places all over Ghana to attend funerals in their home

towns, thereby demonstrating kinship ties, factional alliances, political strength, family wealth, individual status, and so on" (297).

55. For descriptions see de Marees 1987:181–182; Rattray 1959:159; and Ulsheimer in Jones 1983:31. Describing customs in the early twentieth century, Ffoulkes (1909:155–156) noted that poorer people were buried in a cloth, whereas wealthier individuals had coffins. The body was reportedly "placed in the coffin, nude if a man, with only a shame-cloth if a women, except, of course, for jewelry."

56. In the 1660s Müller noted both separate cemeteries and burials within town on the central Gold Coast: "For Burying the dead they have special places and cemeteries, which generally lie in front of the village, beneath many beautiful trees, although some people are buried in the village" (in Jones 1983:258). References to in-house burial are found in Bosman 1967:231; Cruickshank 1853, 2:218; Duncan 1847:30–31; and Ffoulkes 1909:156, 159. The locations of several in-house burials were also pointed out during fieldwork (also see Hyland 1970:39; van den Nieuwenhof 1991:55). The practice seems to have become increasingly less common during the twentieth century. Ffoulkes noted: "This burial in huts is fast dying out, and cemeteries are springing up even in bush villages" (1909:156). Christensen indicates: "It was formally the custom to bury an elder under the floor of his house, but this practice has long been forbidden by the government, although a Fanti elder knows in which room of his house a certain ancestor is interred" (1954:69; see also Manoukian 1964:53). The suggestion that only elders were buried in the house is at variance with the archaeological and other documentary data, which clearly indicate juvenile and adolescent, as well as adult, burial within the house. The deceased were reportedly buried in the graveyard of their *abusua* (matrilineage) or in the graveyard of the Christian sect to which they belonged (Christensen 1954:69; see also Manoukian 1964:53). Bosman also discusses a practice whereby a king or important person was left more than a year above ground, in which case "to prevent Putrification, they lay the Corps upon a wooden Utensil like a Grid-Iron; which they put over a very gentle clear Fire, that

by degrees dries it" (1967:231). This account has similarities to the description of the funerals of kings described by Rattray (1959:114–115), who also discusses the defleshing of the skeleton and eventual burial in a coffin. Other early references to funerals in the central Gold Coast seem to suggest separate burial grounds outside town or are ambiguous in the location of the grave (e.g., de Marees 1987:181; Jones 1983:31, 123). There are also references to burial within the house in the Ga and Ahanta areas east and west of the Fante coast (Allen 1874:41; Isert 1992:132–133; Garrard 1980a:106; Römer 1989:91). Isert, writing in the late eighteenth century, noted: "Every single Black is buried in the room in his house where he died" (1992:132–133).

57. Similar graves were noted during archaeological fieldwork. Rattray (1959:162) describes the original Asante grave as an oblong pit with a niche (*ahyenemu*) on one side large enough to receive the body. The niche was then screened off, and the grave shaft filled. This is comparable to burial descriptions given in the Akan area as well as other parts of Ghana. However, the sticks over the top of the grave seem to have been used, at least at some times, in conjunction with the niche.

58. Informants indicated that if an earlier burial is uncovered in digging a grave, earlier bones are pushed to the side. At least in some instances, grave goods associated with earlier interments were removed (e.g., Duncan 1847:27). There is no indication that graves were intentionally located on preexisting ones, but certain areas of cemeteries (and, of course, certain houses) might be associated with particular families. The connection between the living and the dead is illustrated by a request to the colonial secretary, Cape Coast, from Chief Quacoo Andoh, in the name of the people of Elmina, for permission to disinter the bones of those people who were buried in the bombarded portion of the town (Ghana National Archives, Accra, dated September 23, 1873, Elmina, ADM 23/1/36, page 488. I thank Gérard Chouin for this reference). Inasmuch as no lives were lost in the bombardment of the town, the request clearly refers to individuals who had been interred within houses. There is no archaeological evidence that any pre-1873 burials were removed following the request.

59. Evidence for pre-European-contact practices are, however, limited (see the discussion of Sekondi in note 63 below). For references to grave goods, see Allen 1874:41; Barbot 1992:595; Bosman 1967:232; Christensen 1954:71; Cruickshank 1853, 2:218; de Marees 1987:182; Duncan 1847:27; Ffoulkes 1909:155–156; Field 1948:141; Garrard 1980a:106–107; Gordon 1874:45–47; and Müller in Jones 1983:257–258. This practice was also widely noted by informants at Elmina. Wartemberg, describing burial practices of the mid-twentieth century, notes: "The corpse is washed and laid in state, followed by lamentations, and buried within 36 hours of death. It is coffined with articles of clothing, money, etc., a survival of the belief that the dead need, in the spiritual world, the necessities of physical existence in forms corresponding to those of the material plane" (1951:126). He also provides illustration of grave goods included as offerings or libations to the ancestors (Wartemberg 1951:156).

60. See Rattray 1959:161–163 for the use of pots in Asante funerals. The pot used in washing the corpse was reportedly included in the grave. The one local pottery bowl clearly associated with a Locus A burial could have functioned in this context. The forms of some of the imported ceramics found as grave goods would, however, seem to be impractical for this purpose, perhaps indicating they had different functions and meanings.

61. Informants in some instances indicated that specific forms (a brass basin, a delftware ointment pot, or a Rhenish stoneware jug) were placed under the head with a gold offering, but this function was suggested after informants were shown examples or photographs of vessels found archaeologically. The archaeological data leave no doubt that these items functioned in this manner. Numerous examples were noted archaeologically at Elmina and also by *galamsey* workers who extracted gold from these objects when excavating graves at neighboring sites.

62. These practices are widely referenced in documentary accounts and oral traditions as well as in Akan arts. For example, Akan gold weights representing carved elephant ivory trumpets frequently depict human jawbones that were historically attached on the end (Ross 1992:145). For reference to the decapitation of enemies and the placement of the heads with graves, see Barbot 1992:607; Brun in Jones 1983:92–93; de Marees 1987:90–91, 104; Hemmersam in Jones 1983:117; Müller in Jones 1983:197, 199; Römer 1989:103–107, 137; van Dantzig 1978:356; and Vogt 1979:181. Human sacrifices, particularly of slaves, were associated with the death of the chief and royals. Barbot noted: "If I am to believe the people of Comendo, no high-ranking person among them dies without them slaughtering 60 or 80 slaves (of both sexes and of every age), and for a king they kill two thousand" (1992:595). Also see Bosman 1967:231–232; Cruickshank 1853, 2:225–226; de Marees 1987:184; Dupuis 1824:114, 140–141; Ffoulkes 1909:161–163; Gordon 1874:46; Müller in Jones 1983:179; Rattray 1959:105–112; Ricketts 1831:108–109; Römer 1989:74–75, 169–170; Thompson 1937:57; and Ulsheimer in Jones 1983:31. At the death of Asantehene Kwaku Dua Panin in 1867, 1,400–3,600 people may have been killed in Kumasi (McCaskie 1989:433–435).

It is possible that evidence for such practices was recovered archaeologically but unrecognized. Many unarticulated cranial fragments were recovered during excavations. Because evidence of secondary and tertiary interments and/or evidence of disturbance by construction were generally present and postcranial bone was also recovered, these fragments were interpreted as having come from disturbed burials. It is, however, possible that sacrifices are represented. This is a question that may be addressed by further study of the skeletal remains.

63. The only pre-European-contact burials within the region are from Sekondi (Davies 1956). Unfortunately, the age of the burials and the site as a whole can only be estimated, and the interments may be of substantially different ages. The stone tools, ceramics, and lack of iron artifacts suggest that the burials are early, perhaps predating the arrival of iron metallurgy on the coast. The ceramics are not immediately similar in form and decorative inventory to those found in the Elmina area. The burials present some general features similar to later burial practices noted in the archaeological and documentary information presented here, including burial shafts, grave goods, and evidence for secondary and tertiary burials in the same grave. On the other hand, they also present a number of features that are impossible to assess given the available informa-

tion, including possible ritual surfaces and stone cairns.

64. The location where the pots and figures were placed within the burial ground is termed *asensie*, "the place of the pots." The principal ethnographic source remains Rattray 1959; see also references and discussions in Bellis 1982; Gilbert 1989; Quarcoopome 1977; Sieber 1972; and Vivian 1992.

65. For other historical references to clay figurines on the central Gold Coast, see Barbot 1992:380, 595; Bosman 1967:232; Cruickshank 1853, 2:270; and Müller in Jones 1983:257–258. Available information would seem to suggest that the terracotta traditions of the neighboring Akan groups in southwestern Ghana and southeastern Ivory Coast have a similar temporal range (Quarcoopome 1977; Soppelsa 1982).

66. Portions of terracotta figures may be represented at Elmina, but the pieces are so fragmentary that identification is impossible. One of the Elmina potters interviewed by Tetrault (1998) reported that she had made clay figurines in the past that were used by the fetish priest to communicate with the gods, but it is unclear if these were used in mortuary rituals. Tetrault also observed figurines for sale. Numerous fragments of pots comparable to those associated with *asensie*, including various pedestal bowls, *mmukyia* (hearth pots), and red-slipped vessels, were recovered.

67. Although Barbot may have viewed Elmina Castle from the sea in 1679, his firsthand knowledge of the town must have come from a two-day visit in 1682 (Barbot 1992:383 n. 2). The quotation here is Hair and colleagues' translation of the original French version of the manuscript, probably written in the 1680s. Barbot himself translated and expanded his French text, which was published posthumously in 1732. This version provides a slightly more detailed discussion of the Elmina graves: " . . . several tombs or little monuments, with abundance of puppets and antick ridiculous figures, which, as I was told, are of some kings, and other notable persons buried there, all adorn'd with imagery and other baubles" (Barbot 1992:387 n. 25). He later elaborates and discusses the associated mortuary ritual.

68. The nineteenth-century comment by Cruickshank suggests that both the deceased and his at-tendants are represented: "They also mould images from clay, and bake them. We have seen curious groups of these in some parts of the country. Upon the death of a great man, they make representations of him, sitting in state, with his wives and attendants seated around him" (1853, 2:270). Cruickshank describes the figures as very natural in appearance with different colors from jet black to tawny red, "according to the complexion of the originals," but this would seem to refer possibly to the shades of the fired clay, not to painted colors.

69. Rattray (1959:165) clearly describes the *asensie* as a separate portion of the cemetery, whereas Sieber's (1972) work indicates that pots and figurines were placed directly on the graves. Archaeological work on several seventeenth- and eighteenth-century archaeological sites is consistent with Rattray's description of *asensie* as separate areas (Bellis 1982:24–27; Vivian 1992).

70. In addition to de Marees (1987:184) and Barbot (1992:595), Müller describes painted figures: "They also make male and female figures out of clay and paint them red and white. These are supposed to represent the deceased" (in Jones 1983:258). Bosman (1967:232) only notes "Earthen Images on the Graves" that were washed up to a year after the funeral.

71. However, de Marees's 1602 description suggests that the tradition was established before the start of the seventeenth century. Thermoluminescence dates are also consistent with late sixteenth-century through late eighteenth-century ages (Garrard 1981:2), and a similar age has been suggested on the basis of Aowin stool lineages in southwestern Ghana (Quarcoopome 1977:84). Garrard (1981, 1983a:46–47) suggested that a terracotta figurine cult emerged in southern Ghana as a direct result of Portuguese missionary activity during the 1570s and that this tradition spread inland in the early seventeenth century. He specifically linked the tradition to the Ntona cult, said to relate to the figure of St. Anthony (also see Wartenberg 1951:152–153). Jones (1994:359–360) is rightly critical of the limited historical and archaeological data on which these suppositions are based, and it is clear that additional archaeological research is needed. Information is, however, gradually accumulating, the most notable addition being the four *asensie* excavated in

Asante, dating between the first half of the seventeenth century and the present century (Vivian 1992). The specific role of Portuguese missionary activity and the presence of a "cult of figurines" are more difficult to assess. Even if directly derived from imagery in Catholic ritual, the figurines may have been incorporated into existing Akan ritual structures.

72. Vivian (1992) documents a transformation in the perception of *asensie* and in the function of the terracottas, which he sees as a transition from sacred to secular, in part resulting from Christian influences.

73. Unfortunately the archaeological finds were not associated with any features.

74. Coffins were in use in the Central Region, particularly in Cape Coast, by the mid-nineteenth century (e.g., Allen 1874:117; Gordon 1874:45). In the Ga area, coffins of a "sort" were used for rich people by the late eighteenth century (Isert 1992:132–133; see also Garrard 1980a:106). For discussion of twentieth-century practices in Elmina, see Wartemberg 1951:127, 156.

75. These observations raise serious conceptual issues with generalized methods for extrapolating cultural patterns from archaeological data, a case in point being the pattern-recognition studies first developed by South (1977a, b, 1978) using data from eighteenth-century Anglo-American sites. South divided artifacts into several classes that were "based on functional activities related to the systemic context reflected by the archaeological record" (1977a:93). Although South saw this as a point of departure for the investigation of archaeological patterns, researchers have at times used the classification scheme as an end itself, thereby obscuring the very patterns they would hope to uncover.

REFERENCES

ARCHIVAL SOURCES AND MUSEUM COLLECTIONS

Algemeen Rijksarchief. The Hague, the Netherlands.

Balme Library. University of Ghana, Legon.

   Furley Collection. Gold Coast Tribal States Notebooks, 1707–15.

Bibliotheek der Rijkuniversiteit te Leiden. Leiden, the Netherlands.

British Library. Department of Manuscripts. London.

Cambridge Museum of Archaeology. Cambridge University, Cambridge.

Centre des Archives d'Outre-Mer. Aix-en-Provence, France.

   Dépôt des Fortifications des Colonies, Côtes d'Afrique.

Charles E. Young Research Library, Department of Special Collections. University of
   California, Los Angeles.

Corning Museum of Glass. Corning, New York.

Fowler Museum of Cultural History. University of California, Los Angeles.

Ghana National Archives. Accra, Ghana.

Ghana National Archives. Cape Coast, Ghana.

Ghana National Museum. Accra, Ghana.

Illustrated London News Picture Library. London.

Koninklijk Instituut voor Taal-, Land- en Volkenkunde. University of Leiden, the
   Netherlands.

Military Museum. Kumasi, Ghana.

National Army Museum, Department of Weapons, Equipment, and Vehicles.
   Chelsea, London.

National Museum of African Art. Smithsonian Institution, Washington, D.C.

National Museum of Natural History. Smithsonian Institution, Washington, D.C.

Public Record Office. Kew, Richmond, Surrey, England.

Rijksmuseum. Amsterdam, the Netherlands.

University of Ghana, Department of Archaeology. Legon, Ghana.

   Archaeological collections and unpublished fieldnotes.

West African Historical Museum. Cape Coast, Ghana.

OTHER SOURCES

Abraham, William
   1964   The Life and Times of Anton Wilhelm Amo. Transactions of the Historical
          Society of Ghana 7:60–81.

Abrahams, Gabeba
   1987   Seventeenth and Eighteenth Century Glass Bottles from Fort de Goede
          Hoop, Cape Town. Annals of the South African Cultural History Museum
          1(1).

   1996   Foodways of the mid-18th Century Cape: Archaeological Ceramics from

the Grand Parade in Central Cape Town.
Ph.D. thesis, Department of Archaeology,
University of Cape Town.

Adams, John
1822   Sketches Taken during Ten Voyages to
Africa, between the Years 1786 and 1800; Including Observations on the Country between Cape Palmas and the River Congo.
London: Hurst, Robinson and Company.

Agbodeka, Francis
1971   African Politics and British Policy in the
Gold Coast 1868–1900. London: Longman.

Agorsah, Emmanuel Kofi
1975   Unique Discoveries at Efutu, Ghana.
Sankofa 1:88.

1983a   Social Behavior and Spatial Context.
African Study Monographs 4:119–128.

1983b   An Ethnoarchaeological Study of Settlement and Behavior Patterns of a West
African Traditional Society: The Nchumuru of Banda-Wiae in Ghana. Ph.D. dissertation, Department of Anthropology,
University of California, Los Angeles.

1985   Archaeological Implications of Traditional
House Construction among the Nchumuru
of Northern Ghana. Current Anthropology
26(1):103–115.

1986   House Forms in Northern Volta Basin,
Ghana: Evolution, Internal Spatial Organization and the Social Relationships Depicted. West African Journal of Archaeology 16:25–51.

1993   Archaeology and Resistance in the
Caribbean. African Archaeological Review
11:175–195.

Aitken, W. C.
1866a   Brass and Brass Manufactures. In The Re-
sources, Products and Industrial History of
Birmingham and the Midland Hardware
District. S. Timmins, ed. Pp. 225–380.
London.

1866b   Coffin-Furniture Manufacture. In The Resources, Products and Industrial History of
Birmingham and the Midland Hardware
District. S. Timmins, ed. Pp. 704–708. London: Robert Hardwicke.

Ajayi, J. F. Ade, ed.
1989   General History of Africa, vol. 6. Africa in
the Nineteenth Century until the 1880s.
Berkeley: University of California Press.

Ajayi, J. F. Ade, and Michael Crowder, eds.
1976   History of West Africa, vol. 1. New York:
Columbia University Press.

1984   History of West Africa, vol. 2. Hong Kong:
Longman.

Alexander, John
1993   The Salt Industries of West Africa: A Pre-
liminary Study. In The Archaeology of
Africa: Food, Metals and Towns. Thurstan
Shaw, Paul Sinclair, Bassey Andah, and Alex
Okpoko, eds. Pp. 652–657. New York:
Routledge.

Alexandre, Pierre
1972   Languages and Language in Black Africa.
Evanston, Ill.: Northwestern University
Press.

Allen, Marcus
1874   The Gold Coast or, A Cruise in African Waters. London: Hodder and Stoughton.

Alpern, James
1992   The European Introduction of Crops into
West Africa in Precolonial Times. History
in Africa 19:13–43.

1995   What Africans Got for Their Slaves: A Master List of European Trade Goods. History
in Africa 22:5–43.

Amissah, P. Ebo
1975   The History of the Asafo Company of
Elmina. Unpublished B.A. thesis, history,
University of Ghana, Legon.

Anquandah, James
1982   Rediscovering Ghana's Past. Harlow,
England: Longman.

1992   Archaeological Investigations at Fort St.
Jago, Elmina, Ghana. Archaeology in
Ghana 3:38–45.

1993   Fort St. Jago, Elmina Ghana: Archaeologi-
cal Reconnaissance Report. Cape Coast,
Ghana: Central Region Development
Commission.

1997   Cape Coast Castle and Fort St. Jago,
Elmina, Ghana: Archaeological Reconnais-
sance Survey Phase Two. Cape Coast,
Ghana: Central Region Development
Commission.

Anquandah, Kwesi J.
1999   Castles and Forts of Ghana. Paris: Atalante.

Arhin, Kwame
1966   Diffuse Authority among Coastal Fanti.
Ghana Notes and Queries 9:66–70.

Atkinson, D. R., and Adrian Oswald
1972   A Brief Guide for the Identification of Dutch Clay Tobacco Pipes Found in England. Post-Medieval Archaeology 6:175–182.

Austen, Ralph A.
1987   African Economic History. London: James Currey.

Baart, J., and R. S. Caladro
1987   Portuguese Faience. Amsterdam: Amsterdam Historisch Museum.

Baart, J. M., W. Krook, and A. C. Lagerweij
1986   Opgravingen ann de Oosterburggermiddenstraat. Utrecht: Matrijs.

Baesjou, Rene, ed.
1979a   An Asante Embassy on the Gold Coast: The Mission of Akyempou Yaw to Elmina, 1869–1872. African Social Research Documents, vol. 11. Cambridge: African Studies Centre.
1979b   Dutch "Irregular" Jurisdiction on the Nineteenth-Century Gold Coast. African Perspectives 2:21–66.

Baker, T. Lindsey, and Billy R. Harrison
1986   Adobe Walls: The History and Archaeology of the 1874 Trading Post. College Station: Texas A & M University Press.

Ballong-Wen-Mewuda, J. Bato'ora
1984   Sao Jorge da Mina (Elmina) et son contexte socio-historique pendant l'occupation portugaise (1482–1637). These de doctorat, Centre de Recherches Africaines, Université de Paris, Paris.
1993   La Vie d'un comptoir portugais en Afrique Occidentale. Lisbon and Paris: École des Hautes Études en Sciences Sociales, Centre d'Études Portugaises: Fondation Calouste Gulbenkian/Commission Nationale por les Commémorations des Décourvertes Portgaises.

Barbot, J.
1732   Description of the Coast of North and South Guinea. In A Collection of Voyages and Travels, vol. 5. A. Churchill, ed. London. (Barbot's own English translation of his original French text, written in the 1680s and published posthumously.)
1992   Barbot on Guinea: The Writings of Jean Barbot on West Africa, 1678–1712. P. E. H. Hair, Adam Jones, and Robin Law, trans. and eds. London: Hakluyt Society. (Translation of Barbot's original French text, showing comparisons with and annotations regarding Barbot's 1732 English translation.)

Barros, João de
1967   The Asia of Joao de Barros. In The Voyages of Cadamosto. G. R. Crone, ed. Pp. 103–147. Nendeln, Liechtenstein: Kraus Reprint.

Bascom, William R., and Melville J. Herskovits, eds.
1963   Continuity and Change in African Cultures. Chicago: University of Chicago Press.

Bean, Richard
1974   A Note on the Relative Importance of Slaves and Gold in West African Exports. Journal of African History 15(3):351–356.

Beaton, Alfred Charles
1873   The Ashantees: Their Country, History, Wars, Government, Customs, Climate, Religion, and Present Position; with a Description of the Neighbouring Territories. London: Blackwood.

Beaudry, Mary C., ed.
1988   Documentary Archaeology in the New World. Cambridge: Cambridge University Press.

Bech, Niels, and A. D. C. Hyland
1978   Elmina: A Conservation Study. Faculty of Architecture, University of Science and Technology, Kumasi, Occasional Report, 17.

Bellefond, Villault de
1669   Relation des costes d'Afrique appeleé Guinée. Paris.

Bellis, James Oren
1972   Archaeology and the Culture History of the Akan of Ghana. Ph.D. dissertation, anthropology, Indiana University, Bloomington.
1982   The "Place of Pots" in Akan Funerary Custom. African Studies Program, Indiana University, Bloomington.
1987   A Late Archaeological Horizon in Ghana: Proto-Akan or Pre-Akan. In The Golden Stool: Studies of the Asante Center and Periphery. E. Schildkrout, ed. Pp. 36–50. Anthropological Papers of the American Museum of Natural History, vol. 65. New York.

Ben-Amos, Paula
1980   The Art of Benin. London: Thames and Hudson.

Bennett, Norman R., and George E. Brooks, eds.

1965   New England Merchants in Africa: A History through Documents. Boston University African Research Studies, vol. 7. Boston.

Bickerton, L. M.

1986   Eighteenth Century English Drinking Glasses: An Illustrated Guide. Woodbridge, Suffolk: Antique Collectors' Club.

Birmingham, David

1970   The Regimento de Mina. Transactions of the Historical Society of Ghana 9:1–7.

Blake, John William

1942   Europeans in West Africa, 1450–1560. London: Hakluyt Society.

1977   West Africa: Quest for God and Gold, 1454–1578. London: Curzon Press Ltd.

1987   O Castello de São Jorge da Mina or Elmina Castle: Reflections on Its History under the Portuguese Arising from Some Recent Advances in Knowledge. *In* Vice-Almirante A. Teixeira da Mota in Memorium, vol. 1. Lisbon: Academia de Marinha and Instituto de Investigação Científica Tropical.

Blakely, Allison

1993   Blacks in the Dutch World: The Evolution of Racial Imagery in Modern Society. Bloomington: Indiana University Press.

Boachie-Ansah J.

1986   An Archaeological Contribution to the History of Wenchi. African Occasional Papers, No. 3. Calgary: University of Calgary Press.

Boahen, A. Adu

1991   African Perspectives on Colonialism. Baltimore: Johns Hopkins University Press.

Booth, A. H.

1960   Small Mammals of West Africa. Harlow, England: Longman.

Bosman, Willem

1704   Nauwkeurige beschryving van de Guinese Goud-, Tand- en Slave-kust. Utrecht.

1967   A New and Accurate Description of the Coast of Guinea: Divided into the Gold, the Slave, and the Ivory Coasts. Facsimile ed., with an introduction by John Ralph Willis and notes by J. D. Fage and R. E. Bradbury. London: Frank Cass. Original English-translation edition, London, 1705.

Bouët-Willaumez, Louis Edouard

1848   Commerce et traite des noirs aux côte occi-

dentales d'Afrique. Paris: Imprimerie Nationale.

Bourque, Nicole Marie

1997   An Analysis of Faunal Remains from Elmina, Ghana. B.A. honors thesis, Department of Anthropology, Syracuse University.

Bowdich, T. Edward

1966   A Mission from Cape Coast to Ashantee. London: Frank Cass.

Boxer, C. R.

1972   Four Centuries of Portuguese Expansion, 1415–1825. Berkeley: University of California Press.

1990   The Dutch Seaborne Empire, 1600–1800. New York: Penguin.

Bovill, Edward William

1958   The Golden Trade of the Moors. London: Oxford University Press.

Boyle, Frederick

1874   Through Fanteeland to Comassie. London: Chapman and Hall.

Brain, Jeffrey P.

1979   Tunica Treasure. Papers of the Peabody Museum of Archaeology and Ethnology, Harvard University, 71.

Bredwa-Mensah, Yaw

1996   Slavery and Plantation Life at the Danish Plantation Site of Bibease, Gold Coast (Ghana). Ethnographisch-Archäologische Zeitschrift 38:445–458.

Breunig, Peter

1996   The 8000-Year-Old Dugout Canoe from Dufuna (NE Nigeria). *In* Aspects of African Archaeology: Papers from the 10th Congress of the PanAfrican Association. Gilbert Pwiti and Robert Soper, eds. Pp. 461–468. Harare: University of Zimbabwe.

British Parliamentary Papers

1970a   Correspondence Concerning the Gold Coast and the Ashantee Invasion, 1873–1874. Irish University Press Series of British Parliamentary Papers, Colonies Africa, vol. 58.

1970b   Further Correspondence Respecting the Ashantee Invasion, 1873–1874. Irish University Press Series of British Parliamentary Papers, Colonies Africa, vol. 59.

Brooks, George E.

1962   The Letter Book of Captain Edward Harrington. Transactions of the Historical Society of Ghana 6:71–77.

Brukum, N. J. K.
1985 Afro-European Relations on the Gold Coast, 1791–1844. M.A. thesis, history, University of Ghana, Legon.

Brun, Samuel
1624 Samuel Brun, des Wundartzt und Burgers zu Basel, Schiffarten. Translated as Samuel Brun's Voyages of 1611–1620 in German Sources for West African History 1599–1669. Adam Jones, trans. and ed. Pp. 44–96. Studien zur Kulturkunde, vol. 64 (1983).

Bruner, Edward M.
1996 Tourism in Ghana: The Representation of Slavery and the Return of the Black Diaspora. American Anthropologist 98(2):290–304.

Burton, Richard
1863 Wanderings in West Africa from Liverpool to Fernando Po. London: Tinsley Brothers.

Busia, Kofi Abrefa
1951 The Position of the Chief in the Modern Political System of Ashanti. New York: Oxford University Press.

Calvocoressi, David
1968 European Traders on the Gold Coast. West African Archaeological Newsletter 10:16–19.
1975a European Trade Pipes in Ghana. West African Journal of Archaeology 5:195–200.
1975b Excavations at Komenda, Ghana. West African Journal of Archaeology 5:153–164.
1977 Excavations at Bantama, near Elmina, Ghana. West African Journal of Archaeology 7:117–141.

Cameron, Catherine M., and Steve A. Tomka, eds.
1996 Abandonment of Settlements and Regions: Ethnoarchaeological and Archaeological Approaches. Cambridge: Cambridge University Press.

Carney, Judith
1996 Landscapes of Technology Transfer: Rice Cultivation and African Continuities. Technology and Culture 37(1):5–35.

Carr, Christopher
1995 Mortuary Practices: Their Social, Philosophica-Religious, Circumstantial, and Physical Determinants. Journal of Archaeological Method and Theory 2(2):105–200.

Cave, Rosemary
1961 Gold Coast Forts. New York: Thomas Nelson and Sons.

Chase-Dunn, Christopher, and Thomas D. Hall
1991 Core/Periphery Relations in Precapitalist Worlds. Boulder: Westview.

Chastanet, M., ed.
1998 Plantes et paysages d'Afrique: Une histoire à explorer. Paris: Karthala-CRA.

Chouin, Gérard
1996 Tentation patrilinéaire, guerre et conflits lignagers en milieu akan: Une contribution à l'histoire de la transmission du pouvoir royal en Eguafo (XVII–XXe siècle). Identity and Power in West Africa, International Symposium in Akan Studies, May 9–11, Università degli Studi di Urbino, Urbino, Italy.
1998a Eguafo: Un Royaume Africain "au Cœur François" (1637–1688). Paris: AFERA Éditions.
1998b Looking through the Forest: Sacred Groves as Historical and Archaeological Clues in Southern Ghana: An Approach. Paper presented at the 14th Biennial Conference of the Society of Africanist Archaeologists, Syracuse, New York.
n.d.-a Mapping the Unknown: GIS and Mental Mapping in Seventeenth Century Guinea. Manuscript in preparation.

Chouin, Gérard, ed.
n.d.-b Le "Tourbillon" sur les Côtes de Guinée (1670–1671): Une édition comparée des relations de voyage de Louis d'Hally et Louis Ancelin de Gémosat, extract LXXXVII. Manuscript in preparation. African Studies Department, University of Wisconsin–Madison.

Christaller, J. G.
1881 A Dictionary of the Asante and Fante Language, Called Tschi. Basel.
1985 Twi Mmebusɛm Mpensa-Ahansia Mmoaano—A Collection of Three Thousand and Six Hundred Tshi Proverbs. Translated by Abetifi-Kwaku. Typescript. Frobenius-Institut, Frankfort on Main. Original Twi version, 1879.

Christensen, James Boyd
1954 Double Descent among the Fanti. New Haven, Conn.: Human Relations Area Files.

Chukwukere, I.

1970   Cultural Resilience: The Asafo Company System of the Fanti. Cape Coast: University Press.

1978   Akan Theory of Conception—Are the Fante Really Aberrant? Africa 48(2):135–148.

1980   Perspectives on the *Asafo* Institution in Southern Ghana. Journal of African Studies 7(1):13–17.

1981   A Coffin for "The Loved One": The Structure of Fante Death Rituals. Current Anthropology 22(1):61–68.

Clark, Edie

1983   The Last American Flint Knapper. Yankee (May):15.

Clark, J. Desmond

1963   Prehistoric Cultures of Northeast Angola and Their Significance in Tropical Africa. Publicações Culturais 62:171–183.

1984   Old Stone Tools and Recent Knappers: Late Pleistocene Stone Technology and the Current Flaking Techniques in the Zaire Basin. Zimbabwea 1:1–22.

Clark, J. Desmond, and Steven A. Brandt, eds.

1984   From Hunters to Farmers: The Causes and Consequences of Food Production in Africa. Berkeley: University of California Press.

Colburn's United Service Magazine

1850   Reminiscences of the Gold Coast: Being Extracts from Notes Taken during a Tour of Service in 1847–48. Colburn's United Service Magazine, part 3:67–84, 400–418, 573–588.

Cole, Herbert M.

1979   Art Studies in Ghana. African Arts 13(1):26–27.

Cole, Herbert M., and Doran H. Ross

1977   The Arts of Ghana. Los Angeles: University of California Press.

Colton, Harold S.

1942   Archaeology and the Reconstruction of History. American Antiquity 1:33–40.

Connah, Graham

1975   The Archaeology of Benin. Oxford: Clarendon Press.

1987   African Civilizations. New York: Cambridge University Press.

Connolly, R. M.

1897   Social Life in Fanti-Land. Journal of the Royal Anthropological Institute of Great Britain and Ireland 26:128–153.

Coombs, Douglas

1963   The Gold Coast, Britain and the Netherlands, 1850–1874. London: Oxford University Press.

Cortesão, Armando, and Avelino Teixeira da Mota

1960   Portugaliae monumenta cartographica, vols. 1–6. Lisbon: Comemoracoes do V Centenario da Morte do Infante d. Henrique.

Cowgill, George L.

1993   Distinguished Lecture in Archeology: Beyond Criticizing New Archaeology. American Anthropologist 95(3):551–573.

Craddock, P. T., and D. R. Hook

1995   Copper to Africa: Evidence for the International Trade in Metal with Africa. *In* Trade and Discovery: The Scientific Study of Artefacts from Post-Medieval Europe and Beyond. D. R. Hook and D. R. M. Gaimster, eds. Pp. 181–193. British Museum Occasional Paper 109.

Crone, G. R.

1937   Cadamsoto and Other Documents on Western Africa in the Second Half of the Fifteenth Century. Series 2, vol. 80. London: Hakluyt Society.

Crooks, J. J.

1923   Records Relating to the Gold Coast Settlements 1750–1874. Belfast: Browne and Nolan.

Crosby, Alfred W.

1986   Ecological Imperialism: The Biological Expansion of Europe, 900–1900. New York: Cambridge University Press.

Crossland, L. B.

1973   A Study of Behgo Pottery in the Light of Excavations Conducted at the Begho-B2 Site. M.A. thesis, archaeology, University of California, Los Angeles.

1989   Pottery from the Behgo-Be Site, Ghana. African Occasional Papers, 4. Calgary: University of Calgary Press.

Cruickshank, Brodie

1853   Eighteen Years on the Gold Coast of Africa, Including an Account of the Native Tribes, and Their Intercourse with Europeans. 2 vols. London: Hurst and Blackett.

Curtin, Philip D.

1961   The White Man's Grave: Image and Reality, 1750–1850. Journal of British Studies: 94–110.

1975 Economic Change in Precolonial Africa: Senegambia in the Era of the Slave Trade. Madison: University of Wisconsin Press.

1986 Cross-Cultural Trade in World History. New York: Cambridge University Press.

1998 Disease and Empire: The Health of European Troops in the Conquest of Africa. New York: Cambridge University Press.

Curtin, Philip D., ed.

1972 Africa and the West: Intellectual Responses to European Culture. Madison: University of Wisconsin Press.

Cusick, James G., ed.

1998 Studies in Culture Contact: Interaction, Culture Change, and Archaeology. Occasional Paper 2. Center for Archaeological Investigations, Southern Illinois University, Carbondale.

Daaku, Kwame Yeboa

1970 Trade and Politics on the Gold Coast 1600–1720. London: Oxford University Press.

Daaku, Kwame Yeboa, and Albert Van Dantzig

1966 Map of the Regions of the Gold Coast in Guinea. Ghana Notes and Queries 9:14–15.

Daget, J., and Z. Ligers

1962 Une ancienne industrie Malienne: Les pipes en terre. Bulletin de l'IFAN 24(1 and 2):12–53.

Dahmen, Rene, and Servaas van Elteren

1992 Forts and Castles of Ghana: The Future of Fort Batenstein. Faculty of Architecture, Delft University of Technology, Delft.

Daily News Special Correspondent

1874 The Ashantee War: A Popular Narrative. London: Henry S. King.

Danquah, J. B.

1928 Akan Laws and Customs. London: Routledge and Sons.

Dapper, Olfert

1676 Naukeurige beschrijvinge der Afrikaensche gewesten. 2d ed. Amsterdam.

da Silva Rego, A.

1959 Portuguese Colonization in the Sixteenth Century: A Study of the Royal Ordinances (Regimentos). Publications of the Ernest Oppenheimer Institute of Portuguese Studies of the University of the Witwatersrand 1.

Datta, Ansu K., and R. Porter

1971 The Asafo System in Historical Perspective. Journal of African History 12(2):279–297.

David, Nicholas

1971 The Fulani Compound and the Archaeologist. World Archaeology 3(2):111–131.

David, Nicholas, Judy Sterner, and Kodzo Gavua

1988 Why Pots Are Decorated. Current Anthropology 29:365–389.

Davies, K. G.

1957 The Royal African Company. London

1970 The Royal Africa Company. New York: Atheneum.

Davies, Oliver

1955 Excavation at Mampongtin, 1955: A Corpus of Eighteenth Century Ashanti Pottery. Department of Archaeology, University of Ghana, Legon.

1956 Excavations at Sekondi, Ghana in 1954 and 1956. Report on file, Department of Archaeology, University of Ghana, Legon.

1961a Archaeology in Ghana. London: Thomas Nelson.

1961b Native Culture on the Gold Coast at the Time of Portuguese Discoveries. Congresso International de Historia dos Descombrimentos 3:97–109.

1967 West Africa before the Europeans. New York: Methuen.

1976 Field Notes Ghana, part 4. Southern Ghana. Legon: University of Ghana.

Davison, Claire

1970 Are Cori Beads Cordierite? West African Archaeological Newsletter 12:49–52.

Davison, Claire, Robert Giaque, and J. Desmond Clark

1971 Two Chemical Groups of Dichroic Glass Beads from West Africa. Man 6(4):645–659.

Day, Joan

1973 Bristol Brass, a History of the Industry. Newton Abbot: David and Charles.

Deagan, Kathleen

1982 Avenues of Inquiry in Historical Archaeology. Advances in Archaeological Method and Theory 5:151–155

1983 Spanish in St. Augustine: The Archaeology of a Colonial Creole Community. New York: Academic Press.

1987 Artifacts of the Spanish Colonies of Florida and the Caribbean, 1500–1800. Washington, D.C.: Smithsonian Institution Press.

de Barros, Philip

1988 Societal Repercussions of the Rise of

Large-Scale Traditional Iron Production: A West African Example. African Archaeological Review 6:91–113.

DeCorse, Christopher R.

1980   An Archaeological Survey of Protohistoric Defensive Sites in Sierra Leone. Nyame Akuma 17:48–53.

1987a   Excavations at Elmina, Ghana. Nyame Akuma 28:15–18.

1987b   Historical Archaeological Research in Ghana, 1986–1987. Nyame Akuma 29:27–32.

1988   Ghana. Society for Historical Archaeology Newsletter 21(2):40.

1989a   An Archaeological Study of Elmina, Ghana: Trade and Culture Change on the Gold Coast between the Fifteenth and Nineteenth Centuries. Ph.D. dissertation, anthropology, University of California, Los Angeles.

1989b   Beads as Chronological Indicators in West African Archaeology: A Reexamination. Beads: Journal of the Society of Bead Researchers 1:41–53.

1989c   Material Aspects of Limba, Yalunka and Kuranko Ethnicity: Archaeological Research in Northeastern Sierra Leone. In Archaeological Approaches to Cultural Identity. Stephen Shennan, ed. Pp. 125–140. London: Unwin Hyman.

1991   West African Archaeology and the Atlantic Slave Trade. Slavery and Abolition 12(2):92–96.

1992a   Archaeological Research at Elmina. Archaeology in Ghana 3:23–27.

1992b   Culture Contact, Continuity, and Change on the Gold Coast, AD 1400–1900. African Archaeological Review 10:163–196.

1993   The Danes on the Gold Coast: Culture Change and the European Presence. African Archaeological Review 11:149–173.

1996   Documents, Oral Histories, and the Material Record: Historical Archaeology in West Africa. World Archaeological Bulletin 7:40–50.

1997   Western African Historical Archaeology. In Encyclopedia of Precolonial Africa: Archaeology, History Language, Cultures, and Environments. Joseph O. Vogel, ed. Pp. 545–549. Walnut Creek, Calif.: Altimira Press.

1998a   African Historical Archaeology: Coastal Ghana. Society for Historical Archaeology Newsletter 31(4):28–29.

1998b   Culture Contact and Change in West Africa. In Studies in Culture Contact. James Cusick, ed. Pp. 358–377. Carbondale: Southern Illinois University Press.

1998c   The Europeans in West Africa: Culture Contact, Continuity and Change. In Transformations in Africa: Essays on Africa's Later Past. Graham Connah, ed. Pp. 219–244. London: Leicester University Press.

1999   Oceans Apart: Research and Objectives in African and African-American Archaeology. In I, Too, Am America. Theresa Singleton, ed. Pp. 132–155. Charlottesville: University of Virginia Press.

2000a   Central Region Project Field Manual. Photocopy. On file at Syracuse University, Department of Anthropology, and at the Ghana Museums and Monuments Board, Cape Coast.

DeCorse, Christopher R., ed.

2000b   West Africa during the Atlantic Slave Trade: Archaeological Perspectives. New York: Continuum.

Deetz, James

1996   In Small Things Forgotten: An Archaeology of Early American Life. New York: Anchor.

Deffontaine, Yann

1993   Guerre et société au royaume de Fetu, Ghana: 1471–1720. Ibaden: Institute of African Studies.

1996   Européens et Africains en Efutu et sur la Côte de l'Or: Les acteurs du commerce atlantique et leurs stratégies durant un siècle de relations afro-européennes sur la Côte de l'Or (Ghana, 1650–1750). These de doctorat en histoire, Centre de Recherches Africaines, Université de Paris, I Panthéon-Sorbonne.

de Graft-Johnson, J. C.

1932   The Fanti Asafu. Africa 5(3):307–322.

1969   The Population of Ghana 1846–1967. Transactions of the Historical Society of Ghana 10:1–12.

Dei, George J. S.

1989   The Economics of Death and Funeral Celebration in a Ghanaian Akan Community. Culture 9(1):49–62.

Deith, Margaret R.
  1988 A Molluscan Perspective on the Role of
       Foraging in Neolithic Farming Economies.
       In The Archaeology of Prehistoric Coast-
       lines. Geoff Bailey and John Parkington,
       eds. Pp. 116–124. New York: Cambridge Uni-
       versity Press.
Delaroziere, Marie-Francoise
  1985 Les perles de Mauretania. La Calade: Edisud.
Delaunay, Karine
  1994 Voyages à la Côte l'Or (1500–1750): Étude
       historiographique des relations de voyage
       sur le littoral ivoirien et ghanéen. Paris:
       AFERA Éditions.
de Lotbiniere, Seymour
  1980 English Gunflint Making in the Seven-
       teenth and Eighteenth Centuries. Min-
       nesota Archaeologist 39(2):54–69.
  1984 Gunflint Recognition. International Journal
       of Nautical Archaeology and Underwater
       Exploration 13(3):206–209.
de Marees, Pieter
  1602 Beschryvinge ende historishche verhael,
       van Gout Koninckrijck van Guinea.
       Amsterdam.
  1987 Description and Historical Account of the
       Gold Kingdom of Guinea (1602). Translated
       and annotated by Albert van Dantzig and
       Adam Jones. Oxford: Oxford University Press.
de Marrée, J. A.
  1818 Reizen op en Beschrijving van de Goudkust
       van Guinea. The Hague, Netherlands.
Denteh, A. C.
  1967 Ntorɔ and ntɔn. University of Ghana, Insti-
       tute of African Studies, Research Review
       3(3):91–96.
Denyer, Susan
  1978 African Traditional Architecture: An His-
       torical and Geographical Perspective. New
       York: Africana Publishing Company.
de Oliveira Marques, A. H.
  1972 History of Portugal, vol. 1. From Lusitania
       to Empire. New York: Columbia University
       Press.
Descamps, C., G. Thilmans, and Y. Thommeret
  1974 Donnees sur l'edification de l'amas coquil-
       lier de Dioron Boumak (Sénégal). Bulletin
       de Liaison, Association Sénégalaise pour
       l'Étude du Quaternaire de l'Ouest Africain
       41: 67–83.

Descamps, C., G. Thilmans, J. et Y. Thommeret, and
     E. F. Hauptmann
  1977 Donnees sur l'age et la vitesse d'edification
       de l'amas coquillier de Faboura (Sénégal).
       Bulletin de Liaison, Association Sénégalaise
       pour l'Étude du Quaternaire de l'Ouest
       Africain 51:23–32.
Dickey, Thomas, and Peter C. George
  1980 Field Artillery Projectiles of the American
       Civil War. Atlanta: Arsenal Press.
Dike, K. Onwuka
  1966 Trade and Politics in the Niger Delta,
       1830–1885. Oxford: Clarendon.
Dolphyne, F. A., and M. E. Kropp Dakubu
  1988 The Volta-Comoé Languages. *In* The Lan-
       guages of Ghana. M. E. K. Dakubu, ed. Pp.
       50–90. London: Kegan Paul.
Doortmont, Michel R.
  n.d. A Ghanaian Photo Album—Cape Coast
       and Elmina in 1890: Description and Cata-
       logue of a Collection of Photos Brought
       Together by Hendrik Pieter Nicolaas
       Muller during His Trip to the Gold Coast in
       1890. Work in preparation.
Dubin, Lois Sherr
  1987 The History of Beads. New York: Henry N.
       Abrams.
Duncan, John
  1847 Travels in Western Africa in 1845 & 1846,
       vol. 1. London: Richard Bentley.
Dupuis, Joseph
  1824 Journal of a Residence in Ashantee. Lon-
       don: Henry Colburn.
Edmunds, Janet
  1977 Sea Shells and Other Molluscs Found on
       West African Shores and Estuaries. Accra:
       Ghana Universities Press.
Effah-Gyamfi, Kwaku
  1979 Some Archaeological Reflections on Akan
       Traditions of Origin. West African Journal
       of Archaeology 9:187–199.
  1985 Bono Manso: An Archaeological Investiga-
       tion into Early Akan Urbanism. African
       Occasional Paper, 2. Department of Ar-
       chaeology, University of Calgary.
Ehret, Christopher, and Merrick Posnansky, eds.
  1982 The Archaeological and Linguistic Recon-
       struction of the African History. Berkeley:
       University of California Press.

Ehrlich, Martha J.
1989 Early Akan Gold from the Wreck of the
Whydah. African Arts 22(4):52–57.

Eisenstadt, S. N., M. Abitol, and N. Chazan, eds.
1988 The Early State in African Perspective.
Studies in Human Society, vol. 3. New York:
E. J. Brill.

Elbl, Ivana
1986 The Portuguese Trade with West Africa,
1440–1521. Ph.D. dissertation, University of
Toronto.
1997 The Volume of the Early Atlantic Slave
Trade, 1450–1521. Journal of African History
38(1):31–75.

Ellis, Alfred Burdon
1893 A History of the Gold Coast of West
Africa. London: Chapman and Hall.

Eltis, David
1994 The Relative Importance of Slaves and
Commodities in the Atlantic Trade of
Seventeenth-Century Africa. Journal of
African History 35(2):237–249.

Eltis, David, and David Richardson, eds.
1997 Routes to Slavery: Direction, Ethnicity and
Mortality in the Atlantic Slave Trade. Port-
land, Oreg.: Frank Cass.

Eluyemi, Omotoso
1975 Tobacco Pipes Excavated at Isoya (Ife).
Ikenga 3(1 and 2):108–118.

Ephson, Isaac S.
1970 Ancient Forts and Castles of the Gold
Coast. Accra: Ilen Publications.

Erlandson, Jon M.
1988 The Role of Shellfish in Prehistoric
Economies: A Protein Perspective. American Antiquity 53(1):102–109.

Fage, J. D.
1959 A New Check List of the Forts and Castles
of Ghana. Transactions of the Historical
Society of Ghana 4(pt. 1):57–67.
1962 Some Remarks on the Beads and Trade in
Lower Guinea in the Sixteenth and Seventeenth Centuries. Journal of African History 3(2):343–347.
1973 Portuguese Gold Trade: An Account
Ledger From Elmina, 1529–1531. Transactions of the Historical Society of Ghana
19(1):93–103.
1980 A Commentary on Duarte Pacheco

Pereira's Account of the Lower Guinea
Coastlands in His *Esmeraldo de Situ Orbis*,
and Some Other Early Accounts. History in
Africa 7:47–79.
1987 A Guide to Original Sources for Precolonial
Western Africa Published in European Languages. African Studies Program, University of Wisconsin–Madison.
1992 A Supplement to a Guide to Original
Sources for Precolonial Western Africa:
Corrigenda et Addenda. History in Africa
19:201–236.

Fairbanks, Charles H.
1966 A Feldspar-Inlaid Ceramic Type from Spanish Colonial Sites. American Antiquity
31(3):430–432.

Farrar, Vincent Kenneth
1988 Traditional Akan Architecture and Building
Construction: A Technological and Historical Study. Ph.D. dissertation, anthropology,
University of California, Berkeley.
1996 Building Technology and Settlement Planning in a West African Civilization. Lewis-
ton: Mellen University Press.

Faulkner, Alaric, and Gretchen Faulkner
1987 The French at Pentagoet 1635–1674. Occasional Publications in Maine Archaeology
No. 5. Arthur Spiess, series ed. Augusta:
Maine Archaeological Society.

Feinberg, Harvey Michael
1969 Elmina, Ghana: A History of Its Development and Relationship with the Dutch in
the Eighteenth Century. Ph. D. dissertation, Boston University. Ann Arbor: University Microfilms.
1970a An Incident in Elmina-Dutch Relations, the
Gold Coast (Ghana), 1739–1740. African Historical Studies 3(2):359–372.
1970b Who Are the Elmina? Ghana Notes and
Queries 11:20–26.
1974 New Data on European Mortality in West
Africa: The Dutch on the Gold Coast,
1719–1760. Journal of African History
15(3):357–371.
1979 An Eighteenth-Century Case of Plagiarism:
William Smith's *A New Voyage to Guinea*.
Journal of African History 6:45–50.
1989 Africans and Europeans in West Africa:
Elmina and Dutchmen on the Gold Coast

during the Eighteenth Century. Transactions of the American Philosophical Society 79(pt. 7).

Ffooks, Oliver
1969 Opaque Twist Soda Glasses: Are They English or Continental Provenance? Antique Collector (February):27–30.

Ffoulkes, Arthur
1907 The Company System in Cape Coast Castle. Journal of the Royal African Society 7(27):261–277.
1909 Funeral Customs of the Gold Coast Colony. Journal of the African Society 8(30):154–164.

Field, M. J.
1948 Akim-Kotoku: An Oman of the Gold Coast. London: Crown Agents for the Colonies.

Fike, Richard E.
1987 The Bottle Book: A Comprehensive Guide to Historic, Embossed Medicine Bottles. Salt Lake City, Utah: Peregrine Smith.

Finlayson, R. W.
1972 Portneuf Pottery. Ontario: Longman.

Firman-Sellers, Kathryn
1996 The Transformation of Property Rights in the Gold Coast. New York: Cambridge University Press.

Fisher, Humphrey J., and Virginia Rowland
1971 Firearms in the Central Sudan. Journal of African History 12(2):215–239.

Fleming, J Arnold Maclehouse
1923 Scottish Pottery. Glasgow: Jackson.

Fletcher, Roland
1975 House Form and Function. Institute of African Studies, Legon Family Research Papers 1:305–325.

Flight, Colin
1968 The "French Battery" at Elmina. West African Archaeological Newsletter 10:20–23.

Flin, J. E., ed.
1976 Cambridge History of Africa, vol. 5. From c. 1790 to c. 1870. Cambridge: Cambridge University Press.

Ford, John
1931 The Letters of John III. Cambridge, Mass.: Harvard University Press.

Fortes, Meyer
1970 Kinship and Marriage among the Ashanti.
In African Systems of Kinship and Marriage. A. R. Radcliffe-Brown and Daryll Forde, eds. Pp. 252–284. London: Oxford University Press.

Fortes, M., and E. E. Evans-Pritchard, eds.
1940 African Political Systems. London: Oxford University Press.

Frank, Susan
1982 Glass and Archaeology. New York: Academic Press.

Freeman, Richard Austen
1898 Travels and Life in Ashanti and Jaman. Westminster: Archibald Constable.

Friedman, Kajsa Ekholm
1991 Catastrophe and Creation: The Transformation of an African Culture. Philadelphia: Harwood Academic Publishers.

Fynn, John
1971 Asante and Its Neighbors 1700–1807. London: Longman.
1974a Abrem. Oral Traditions of the Fante States, 1. Legon: Institute of African Studies.
1974b Edina (Elmina). Oral Traditions of the Fante States, 4. Legon: Institute of African Studies.
1974c Eguafo. Oral Traditions of the Fante States, 2. Legon: Institute of African Studies.

Garrard, Timothy F.
1973 Studies in Akan Goldweights (IV): The Dating of Akan Goldweights. Transactions of the Historical Society of Ghana 14(2):36–43.
1979 Akan Metal Arts. African Arts 13(1):36–43.
1980a Akan Weights and the Gold Trade. New York: Longman.
1980b Brass in Akan Society to the Nineteenth Century: A Survey of Archaeological, Ethnographic and Historical Evidence. M.A. thesis, Department of Archaeology, University of Ghana, Legon.
1981 Figurine Cults of the Southern Akan. Paper presented at the Symposium on African Art, University of Iowa.
1983a A Corpus of 15th to 17th Century Akan Brass-Castings. In Akan Transformations. D. Ross and T. Garrard, eds. Pp. 30–53. Museum of Cultural History Monograph Series, vol. 21. Los Angeles.
1983b Akan Pseudo-Weights of European Origin. In Akan Transformations. D. Ross and T.

Garrard, eds. Pp. 70–81. Museum of Cultural History Monograph Series, vol. 21. Los Angeles.

1986   Brass Casting among the Frafra of Northern Ghana. Department of History, University of California, Los Angeles.

1989   Gold of Africa: Jewellery and Ornaments from Ghana, Côte d'Ivoire, Mali and Senegal in the Collection of the Barbier-Mueller Museum. Munich: Prestel.

Geary, Christraud M., and Andrea Nicolls

1992   Elmina: Art and Trade on the West African Coast. Washington, D.C.: National Museum of African Art, Smithsonian Institution.

Geggus, David

1989   Sex Ratio, Age, and Ethnicity in the Atlantic Slave Trade: Data from French Shipping and Plantation Records. Journal of African History 30(1):23–44.

Gemery, Henry A., and Jan S. Hogendorn

1979   The Uncommon Market: Essays in the Economic History of the Atlantic Slave Trade. New York: Academic Press.

Gilbert, Michelle

1988   The Sudden Death of a Millionaire: Conversion and Consensus in a Ghanaian Kingdom. Africa 58(3):291–314.

1989   Akan Terracotta Heads: Gods or Ancestors? African Arts 22(4):34–43, 85–86.

Goggin, G. A.

1963   British Pottery and Porcelain 1780–1850. London: Baker.

Goggin, John M.

1968   Spanish Majolica in the New World. Yale University Publications in Anthropology, 72. New Haven, Conn.

Golden, Bernard

1969   Coastal Survey—1969: Field Notes and Records. Manuscript on file, Department of Archaeology. Legon: University of Ghana.

Gordon, Charles Alexander

1874   Life on the Gold Coast. London: Baillière, Tindall and Cox.

Graham, C. K.

1976   The History of Education in Ghana. Accra: Ghana Publishing Corporation.

Gramberg, J. S. G.

1861   Schetsen van Afrika's Westkust. Amsterdam.

Gray, R., ed.

1975   Cambridge History of Africa, vol. 4. From 1600 to 1790. Cambridge: Cambridge University Press.

Greenberg, Joseph H.

1966   The Languages of Africa. Bloomington: Indiana University Press.

Greene, Sandra E.

1988   Social Change in Eighteenth-Century Anlo: The Role of Technology, Markets and Military Conflict. Africa 58(1):70–86.

Groll, C. L. Temminck

1968   De Momumenten van Europese Oorsprong in Ghana. Bulletin van de Koninklijke Nederlandse Oudheidkundige Bond 67(5):103–121.

Gusset, Gerard

1984   Stoneware Containers from Some Canadian Prairie Sites. Parks Canada Research Bulletin, 221. Ottawa.

Gyekye, Kwame

1987   An Essay on African Philosophical Thought: The Akan Conceptual Scheme. New York: Cambridge University Press.

Hailey, Lord

1935   An African Survey. New York: Oxford University Press.

Hair, Paul Edward Hedley

1966   The Use of African Languages in Afro-European Contacts in Guinea: 1440–1560. Sierra Leone Language Review 5:5–26.

1967a   An Ethnolinguistic Inventory of the Upper Guinea Coast before 1700. African Language Review 6:32–70.

1967b   Ethnolinguistic Continuity on the Guinea Coast. Journal of African History 8:247–268.

1968   An Ethnolinguistic Inventory of the Lower Guinea Coast before 1700: Part I. African Language Review 7:47–73.

1969   An Ethnolinguistic Inventory of the Lower Guinea Coast before 1700: Part II. African Language Review 8:225–256.

1974   Early Sources on the Religion and Social Values in the Sierra Leone Region (2) Eustache de la Fosse. Africana Research Bulletin 4(3):49–54.

1989   The Atlantic Slave Trade. Liverpool: Liverpool University Press.

1990   Columbus from Guinea to America. History in Africa 17(113–129).

1994a   The Early Sources on Guinea. History in Africa 21:87–126.

1994b   The Founding of the Castelo de São Jorge da Mina: An Analysis of the Sources. African Studies Program, University of Wisconsin–Madison.

Hair, Paul Edward Hedley, ed.

1990   Black Africa in Time-Perspective: Four Talks. Liverpool: Liverpool University Press.

Hair, Paul Edward Hedley, and Cecil H. Clough, eds.

1994   The European Outthrust and Encounter: The First Phase c. 1400–c. 1700. Liverpool: Liverpool University Press.

Hakluyt, Richard

1589   The Principall Navigations . . . of the English Nation. London. Facsimile ed., D. B. Quinn and R. A. Skelton, eds. London: Hakluyt Society, 1965.

Hall, Martin

1993   The Archaeology of Colonial Settlement in Southern Africa. Annual Review of Anthropology 22:177–200.

Hamilton, Henry

1967   The English Brass and Copper Industries to 1800. London: Frank Cass.

Hamilton, T. M.

1980   Colonial Frontier Guns. Chadron, Nebr.: Fur Press.

Happold, D. C. D.

1973   Large Mammals of West Africa. Harlow, England: Longman.

Haring, Clarence Henry

1964   Trade and Navigation between Spain and the Indies in the Time of the Hapsburgs. Gloucester: Peter Smith.

Harrington, J. C.

1954   Dating Stem Fragments of Seventeenth and Eighteenth Century Clay Tobacco Pipes. Quarterly Bulletin of the Archaeological Society of Virginia 9(1):1–5.

Hassan, Fekri A.

1981   Demographic Archaeology. New York: Academic Press.

Haviser, Jay, and Christopher R. DeCorse

1991   African-Caribbean Interaction: A Research Plan for Curaçao Creole Culture. Proceedings of the Thirteenth International Congress for Caribbean Archaeology, Curaçao, Netherlands Antilles. Reports of the Archaeological-Anthropological Institute of the Netherlands Antilles 9:326–337.

Hawthorne, Nathaniel, ed.

1845   Journal of an African Cruiser. London: Wiley and Putnam.

Hay, Sir John Charles Dalrymple

1874   Ashanti and the Gold Coast and What We Know of It. London: Edward Stanford.

Hayford, Casely

1903   Gold Coast Institutions. London: Sweet and Maxwell.

Headrick, Daniel R.

1981   Tools of Empire: Technology and European Imperialism in the Nineteenth Century. Oxford: Oxford University Press.

Heintze, Beatrix, and Adam Jones, eds.

1987   European Sources for Sub-Saharan Africa before 1900: Use and Abuse. Frankfort on Main: Frobenius-Institut E.V.

Hemmersam, Michael

1663   Guineische und West-Indianische Reissbeschreibung de An: 1639 biss 1645 von Amsterdam nach St. Joris de Mina. Translated as Description of the Gold Coast, 1639–45 in German Sources for West African History 1599–1600. Adam Jones, trans. and ed. Pp. 97–133. Studien zur Kulturkunde, vol. 64 (1983).

Henige, David P.

1973   The Problem of Feedback in Oral Tradition: Four Examples from the Fante Coastlands. Journal of African History 14(2):223–235.

1974   Kingship in Elmina before 1869: A Study in "Feedback" and the Traditional Idealization of the Past. Cahiers d'Études Africaines 14(3):499–520.

1982   Oral Historiography. London: Longman.

Henige, David, and T. C. McCaskie

1990   West African Economic and Social History. African Studies Program, University of Wisconsin–Madison.

Herbert, Eugenia W.

1984   Red Gold of Africa: Copper in Precolonial History and Culture. Madison: University of Wisconsin Press.

Hernaes, Per
    1998   Asafo History: An Introduction. Transac-
            tions of the Historical Society of Ghana
            (n.s.) 2:1–5.
Herskovits, Melville J.
    1962   The Human Factor in Changing Africa.
            New York: Alfred A. Knopf.
Herskovits, Robert M.
    1978   Fort Bowie Material Culture. Anthropolog-
            ical Papers of the University of Arizona, 31.
            Tucson: University of Arizona Press.
Hodasi, J. K. M.
    1995   Snails in the National Economy. Legon:
            School of Communication Studies Press.
Holl, Augustin
    1993   Transition from Late Stone Age to Iron Age
            in the Sudano-Sahelian Zone: A Case Study
            from the Perichadian Plain. In The Archae-
            ology of Africa: Food, Metals and Towns.
            Thurstan Shaw, Paul Sinclair, Bassey
            Andah, and Alex Okpoko, eds. Pp. 330–343.
            New York: Routledge.
    1997   Metallurgy, Iron Technology and African
            Late Holocene Societies. In Traditionelles
            Eisenhandwerk in Afrika. Reinhard Klein-
            Arendt, ed. Pp. 13–54. Cologne: Heinrich-
            Barth-Institut.
    2000   500 Years in the Cameroons: Making Sense
            of the Archaeological Record. In West
            Africa during the Atlantic Slave Trade: Ar-
            chaeological Perspectives. C. R. DeCorse,
            ed. New York: Continuum.
Hopkins, Anthony G.
    1973   An Economic History of West Africa. New
            York: Columbia University Press.
Howison, John
    1834   European Colonies, in Various Parts of the
            World, Viewed in Their Social, Moral, and
            Physical Condition, vol. 1. London.
Huey, Paul
    1988   Aspects of Continuity and Change in
            Colonial Dutch Material Culture at Fort
            Orange. Ph.D. dissertation, Department
            of Anthropology, University of Penn-
            sylvania.
Hughes, Bernard, and Therle Hughes
    1968a   The Collector's Encyclopedia of English
            Ceramics. London: Abbey Library.
    1968b   English Porcelain and Bone China:
            1743–1850. New York: Praeger.

Hurst, J. G.
    1977   Spanish Pottery Imported into Medieval
            Britain. Journal of Medieval Archaeology
            21:68–105.
Hutton, William
    1821   A Voyage to Africa. London.
Hyland, A. D. C.
    1970   Documentation and Conservation. Faculty
            of Architecture, University of Science and
            Technology, Kumasi, Occasional Report, 13.
    1971   The Castles at Elmina. Ghana Museums
            and Monuments Board Series, 3.
    1995   Monuments Conservation Practice in Ghana:
            Issues of Policy and Management. Journal of
            Architectural Conservation 2:45–62.
Inikori, J. E.
    1976a   Measuring the Atlantic Slave Trade: An As-
            sessment of Curtin and Anstey. Journal of
            African History 17(2):197–233.
    1976b   Measuring the Atlantic Slave Trade. Journal
            of African History 18(4):607–627.
Inikori, J. E., ed.
    1982   Forced Migration: The Impact of the Ex-
            port Slave Trade on African Societies. New
            York: Africana Publishing.
Insoll, Timothy
    1995   A Note on a 16th–17th Century Sherd of
            Chinese Stoneware Found at Gao, the Re-
            public of Mali, West Africa. Oriental Ce-
            ramic Society Newsletter 3:11–13.
Iselin, Regula
    1994   Reading Pictures: On the Value of the Cop-
            perplates in the Beschryvinghe of Pieter de Ma-
            rees (1602) as Source Material for Ethnohistor-
            ical Research. History in Africa 21:147–170.
Isert, Paul Erdmann
    1992   Journey to Guinea and the Caribbean Islands
            in Columbia (1788). Selena Axelrod Wisnes,
            trans. Oxford: Oxford University Press.
Jobson, Richard
    1999   The Discovery of the River Gambra (1623).
            David P. Gamble and P. E. H. Hair, eds. and
            trans. London: Hakluyt Society.
Johnson, Marion
    1977a   Census, Map, and Guestimate: The Past
            Population of the Accra region. In African
            Historical Demography 1: Proceedings of a
            Seminar Held in the Centre of African
            Studies, University of Edinburgh, April
            1977. Edinburgh: Centre of African Studies.

1977b   Elephants for Want of Towns. *In* African
         Historical Demography 2: Proceedings of a
         Seminar Held in the Centre of African
         Studies, University of Edinburgh, April
         1981. Edinburgh: Centre of African Studies.
1982   Two Pottery Traditions in Southern Ghana.
         In Earthenware in Asia and Africa. J. Picton,
         ed. Pp. 208–218. University of London Col-
         loquies on Art and Archaeology, vol. 12.
         London.

Jones, Adam
1980   William Smith the Plagiarist: A Rejoinder.
         History in Africa 7:327–328.
1983   German Sources for West African History
         1599–1669. Studien zur Kulturkunde, vol.
         64. Wiesbaden: Franz Steiner Verlag.
1985   Brandenburg Sources for West African His-
         tory 1680–1700. Studien zur Kulturkunde,
         vol. 77. Wiesbaden: Franz Steiner Verlag.
1986   Semper Aliquid Veteris: Printed Sources for
         the History of the Ivory and Gold Coasts,
         1500–1750. Journal of African History
         27:215–235.
1987   Raw, Medium, Well Done: A Critical Re-
         view of Editorial and Quasi-Editorial Work
         on European Sources for Sub-Saharan
         Africa, 1960–1986. African Studies Program,
         University of Wisconsin–Madison.
1988   Drink Deep, or Taste Not: Thoughts on the
         Use of Early European Records in the
         Study of African Material Culture. Paper
         presented at the Workshop on Resources
         and Documentation in the Study of African
         Material Culture, Bellagio, May 25–27.
1990   Zur Quellenproblematik der Geschichte
         Westafrikas, 1450–1900. Studien zur Kul-
         turkunde, vol. 99. Wiesbaden: Franz Steiner
         Verlag.
1994   Drink Deep, or Taste Not: Thoughts on the
         Use of Early European Records in the
         Study of African material Culture. History
         in Africa 21:349–370.

Jones, Adam, ed.
1995   West Africa in the Mid-Seventeenth Cen-
         tury: An Anonymous Dutch Manuscript.
         African Historical Studies, vol. 10. N.p.:
         African Studies Association Press.

Jones, Olive
1985   Glass of the British Military, 1755–1820. Ot-
         tawa: Parks Canada.

Joseph, J. W.
1989   Pattern and Process in the Plantation Ar-
         chaeology of the Low Country of Georgia
         and South Carolina. Historical Archaeology
         23(1):55–68.

Joustra, A. K., and D. Six
1988   De oud-Europese Forten aan de Westkust
         van Afrika. Bulletin van de Koninklijke
         Nederlandse Ouheidkundige Bond
         87(6):256–260.

Juhe-Beaulaton, D.
1990   "La diffusion du maïs sur les Côtes de l'Or
         et des Esclaves au XVIIème et XVIIIème
         siècles." Revue Française d'Histoire
         d'Outre-Mer77(287): 177–198.

Kalous, Milan
1966   A Contribution to the Problem of Akori
         beads. Journal of African History 7(1):61–66.
1979   Akorite? Journal of African History
         20:203–217.

Kankpeyeng, Benjamin Warinsie
1996   Archaeological Resources Management in
         Ghana. M.A. thesis, anthropology, Syracuse
         University.

Karklins, Karlis
1981   The Old Fort Point Site: Fort Wedderburn
         II? Canadian Historic Sites Occasional Pa-
         pers in Archaeology and History 26. Ot-
         tawa: Parks Canada.

Kea, Ray
1971   Firearms and Warfare on the Gold and
         Slave Coasts from the Sixteenth to the
         Nineteenth Centuries. Journal of African
         History 12(2):185–213.
1982   Settlements, Trade and Politics in the
         Seventeenth-Century Gold Coast. Balti-
         more: Johns Hopkins University Press.
1996   "When I die, I shall return to my own land."
         In The Cloth of Many Colored Silks: Papers
         on History and Society Ghanaian and Is-
         lamic in Honor of Ivor Wilks. John Hunwick
         and Nancy Lawler, eds. Pp.159–193. Evan-
         ston, Ill.: Northwestern University Press.

Kelly, Kenneth G.
1997a   The Archaeology of African-European In-
         teraction: Investigating the Social Roles of
         Trade, Traders, and the Use of Space in the
         Seventeenth- and Eighteenth-Century
         Hueda Kingdom, Republic of Bénin. World
         Archaeology 28(3):351–369.

1997b   Using Historically Informed Archaeology: Seventeenth and Eighteenth Century Hueda/European Interaction on the Coast of Benin. Journal of Archaeological Method and Theory 4(3-4):353–366.

Kense, F. J.
1987   The Impact of Asante on the Trade Patterns of Northern Ghana and Ivory Coast. *In* The Golden Stool: Studies of the Asante Center and Periphery, Anthropological Papers of the American Museum of Natural History 65, Part 1, ed. E. Schildkrout, 29–35. New York: American Museum of Natural History.

Kense, F. J., and J. Ako Okoro
1993   Changing Perspectives on Traditional Iron Production in West Africa. *In* The Archaeology of Africa: Food, Metals and Towns. P. S. Thurstan Shaw, Bassey Andah, and Alex Okpoko, eds. Pp. 449–458. London: Routledge.

Kent, Susan
1983   The Differential Acceptance of Culture Change: An Archaeological Test Case. Historical Archaeology 17(2):56–63.

Kerkdijk, L
1978   Reisjournaal van Lodewijk Kerdijk: West Africa 1857–1858. Schiedam, Netherlands: Interbook International.

Ketchum, William C.
1983   Pottery and Porcelain. New York: Knopf.
1987   American Country Pottery: Yellowware and Spongeware. New York: Knopf.

Kirkman, James
1974   Fort Jesus: A Portuguese Fortress on the East African Coast. Oxford: Clarendon.

Kiyaga-Mulindwa, David
1978   The Earthworks of the Birim Valley, Southern, Ghana. Ph.D. dissertation, Johns Hopkins University.
1980   The "Akan" Problem. Current Anthropology 21(4):503–506.
1982   Social and Demographic Changes in the Birim Valley, Southern Ghana, c. 1450 to c. 1800. Journal of African History 23:63–82.

Klose, Jane
1992   Excavated Oriental Ceramics from the Cape of Good Hope. Transactions of the Oriental Ceramic Society 57:69–81.
1997   Analysis of Ceramic Assemblages from Four Cape Historical Sites Dating from the Late

Seventeenth Century to the Mid-Nineteenth Century. M.A. thesis, archaeology, University of Cape Town, South Africa.

Krieger, Kurt
1943   Studien uber afrikanische Kunstperlen. Baessler-Archive 25(2):53–103.

Lamb, H. Alastair
1976   Krobo Powder Glass Beads from Ghana. African Arts 9(3):32–39.
1978   Some 17th-Century Glass Beads from Ghana, West Africa. Bead Journal 3(3-4):23–27.

Lamb, H. A., and R. N. York
1972   A Note on Trade Beads as Type Fossils in Ghanaian Archaeology. West African Journal of Archaeology 2:109–113.

Landewijk, J. E. J. M. van
1970   What Was the Original Aggrey Bead? Ghana Journal of Sociology 6(2):89–99.

Latham, M. C.
1979   Human Nutrition in Tropical Africa. Food and Agriculture Organization of the United Nations, Rome.

Lawrence, A. W.
1963   Trade Castles and Forts of West Africa. London: Jonathan Cape.

Lawson, Rowena M.
1968   The Transition of Ghana's Fishing from a Primitive to a Mechanized Industry. Transactions of the Historical Society of Ghana 9:90–104.

Lebeuf, J. P.
1962   Pipes et plantes a fumer chez les Kotoko. Notes Africaines 93:16–17.

Leibowitz, Joan
1985   Yellowware: The Transitional Ceramic. Exton, Pennsylvania: Schiffer.

Lever, J.
1970   Mulatto Influence on the Gold Coast in the Early Nineteenth Century: Jan Neiser of Elmina. African Historical Studies 3(2):253–261.

Lévi-Strauss, C., and D. Eribon
1991   Conversations with Claude Lévi Strauss. P. Wissing, trans. Chicago: University of Chicago Press.

Levtzion, Nehemia, and J. F. P. Hopkins, eds.
1981   Corpus of Early Arabic Sources for West African History. New York: Cambridge University Press.

Lewicki, Tadeusz
1974 West African Food in the Middle Ages: According to Arabic Sources. New York: Cambridge University Press.

Lightfoot, Kent G.
1995 Culture Contact Studies: Redefining the Relationship between Prehistoric and Historical Archaeology. American Antiquity
60(2):199–217.

Lightfoot, Kent G., Antoinette Martinez, and Ann M.
Schiff
1998 Daily Practice and Material Culture in Plu-
ralistic Social Settings: An Archaeological
Study of Culture Change and Persistence
from Fort Ross, California. American Antiquity 63(2):199–222.

Linares da Sapir, Olga
1971 Shell Middens of the Lower Casamance
and Problems of Diola Protohistory. West
African Journal of Archaeology 1:23–54.

Lister, Florence C., and Robert H. Lister
1976 A Descriptive Dictionary of 500 Years of
Spanish-Tradition Ceramics, 13th through
18th Centuries. Society for Historical Archaeology, Special Publication Number
Series 1. N.p.: Society for Historical
Archaeology.
1987 Andalusian Ceramics in Spain and New
Spain. Tucson: University of Arizona Press.

Little, Barbara J.
1994 People with History: An Update on Historical Archaeology in the United States. Journal of Archaeological Method and Theory
1(1):5–40.

Lofstrom, E., J. P. Tordoff, and D. C. George
1982 A Seriation of Historic Earthenwares in the
Midwest, 1780–1870. Minnesota Archaeologist 41(1):3–29.

Logan, Herschel C.
1959 Cartridges—A Pictorial Digest of Small
Arms Ammunition. New York: Bonanza
Books.

Lonsdale, John
1981 States and Social Processes in Africa: A Historical Survey. African Studies Review
24(2–3):139–225.

Lovejoy, Paul E.
1983 Transformations in Slavery: A History of
Slavery in Africa. Cambridge: Cambridge
University Press.
1989 The Impact of the Atlantic Slave Trade on
Africa: A Review of the Literature. Journal
of African History 30(3):365–394.

Lübelfing, Johann von
1612 Ein schön lustig Reissbuch. Translated as
Voyage of 1599–1600 in German Sources for
West African History 1599–1669. Adam
Jones, trans. and ed. Pp. 9–17. Studien zur
Kulturkunde, vol. 64 (1983).

Lui, Robert K.
1974 African Mold-Made Glass Beads. Bead Journal 1(2):8–14.
1995 Collectable Beads: A Universal Aesthetic.
Vista, Calif.: Ornament.

Lynn, Martin
1989 From Sail to Steam: The Impact of the
Steamship Services on the British Palm Oil
Trade with West Africa, 1850–1890. Journal
of African History 30(2):227–245.

McCaskie, T. C.
1989 Death and the Asantehene: A Historical
Mediation. Journal of African History
30(3):417–444.
1995 State and Society in Pre-Colonial Asante.
Cambridge: Cambridge University Press.

McDougall, E. Ann
1990 Salts of the Western Sahara: Myths, Mys-
teries, and Historical Significance. International Journal of Historical Studies
23(2):231–257.

MacEachern, Scott
1993 Selling Iron for Their Shackles: Wandala-
Montagnard Interactions in Northern
Cameroon. Journal of African History
33(2):241–270.

McIntosh, Roderick
1976 Finding Lost Walls on Archaeological
Sites—The Hani Model. Sankofa 2:45–53.
1977 The Excavation of Mud Structures: An
Experiment from West Africa. World
Archaeology 9:185–199.

McIntosh, Susan Keech
1999 Beyond Chiefdoms: Pathways to Complexity in Africa. New York: Cambridge University Press.

McLynn, Frank
1992 Hearts of Darkness: The European Exploration of Africa. New York: Carroll and
Graf Publishers.

McNulty, Robert H.

1971 Common Beverage Bottles: Their Production, Use, and Forms in Seventeenth- and Eighteenth-Century Netherlands, Part 1. Journal of Glass Studies 13:91–119.

Majewski, Teresita, and Michael J. O'Brien

1987 The Use and Misuse of Nineteenth-Century English and American Ceramics in Archaeological Analysis. *In* Advances in Archaeological Method and Theory, vol. 11. M. Schiffer, ed. Pp. 97–209. New York: Academic Press.

Manning, Patrick

1990 Slavery and African Life: Occidental, Oriental, and African Slave Trades. Cambridge: Cambridge University Press.

Manoukian, Madeline

1964 Akan and the Ga-Adangme Peoples. Ethnographic Survey of Africa. Western Africa, Part 1. Daryll Forde, series ed. London: International African Institute.

Marcus, George E.

1995 Ethnography in/of the World System: The Emergence of Multi-Sited Ethnography. Annual Review of Anthropology 24:95–117.

Martin, Colin J. M.

1979 Spanish Armada Pottery. International Journal of Nautical Archaeology 8(4):279–302.

Mauny, Raymond

1949 Que faut il appeler "pierres" d'aigiris? Notes Africaines 42:33–35.

1950 Les pre'tendues navigations dieppoises a'la Côte occidentale d'Afrique au XIVe siècle. Institute Française d'Afrique Noire, Bulletin 12:122–134.

1954 Notes historiques sur les plantes cultivées d'Afrique occidentale. Institute Française d'Afrique Noire, Bulletin 15(2):684–730.

1958 Akori Beads. Journal of the Historical Society of Nigeria 1(3):210–214.

1961 Tableau geographique. Institute Française d'Afrique Noire, Memoire 61:275–293.

Mbaeyi, P. M.

1973 Arms and Ammunition, and their Embargo in British West African History, 1823–1874. Ikenga 2(2):14–31.

Meredith, Henry

1967 An Account of the Gold Coast of Africa with a Brief History of the Africa Company. London: Frank Cass. Original publication, 1812, London.

Metcalfe, G. E.

1964 Great Britain and Ghana: Documents of Ghana History, 1807–1957. London: Thomas Nelson and Sons.

Meurer, Leonhard

1974 Rheinische Barockkruge in Westafrika. Keramos 66:33–39.

Meyerowitz, Eva L. R.

1952a Akan Traditions of Origin. London: Faber and Faber.

1952b *Review of* Sao Jorge da Mina, by Sylvanus Wartemberg. Africa 22(2):179–180.

1974 The Early History of the Akan States of Ghana. London: Red Candle Press.

Miller, Daniel, and Christopher Tilley

1984 Ideology, Power and Prehistory. New York: Cambridge University Press.

Miller, Duncan E., and Nikolaas J. van der Merwe

1994 Early Metal Working in Sub-Saharan Africa: A Review of the Recent Research. Journal of African History 35(1):1–36.

Miller, Joseph C., ed.

1980 The African Past Speaks: Essays on Oral Tradition and History. Hamden, Conn.: Archon.

Milo, T. H.

1961 Portuguese Trade and Shipping with the Netherlands after the Discoveries. Congresso International de Historia dos Descombrimentos 3:423–432.

Mintz, Sidney

1977 The So-Called World System: Local Initiative and Local Response. Dialectical Anthropology 2:253–270.

Miracle, Marvin P.

1965 The Introduction and Spread of Maize in Africa. Journal of African History 6(1):39–55.

1972 The Elasticity of Food Supply in Tropical Africa during the Pre-Colonial Period. Ghana Social Science Journal 2(2):1–9.

Mizoguchi, Koji

1993 Time in the Reproduction of Mortuary Practices. World Archaeology 25(2):223–235.

Monod, T.

1963 Un Vieux problème: Les navigations dieppoises sur la cote occidentale d'Afrique au

XIV*e* siècle. Bulletin de l'IFAN
25(3–4):427–34.

1969   Le "Ma'den Ijafen," une épave caravanière
        ancienne dans la Majâ al-Kourbrâ. *In* Actes
        du premier colleque internationale d'
        archéologie africaine. Pp. 115–124. Fort-
        Lamy: Institut National Tchadien pour les
        Sciences Humaines.

Moore, David D.

1989   Anatomy of a 17th Century Slave Ship: His-
        torical and Archaeological Investigations of
        "The Henrietta Marie." M.A. thesis, history,
        East Carolina University, Greenville, N.C.

Moseley, Michael E., and Robert A. Feldman

1988   Fishing, Farming, and the Foundations of
        Andean Civilization. *In* The Archaeology of
        Prehistoric Coastlines. Geoff Bailey and
        John Parkington, eds. Pp. 125–134. New
        York: Cambridge University Press.

Müller, Wilhelm Johann

1673   Die afrikanische auf der guineischen Gold
        Cust gelegene Landschafft Fetu. Translated
        as Description of the Fetu Country, 1662–9
        in German Sources for West African His-
        tory 1599–1669. Adam Jones, trans. and ed.
        Pp. 134–259. Studien zur Kulturkunde, vol.
        64 (1983).

Munsey, Cecil

1970   The Illustrated Guide to Collecting Bottles.
        New York: Hawthorne Books.

Murdock, George Peter

1959   Africa, Its Peoples and Their Culture His-
        tory. New York: McGraw-Hill.

Nadel, S. F.

1940   Glass-Making in Nupe. Man 40:85–86.

Nathan, Mathew

1904   The Gold Coast at the End of the Seven-
        teenth Century under Danes and Dutch.
        Journal of the African Society 13(4):1–32.

Newbury, Colin

1978   Trade and Technology in West Africa: The
        Case of the Niger Company, 1900–1920.
        Journal of African History 19:551–575.

Niane, D. T., ed.

1988   General History of Africa, vol. 4. Africa
        from the Twelfth to the Sixteenth Century.
        Berkeley: University of California Press.

Nienhaus, H.

1981   Mineraalwaterkruiken van Gres met Zout-

glazuur, Bron- en fabrikantenmerken.
        Antiek 15(9):489–509.

Nobel, William C.

1973   The Excavation and Historical Identifica-
        tion of Rocky Mountain House. Canadian
        Historic Sites Occasional Papers in Archae-
        ology and History 6. Ottawa: Parks Canada.

Noël Hume, Ivor

1958   German Stoneware Bellarmines—An Intro-
        duction. Antiques 74(5):439–441.

1960   Rouen Faience in Eighteenth-Century
        America. Antiques 78(6):559–561.

1967   Rhenish Gray Stonewares in Colonial
        America. Antiques 92(3):349–353.

1969   Glass in Colonial Willaimsburg's Archaeo-
        logical Collections. Colonial Williamsburg
        Archaeological Series, 1. Williamsburg, Va.:
        Colonial Williamsburg Foundation.

1977   Early English Delftware from London and
        Virginia. Colonial Williamsburg Occasional
        Papers in Archaeology, 2. Williamsburg,
        Va.: Colonial Williamsburg Foundation.

1978   A Guide to Artifacts of Colonial America.
        New York: Knopf.

1992   Martin's Hundred. Charlottesville: Univer-
        sity Press of Virginia.

Nørregård, Georg

1966   Danish Settlements in West Africa,
        1658–1850. Boston: Boston University Press.

Nunoo, R. B.

1957   Excavations at Asebu in the Gold Coast.
        Journal of the West African Science
        Association 3(1):12–44.

1972   A Note on the Scheduling of Monuments
        in Ghana. West African Journal of Archae-
        ology 2:119–120.

Oettinger, Johann Peter

1886   Unter kurbrandenburgischer Flagge: Nach
        dem Tagebuch des Chirurgen Johann Peter
        Oettinger. Translated as Johann Peter Oet-
        tinger's Account of His Voyage to Guinea
        in Brandenburg Sources for West African
        History 1680–1700. Adam Jones, trans. and
        ed. Pp. 180–198. Studien zur Kulturkunde,
        vol. 77 (1985).

Oldendorp, G. G. A.

1987   History of the Mission of the Evangelical
        Brethren on the Caribbean Islands of St.
        Thomas, St. Croix, and St. John. J. J.

Bossard, ed. A. R. Highfield and V. Barac, trans. Ann Arbor: Karoma Publishers. Original German edition, 1777, Barby, Germany.

Oliver, Roland
1966 The Problem of Bantu Expansion. Journal of African History 7: 361–376.

Oliver, R., ed.
1977 Cambridge History of Africa, vol. 3. From c. 1050 to 1600. Paperback ed. Cambridge: Cambridge University Press.

Olmert, Michael
1990 Official Guide to Colonial Williamsburg. Williamsburg, Va.: Colonial Williamsburg Foundation.

O'Neil, B. H. St. J.
1951 Report on Forts and Castles of Ghana. Accra, Ghana: Ghana Museums and Monuments Board.

Oswald, Adrian
1975 Clay Pipes for Archaeologists. British Archaeological Reports 14. Oxford.

Ozanne, Paul
1962 Notes on the Early Historic Archaeology of Accra. Transactions of the Historical Society of Ghana 6:51–70.

1963 Indigenes or Invaders? Antiquity 37(147):229–231.

1964a Notes on the Later Prehistory of Accra. Journal of the Historical Society of Nigeria 3(1):3–23.

1964b Tobacco Pipes of Accra and Shai. Legon. Manuscript. Department of Archaeology, University of Ghana, Legos.

1969 The Diffusion of Smoking in West Africa. Odu 2:29–42.

Pakenham, Thomas
1991 The Scramble for Africa: 1876–1912. New York: Random House.

Palmer, Arlene M.
1976 A Winterthur Guide to Chinese Export Porcelain. New York: Crown Publishers.

Pawson, Michael, and David Buisseret
1975 Port Royal, Jamaica. Oxford: Clarendon Press.

Payne-Gallwey, Ralph
1995 The Book of the Crossbow. New York: Dover Publications.

Pendery, Steven R.
1999 Portuguese Tin-Glazed Earthenware in Seventeenth Century New England: A Preliminary Study. Historical Archaeology 33(4):58–77.

Penfold, D. A.
1972 Excavation of an Iron-Smelting Site at Cape Coast. Transactions of the Historical Society of Ghana 12:1–15.

Pennak, Robert W.
1964 Collegiate Dictionary of Zoology. New York: Ronald Press.

Pereira, Duarte Pacheco
1967 Esmerado de Situ orbis. George H. Kimble, trans. Nendeln, Liechtenstein: Kraus Reprint.

Pettit, Dwight A.
1980 The History of A. van Hoboken & Co., Rotterdam. In Encyclopedia of Black Glass, vol. 1. N.p.

Pezzoli, Gigi, and Danila Brena
1990 Forti e castelli di tratta: Storia e memoria di antichi insediamenti europei sulle coste dell'Africa nera. Milan: Centro Studi Archeologia Africana.

Philips, John Edward
1983 African Smoking and Pipes. Journal of African History 24:303–319.

Phillips, Tom
1996 Africa, the Art of a Continent: 100 Works of Power and Beauty. New York: Guggenheim Museum Publications.

Phillipson, D. W.
1969 Gun-Flint Manufacture in North-Western Zambia. Antiquity 43(172):301–304.

Polanyi, Karl
1966 Dahomey and the Slave Trade: An Analysis of an Archaic Economy. Seattle: University of Washington Press.

Pole, Leonard M., and Merrick Posnansky
1973 Excavation of an Iron-Smelting Site at Cape Coast: Two Comments. Transactions of the Historical Society of Ghana 14(2):263–266.

Pope, Pauline Holman
1969 Cruzan Slavery: An Ethnohistorical Study of Differential Responses to Slavery in the Danish West Indies. Ph.D. dissertation, history, University of California, Davis.

Porter, Robert
1974 European Activity on the Gold Coast, 1620–1667. D. Litt et Phil. thesis, history, University of South Africa, Pretoria.

Posnansky, Merrick
- 1970 Discovering Ghana's Past. Annual Museum Lectures 1969–1970, 18–26.
- 1971 The Origins of West African Trade. Accra: Ghana Universities Press.
- 1973 Aspects of Early West African Trade. World Archaeology 5(2):149–162.
- 1977 Brass Casting and Its Antecedents in West Africa. Journal of African History 18(2):287–300.
- 1979 Dating Ghana's Earliest Art. African Arts 13(1):52–53.
- 1984a Early Agricultural Societies in Ghana. In From Hunters to Farmers: The Causes and Consequences of Food Production in Africa, J. Desmond Clark and Steven A. Brandt, eds. Pp. 147–151. Berkeley: University of California Press.
- 1984b Hardships of a Village. West Africa 3056:2161–2162.
- 1987 Prelude to Akan Civilization. In The Golden Stool: Studies of the Asante Center and Periphery. E. Schildkrout, ed. Pp. 14–22. Anthropological Papers of the American Museum of Natural History, vol. 65. New York.

Posnansky, Merrick, and Christopher DeCorse
- 1986 Historical Archaeology in Sub-Saharan Africa: A Review. Historical Archaeology 20(1):1–14.

Posnansky, Merrick, and Albert Van Dantzig
- 1976 Fort Ruychaver Rediscovered. Sankofa 2:7–18.

Potgieter, Suzanne, and Gabebah Abrahams
- 1984 Gouda Clay Pipes from Excavated Historical Sites in Cape Town. Bulletin of the South African Cultural History Museum 5:42–53.

Price, Cynthia
- 1982 19th Century Ceramics in the Eastern Ozark Border Region. Center for Archaeological Research, Monograph Series 1. Springfield: Southwest Missouri State University.

Priestley, Margaret A.
- 1969 West African Trade and Coast Society. London: Oxford University Press.

Prussin, Labelle
- 1995 African Nomadic Architecture: Space, Place, and Gender. Washington, D.C.: Smithsonian Institution Press.

Quarcoo, Alfred Kofi
- 1994 The Language of Adinkra Patterns. 2d ed. Legon: Sebewie Ventures.

Quarcoo, A. K., and Marion Johnson
- 1968 Shai Pots, the Pottery Industry of the Shai People of Southern Ghana. Baessler Archiv 16:47–87.

Quarcoopome, Ebenezer Nii Otokunor
- 1977 A Morphological Classification of Funerary Terracotta Heads in Ghana and a Case Study of the Western Region. B.A. honors thesis, social science, University of Ghana, Legon

Quimby, Ian M. G.
- 1980 Ceramics in America. Charlottesville: University Press of Virginia.

Rattray, R. S.
- 1959 Religion and Art in Ashanti. Facsimile ed. London: Oxford University Press. Original publication, 1927.

Redman, Charles
- 1978 Late Medieval Ceramics from Qsar es-Seghir. Colloques Internationaux Centre National de la Recherche Scientifique, 584.
- 1979 La ceramique du moyen-age tardif a Qsar es-Seghir. Bulletin d'Archaeologie Marocaine 12:292–305.
- 1986 Qsar es-Seghir: An Archaeological View of Medieval Life. New York: Academic Press.

Reineking–von Bock, Gisela
- 1971 Steinzeug. Koln: Kunstgewerbemuseum.

Reynolds, Edward
- 1974 Trade and Economic Change on the Gold Coast, 1804–1874. London: Longman.

Rice, Prudence M.
- 1987 Pottery Analysis: A Sourcebook. Chicago: University of Chicago Press.

Richards, W. A.
- 1980 The Import of Firearms into West Africa in the Eighteenth Century. Journal of African History 21:43–59.

Ricketts, Major
- 1831 Narrative of the Ashantee War; with a View of the Present State of the Colony of Sierra Leone. London: Simpkin and Marshall.

Rivallain, Josette
- 1994 Échanges et pratiques monetaires in Afrique du XVe au XIXe siècles a travers les récits de voyageurs. Musée de l'Homme,

Paris, and Association des Amis du Musée de l'Imprimerie et de la Banque, Lyon.

Robaker, E. F., and A. F. Robaker
1978 Spatterware and Sponge. New York: Barnes.

Robertshaw, Peter
1999 Sibling Rivalry? The Intersection of Archaeology and History. Electronic document. http://h-net2.msu.edu/~africa/africaforum/Robertshaw.html.

Robertson, G. A.
1819 Notes on Africa. London.

Rodney, Walter
1965 Portuguese Attempts at Monopoly on the Upper Guinea Coast, 1580–1650. Journal of African History 6(3):307–322.
1969 Gold and Slaves on the Gold Coast. Transactions of the Historical Society of Ghana 10:13–28.
1970 A History of the Upper Guinea Coast. New York: Monthly Review Press.
1983 How Europe Underdeveloped Africa. London.

Rogers, J. Daniel, and Samuel M. Wilson, eds.
1993 Ethnohistory and Archaeology: Approaches to Postcontact Change in the Americas. New York: Plenum Press.

Rohrer, Von E.
1947 Tabakpfeifenkopfe und Sprichworter der Asante. Jahrbuch des Bernischen Historischen Museums in Bern 26:7–24.

Römer, L. F.
1989 Le Golfe de Guinée, 1700–1750. Paris: Editions L'Harmattan.

Ross, Doran H.
1974 Ghanaian Forowa. African Arts 8(1):40–49.
1983 Four Unusual *Forowa* from the Museum of Cultural History. *In* Akan Transformations. D. H. G. Ross and F. Timothy, eds. Pp. 54–59. Museum of Cultural History Monograph Series, vol. 30. Los Angeles.

Ross, Doran H., ed.
1992 Elephant: The Animal and Its Ivory in African Culture. Los Angeles: Fowler Museum of Cultural History, University of California.

Roussier, Paul
1935 L'Établissement d'Issiny, 1687–1702. Publications du Comité d'Études Historiques et Scientifiques de L'Afrique Occidentale Française, série A, no. 3. Paris: Librairie Larose.

Sahlins, Marshall
1985 Islands of History. Chicago: University of Chicago Press.
1991 The Return of the Event, Again. *In* Clio in Oceania: Toward a Historical Anthropology. Aletta Biersack, ed. Pp. 37–99. Washington, D.C.: Smithsonian Institution Press.

Sanders, James
1979 The Expansion of the Fante and the Emergence of Asante in the Eighteenth Century. Journal of African History 20(3):349–364.

Sarbah, John Mensah
1968 Fanti National Constitution. London: Frank Cass.

Savage, George, and Harold Newman
1976 An Illustrated Dictionary of Ceramics. New York: Van Nostrand Reinhold Company.

Schiffer, Michael B.
1987 Formation Processes of the Archaeological Record. Albuquerque: University of New Mexico Press.

Schildkrout, Enid, ed.
1987 The Golden Stool: Studies of the Asante Center and Periphery. Anthropological Papers of the American Museum of Natural History, 65, part 1. New York.

Schmidt, Peter
1978 Historical Archaeology: A Structural Approach in an African Culture. Westport, Conn.: Greenwood Press.
1990 Oral Traditions, Archaeology, and History: A Short Reflective History. *In* A History of African Archaeology. Peter Robertshaw, ed. Pp. 252–270. London: James Curry.
1996 The Culture and Technology of African Iron Production. Gainesville: University of Florida Press.

Schrire, Carmel
1996 Digging through Darkness: Chronicles of an Archaeologist. Charlottesville: University Press of Virginia.

Schrire, Carmel, James Deetz, David Lubinsky, and Cedric Poggenpoel
1990 The Chronology of Oudepost I, Cape, as Inferred from an Analysis of Clay Pipes. Journal of Archaeological Science 17:269–300.

Schuyler, Robert L.
  1978   Historical Archaeology: A Guide to Sub-
          stantive and Theoretical Contributions.
          Farmingdale, N.Y.: Baywood Publishing.
Serageldin, Ismail, and June Taboroff
  1994   Culture and Development in Africa. Wash-
          ington, D.C.: World Bank.
Service, Elman
  1971   Primitive Social Organization: An Evolu-
          tionary Perspective. New York: Random
          House.
Shaw, Thurstan
  1945   Bead-Making with a Bow Drill in the Gold
          Coast. Journal of the Royal Anthropologi-
          cal Institute of Great Britain and Ireland
          75(1–2):45–50.
  1960   Early Smoking Pipes: In Africa, Europe,
          and America. Journal of the Royal Anthro-
          pological Institute of Great Britain and Ire-
          land 90(2):272–305.
  1961   Excavation at Dawu. New York: Thomas
          Nelson and Sons.
  1970   Igbo-Ukwu: An Account of Archaeological
          Discoveries in Eastern Nigeria. Evanston,
          Ill.: Northwestern University Press.
Shaw, Thurstan, Paul Sinclair, Bassey Andah, and Alex
    Okpoko, eds.
  1993   The Archaeology of Africa: Food, Metals,
          and Towns. New York: Routledge.
Shennan, Stephen J., ed.
  1989   Archaeological Approaches to Cultural
          Identity. Boston: Unwin Hyman.
Shinnie, Peter L., and F. J. Kense
  1989   Archaeology of Gonja, Ghana. Calgary:
          University of Calgary Press.
Shinnie, P. L., and P. C. Ozanne
  1962   Excavations at Yendi Dabari. Transactions
          of the Historical Society of Ghana 6:87–118.
Shinnie, Peter L., and Brian C. Vivian
  1991   Asante Research Project. Nyame Akuma
          36:2–6.
Sieber, Roy
  1972   Kwaku Terracottas, Oral Tradition, and
          Ghanaian History. In African Art and Lead-
          ership. D. Fraser and H. Cole, eds. Pp.
          173–183. Madison: University of Wisconsin
          Press.
Silverman, Raymond
  1983a   Akan Kuduo: Form and Function. In Akan
          Transformations. D. H. G. Ross and F.

Timothy, eds. Pp. 10–29. Museum of Cul-
          tural History Monograph Series, vol. 30.
          Los Angeles.
  1983b   History, Art and Assimilation: The Impact
          of Islam on Akan Material Culture
          (Ghana). Ph.D. dissertation, fine arts, Uni-
          versity of Washington, Seattle.
Simmonds, Doig
  1973   A Note on the Excavations in Cape Coast
          Castle. Transactions of the Historical So-
          ciety of Ghana 14(2):267–269.
Sinclair, G. E.
  1939   A Method of Bead Making in Ashanti. Man
          39:128.
Skertchly, Sydney B. J.
  1879   The Manufacture of Gun Flints. London.
Smith, Roger C.
  1993   Vanguard of Empire: Ships of Exploration
          in the Age of Columbus. New York: Oxford
          University Press.
Smith, William
  1967   A New Voyage to Guinea. London: Frank
          Cass.
Soppelsa, Robert T.
  1982   Terracotta Traditions of the Akan of
          Southeastern Ivory Coast. Ph.D. disserta-
          tion, history of art, Ohio State University,
          Columbus.
Sordinas, Augustus
  1964   Modern Koli Beads in Ghana. Man
          64:75–76.
  1965   A Report on the Manufacture and Market-
          ing of the Adjagba Beads in Ghana. Journal
          of Glass Studies 7:114–119.
South, Stanley
  1977a   Method and Theory in Historical Archaeol-
          ogy. New York: Academic Press.
  1977b   Research Strategies for Archaeological Pat-
          tern Recognition on Historic Sites. World
          Archaeology 10(1):36–50.
  1978   Pattern Recognition in Historical Archae-
          ology. American Antiquity 43(2):223–230.
South, S., R. K. Skowronek, and R. E. Johnson
  1988   Spanish Artifacts from Santa Elena. South
          Carolina Institute of Archaeology and An-
          thropology, Anthropological Studies, 7.
Stahl, Ann Brower
  1992   The Culture History of the Central Volta
          Basin. In An African Commitment: Essays
          in Honour of Peter Lewis Shinnie. Judy

Sterner and Nicholas David, eds. Pp. 123–155. Calgary: University of Calgary Press.

1993a   Concepts of Time and Approaches to Analogical Reasoning in Historical Perspective. American Antiquity 58(2):235–260.

1993b   Intensification in the West African Late Stone Age: A View from Central Ghana. In The Archaeology of Africa: Food, Metals and Towns. Thurstan Shaw, Paul Sinclair, Bassey Andah, and Alex Okpoko, eds. Pp. 261–273. New York: Routledge.

1999   The Archaeology of Global Encounters Viewed from Banda, Ghana. African Archaeological Review 16(1):5–81.

Stanley, Henry Morton

1874   Coomassie and Magdala: The Story of Two British Campaigns in Africa. New York: Harper Brothers.

Steward, Julian

1972   Three African Tribes in Transition. Urbana: University of Illinois Press.

Stone, Lyle M.

1974   Fort Michilimackinac 1715–1781: An Archaeological Perspective on the Revolutionary Frontier. Publications of the Museum. Michigan State University, East Lansing.

Sullivan, Catherine

1986   Legacy of the Machault: A Collection of 18th Century Artifacts. Canadian National Historic Parks and Sites, Studies in Archaeology, Architecture, and History. Ottawa: Parks Canada, National Historic Parks and Sites Branch, Ministry of the Environment.

Sundstrom, Lars

1965   The Trade in Guinea. Studia Ethnographica Upsaliensia 24.

Super, John C.

1988   Food, Conquest, and Colonialization in Sixteenth-Century Spanish America. Albuquerque: University of New Mexico Press.

Sutton, I. B.

1981   The Volta River Salt Trade: The Survival of an Indigenous Industry. Journal of African History 22:43–61.

Tchakirides, Tiffany Forbes

1999   Isotopic Composition of Lead in Sheet Brass as an Indicator of the Provenance of Ghanaian Ceremonial Objects. Honors thesis, geology, Syracuse University.

Teixeira da Mota, A., and P. E. H. Hair

1988   East of Mina: Afro-European Relations on the Gold Coast in the 1550s and the 1560s. African Studies Program, University of Wisconsin–Madison.

Tenkorang, S.

1968   The Importance of Firearms in the Struggle between Ashanti and the Coastal States. Transactions of the Historical Society of Ghana 9:1–16.

Terray, Emmanuel

1995   Une histoire du royaume abron du Gyaman: Des origines a la conquete coloniale. Hommes et societes serie. Paris: Karthala-CRA.

Tessler, Mark A., William M. O'Barr, and David H. Spain

1973   Tradition and Identity in Changing Africa. New York: Harper and Row.

Tetrault, Tara Lilian

1998   The Elmina Pottery Project: An Ethnoarchaeological Study of Pottery Manufacture and Use. M.A. paper, anthropology, University of Maryland, College Park.

Thilmans, Guy

1968   Sur l'existence, fin XVIe, de comptoirs Neerlandais a Joal et Portudal (Sénégal). Notes Africaines 117:17–18.

Thomas, Nicholas

1991   Entangled Objects, Exchange, Material Culture and Colonialism in the Pacific. Cambridge, Mass.: Harvard University Press.

Thompson, Thomas

1937   An Account of Two Missionary Voyages. London: Society for Promoting Christian Knowledge.

Thornton, John

1995   Africa and Africans in the Making of the Atlantic World, 1400–1680. Cambridge: Cambridge University Press.

1999   Forum on Vansina: Reply. Electronic document. http://h-net2.msu.edu/log.

Tomlinson, Regina Johnson

1970   The Struggle for Brazil: Portugal and the French Interlopers (1500–1550). New York: Las Americas Publishing.

Towerson, William

1967   William Towerson's First Voyage to Guinea, 1555–6. In Europeans in West

Africa, 1450–1560. J. W. Blake, ed. Pp. 360–392. Nendeln, Liechtenstein: Kraus Reprint.

Ulsheimer, Andreas Josua

1616   Warhaffte Beschreibung ettlicher Raysen . . . in Europa, Africa, Ostindien, und America. Translated as Samuel Brun's Voyages of 1611–1620 *in* German Sources for West African History 1599–1669. Adam Jones, trans. and ed. Pp. 18–43. Studien zur Kulturkunde, vol. 64 (1983).

Valentin, Peter

1976   Les pipes en terre des Ashanti. Arts d'Afrique Noire 19:8–13.

van Dantzig, Albert

1975   English Bosman and Dutch Bosman: A Comparison of Texts, I. History in Africa 2:185–215.

1976   English Bosman and Dutch Bosman: A Comparison of Texts, II. History in Africa 3:92–126.

1977   English Bosman and Dutch Bosman: A Comparison of Texts, III. History in Africa 4:248–273.

1978   The Dutch and the Guinea Coast 1674–1742: A Collection of Documents from the General State Archives the Hague. Accra, Ghana: Ghana Academy of Arts and Sciences.

1980a   Forts and Castles of Ghana. Accra: Sedco Publishing Limited.

1980b   Les Hollandais sur la Côte de Guinée: A l'époque de l'essor de l'Ashanti et du Dahomey, 1680–1740. Paris: Société Française d'Histoire d'Outre-Mer.

1982a   Effects of the Atlantic Slave Trade on Some West African Societies. *In* Forced Migration. J. E. Inikori, ed. Pp. 187–201. New York: Africana Publishing.

1982b   English Bosman and Dutch Bosman: A Comparison of Texts, VII. History in Africa 9:286–302.

1990   The Akanists: A West African Hansa. In West African Economic and Social History. David Henige and T. C. McCaskie, eds. Pp. 205–216. African Studies Program, University of Wisconsin–Madison.

n.d.   Selected documents for special paper: Elmina and Its Neighbors, 1836–1876. De-partment of History, University of Ghana, Legon.

van Dantzig, Albert, and Barbara Priddy

1971   A Short History of the Forts and Castles of Ghana. Accra: Liberty Press.

van den Boogaart, Ernst

1992   The Trade between Western Africa and the Atlantic World, 1600–90: Estimates of Trends in Composition and Value. Journal of West African History 33(3):369–385.

van den Nieuwenhof, M. H. L

1991   Four Dutch Merchant's Houses in Elmina, Ghana. M.A. thesis, Eindhoven University of Technology, the Netherlands.

van der Pijl–Ketel, C. L., ed.

1982   The Ceramic Load of the "Witte Leeuw." Amsterdam: Rijkmuseum.

Vansina, Jan

1985   Oral Tradition as History. Madison: University of Wisconsin Press.

1995   Historians, Are Archaeologists Your Siblings? History in Africa 22:369–408.

Varley, W. J.

1952   The Castles and Forts of the Gold Coast. Transactions of the Gold Coast and Togoland Historical Society 1:1–15.

Vivian, Brian

1992   Sacred to Secular: Transitions in Akan Funerary Customs. *In* An African Commitment: Essays in Honour of Peter Lewis Shinnie. Judy Sterner and Nicholas David, eds. Pp. 157–167. Calgary: University of Calgary Press.

Vogt, John

1971   The Early São Tomé–Príncipe Slave Trade with Mina, 1500–1545. International Journal of African Historical Studies 6(3):453–467.

1973a   The Early São Tomé–Príncipe Slave Trade with Mina, 1500–1540. International Journal of African Historical Studies 6(3):453–467.

1973b   Portuguese Gold Trade: An Account Ledger from Elmina. Transactions of the Historical Society of Ghana 14(1):93–103.

1974   Private Trade and Slave Sales at São Jorge da Mina: A Fifteenth Century Document. Transactions of the Historical Society of Ghana 15(1):103–110.

1979   Portuguese Rule on the Gold Coast 1469–1682. Athens, Ga.: University of Georgia Press.

Vollbrecht, Judith Ann

1978   Structure and Communitas in an Ashanti
        Village: The Role of Funerals. Ph.D. disser-
        tation, anthropology, University of
        Pennsylvania.

Walker, Iain C.

1965   Some Thoughts on the Harrington and
        Binford Systems for Statistically Dating
        Clay Pipes. Quarterly Bulletin of the Ar-
        chaeological Society of Virginia 20(2):
        60–64.

1966   TD Pipes—A Preliminary Study. Quarterly
        Bulletin of the Archaeological Society of
        Virginia 20(4):86–102.

1973   Cojote—A Franco-African Word for Tobacco-
        Pipe? West African Journal of Archaeology
        3:239–243.

1975   The Potential Use of European Clay To-
        bacco Pipes in West African Archaeological
        Research. West African Journal of Archae-
        ology 5:165–193.

1977   Clay Tobacco-Pipes, with Particular Refer-
        ence to the Bristol Industry. Studies in Ar-
        chaeology, Architecture, and History, vol.
        11A–D. Ottawa: Parks Canada, National
        Historic Parks and Sites Branch, Ministry of
        the Environment.

Wallerstein, Immanuel

1966   Social Change: The Colonial Situation.
        New York: John Wiley.

1976a   The Modern World System: Capitalist Agri-
        culture and the Origins of the European
        World-Economy in the Sixteenth Century.
        New York: Academic Press.

1976b   The Political Economy of Contemporary
        Africa. Beverly Hills: Sage.

1980   The Modern World System: Mercantilism
        and the Consolidation of the European
        World-Economy, 1600–1750. New York: Aca-
        demic Press.

1986   Africa and the Modern World. Trenton,
        New Jersey: Africa World Press.

Ward, W. E. F.

1958   A History of Ghana. London: Allen and
        Unwin.

Warren, Dennis Michael

1973   Disease, Medicine, and Religion among the
        Techiman-Bono of Ghana: A Study in Cul-
        ture Change. Ph.D. dissertation, anthro-
        pology, Indiana University, Bloomington.

Warren, Dennis Michael, ed.

1990   Akan Arts and Aesthetics: Elements of
        Change in a Ghanaian Indigenous Knowl-
        edge System. Studies in Technology and So-
        cial Change, 14. Ames: Iowa State University.

Wartemberg, J. Sylvanus

1951   Sao Jorge d' El Mina, Premier West
        African European Settlement: Its Tradi-
        tions and Customs. Ilfracombe, England:
        Stockwell Ltd.

Watson, Patty Jo

1995   Archaeology, Anthropology, and the Cul-
        ture Concept. American Anthropologist
        97(4):683–694.

Werz, Bruno E. J. S., and Jane E. Klose

1994   Ceramic Analysis from the VOC Ship Oost-
        erland (1697). South African Journal of Sci-
        ence 90:522–526.

Westergaard, W.

1917   The Danish West Indies under Company
        Rule (1671–1754). New York.

Whitford, John

1877   Trading Life in Western and Central Africa.
        Liverpool: Porcupine Office.

Whitley, David S., Joseph M. Simon, and Ronald I.
        Dorn

1999   The Vision Quest in the Coso Range.
        American Indian Rock Art 25:1–31.

Wild, R. P.

1937   A Method of Bead Making Practiced on the
        Gold Coast. Man 37:96–97.

Wilkinson, Frederick

1977   Antique Firearms. San Rafael: Presidio Press.

Wilks, Ivor

1957   The Rise of the Akwamu Empire. Transac-
        tions of the Historical Society of Ghana
        3(2):99–136.

1962   A Medieval Trade-Route From the Niger to
        the Gulf of Guinea. Journal of African His-
        tory 3(2):337–341.

1982   Wangara, Akan and the Portuguese in the
        Fifteenth and Sixteenth Centuries II: The
        Struggle for Trade. Journal of African His-
        tory 23(3):463–472.

1993   Forests of Gold: Essays on the Akan and
        the Kingdom of Asante. Athens, Ohio:
        Ohio University Press.

Willet, Frank

1977   Baubles, Bangles and Beads: Trade Con-
        tacts of Medieval Life. The Thirteenth

Melville J. Herskovits Memorial Lecture, Centre of African Studies, Edinburgh University.

Witthoft, John

1966 A History of Gunflints. Pennsylvania Archaeologist 36(1–2):12–49.

Wittop Konig, D. A.

1976 Mineraalwaterkruiken. Antiek 10(9):853:866.

1978 Bitterwaterkruiken. Antiek 13(1):45–47.

Wolf, Eric

1982 Europe and the People without History. Berkeley: University of California Press.

Wood, W. Raymond

1967 An Archaeological Appraisal of Early European Settlement in the Senegambia. Journal of African History 8:39–64.

Yarak, Larry

1986a Elmina and Greater Asante in the Nineteenth Century. Africa 56(1):33–52.

1986b The "Elmina Note": Myth and Reality in Asante-Dutch Relations. History in Africa 13:363–382.

1989 West African Coastal Slavery in the Nineteenth Century: The Case of the Afro-European Slaveowners of Elmina. Ethnohistory 36(1):44–60.

1990 Asante and the Dutch, 1744–1873. Oxford: Oxford University Press.

1993 "Inventing Tradition" in Elmina: A Note on the Bakatue Festival. Akan Studies Council Newsletter 6:3–4.

1995 Early Photography in Elmina. Ghana Studies Council Newsletter 8:9–11.

Yentsch, Anne E.

1994 A Chesapeake Family and Their Slaves. New York: Cambridge University Press.

York, R. N.

1973 Excavations at New Buipe. West African Journal of Archaeology 3:1–189.

Young, Crawford

1993 The African Colonial State in Comparative Perspective. New Haven, Conn.: Yale University Press.

Zur Eich, Hans Jacob

1678 Africanische Reissbeschreibung in die Landschaft Fetu, auf der guineischen Gold-Cust gelegen. Translated as Hans Jacob Zur Eich's Description of the Fetu Country, 1659–69 in German Sources for West African History 1599–1669. Adam Jones, trans. and ed. Pp. 261–268. Studien zur Kulturkunde, vol. 64 (1983).

INDEX

Page numbers in italics indicate figures

A

Abadie. *See* Allade

Abesi, 58

Accra, 5, 21, 68, 71, 117, 141, 142, 164, 166, 167, 176, 183

Ada, 141

Adadie. *See* Allade

Adangme, 28

Adjadie. *See* Allade

African-Europeans. *See* mulattos

Ahanta, 19, 141

Ahinsan, 88

Akan: coast, 117, 118, 146; coastal, 32, 40, 124, 131, 133, 186, 192; cultural homogeneity, 19, 117, 118; cultural tradition, 18, 38, 40, 66, 175, 192; funerary customs, 100, 123, 187–188, 189, 190; hinterland, 33, 113, 166; house construction, 98; languages, 18–19, 49, 176; metal crafts, 124, 126, 127, 128; migration, 112; population of Elmina, 32, 33, 49; religious beliefs, 66, 180; states, 42, 112. *See also* Asante; ceramics, Akan; Fante

Akani, 33

Akim: group, 33; ward, 58

Akrampa, 37, 41, 58–59

Akwamu, 28

Aldea das Duas Partes. *See* Village of Two Parts

Allade, 58

Ampenyi, 42, 140

Ankobia, 58

Ankobra, 137

Ankwanda, 42

animals: in documentary accounts, 110–111; domesticated, 111; introduced, 32, 111; remains of, 10, 79, 105, 108, 111, 113–114, 178, 186; wild, as food, 104, 112–114. *See also* diet; shell; shellfish

Anlo-Ewe, 140

Anomabu, 92; fort, 91, 164

Anona clan, 39

antiquities program, 69, 70

Aowin, 143

Apendjafoe, 58

archaeological research, methods used at Elmina, 73–75. *See also* temporal phases used at Elmina

Arguim, 34

artifacts: American, 148; British-period, 78, *78*, 79; chronologies of, 4, 73; clothing-related, 150; collected from Fort Java, 80; dating of, 5, 6, 76, 101; diagnostic, 5; education-related, 150; European, 18, 146; frequency of types of, 76, 79; inventory of, 6, 15, 16, 18, 26, 192

artillery, 24, 31, 51, 56, 173

asafo, 35, 37, 39, 40–41, 57–58, 59, 186, 187, 192

asaman, 66, 180

Asante (Ashanti): army, 31, 169, 172–173; bead technology, 136; community in Elmina, 59; Empire, 118; as middlemen, 42; relations with Elmina, 42–43; state, 19, 33, 42–43, 168; traders and officials at Elmina, 33, 140; War, 2. *See also* ceramics, Asante forms/influences

asantehene, 118

Asebu, 5, 23, 118, 121, 139, 143, 149, 168

asuman, 180, 182–183, 189

Atabadze, 42

Axim, 21, 25, 108, 164

Azambuja, Diogo de. *See* de Azambuja, Commander Diogo